COMMERCIAL BUILDINGS

COMMERCIAL BUILDINGS

AN ARCHITECTURAL RECORD BOOK

OFFICE BUILDINGS .

BANKS .

TRANSPORTATION BUILDINGS .

RADIO AND TV BUILDINGS .

THEATERS .

PUBLISHED BY F. W. DODGE CORPORATION, NEW YORK

CONTENTS

INTRODUCTION

It comes as something of a surprise to look back just five years—the time-span of the work illustrated here—and to see what architects have actually accomplished in designing various kinds of commercial buildings. The buildings we erect for office work, finance, the entertainment and transportation industries have all changed, in some cases greatly, in some to a lesser extent. At the end of World War II there were portents of developments to come, mostly in the form of design preliminaries. By 1947, when the earliest example here included was first published in *Architectural Record*, the new ideas were beginning to achieve structural reality. Now it is the exceptional commercial job, generally speaking, that is executed in one of the historical architectural styles.

Not that everything is perfect yet, or that wholly lofty motives have fostered the change. The architect's historic antagonists are still active: climate, the rain, wind, temperature and sun which he has always had to combat. Not all the new solutions to building problems have yet been made weatherproof; on the other hand, traditional masonry leaks, too!

The changes in building techniques that contemporary design seeks to express have been fostered almost entirely by the need for economy. It is no news that costs are astronomical; but not many realize how much higher they might be if we persisted in putting up buildings adorned with the fripperies we once considered appropriate. We have gone farther; we have begun to give reality to such concepts as the integration of mechanical and structural elements and the rationalization of the structure itself.

In other fields, notably television and air transport, types of buildings are being developed which, in 1947, were at best embryonic, often unheard-of. The television studio, growing out of the theater, radio and the movies, has become a type distinct from its progenitors. Airport buildings, despite a few attempts at organizing their complex circulation problems, have only recently begun to demonstrate satisfactory solutions.

Naturally there are many more examples, in these and related fields, than can be shown in a book of this kind. We bring you here a fair cross-section, not of the entire activity but of those recent buildings which best demonstrate the kind of advance which has characterized postwar commercial construction.

Frank G. Lopez

SENIOR ASSOCIATE EDITOR,
ARCHITECTURAL RECORD

Section I

OFFICE BUILDINGS

ALCOA BUILDING: INNOVATIONS IN ALUMINUM

Harrison & Abramovitz, Architects
Mitchell & Ritchey and Altenhof & Bown, Associate Architects
Edwards & Hjorth, Consulting Structural Engineers
Jaros, Baum & Bolles, Consulting Mechanical Engineers
Edward E. Ashley, Consulting Electrical Engineer
Moran, Proctor, Mueser & Rutledge, Consultants on Foundations
George A. Fuller Co., General Contractor

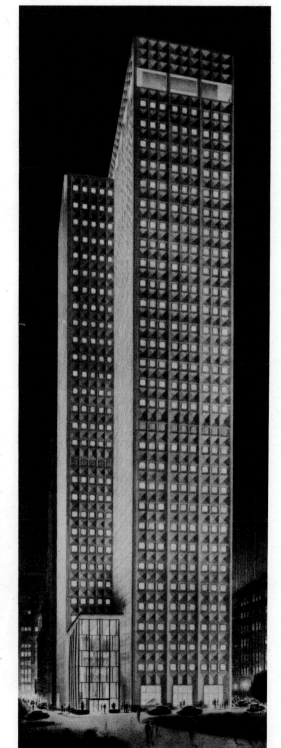

THIS ALUMINUM TOWER, now nearing completion in Pittsburgh's famed Golden Triangle, has proved an unusual opportunity for its team of architects, engineers, builders and owners to experiment with new ideas, materials and methods in such a large project.

In addition to housing its now-scattered Pittsburgh offices, the Aluminum Company of America expressly wished the building to serve as a demonstration of both standard and new uses of aluminum in construction. The result, after several years of study and revision, is the lightest-weight building of its size to date and incorporates a great number of new developments. The structural steel frame is fireproofed with foam concrete, which was also used for floor slabs in the mechanical core areas. The remainder of the flooring is of cellular steel panels surfaced with concrete fill and plastic tile or carpet, and fireproofed beneath with perlite-plaster.

Exterior walls are thin, stamped aluminum panels bolted to angles on the spandrel beams, and backed up with 4 in. of perlite-concrete sprayed on slotted aluminum lath and reinforcing bars. Ceilings are aluminum radiant heating and cooling panels designed to provide all the winter heating and half of the summertime sensible cooling. Air for ventilation and the rest of the cooling is distributed through aluminum ducts to ceiling diffusers. All electrical wiring, conduit and sector busses, and most piping are also of aluminum.

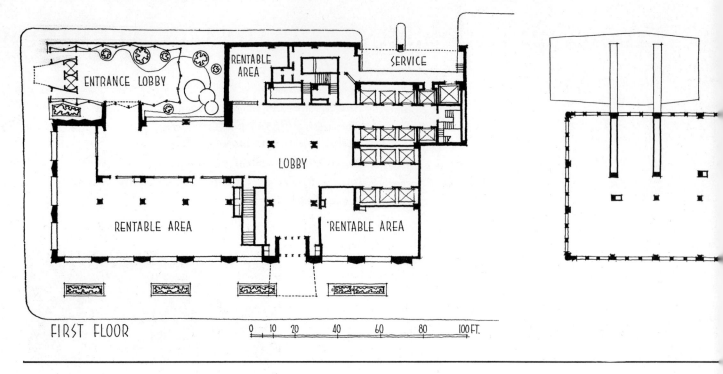

FIRST FLOOR

0 10 20 40 60 80 100 FT.

The building is 30 stories high, plus a penthouse and two basements. The lower five floors are for rental; Alcoa will occupy the rest. Mechanical equipment is located in sub-basement, 14th floor and penthouse; each floor has small utility core containing fan room, electrical equipment, fire stairs, wash rooms, dumbwaiters for mail distribution

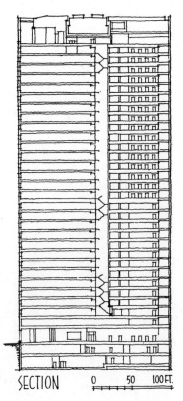

SECTION

0 50 100 FT.

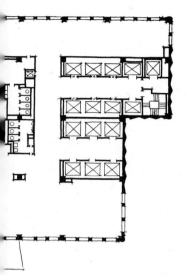

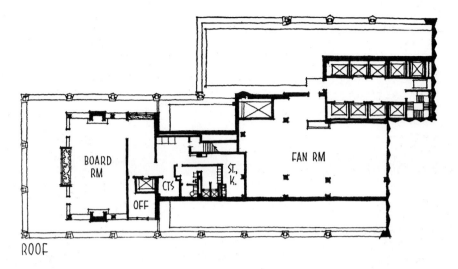

BOARD
RM

OFF

CTS

ST.,
K.

FAN RM

ROOF

Building plan shape was calculated to give maximum number of outside offices (see fifth floor plan above center). Photos at right show mock-ups of typical offices; below, present stage of interiors

Opposite page: erection of stamped aluminum exterior panels. These are backed by aluminum lath (above) and lightweight concrete. Special windows are double glazed, with heat resisting exterior panes, are reversible for cleaning, and are sealed with pneumatic synthetic-rubber tubes around edges. Sketch shows lower floor fenestration

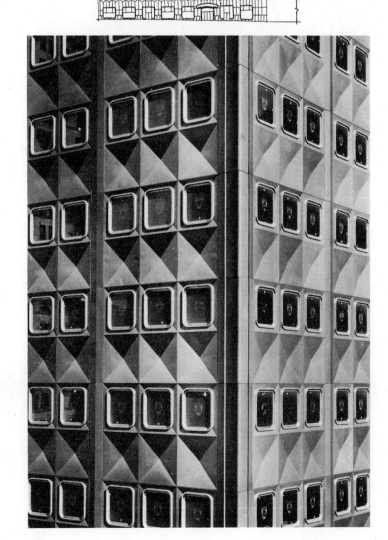

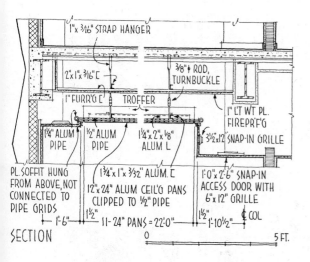

Four and one-half story entrance lobby is suspended from two huge cantilever beams at fifth floor level (above left). The tall aluminum glazed framing members (above) will hold lights of double-glazed plate glass similar to sketch, left

Labor-saving devices were developed and used throughout the project. Typical is tool (right) for fastening special aluminum ceiling panels directly to heating and cooling coils. A glass fiber blanket is placed above coils for acoustical insulation. Photos and sketches, far right, show details of ceiling panels. Windows have pockets for aluminum blinds

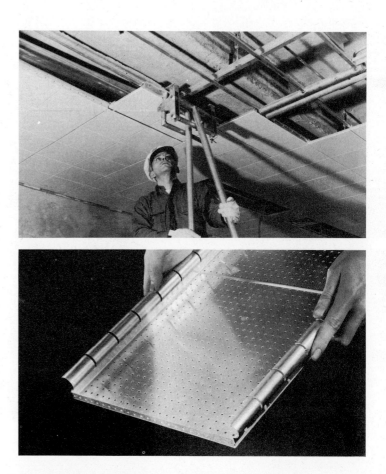

1"x ³⁄₁₆" STRAP HANGER

2"x1"x³⁄₁₆" C

3⁄8"⌀ ROD, TURNBUCKLE

1" FURR'G C TROFFER

1" LT WT PL. FIREPRF'G

1¼" ALUM PIPE

½" ALUM PIPE

1¼"x 2"x⅛" ALUM L

3½"x12" SNAP-IN GRILLE

PL. SOFFIT HUNG FROM ABOVE, NOT CONNECTED TO PIPE GRIDS

1¾"x1"x³⁄₃₂" ALUM. C

12"x 24" ALUM CEIL'G PANS CLIPPED TO ½" PIPE

1'-0"x 2'-6" SNAP-IN ACCESS DOOR WITH 6"x12" GRILLE

1'-6"   ½"   11-24" PANS = 22'-0"   ½"   1'-10½"   ₵ COL

SECTION

0   5 FT.

HUNG PLASTER CONSTRUCTION
TYPICAL BAY   0   5   10 FT.

2" x 1" x 3/16" Ls
4'-0" O.C.

1" FURRING Ls
16" O.C.

PL. SOFFIT
CONSTRUCTION

PLAN OF PIPE GRIDS ABOVE ALUMINUM CEILING
TYPICAL BAY   0   5   10 FT

1 1/4" ALUMINUM
PIPE

1 1/2 ALUMINUM
PIPE 12" O.C.

1 1/4" x 2" x 1/8" ALUM. L

1 1/2" x 1" x 3/32" ALUM C

12" x 12" AIR TRANSFER GRILLES IN PLASTER SOFFIT

1'-0" WIDE TROFFERS
4'-0" & 6'-0" LONG

1'-0" x 2'-0" ACCESS
DOORS WITH
6" x 12" GRILLES

12" x 12" PERFORATED
ALUMINUM PANELS
BETW'N TROFFERS

12" x 12" CEILING
DIFFUSER

12" x 24" PERFORATED
ALUM CEIL'G PANS

PLASTER SOFFIT

REFLECTED CEILING PLAN
TYPICAL BAY   0   5   10 FT.

OFFICE DESIGN

Prepared by Caleb Hornbostel, Architect

DUE TO THE SHORTAGE of office space in most cities since the start of World War II, tenants have gradually accepted the responsibility and cost of alteration in order to obtain satisfactory quarters. The architect found that he was being called in not only when a new structure was planned but also for remodeling and interior redesign. With the continuing heavy demand for office space, his practice may include anything from the layout for a one-room office to altering several floors of a large building and even designing specialized small buildings in situations that are often not satisfactory. Basic layout for office space, be it large or small, usually includes the following areas: reception, waiting or display; main or executive business offices; and subsidiary office space, including work areas, pertinent to the business itself.

An office generally presents much the same requirements as a classroom. The problems in lighting both natural and artificial, of the acoustics of the area as a whole and of soundproofing individual offices, of storage space, of the use of color, and of flexibility in internal arrangements, are common to both. The main design problem usually is to fit the client's office and circulation needs into the limitations imposed by existing conditions. What is interesting is how the difficulties themselves are often turned into design assets.

ORIENTATION

TODAY's client has become conscious of comfort. In other words, he is now aware how important it is to make his office a pleasant place to work in. Therefore, orientation is the first factor the architect will consider in arriving at his final design. If he may determine the location, he can avoid many of the troubles by selecting a northern or eastern exposure. If the orientation is of necessity southern or western, he must somehow eliminate the effects of solar heat and glare, using perhaps double glazing, heat-resistant glass, drapes or screens, venetian blinds or interior or external louvers, now available in a variety of designs and materials.

Air conditioning, too, is influenced by orientation. For example, southern or western exposures may require a larger number and higher capacity of units than either northern or eastern exposures.

In short, orientation influences the basic pattern for both large aspects and details of office design.

AIR CONDITIONING

AIR conditioning today is usually installed either as localized units or as a central unit with a duct system. The local unit has the advantage of flexibility, but may demand a special power outlet. Some types require water and drainage and therefore are impractical wherever water restrictions exist. Cost is also a factor, depending on how many units are used.

The central unit with a duct system for each office group, although more economical from the viewpoint of equipment costs, can create other problems. First, as a cost factor, the system of ducts has to be distributed throughout the entire office space, and much of the ceiling area often has to be furred. Second, in the design, the ducts must not cut down too much on ceiling height.

Finally, localized control for individual conditions within the office is usually ruled out by cost. Nonetheless, the central unit remains the best type for a large yet compact office.

In some of the newer large office buildings a central plant supplies refrigerant and heat to every office area. The advantages of these systems are many; foremost among them are complete flexibility, individual control, and a mechanical simplification of air conditioning equipment, which represents a great reduction in cost.

Extensive research is being done on the "heat pump" type of equipment which will, when we know more about its cost under all conditions, supply atmospheric conditions to order the year around.

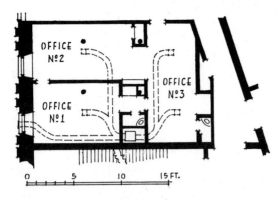

This alteration, a business office for The Cooper Union in New York designed by Esmond Shaw, is uncomplicated and succeeds in using the peculiarities of this old building, one of the first steel structures put up in America, to advantage. Central air conditioning with a duct system helped cut down ceilings — too high to begin with. The cast iron Corinthian column, painted green, is actually one of the original main supporting structural members and not just a decorative note

Alexander Demaras

REMODELING

Bob Bailey

THE problems of office alteration are perhaps best explained by taking a specific example, designed by Kenneth Franzheim, Architect, and following the changes made to reach a final scheme (see photos right).

The original San Jacinto Hotel Building, built in 1910, proved a real conversion headache, as original structural drawings were not available and the skeleton had to be exposed before planning could begin.

At the start, the owner, thinking it possible to salvage the upper floors by simply changing the layout from bedrooms to offices, leased the lower four floors with sub-basement, complete from street to street. This forced relocation of elevators to the side street property line. As demolition proceeded, it became evident that only the original structural steel could be salvaged; heavy floor slabs had to go. Since this was in June 1950 when steel was scarce, conversion, instead of rebuilding, went ahead even though the fenestration also proved unsuitable and the entire facade had to be removed.

Office planning within the existing framework and with front location of elevators proved to be unsound economically, as the proportion of rental area to gross area was very low. The owners were then persuaded to extend the building through the block, to bring net rentable area to 80 per cent of the gross. Since the building is air conditioned all year and had good artificial light, the entire lot area was covered, leaving no rear light courts.

This move proved a sound one. The building is almost fully rented at profitable rates, with tenants paying for partitions and individual construction costs.

Stuart Wiener

INTERIOR PLANNING OF A

Office for Dean of School of Architecture

University of Southern California

Los Angeles, California

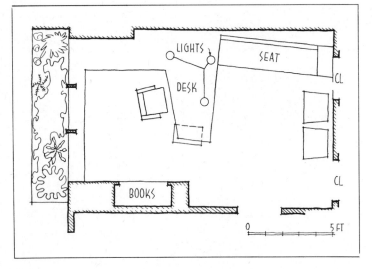

THE STUDENTS IN INDUSTRIAL DESIGN at the University of Southern California undertook the remodeling of their dean's office as an extracurricular project, with results that speak for themselves. What was just a 10 by 15 ft cubicle of office space, with four plaster walls and a narrow strip window at one end, was turned into a very pleasant room. The only set requirement had been a 28 in. high desk with large working surface. Otherwise the design and plan were to be the students' own. The labor was theirs also, as were the design and cabinet work for all the furniture except the two Eames chairs. One wall was faced with ½ by 4 in. oak strips separated by a ½ in. space backed by a strip of industrial cork. This simple device greatly improved the acoustics of the room, which were decidedly poor prior to remodeling. The broad ell-shaped desk with brown plastic top aids the horizontal effect in the very small room. The color scheme is natural oak, brown leather, brown plastic and a blue-green wall opposite the window.

SPATIAL ORGANIZATION

Using furniture to subdivide space

ACOUSTICS

Improved acoustics by clever use of materials

FURNISHINGS

Everything built-in except three chairs

ONE-ROOM OFFICE

The complete end wall of the office was removed and replaced by a glass wall opening onto a private patio; ventilating units are at the floor and above the trellis at the ceiling. Beyond the glass wall is a planting area in the patio

The tiny lobby and receptionist's area holds only a desk reduced to barest essentials; the switchboard, files and other office needs are concealed in the small alcove to the left. Below is the cantilevered desk in the semiprivate alcove

THREE-IN-ONE OFFICE FOR

H. B. Humphrey Company, Inc.
New York, New York

HERE IS AN ADMIRABLY SIMPLE LAYOUT that was worked out for a small commercial office area. Yet this mere "hole in the wall," to use 'the words of the advertising firm which had its start here (the company has expanded and merged with Alley & Richards, Inc.; it is now H. B. Humphrey, Alley & Richards, Inc.), was so carefully scaled and stripped to the bone that it gives the impression of being much larger than it actually is. The basic requirements for three separate work areas — reception, work and private conference — were met by using only three partitions: one a solid wall; one a screen wall of glass above and fiber board below, which can be

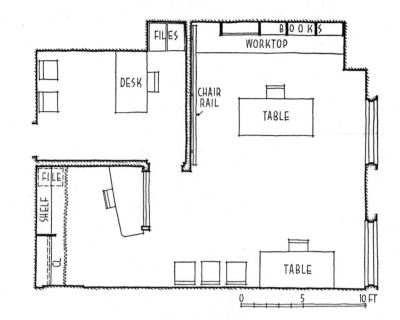

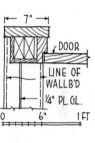

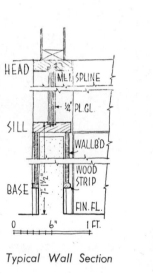

HEAD · ML · SPLINE

¼" PL. GL.

SILL

WALLB'D

BASE · 7'·1½" · WOOD STRIP

FIN. FL.

0 · 6" · 1 FT.

Typical Wall Section

7"

DOOR

LINE OF WALLB'D

¼" PL. GL.

0 · 6" · 1 FT.

Jamb Details at Partition (above), at Desk (below)

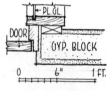

PL. GL.

DOOR

GYP. BLOCK

0 · 6" · 1 FT.

ADVERTISING AGENCY

Ketchum, Gina & Sharp, Architects

used for display on both sides; and one a floor-to-ceiling glass panel between the main working area and the ell of space on the other side of the solid partition setting apart the receptionist's area. This alcove serves for conferences with individual clients and gives a certain amount of privacy. The large work area can also be used for conferences by pushing the two large table desks together to form one long table. The old radiators were left in place and only venetian blinds were added to the windows at the outside wall. The drape across the entire length of the semiprivate alcove hides a coat closet and a surprising amount of storage space.

INTERNAL CIRCULATION

One door controls inside circulation

STORAGE

In existing niche, in hung cabinets and behind a curtain

PARTITION

Use of minimum partitions to sub-divide space

Gottscho-Schleisner

Corner office, marked A in General Plan, with two false walls. Wood panelled wall holds bar, closet, refrigerator, storage units and air conditioning equipment. Two hinged panels cover bar

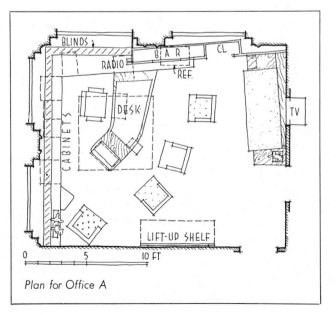

Plan for Office A

WITH "PROBLEM" WINDOWS

Offices for Holly Stores, Inc.
New York, New York

Morris Lapidus, Architect

SCREEN WALLS

Three methods of treating poor fenestration

LIGHTING

Natural over-all lighting supplemented with skylight-type fixture

EQUIPMENT

Complex facilities for business, conference and entertaining

WHERE THE EXTERIOR WINDOWS are as unattractive and badly situated as they were here, and whenever the orientation is poor, the best answer often is to close off the original external walls with false screen walls. These two offices illustrate three different solutions to the problem. In the one office (A in General Plan) shown on the facing page, vertical cloth louvers screen the upper section of one wall and part of the adjoining wall, yet permit daylight to filter through. The lower wood-panelled portion that extends along both false walls holds drawers, storage space and special equipment. In the other office (B in General Plan), there is only one screen wall, back of which are the radiator, air conditioning and additional storage compartments.

Both offices are elaborately appointed to serve the needs of top-level business executives. The larger and more complex of the two (office A) has facilities for business conference and entertaining which include a bar, radio and television. The desks in both offices have been specially designed and integrated with the other fittings of the room. The ceilings are hung acoustical plaster, with skylight-type fixtures over the desks.

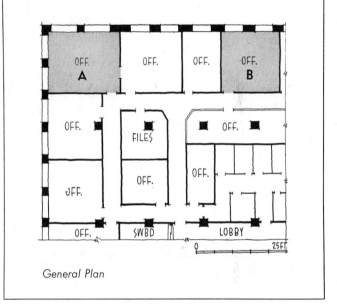

General Plan

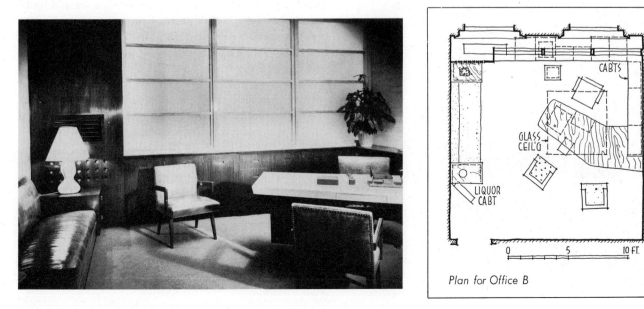

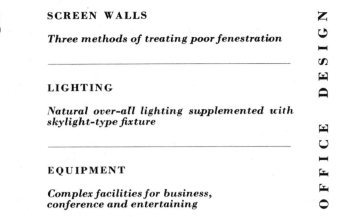

Plan for Office B

AIR CONDITIONING

*Central ceiling area furred and used
as plenum for perimeter offices*

FURNISHINGS

*Basic theme incorporated into design
of each item*

SPATIAL ORGANIZATION

*Executive offices surround parti-
tioned central work area*

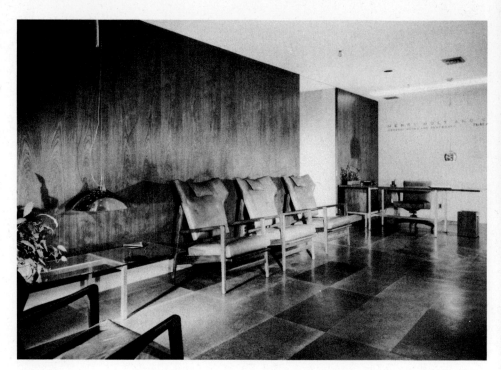

OFFICES FOR A PUBLISHING FIRM

Offices of Henry Holt and Company

New York, New York

*Maurice and Joseph Mogulescu
and Gerald Luss of
Designs For Business, Inc., Designers*

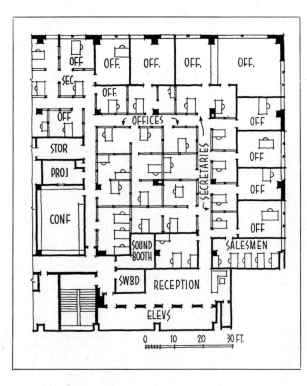

ESPECIALLY EFFECTIVE LIGHTING is achieved throughout these offices by the use of a combination of indirect fluorescent lighting, incandescent recessed baffle
downlights with baffles painted same as ceiling to conceal the source, and direct light from adjustable pulley-
type suspended fixtures for desk work. The result is
soft diffused shadowless general illumination and pools
of warm light at key desk areas.

Clear glass and metal form movable partitions which
divide individual offices in the central work area. A
flush acoustical ceiling reflects light from low-brightness
tubes to give 65-ft candle illumination.

The president's office has an interior adapted to the
specific working needs of a publisher. The 20-ft desk is
broken by its L-shaped contour.

The receptionist's desk repeats the above design. In
all the desks any massive feeling is overcome by a system of suspending the working units and floating the
desk surface to give a light airy feeling.

The related color scheme uses muted tones ranging
from off-white to warm walnut.

Above: Combination library and conference room. Standard steel shelves hold firm's first editions. During conferences sliding walnut panels hide books. Back of one panel is a film projector, and on opposite wall a recessed screen. At right and below: President's office with desk-conference table which houses working equipment

Ben Schnall

LEVER

Architects: Skidmore, Owings & Merrill

Structural Engineers: Weiskopf & Pickworth

Mechanical Engineers: Jaros, Baum & Bolles

HOUSE, NEW YORK: GLASS AND STEEL WALLS

Interior Design: Raymond Loewy Associates

Contractor: George A. Fuller Company

THE EXTERIOR OF LEVER HOUSE — 24 stories of blue-green heat-resistant glass and stainless steel — was a technical design problem which required the joint efforts of architects, engineers, general contractors and sub-contractors. Its glass-paned skin is designed to be kept sparkling clean (Lever Brothers, manufacturers of soaps and detergents, are naturally pleased at this) with minimum difficulty or expense. The building has no openable sash. This not only prevents the entrance of the big city's dirt and grime, but is a means of reducing the total air conditioning load. It also lessens interior maintenance.

The heat-resistant glass likewise reduces both the air conditioning load and sun or sky glare. Wire glass faces the spandrels, which the building code required to be of masonry. The structure itself is of conventional steel frame, with tower bays so laid out that only narrow vertical mullions, formed of paired channel shapes, interrupt the glass. Horizontal mullions and muntins are similarly light in section; all are sheathed with 16-ga Type 302 stainless steel which is secured to the exterior glazing channels with hand-driven screws. Glazing channels were in turn screwed to structural mullions; the operation (see details on following pages) took time and was obviously expensive. However, this office building was designed for sole occupancy by Lever Brothers — even its ground floor has no tenants; a reasonably high construction cost, commensurate with the aim of providing an imposing, almost institutional, edifice, was not inappropriate.

The openness of the ground floor (where much of the area is garden and pedestrian walks with only the essentials enclosed in glass) is also somewhat monumental, if not in expression certainly in its fundamental regard

Photo **opposite:** Ben Schnall

LEVER HOUSE

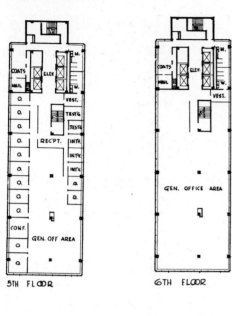

5TH FLOOR   6TH FLOOR

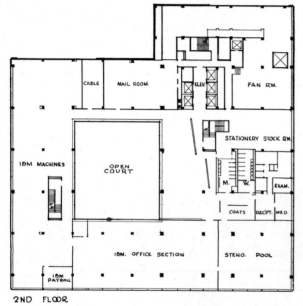

2ND FLOOR

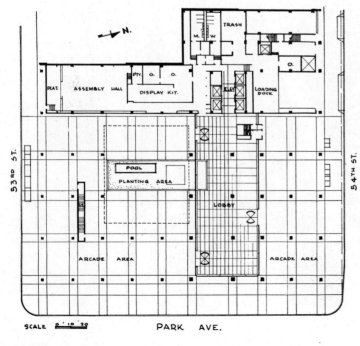

SCALE   PARK AVE.

Photo courtesy Geo. A. Fuller Co.

for the citizens of New York. In this aspect, the entire structure is thoughtful, pleasant and a decided advance over the average speculative building. Above the few lower stories the tower is so designed that its slim bulk permits what it can of a city vista — an impression heightened by the contrasting surroundings. This is something to be grateful for. Like the U. N. Secretariat, like the new Carnegie building now under construction (see pp. 31 through 39), it is a narrow slab, which means that the typical office floor will contain few dark cubicles. The design is an enlightened venture in public relations, and is to be applauded; the glass and metal skin, also a source of public interest, becomes rather a stunt by comparison.

In plan, the enclosed ground-floor area contains display and reception space, waiting areas for visitors, a demonstration kitchen and an auditorium. On the second floor are employees' lounge, medical suite, general office facilities. On the third floor, lowest of the tower, is the employees' cafeteria overlooking roof terraces. The remaining floors, up through the 21st, house offices of the parent and subsidiary companies. Above are the equivalent of three floors of mechanical equipment. In addition to complete air conditioning, the building is fitted with what has been called "the most modern fire alarm equipment"; and with a conveyor system, newly developed, which not only picks up internal and outside communications and distributes them vertically, but also transports them horizontally to the mail room. In such technical aspects, Lever House is marvelously ingenious.

Applying the glass-and-steel skin: facing page, fundamental structure complete, stainless steel being applied, June 1, 1951. Above, left, setting stainless steel (note hand tools bottom of photo); center, close-up at spandrel, viewed from window-washing gondola; right, stainless steel interior sills, flush with spandrel members, are also outlets for high-velocity air conditioning system. In details, note cap, shield and sleeve flashings

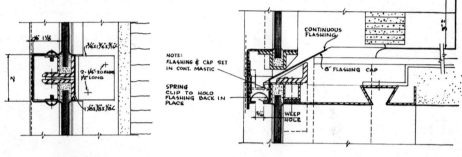

SPANDREL MUNTIN

NOTE:
FLASHING & CAP SET IN CONT. MASTIC

SPRING CLIP TO HOLD FLASHING BACK IN PLACE

CONTINUOUS FLASHING

8" FLASHING CAP

WEEP HOLE

HORIZONTAL MULLION

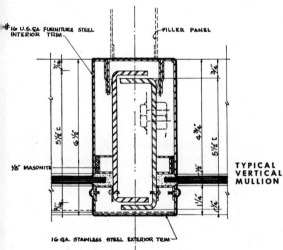

#16 U.S.GA. FURNITURE STEEL INTERIOR TRIM

FILLER PANEL

1/8" MASONITE

16 GA. STAINLESS STEEL EXTERIOR TRIM

TYPICAL VERTICAL MULLION

EXPLODED DIAGRAM, juncture of horizontal mullion and vertical rail which guides window-washing gondola

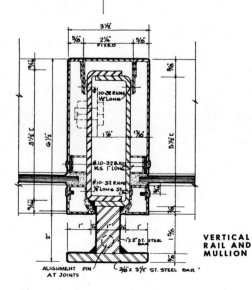

FLASHING SLEEVE

FLASHING SHIELD

FLASHING CAP

CONTINUOUS MONEL METAL FLASHING

WEEP HOLE COVER
WEEP HOLE

#10-32 RHMS 1/2" Long

#10-32 B.H.MS 1" Long

#10-32 R.H.MS 1/2" Long St.

VERTICAL RAIL AND MULLION

ALIGNMENT PIN AT JOINTS

3/8" x 3 1/2" ST. STEEL BAR

1 1/2" x 5" ST. STEEL

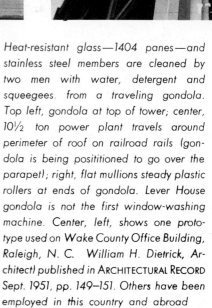

Joseph W. Molitor

Heat-resistant glass—1404 panes—and stainless steel members are cleaned by two men with water, detergent and squeegees. from a traveling gondola. Top left, gondola at top of tower; center, 10½ ton power plant travels around perimeter of roof on railroad rails (gondola is being posititioned to go over the parapet); right, flat mullions steady plastic rollers at ends of gondola. Lever House gondola is not the first window-washing machine. Center, left, shows one prototype used on *Wake County Office Building, Raleigh, N. C. William H. Dietrick, Architect)* published in ARCHITECTURAL RECORD Sept. 1951, pp. 149–151. Others have been employed in this country and abroad

Stainless steel is also employed extensively inside the building. Left, stainless steel revolving door and housing, with air conditioning outlet in jamb; above, stainless-steel-sheathed columns at sidewalk arcade; note open ground floor

Photo opposite, Ben Schnall

INSURANCE COMPANY
OFFICES IN HONOLULU, T. H.

Security Insurance Agency, Ltd., Agents for
Occidental Life Insurance Company of California

Cyril W. Lemmon, Architect; Douglas Freeth, Associate
Ernest H. Hara, Associate Architect
Thompson and Thompson, Landscape Architects

R. Wenkam

Main entrance (opposite page) faces landscaped parking area, at each end of which are stairs leading to lanai connecting second-floor offices. Building is reinforced concrete with exterior walls of Arizona sandstone and plaster

WHILE THIS BUILDING was in the early planning stage the architects made a careful analysis of the office needs of the 40 agents on the staff. Individual desks were ruled out: they would have required an area of about 2400 sq ft, in use for only a small part of the day. The owners recommended a series of conference tables to which the agents could take their documents and papers from individual filing cabinets; this idea was vetoed by the architects because a large room full of unused conference tables "could easily be somewhat institutional in appearance," and because the large tables would have been in the way when the space was needed for general meetings.

The solution to the problem was based on the fact that, except in rare instances, not more than eight or ten agents would need desk space at the same time. Eight reference tables were ranged along the wall of the corridor leading to an agents' lounge. The tables are for reference only, and do not have drawers — the architects reasoned that this would prevent an agent from staking a claim to a particular table, and would force him to return his papers to his own individual file. If more than eight agents need reference space at one time, the large table in the school room at one end of the lounge can be pressed into service.

For discussions between agents and their clients, the architects felt strongly that an informal and friendly atmosphere must be provided. Hence the large and airy lounge where several agents may hold conferences at the same time. With the furniture rearranged and sup-

INSURANCE BUILDING

plemented by folding chairs (stored in cabinets along the wall), the lounge can be converted to a meeting room with a seating capacity of 110. Three small conference rooms, a file room and a secretaries' office are also provided.

The balance of the ground floor is given over to private and general offices, lobby and a library. Doctors' and dentists' offices and a laboratory occupy the second floor. Stairs at each end of the parking area, and an elevator adjacent to the main entrance, lead to a lanai-corridor serving the entire second floor.

R. Wenkam

Switchboard-reception desk faces main entrance

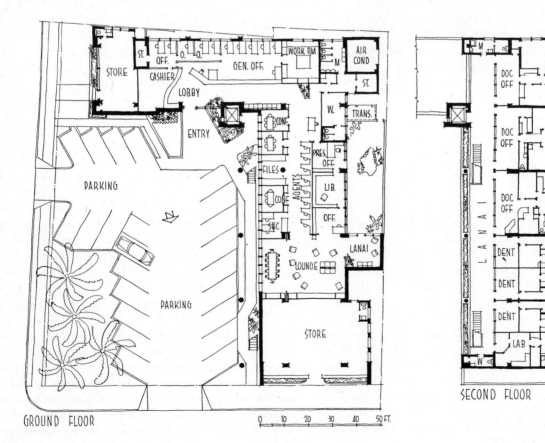

GROUND FLOOR

SECOND FLOOR

0   10   20   30   40   50 FT.

Above: left, cashier's desk; right, general office   Below: agents' tables, secretaries' office and phone booths

R. Wenkam

Above, left: another view of agents' quarters with lounge in background, president's office at left. Above, right: president's office has own small reception area. Below, left: school at end of agents' lounge can be closed off by folding doors, or left open for agents' use. Below, right: reference tables do not have telephones; instead, sound-proofed telephone alcoves are provided outside adjacent conference rooms

OFFICE BUILDINGS

THE OFFICE SPACE within which this country's business is carried on has changed quite radically in recent years. In metropolitan centers the skyscraper concept remains, but the era of bigness for bigness' sake which reached a dubious fruition just at the time of the 1929 market crash does not now exist. Costs of construction and the emergence of different materials, of advanced design techniques, of mechanical equipment whose potentialities were barely foreseen two or three decades ago, are two reasons for the change. The emphasis is increasingly on quality of accommodation at relatively low cost.

The speculatively built office building (that is, one erected for a multiplicity of anonymous tenants) has not pioneered many of these changes. One would hardly expect it to; the speculator, who by definition takes the huge risk of building the structure at all, cannot afford to gamble in the smaller matters. Like the speculative builder of houses for sale, he believes he must employ the tried architectural devices. We find on the other hand that the client who builds for his own use is more bold; his buildings are the pioneers; sometimes, as in the case of Harris Armstrong's American Stove Company Building, in Lever House, the Alcoa Building, the U. N. Secretariat, the Carnegie Building and other recent examples, the private owner sees in these new ideas a means of impressing himself, his company or his product indelibly on the public consciousness. The U. N. Secretariat is also a symbol, of a somewhat different sort.

It is also significant that the comfort of the occupants of these pioneer buildings is considered important. The tenant is given light, views, air at its mechanically controlled best; he is transported vertically and his mail is whisked away with automatic precision and speed that are awesome. Something of this filters down from the skyscraper even to the two-story taxpayer; in fact, it is characteristic of smaller office structures that they provide control of sun, glare, heat, cold and air movement or else, generally speaking, their occupancy records are not so good. The demand for economical construction has led to thin membrane walls — some of them hard to justify solely on the basis of economy — and to experimentation with framing systems, even to fairly complete integration of equipment in the structure. One of the most advanced of these concepts is contained in the new building of the Carnegie Endowment for International Peace, an analysis of which is presented in the following pages.

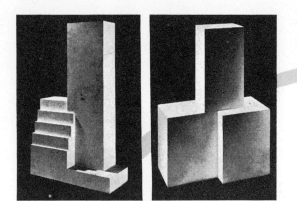

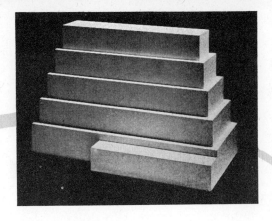

CARNEGIE

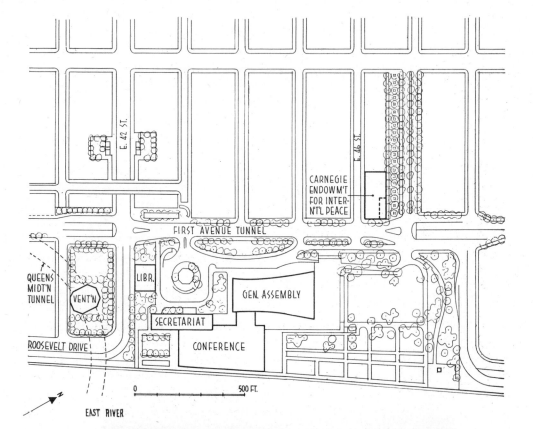

E. 42 ST.

E. 47 ST.

CARNEGIE
ENDOWM'T
FOR INTER-
N'T'L PEACE

FIRST AVENUE TUNNEL

QUEENS
MIDT'N
TUNNEL

VENT'N

LIBR.

GEN. ASSEMBLY

SECRETARIAT

ROOSEVELT DRIVE

CONFERENCE

0   500 FT.

EAST RIVER

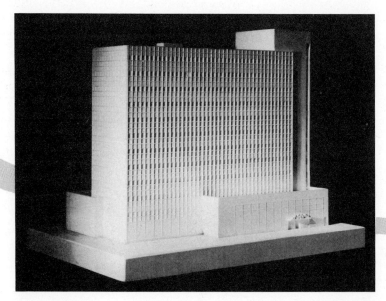

Harrison & Abramovitz, Goldstone & Abbe, Architects

James Dawson, Supervising Engineer

ENDOWMENT FOR INTERNATIONAL PEACE

Severud, Elstad & Krueger, Structural Engineers

Syska & Hennessy, Mechanical and Electrical Engineers

Cauldwell-Wingate Co., General Contractors

THE BUILDING FOR THE CARNEGIE ENDOWMENT for International Peace, now rising opposite the entrance to the United Nations enclave on First Avenue in New York, is unusual in occupancy, site and design. Many of its characteristics are not apparent to the casual observer; almost all of them are important, at least in principle, as concepts for careful study.

Regarding occupancy: Above the ground floor, the Carnegie Peace Building is to be occupied entirely by international organizations and agencies of non-governmental types — charitable, cultural, professional, social, commercial, etc. — such as the Endowment itself, Rotary International, and many other familiar bodies. These all have a common trait. They are strictly limited as to the amount they can spend for housing their own organizations. Consequently the Carnegie Peace Building had to be designed to squeeze the maximum of rentable floor area out of the minimum building envelope — a factor in designing the average speculative building but here even more potent, and, since the owner was not afraid to pioneer, an actual stimulus to design progress. Also, these organizations are tax-exempt. In order to reduce rentals even further than extreme design economy would permit, it was decided to lease most of the ground floor to commercial tenants; on this portion of income the owner will have to pay taxes. However, the structure is not intended to make a profit.

The site, fronting on First Avenue (United Nations Plaza) and running through from 46th St. to the park-like widening of 47th St. which will form the public approach to the U.N., was assembled like any other real estate holding. Not until design had been completed and excavation begun did the northeast corner lot become available. This helped determine column spacing

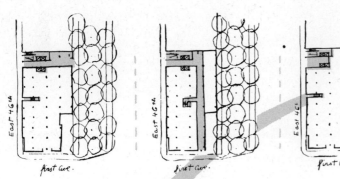

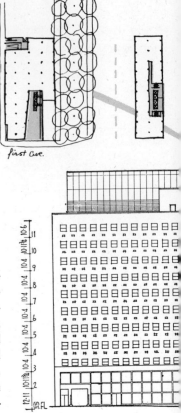

CARNEGIE PEACE BUILDING

Plan, like the building envelope, underwent many evolutionary steps of which a few (not in exact order) appear above. Left, early first floor scheme with services at west, main entrance on widened 47th St. Next, after 47th St. access was denied, services still at west, entrances on 46th St. and First Ave. Next, another scheme with westerly service core, 46th St. entrance only. Next, typical floor required for all three lower floors to left; note long travel to elevators, secondary stair. Two right-hand sketches, scheme with service core on north side of tower, main entrance on First Ave., minor trucking entrance (primarily for restaurant) on 46th St. This conception sacrificed much of the most valuable ground floor rental space on First Ave. and was abandoned despite advantages

Final plan has main entrance on 46th St., utilizes all First Ave. frontage for commercial rental space. Secondary entrance on 46th St. is for trucks and service to both commercial and private restaurants. The single cellar floor is quite crowded; to obtain even the small amount of tenant storage space sidewalk vaults were necessary. Advantages of final scheme include an impressive 2-story lobby connecting directly with the International Center on the second floor, plus the simplicity of the typical tower floor loft space. In tower, note that service core is concentrated, corridor distances can be at minimum, toilets have outside windows. Carnegie Endowment offices are to be on 11th and penthouse floors. On all tower floors, duct spaces at east and west ends of service core carry the limited air conditioning supplies needed for the few possible interior offices. Column spacing is such that, on the north, single-row offices can be one bay deep; on south, bays accommodate typical anteroom plus private office

and tower placement in plan. At first, the main entrance was to be from 47th St., on the north. However, the city's Park Department, which has jurisdiction over the park strip that widens 47th St., denied the Endowment access (in line with usual city policy) and the plan had to be restudied (see sketches). The location is most important. The agencies housed have fairly close liaison with the U.N.; in fact, at one time in U.N.'s development they were to be accommodated in the northernmost U.N. building, the one which was later eliminated.

The architects and engineers worked closely in designing the Carnegie Peace Building. Structure, mechanical equipment and electrical systems are thoroughly integrated. In the 9-in. structural flat slab are contained all electrical ducts and conduits;

CELLAR   GROUND FLOOR   0 10 20   40   60 FT

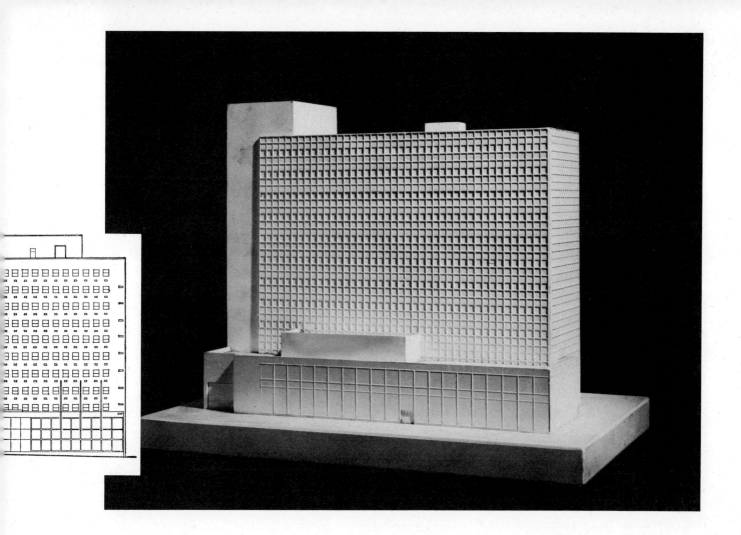

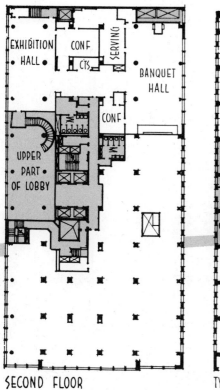

Above, photo of model as it was developed when three sides of building were metal and glass. Left, south elevation (north similar) after these walls were changed to masonry and windows. Two lower floors remain glass, metal

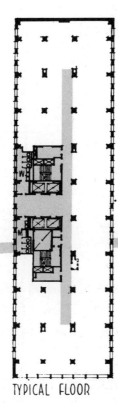
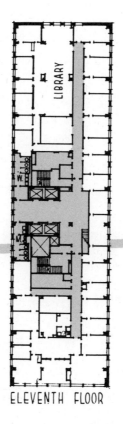
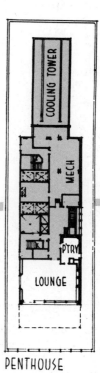

SECOND FLOOR   TYPICAL FLOOR   ELEVENTH FLOOR   PENTHOUSE

COST ANALYSES OF STRUCTURAL SYSTEMS

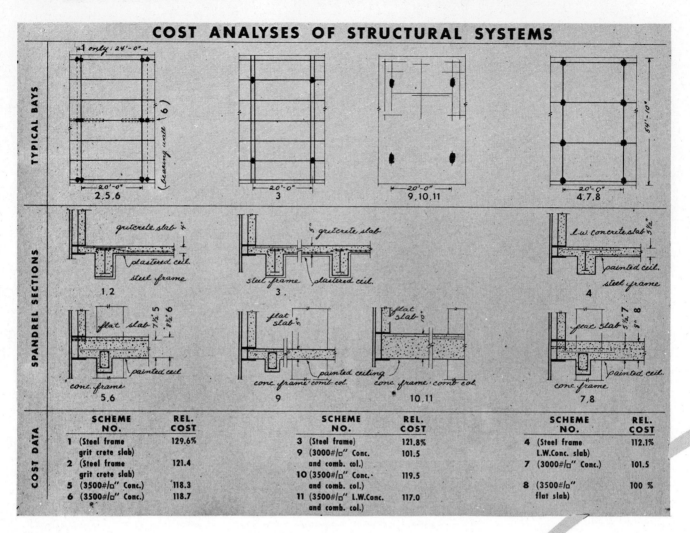

TYPICAL BAYS

2,5,6 — 3 — 9,10,11 — 4,7,8

SPANDREL SECTIONS

gritcrete slab — plastered ceil. — steel frame — 1,2

5" gritcrete slab — steel frame — plastered ceil. — 3

l.w. concrete slab — painted ceil. — steel frame — 4

flat slab — painted ceil. — conc. frame — 5,6

flat slab — painted ceiling — conc. frame comb. col. — 9

flat slab-10 — conc. frame comb. col. — 10,11

peac slab — painted ceil. — conc. frame — 7,8

COST DATA

SCHEME NO.	REL. COST		SCHEME NO.	REL. COST		SCHEME NO.	REL. COST
1 (Steel frame grit crete slab)	129.6%		3 (Steel frame)	121.8%		4 (Steel frame L.W.Conc. slab)	112.1%
2 (Steel frame grit crete slab)	121.4		9 (3000#/□" Conc. and comb. col.)	101.5		7 (3000#/□" Conc.)	101.5
5 (3500#/□" Conc.)	118.3		10 (3500#/□" Conc. and comb. col.)	119.5		8 (3500#/□" flat slab)	100 %
6 (3500#/□" Conc.)	118.7		11 (3500#/□" L.W.Conc. and comb. col.)	117.0			

Above, analysis of eleven different structural schemes prepared by the engineers during design process, arranged according to column layout. Cheapest scheme, Number 11, uses concrete columns, an 8-in. flat slab flush on underside except for continuous peripheral beam. When all electrical services were built into structural slab, thickness had to be made 9 in. Left, detail of air conditioners which eliminated most ducts

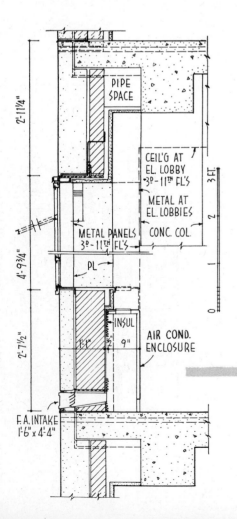

PIPE SPACE

CEIL'G AT EL. LOBBY 3ᴰ-11ᵀᴴ FL'S

METAL AT EL. LOBBIES

CONC. COL.

METAL PANELS 3ᴰ-11ᵀᴴ FL'S

PL

INSUL 1"

AIR COND. ENCLOSURE 9"

F. A. INTAKE 1'-6" x 4'-4"

2'-11¼" — 4'-9¾" — 2'-7½"

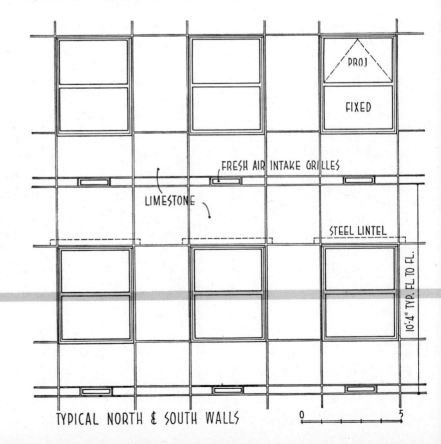

PROJ

FIXED

FRESH AIR INTAKE GRILLES

LIMESTONE

STEEL LINTEL

10'-4" TYP. FL. TO FL.

TYPICAL NORTH & SOUTH WALLS

0 ___ 5

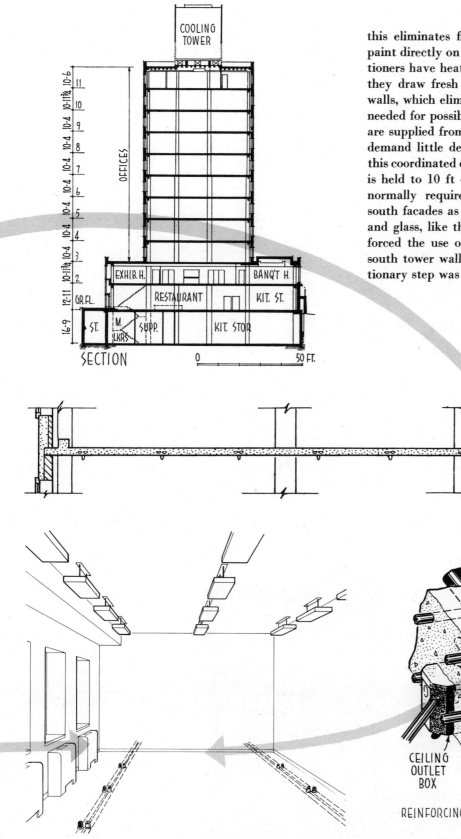

SECTION

0   50 FT.

this eliminates floor fill and ceiling finish other than paint directly on the concrete. The individual air conditioners have heating and cooling media piped to them; they draw fresh air directly through north and south walls, which eliminates most air ducts (the small ducts needed for possible conditioning the few interior spaces are supplied from vertical ducts in the service core and demand little depth of ceiling furring). As a result of this coordinated design, floor-to-floor height in the tower is held to 10 ft 4 in. — in contrast to the 11 to 12 ft normally required. Until final estimates, north and south facades as well as the east face were to be metal and glass, like the U.N. Secretariat. Construction cost forced the use of limestone facades on the north and south tower walls; an added benefit of this last evolutionary step was reduction in air conditioning load.

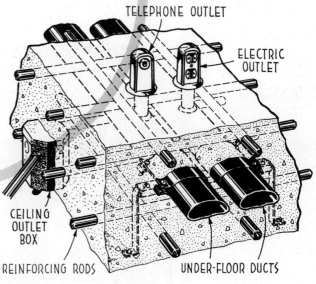

TELEPHONE OUTLET

ELECTRIC OUTLET

CEILING OUTLET BOX

REINFORCING RODS

UNDER-FLOOR DUCTS

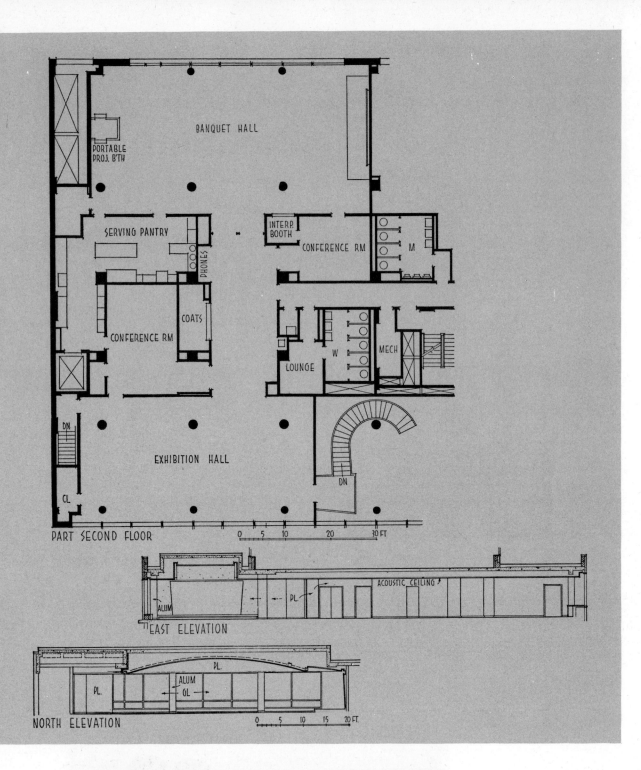

BANQUET HALL

PORTABLE PROJ. B'TH

SERVING PANTRY

INTERP. BOOTH

CONFERENCE RM

M

PHONES

COATS

CONFERENCE RM

LOUNGE

W

MECH

DN

EXHIBITION HALL

DN

CL

PART SECOND FLOOR

0   5   10   20   30 FT.

ACOUSTIC CEILING

PL.

ALUM

EAST ELEVATION

PL.

PL.

ALUM GL

NORTH ELEVATION

0   5   10   15   20 FT.

Left, study model, 46th St. Lobby, showing stair to International Center. Probably to be finished in wood, it is intended to have both warmth and scale

CARNEGIE PEACE BUILDING

Right, plan and elevations of Carnegie Endowment Lounge on penthouse floor. Interior design has not been finally determined

Left, plan and elevations, International Center on second floor. Note the physical connection by stair with the 2-story lobby on the 46th St. side. Service elevator (far left) connects with first-floor service entrance, restaurant kitchen, and kitchen storage in basement. Since these drawings were made the Center has been expanded; a Lounge has been added to the right of the Banquet Hall, with its entrance directly from the elevator lobby (not shown). Below, construction status early in May, 1952

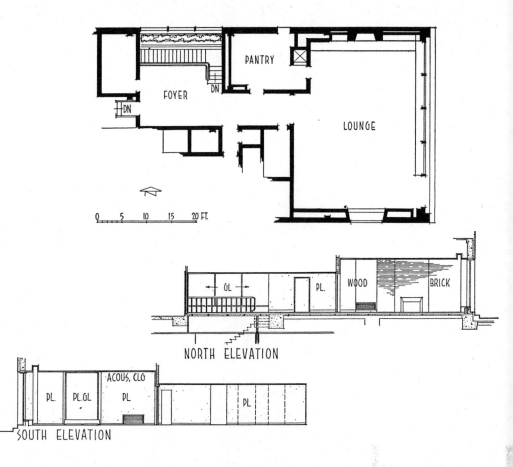

FOYER   PANTRY   DN

LOUNGE

0 5 10 15 20 FT.

GL   PL.   WOOD   BRICK

NORTH ELEVATION

PL.   PL.GL   ACOUS. CLG   PL   PL

SOUTH ELEVATION

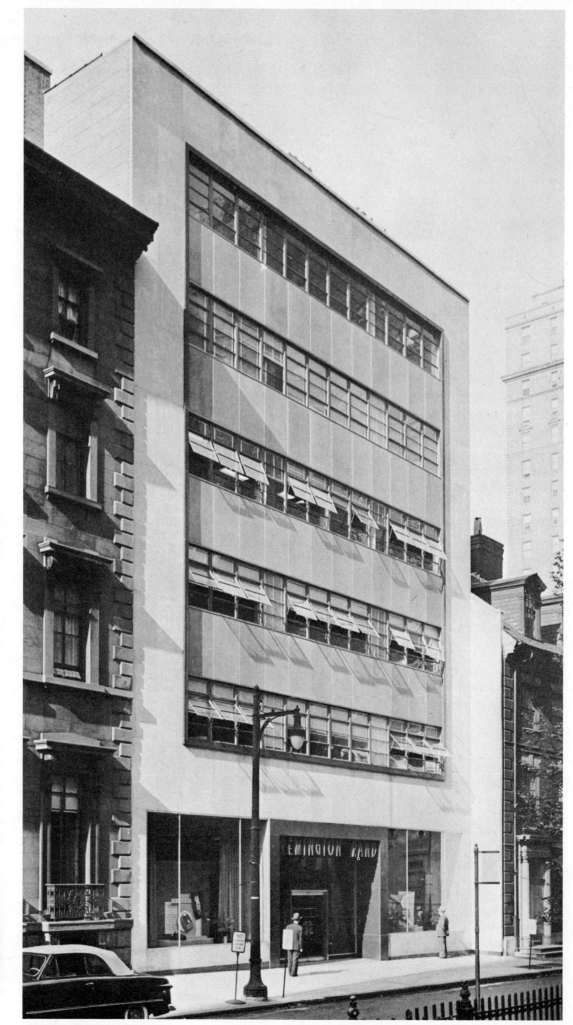

Cortland V. D. Hubbard

The first floor of the Remington-Rand building (plan below) houses main sales area, utilizes secondary street at rear for shipping and receiving

OFFICES CONSOLIDATE ACTIVITIES
FOR BUSINESS MACHINE SALES

Philadelphia, Pennsylvania

Thalheimer and Weitz, Architects

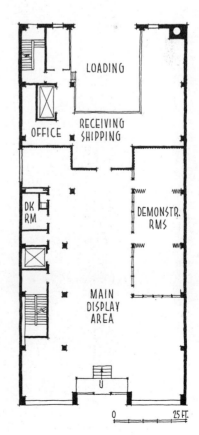

THE MULTIPLE ACTIVITIES of a business machine sales office — display, demonstration, administration, stock storage and maintenance — have been brought together here in a building almost as neatly styled as the machines it exhibits. The architects have circumvented the often heard debate on whether a multi-story building — even a small one as this — should be expressed vertically or horizontally, and have simply grouped windows and aluminum spandrels into a large panel with a cast granite frame.

All six floors are similar in plan, with utilities and toilets grouped on the stair wall. The rest of the areas are divided into offices and general stock space on the 2nd, 3rd and 4th floors, a maintenance division on the 4th, and stock and supply storage on the 5th and 6th. The building is constructed with steel frame, common brick exterior walls, concrete floor slabs. The facade is faced with limestone. Interiors have painted plaster walls, asphalt tile floors and hung plaster ceilings.

ESQUIRE-
CORONET
OFFICES

Hedrich-Blessing

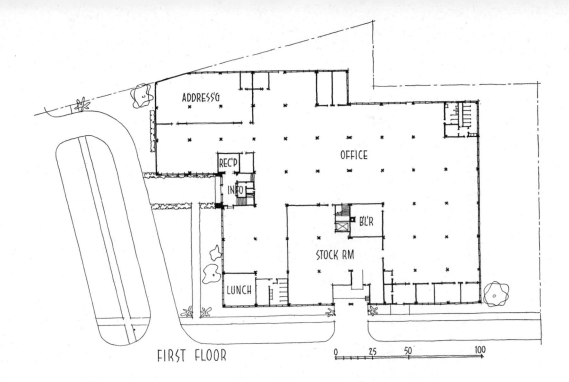

FIRST FLOOR

0   25   50   100

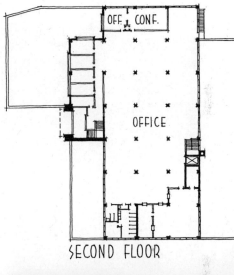

SECOND FLOOR

LOW COST OFFICES FOR
A MAGAZINE DIVISION

Boulder, Colorado

Ralph Stoetzel, Architect

THESE EFFICIENT, PLEASANT OFFICES for Esquire-Coronet Publications' Circulation Department are typical of an apparently growing trend for large organizations to relocate many of their activities in less congested cities — a trend which gives mutual benefit both to the cities and the businesses concerned. In this case, Esquire-Coronet desired to increase its operating efficiency by transferring the Circulation Department from company headquarters in Chicago. To attract an operation of this type, and thereby increase employment and revenues, the City of Boulder and its Chamber of Commerce donated a site for the offices. The architect was given the problem of designing a suitable office building at the cost of an industrial type building. This was solved by providing an open, flexible plan and a structure of reinforced concrete. Exterior walls are natural finish concrete, with some use of stone and brick at the entrance. Office interiors are finished with glazed tile walls, asphalt tile floors and acoustic tile ceilings. A curved driveway and a two-story, open-front lobby were used to ease the transition from the main street, which lies 10 to 15 feet above average property grade.

Ben Schnall

FRANK STAMATO
& CO.
OFFICES

OFFICES FOR AN AGREEABLE

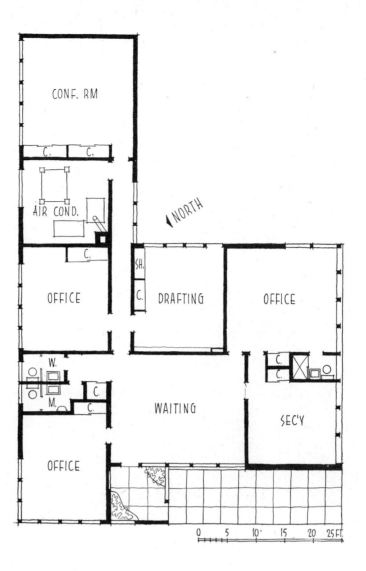

CONTRACTOR

Lodi, New Jersey

George Cooper Rudolph, Architect

THE OWNER of this office building, a New Jersey road builder and garbage collection contractor, requested only three things of the architect: the correct number and sizes of offices, air conditioning, and his name visible from a highway 200 yds to the south. All questions of design, esthetics and furnishings were left in the architect's hands. After completion of the contract, Mr. Rudolph says of his client, "Of course now he is broke, but very proud."

Ben Schnall

The building amply fulfills the client's few stipulations and provides extremely comfortable and pleasant areas for staff employees and clients. A planted entry leads into the waiting room, which joins directly with the large-size offices and the drafting room. The conference room is placed at the end of an ell for greater privacy and quietness. Construction is straightforward and simple (see wall section, right). Exterior walls are concrete block painted white, stone, and cedar-stained vertical wood siding. The large sign is on an extended wall to integrate it with the general design — and is quite visible from the highway. Interior partitions are wood frame, finished with plaster or wood veneer. Floors are rubber tile. Acoustical plaster is used on the waiting room ceiling. Landscaping for the project was done by Janet Darling.

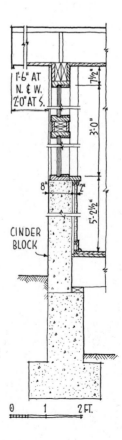

The interiors were designed by Alexander
R. Stavenitz, an associate of the architect,
and include furniture by George Nakashima,
a gesso mural by Louis Ross

BREWERY OFFICES DESIGNED

Hedrich-Blessing

MILLER
BREWING
COMPANY
OFFICES

TO BETTER PUBLIC RELATIONS

Milwaukee, Wisconsin

Brooks Stevens Associates, Designers

*Arthur L. and Arthur W. Seidenschwartz,
Architectural Consultants*

Dailey, Brenner & Schreiber, Management Engineers

THE CONSCIOUSLY DRAMATIC LIGHTING and lobby design of this new administration building for the Miller Brewing Company were planned to serve as an arresting focal point in the midst of the older, traditionally-styled plant buildings. The owners desired the building to be of the same basic materials — beige brick with limestone trim — as the others, but also wished it to be modern, functional, and to have as much merchandising and public relations value as possible. With this in mind, the designers, who also serve as consultants to the firm on all phases of merchandising design, were commissioned to give "complete consideration" to the general architecture, furniture design, fabrics, colors, *objets d'art*, and general planning for the industrial murals executed by Edmund Lewandowski.

The main floors of the building are planned around a central open area for general clerical groups, with executive offices ranging the outer perimeter. Most of these outer offices are designed with movable metal partitions, and can be altered in size on 4-ft modules. A penthouse-type office with balcony for the president is located above the corner lobby and an auditorium equipped for movies is in the basement. The building is of steel frame construction with brick exterior. Interior partitions are cinder block, plastered and painted.

Principal executives' offices (above, directly at right) and Board Room (right center) have specially designed plastic-surfaced furniture, oak veneer paneling, gold carpets. Other colors — gray greens, tile red, amber — were picked from the company's packaging colors. All metal work is two-tone brass and stainless steel to recall the brass beer and steel foam of an abstract symbol on the facade. The new building has resulted in a sharp rise in Brewery tour attendance

Central clerical area (above) is made comfortable
with fluorescent lighting, air conditioning, acoustic
ceilings. Below: basement auditorium

NEW OFFICES EMPHASIZE COORDINATION

Offices of Sterling Advertising Agency, Inc.   *New York City*

Ben Schnall

THE PLANNING OF THIS SUITE OF OFFICES was complicated by the fact that the agency was moving from four small floors to one large one. The architects' first task, therefore, was to set up a logical and space-saving traffic pattern for interdepartmental operations. In addition, they were asked to provide a new centralized filing system for art work, etc., and to give the account executives attractive and functional quarters. The architects also served as decorators, and designed much of the furniture for the executive offices (see pages 54-55).

Louis Hatkoff Associates
Architects

Above: left, conference room; right, corridor between offices of account executives and their assistants. Opposite and below: reception room and entrance foyer. Ceilings throughout are suspended, with acoustical tile block. Floors are rubber tile in reception room, corridors and work areas, carpeted in executive offices

For the executive offices the architects designed special units for various kinds of storage. Wall unit above and below provides space for everything from coats to hospitality items

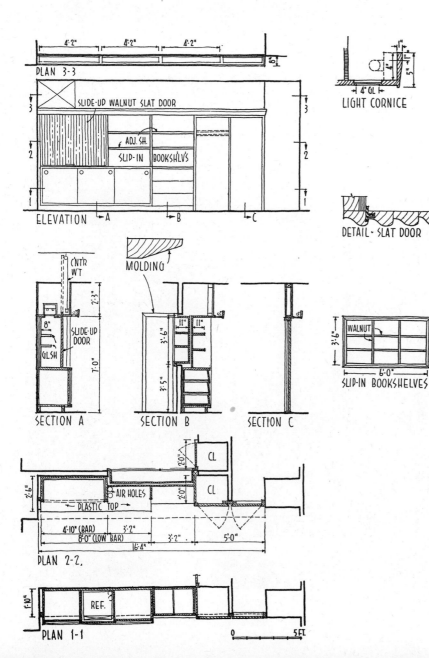

PLAN 3-3

4'-2" 4'-2" 4'-2" 8"

ELEVATION

SLIDE-UP WALNUT SLAT DOOR

ADJ. SH.

SLID-IN BOOKSHLV'S

A B C

LIGHT CORNICE

4" GL 5" 4"

DETAIL - SLAT DOOR

MOLDING

CNTR WT

2'-3"

8" SLIDE-UP DOOR

GL SH

7'-0"

SECTION A

3'-6" 11" 11"

3'-5"

SECTION B

SECTION C

WALNUT

3'-6"

6'-0"

SLID-IN BOOKSHELVES

CL

2'-0"

AIR HOLES

CL

2'-0"

2'-6"

PLASTIC TOP

4'-10" (BAR) 3'-2"

8'-0" (LOW BAR) 3'-2" 5'-0"

16'-4"

PLAN 2-2.

REF.

1'-10"

PLAN 1-1

0 5 FT.

The typical account executive's office (above and opposite) has wall rack and cork bulletin board for presentations and display. Art department (below) is partitioned into individual cubicles to give each member of the staff privacy and tack-up space

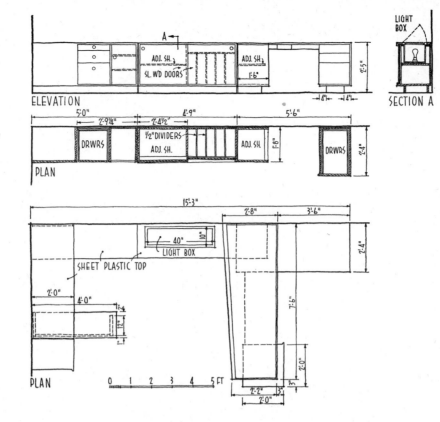

ELEVATION

ADJ. SH.

SL. W'D DOORS

ADJ. SH.

1'-6"

2'-5"

4" 4"

LIGHT BOX

SECTION A

5'-0"

2'-9¼"

2'-4½"

4'-9"

5'-6"

DRWRS

½"DIVIDERS

ADJ. SH.

ADJ. SH.

DRWRS

1'-8"

2'-4"

PLAN

15'-3"

2'-8"

3'-6"

40"

10"

LIGHT BOX

SHEET PLASTIC TOP

2'-4"

2'-0"

4'-0"

7'-6"

12"

2'-0"

PLAN

0   1   2   3   4   5 FT

2'-2"

3"

2'-0"

Account executives' work area, specially designed by the architects, consists of work desk with drawers and storage space, a 7-ft long conference desk, vertical and horizontal storage cabinets, and a built-in light table

Ben Schnall

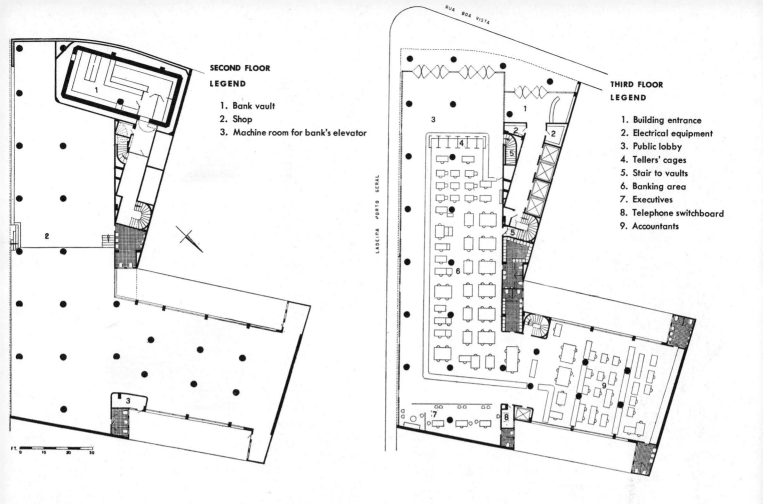

SECOND FLOOR

LEGEND

1. Bank vault
2. Shop
3. Machine room for bank's elevator

THIRD FLOOR

LEGEND

1. Building entrance
2. Electrical equipment
3. Public lobby
4. Tellers' cages
5. Stair to vaults
6. Banking area
7. Executives
8. Telephone switchboard
9. Accountants

OFFICE BUILDING FOR SÃO PAULO, BRAZIL

Rino Levi, Architect

Roberto Cerqueira Cezar, Associate Architect

ALTHOUGH it stems from a concept similar to that of many recent structures, this glass-walled, fifteen-story office building in São Paulo introduces several well thought out planning factors which distinguish it from the average example.

The program requirements were familiar ones: a simple, easy-to-maintain building that would fill the maximum building envelope allowed by the city, and whose structure would give great flexibility in arrangement of office areas in the top eleven floors. These floors were to be subdivided and sold as cooperatives after completion of the building. A steep site which permitted street access to three floor levels led to the allocation of the two lowest for shops, and the combined third and fourth for the Paulista Bank of Commerce and the building lobby, each with main street entrances.

Unlike the more usual solution, glass curtain walls were used only on the sunless southern facades; walls to the sunny north are completely blank except for a section with wide overhangs in the ell. The fenestration of each floor is divided into three bands, with the lower one of fixed obscured glass protected by a wide interior baseboard which also serves as an electrical duct. The upper panes are clear and open independently for ventilation. Deft use of glass block gives privacy to the banking floor, yet preserves continuity of glazed facade.

Peter Scheier Photos

Peter Scheier Photos

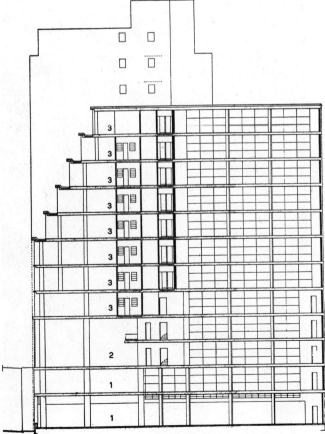

**13TH TO 15TH FLOORS
LEGEND**

1. Elevator hall
2. Office space—to be divided
   with partitions

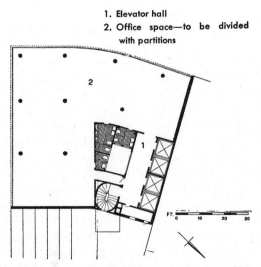

Setbacks of the building follow city regulations. The structure is of reinforced concrete, with brick used in dark areas of section shown left. Numbers indicate floor use: 1. shops; 2. bank; 3. offices. The three top floors follow plan shown above. Utilities are dispersed on each of lower floors to aid in office rearrangement

A slight extension of floor slabs on the exterior (above left) subtly emphasizes the building's structure without destroying the unity of design. The bank interior is richly finished in glass and ceramic mosaic on floors and columns; forthright screen of glass block with window insets gives privacy. Below right: mezzanine office corridor

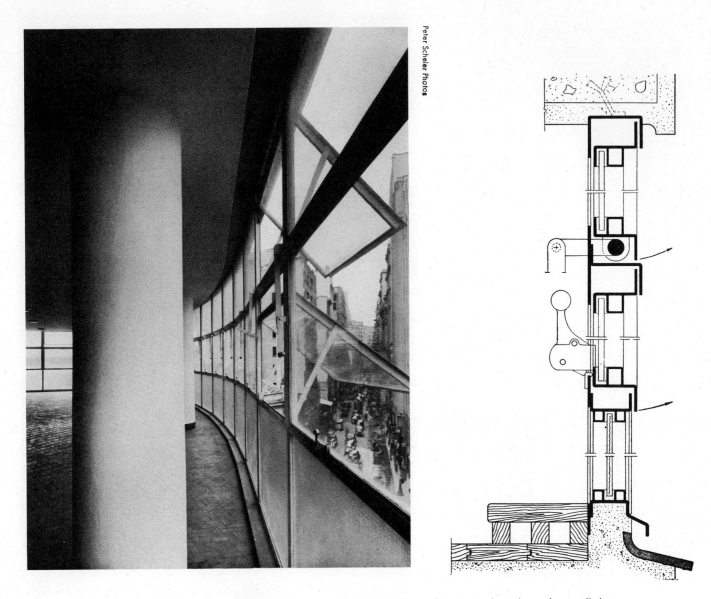

Peter Scheier Photos

Above left: typical office floor. Above right: section through window wall; bottom pane is fixed obscured glass. Below: baseboard detail showing use as electrical duct

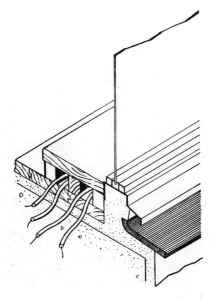

The eleven office floors are planned to be as open as possible, with utilities and toilets ranged along the blank walls to the north. A number of features were incorporated to facilitate the partitioning off and selling of individual office spaces. These include use of regular, short spaced divisions in the windows, and the lack of projecting beams on the ceilings. As it was assumed that most desks would be placed near the window walls, electrical and telephone conduits were run through the protective baseboard, and vertically through the hollow metal window columns. The curve of the front wall follows the bend of the street below. Ceramic tile sills below the windows also serve as finishing caps for the projecting edges of the floor slabs to the exterior. All the office floors are 3.15 meters (about 10 ft 3 in.) high. Flooring is wood parquet glued directly to the concrete slabs with a special mastic.

BIG BUSINESS MOVES TO THE COUNTRY

Pacific Headquarters for Insurance Company of North America, San Jose, Calif.

Wurster, Bernardi and Emmons, Architects
Thomas Church, Landscape Architect

IT HAS frequently been said that the city skyscraper will give way to just such headquarters buildings as this — individual company establishments in smaller towns, with open surroundings, landscaping, parking, and other means of making life more pleasant. This unusually attractive building shows how tempting such considerations can be. The insurance company moved its Pacific Coast headquarters from San Francisco to quiet San Jose, built a handsome but inexpensive building, to "get away from it all."

In plan, large open floor areas were required to permit simplicity of operation and continuity during work processing. The concrete structure with bell-capped columns was developed as the least expensive method of providing open, undivided space, carrying the floor loads and providing a fireproof building to house valuable records. It is designed for an additional floor to be added when needed. There was no effort to conceal the true functions of such things as air ducts on the ceiling, acoustic treatment placed directly on the ceiling slab, elimination of plaster surface on the columns. Attractive appearance of these elements was sought through the use of color: interior walls are gray green, columns darker green, and the lobby and stair hall a still darker green. Heating and ventilating ducts are painted red, as are the door frames ("boldly for decoration"). Sun shields over large window areas and air conditioning contribute to working comfort within the building.

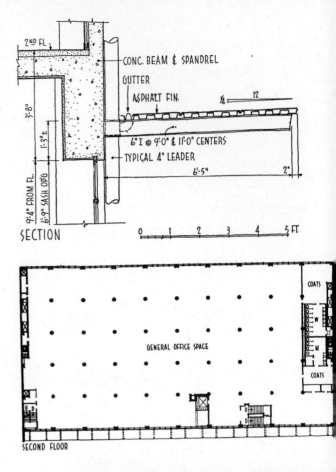

SECTION

CONC. BEAM & SPANDREL
GUTTER
ASPHALT FIN.
6" I @ 9'-0" & 11'-0" CENTERS
TYPICAL 4" LEADER

2ND FL.

3'-8"

1'-3"±

9'-4" FROM FL.

6'-9" SASH OP'G

¼ 12

6'-5" 2"

0 1 2 3 4 5 FT.

GENERAL OFFICE SPACE

COATS

W

M

COATS

SECOND FLOOR

Simple, inexpensive sunshades on the southeast facade give protection against sky glare and solar heat, even though with this orientation full protection is impossible

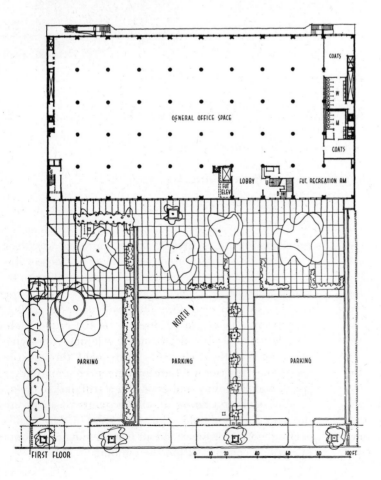

GENERAL OFFICE SPACE

COATS

W

M

COATS

FUT. ELEV.

LOBBY

FUT. RECREATION RM

NORTH

PARKING   PARKING   PARKING

FIRST FLOOR

0 10 20 40 60 80 100 FT

Interiors are simply and boldly done. Ducts and columns
are frankly exposed and gaily painted. Columns are dark
green, walls a lighter green, air conditioning ducts red

Roger Sturtevant Photos

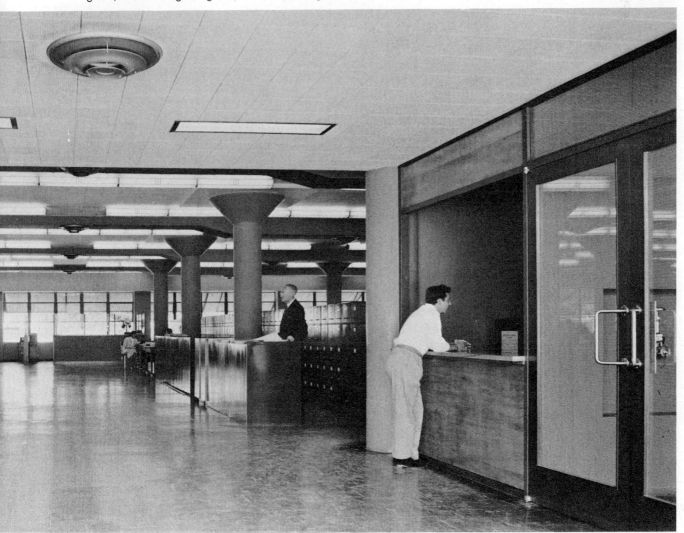

REMODELING SOLVES SPACE PROBLEM

Fidelity Investment Company Offices
Wichita, Kansas

Ramey, Himes & Buchner, Architects

Like many another concern faced with shortage of available office space, as well as building restrictions and high costs, Fidelity Investment Company has secured pleasant, ample quarters through the purchase and remodeling of an old downtown building. The first phase of the project, the ground level, is shown on these pages. Future plans call for remodeling of street elevation and second floor, with addition of stairs.

The architects have succeeded in creating a good sense of space within the confines of the long narrow plan. Generally, divisions of work areas are suggested, rather than completely separated. The exposed brick vault, dropped ceilings, glazed half-partitions, plain surfaces and flush lighting fixtures all serve this end. Clean lines and color also play an important part. To reduce costs, original heating and plumbing locations were not changed, and all materials were selected for ease of maintenance and durability.

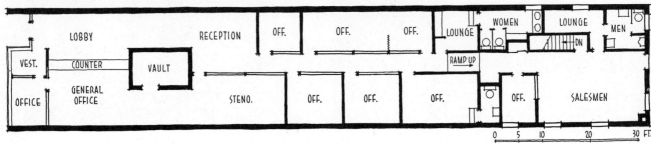

Frankly expressed brick vault serves to define divisions in general office area (left and above). Walls of the room are in quiet, cheerful colors — gray green, lemon yellow, mahogany. Offices off corridor (below) are in blue gray, green gray and mahogany. Floors are gray rubber tile, brown asphalt tile, tan carpeting

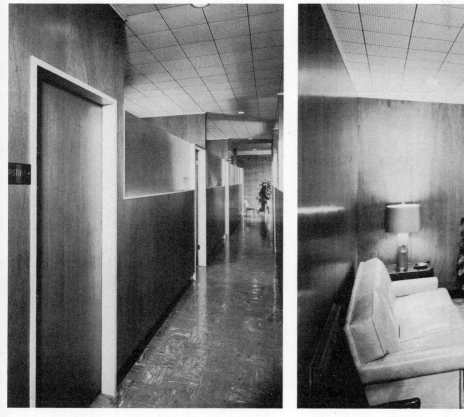

Joseph Molitor

OFFICE FOR BESSEMER IMPROVEMENT CO.

Greensboro, North Carolina

Edward Loewenstein, Architect

WHEN THE REAL ESTATE and development company which owns this building chose the site for the project, it had two main goals in mind: to provide offices away from the center of town and to prove that low, swampy property could be used to good advantage. The site is in the midst of a large area owned by the Bessemer Company. Most of it was 8 ft below the street and several feet below existing sewers; it was partially wooded and generally under water during rainy seasons. Similar sites on the property were not saleable until this building had been completed and it had been proved that construction was possible without great expense and filling.

The original plan was to place the building on a single, central column enclosing the services. The owner considered this too radical, however, and suggested four columns. A block foundation finally was adopted after it had been decided to provide space for heating and air conditioning, plus a garage-work shop at ground level. The original contours of the site were preserved, which is expected to permit easy landscaping and planting in the future.

Half of the building is given over to a private office suite which includes the owner's office, storage space, lounge and light lunch facilities, and a screened sun deck where business may be transacted in good weather. The other half of the building consists of offices for the development company's staff.

Foundation is concrete block, framing is wood stud. Exterior walls are random width pine, painted. Interior walls are plywood, floors are rubber tile over wood, ceilings are acoustical cane fiber tile.

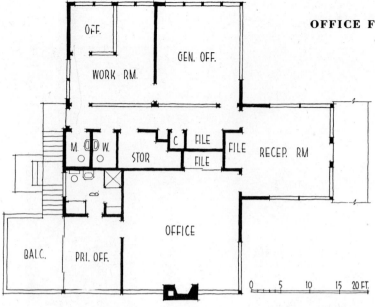

OFFICE FOR BESSEMER IMPROVEMENT CO.

OFF.

GEN. OFF.

WORK RM.

M. | W. | STOR | C | FILE | FILE | RECEP. RM
FILE

B.

OFFICE

BALC. | PRI. OFF.

0   5   10   15   20 FT.

In both plan and section the building is refreshingly simple and well adapted to its swampy site. Opposite page: offices are well lighted and airy; windows are shaded with venetian blinds (top) or split bamboo (bottom). Fireplace wall has marble inserts

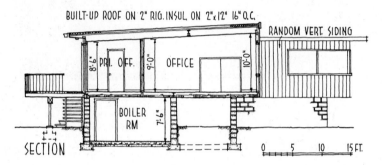

BUILT-UP ROOF ON 2" RIG. INSUL. ON 2"x12" 16" O.C.

RANDOM VERT. SIDING

PRI. OFF. 8'-9" | OFFICE 9'-0" | 10'-0"

BOILER RM. 7'-6"

SECTION

0   5   10   15 FT.

Joseph Molitor

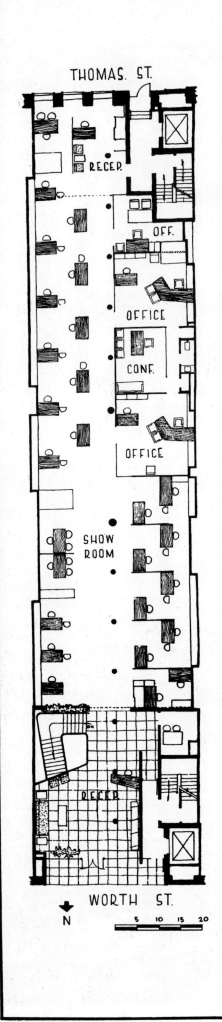

THOMAS ST.

RECEP.

OFF.

OFFICE

CONF.

OFFICE

SHOW ROOM

RECEP.

WORTH ST.

N

5 10 15 20

Greenwood Mills ...

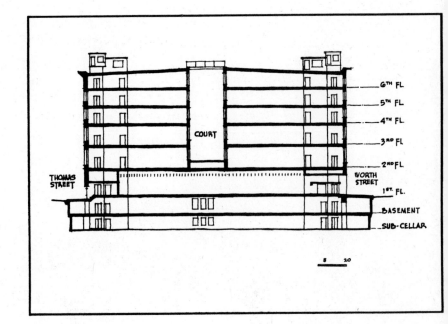

6TH FL
5TH FL
4TH FL
3RD FL
2ND FL

COURT

THOMAS STREET

WORTH STREET

1ST. FL.

BASEMENT

SUB-CELLAR

5   20

GIVE LIFT TO OLD TEXTILE AREA

Photos: Richard Garrison

Beeston and Stott, Architects

Beeston-Stott-Patterson, Designers

THE GROWING TREND of competitors to relocate uptown in the big buildings of New York's congested West 30's and 40's led Greenwood Mills, Inc., to carefully analyze their own position. Their New York sales rooms and offices were housed in a narrow, cast iron front, post Civil War structure that was almost identical to its neighbors. It was located in the heart of the old wholesale textile district where the uptown movement had lessened realty values — and the traffic problem. The final decision to remain and completely remodel the building has helped considerably to add to the prestige of both the district and the firm.

The architects and designers succeeded in providing a series of inviting, open interiors from the long, narrow plan, which had a row of cast iron structural columns through the center. As a light court divided the upper portion of the building, it was decided to provide a separate entrance to the front half so it could be rented. The front of the building was replaced with a new facade of soft blue-green matte-glazed brick and white marble trim. The Thomas Street facade was provided with a new entrance and painted the same blue-green. New stairways, elevators, toilets and air conditioning were installed throughout the building.

REMODELED OFFICES

The reception lobby (below) leads directly into main sales and office area. Interior colors and textures were carefully studied; greens and browns were used throughout, with coral and yellow accents

The stairway shown above and upper right, was planned to be as open and attractive as possible to permit use of basement as a sales area. Besides the general interiors, the design contract included the special louvered ceiling, most of the desks, the wall cabinets, and such accessories as blotter pads, letter trays and waste baskets. Side walls were furred out to hide pipes and pilasters, recess new cabinets

Photos: Richard Garrison

Open planning and glass partitions are also used in upper floors, as in second floor office at right. All floors are surfaced with asphalt tile, rubber tile, or carpet. Walls are plaster, with many surfaced with plastic or textured fabric

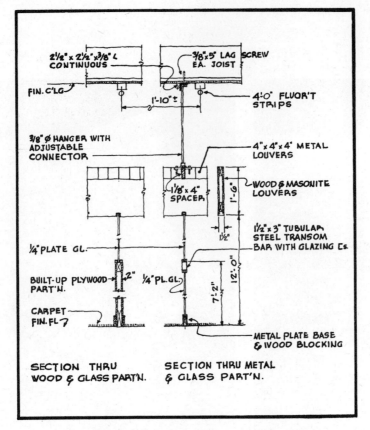

2½" x 2½" x⅜" L
CONTINUOUS

FIN. C'LG.

⅜"x 5" LAG SCREW
EA. JOIST

1'-10"±

4'-0" FLUOR'T
STRIPS

⅜" Ø HANGER WITH
ADJUSTABLE
CONNECTOR

4"x 4"x 4" METAL
LOUVERS

1⅛ x 4"
SPACER

WOOD & MASONITE
LOUVERS

1'-6"

¼" PLATE GL.

½"

1½" x 3" TUBULAR
STEEL TRANSOM
BAR WITH GLAZING Cs.

BUILT-UP PLYWOOD
PART'N.

2"

¼" PL. GL.

7'-2"

12'-0"

CARPET
FIN. FL.

METAL PLATE BASE
& WOOD BLOCKING

SECTION THRU
WOOD & GLASS PART'N.

SECTION THRU METAL
& GLASS PART'N.

*Detail above shows sections through typical office partitions
and through the louvered ceiling of the main floor*

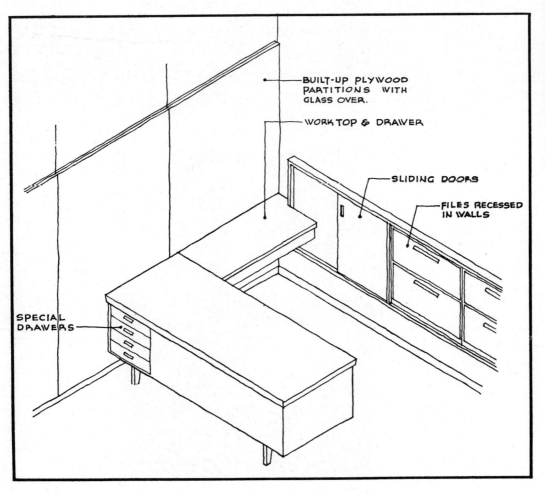

BUILT-UP PLYWOOD
PARTITIONS WITH
GLASS OVER.

WORK TOP & DRAWER

SLIDING DOORS

FILES RECESSED
IN WALLS

SPECIAL
DRAWERS

The president's office (above) is in the center of the main floor, and planned at his request to be as open as possible yet give a reasonable amount of privacy. This was solved by using glass and thin wood screens. Detail of president's custom-designed desk is shown right. Sketch at left shows arrangement of junior executive's desk (visible at right in photo)

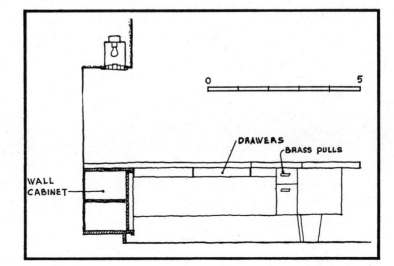

0   5

DRAWERS
BRASS PULLS

WALL
CABINET

SMALL OFFICE BUILDINGS

SMALL OFFICE BUILDINGS is, of course, a loose classification. But it includes a great variety of quite typical assignments for architects. There is, for example, the "taxpayer," long familiar in every American town, but now showing up in new concepts and designs. There are new types of small rental buildings, not taxpayers, and no longer wedded to downtown locations. Also industrial offices, community centers, and so on, all different in purpose and use, but all geared to an age of mobility, an age, too, of fast improvements in concept, equipment, and esthetics.

A trend growing to important proportions is the outward movement of large company headquarters. Once it was considered necessary for a large home office to be in the heart of the city, but now many a large office is moved bodily to outlying areas, where life is not made quite so hectic by noise and traffic and smoke and congestion. An excellent example appears on page 61, a building done by the Wurster firm for the Insurance Company of North America.

Behind a great many of the changes in small office buildings is the automobile. Cars are, of course, the cause of decentralization, and the outward movement, in its turn, is the cause of many changes in building design. Economics change rapidly as property values go down, and buildings tend to go horizontal.

On the other hand, the automobile sometimes works in a contrary way. Many cities now insist that so many square feet of office space must entail parking space for so many cars. So the parking lot becomes bigger than the building. Or, the ground floor space, once considered the *raison d'etre* for the building, now is occupied by parked cars, and the building straddles the parking lot.

Once the auto has had its say, the architect may take over. He may then get busy providing the new comforts and satisfactions, the more positive assets of the times. And usually the success of the whole building venture will devolve upon the architect and the appeals he builds into the project, appeals for customers, tenants, clients or employees. The important thing is that the architect has more scope than ever before. Square foot costs will always be with him, but not necessarily the driving cost equations of high land values. Certainly, away from downtown, he will have more freedom in planning, in materials, in colors, in landscaping, in all matters of design.

GARAGE REMODELED AS OFFICE BUILDING

221 South Church Street Building, Charlotte, N. C.

A. G. O'Dell, Jr., and Associates, Architects and Engineers

WHETHER to remodel or destroy and rebuild? This question is faced by many architects whose clients own speculative buildings which are structurally sound, but located in districts warranting higher rentals and a type of occupancy not possible with the original building. A new building can generally assure easy rental for a considerable period by special planning for the expected tenants. Structural and other difficulties encountered in remodeling are avoided. On the other hand, the shorter life expectancies of older adjoining buildings often warn against heavy new investment.

Such was the case with this small office building, remodeled from a structure formerly used for garages, and on a site adjoining properties which the client also owned. The original two-story building was of mill construction, divided down the center by a continuous brick wall extending to the roof. It was on the property line on all sides, with the exception of a narrow open

Joseph Molitor Photo

Drastic alterations made the old garage building entirely suitable for office use; result: 100 per cent occupancy and higher income

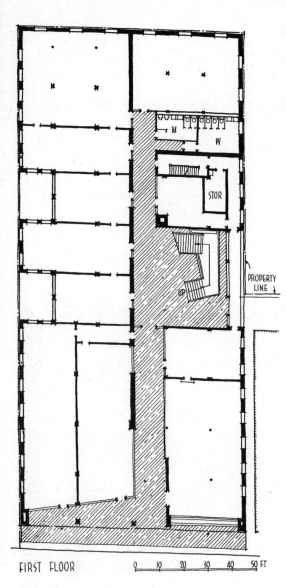

FIRST FLOOR

M

W

STOR

UP

PROPERTY LINE

0   10   20   30   40   50 FT

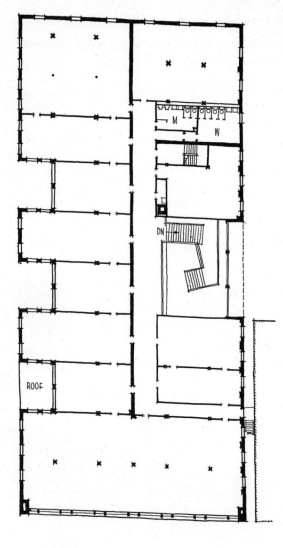

SECOND FLOOR

M

W

DN

ROOF

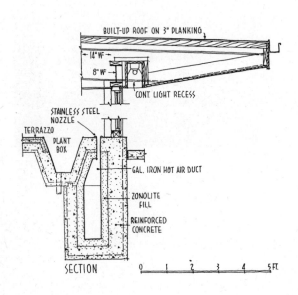

BUILT-UP ROOF ON 3" PLANKING

14" WF

8" WF

CONT. LIGHT RECESS

STAINLESS STEEL NOZZLE

TERRAZZO

PLANT BOX

GAL. IRON HOT AIR DUCT

ZONOLITE FILL

REINFORCED CONCRETE

SECTION

0   1   2   3   4   5 FT.

Joseph Molitor Photo

space and an alley along part of one side. Major problems included how to guarantee rental of second-floor
offices without the expense of providing an elevator,
and how to assure natural light and ventilation to all
offices, particularly on the north side where an existing
parking lot might be built upon in the future.

The final solution seeks to assure economic success of
the building by making it as attractive and comfortable
as possible for the tenants and their customers. Especial
attention was given the entrance and stair lobby. The
latter is two-stories high, and occupies an area larger
than usual, considered by some as wasteful of rental
space. It was the architect's opinion that if the stairs
were not made attractive, the walk-up second floor
office space would be difficult to rent. The building is

now 100 per cent rented and the architect feels "that it
is principally due to the interest of both the tenants and
the public in the open stair lobby."

The exposure of the glass wall in this lobby is southwest, and various means were considered to protect it
from excessive sunlight in the summer months. A roof
overhang extended to the property line helps to shield
this area. Exterior and interior venetian blinds were
considered, but it was finally decided that a few solid
panels would sufficiently cut down the sunlight and in
addition provide interesting shadows and light spots on
the interior of the lobby.

Sections of the dividing center wall were removed or
penetrated in such a way that it is no longer obvious.
All offices are air conditioned.

Joseph Molitor Photo

Joseph Molitor Photos

Extra space and extra design touches combine to make the stair lobby inviting and thus aid in renting upper-floor offices in converted garage building. Corridors and offices have sparkle of modern, clean design, good light

Joseph Molitor Photos

MULTI-PURPOSE BUILDING FOR RURAL COUNTY

Wake County Office Building, Raleigh, N. C.

William Henley Dietrick, Architect

COMFORT and functional requirements are happily combined with economy of structure and maintenance in this simple, straightforward office building. Designed to house a part of the offices and activities of a widely diversified county program, the structure provides facilities for both the government agencies and for the public which they serve. The ground floor includes a large multi-use area for the farm women as a retail curb market for their products on Saturdays and as an assembly room for lectures and demonstrations on other days. The room was provided with ample means of access from the street, parking areas, and main entrances within the building. Due to its location in a relatively non-congested area, a good amount of off-street parking has been provided adjacent to the building.

The first floor houses offices, labor and special equipment rooms for the county health program. Space was provided on the second floor for the County Welfare Department, the County Agricultural Program, Agri-

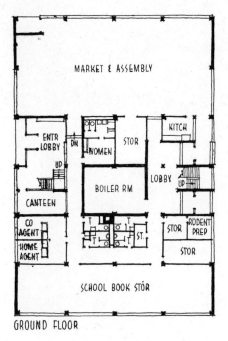

MARKET & ASSEMBLY

ENTR LOBBY · DN · WOMEN · STOR · KITCH

UP · BOILER RM · LOBBY · UP

CANTEEN

CO AGENT · HOME AGENT · ST. · STOR · RODENT PREP · STOR

SCHOOL BOOK STOR

GROUND FLOOR

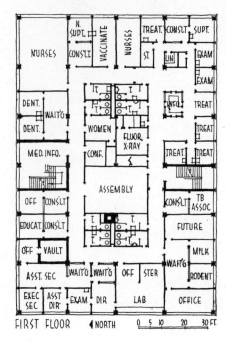

N. SUPT. · VACCINATE · TREAT · CONSLT · SUPT.

NURSES · CONS'LT · NURSES · ST. · LIN · EXAM

EXAM

DENT. · WAIT'G · WOMEN · INFO · TREAT

DENT. · FLUOR. X-RAY · TREAT

MED. INFO. · CONF. · TREAT · TREAT

UP

OFF · CONSLT · ASSEMBLY

EDUCAT. · CONS'LT · CONSLT · TB ASSOC

OFF · VAULT · FUTURE

MILK

WAIT'G · RODENT

ASST. SEC · WAIT'G · WAIT'G · OFF · STER

EXEC SEC · ASST DIR · EXAM · DIR · LAB · OFFICE

FIRST FLOOR ◄NORTH 0 5 10 20 30 FT

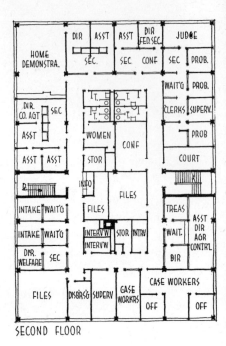

DIR · ASST · ASST · DIR FED. SEC. · JUDGE

HOME DEMONSTRA. · SEC. · SEC. · CONF · SEC · PROB.

WAIT'G · PROB.

DIR CO. AGT · SEC · CLERKS · SUPERV.

ASST · WOMEN · PROB

ASST · ASST · STOR · CONF · COURT

INFO

INTAKE · WAIT'G · FILES · FILES

INTAKE · WAIT'G · INTERVW · STOR · INTRV · WAIT. · TREAS

DIR. WELFARE · SEC · INTERVW · DIR · ASST DIR AGR CONTRL

FILES · DISBRS'G · SUPERV · CASE WORKRS · CASE WORKERS · OFF · OFF

SECOND FLOOR

cultural and Home Demonstration agents, and offices and a small court room for the probation court.

Natural light and ventilation is provided on the interior by continuous window bands of heat resistant glass. Sun glare is tempered by interior venetian blinds.

The steel frame structure has exterior walls of brick cavity construction, with interiors finished with glazed terra cotta and plaster. Brick spandrels are continuous on each facade, with corners finished by 5 by 5 in. steel angles to simplify brick laying. The roof is designed to reduce problems frequently met with parapet construction. Floors are finished in asphalt tile; stairs are exposed steel. All these materials were selected to simplify maintenance. The problem of window washing was met with a special window washing trolley which can be moved around the building on tracks above the window bands.

Interior partitions are concrete block, ceilings are plaster. Interior downspouts are wrought iron. All interior lighting is fluorescent.

Floor plans of this county office building show everything from a combination produce market and assembly room, whatever that is, to health offices and clinics, even a probate court. Must be a busy place on a Saturday in the fall. Note (right) use of a 5-in channel to simplify brick laying at the corner, also trolley for window washing

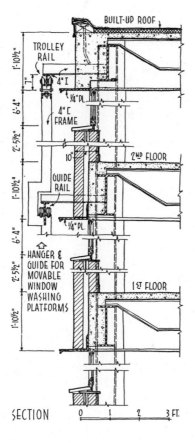

SECTION   0   1   2   3 FT.

Joseph Molitor Photos

INDIVIDUALIZED OFFICES, WITH PARKING

Security Life and Trust Building, Winston-Salem, N. C.

Macklin and Stinson, Architects and Engineers

LARGER private companies are finding it more and more expedient to house their administrative offices in smaller, personally-owned buildings, as in this four-story office building for Security Life and Trust Company. The entire building is devoted to the company's use, with the exception of a small rental area for a bank on the main floor. Entrances to this area are provided off the entrance vestibule and the main lobby.

For the convenience of the personnel, about half the site has been devoted to parking — in a basement area and on the basement roof. The basement also serves as a convenient truck dock for the removal of the large

quantities of waste paper which accumulate in the course of such a business.

The honeycomb facade, augmented with double glazing and venetian blinds, is designed to protect the air-conditioned interior from the glare and heat of the hot summer sun, and still permit ample daylight for the interior, and natural ventilation when desired.

The structure is steel frame, finished in brick and light cream stone. Interior walls are plastered, and painted or papered. Office partitions are of metal, some in wood veneers. Ceilings are of acoustical board. Lobby floor is terazzo; others, asphalt tile.

Joseph W. Molitor Photos

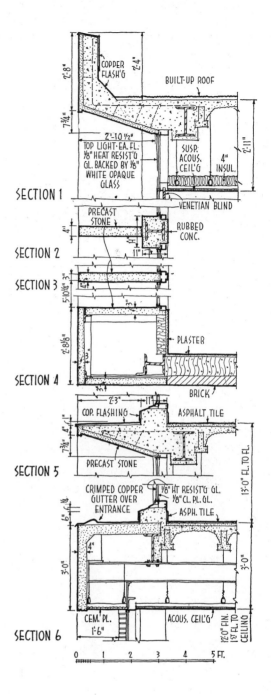

SECTION 1

COPPER FLASH'G
2'-8"
2'-4"
7¾"
2'-10½"
BUILT-UP ROOF
TOP LIGHT·EA. FL. ⅛" HEAT RESIST'G GL. BACKED BY ⅛" WHITE OPAQUE GLASS
SUSP. ACOUS. CEIL'G
4" INSUL.
2'-11"
VENETIAN BLIND

SECTION 2

PRECAST STONE
4"
11"
RUBBED CONC.

SECTION 3

3"
5'-10¼"

SECTION 4

3"
2'-8⅝"
PLASTER
BRICK

SECTION 5

2'-3"
11"
COP. FLASHING
4"
7¾"
PRECAST STONE
ASPHALT TILE
13'-0" FL. TO FL.

SECTION 6

CRIMPED COPPER GUTTER OVER ENTRANCE
6"
6¼"
3'-0"
4"
⅛" HT RESIST'G GL.
⅛" CL. PL. GL.
ASPH. TILE
3'-0"
CEM. PL. 1'-6"
ACOUS. CEIL'G
12'0" FIN. 1ST FL. TO CEILING

0 1 2 3 4 5 FT.

A honeycomb of vertical and horizontal fins of precast stone protect the building against worst of sun heat, without serious loss of daylight, and cut the cooling load

Joseph W. Molitor Photos

Square form is entirely suitable for offices of this insurance and banking firm, where large open offices are the typical space use. Square is economical, and central elevator and utility core keeps space from getting too ''deep'' from windows

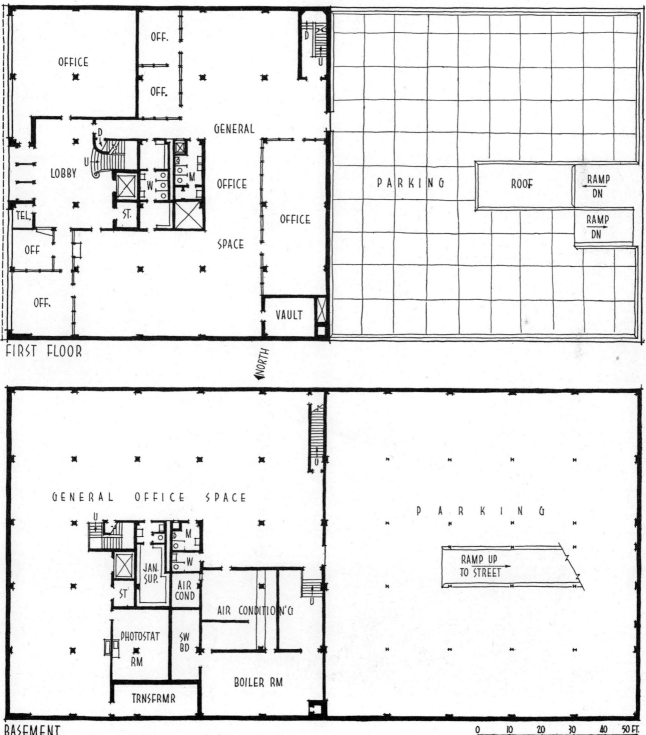

FIRST FLOOR

OFFICE

OFF.

OFF.

GENERAL

OFFICE

OFFICE

SPACE

LOBBY

U D

W M

ST.

TEL.

OFF

OFF.

VAULT

D U

PARKING

ROOF

RAMP DN

RAMP DN

NORTH

BASEMENT

GENERAL OFFICE SPACE

U

M

JAN. SUP.

W

ST.

AIR COND

PHOTOSTAT RM

SW BD

AIR CONDITIO'NG

BOILER RM

TRNSFRMR

D

PARKING

RAMP UP TO STREET

0   10   20   30   40   50 FT.

OFFICE BUILDING FOR AN INSIDE LOT

Herold Building, Oklahoma City, Oklahoma

Vahlberg, Palmer & Vahlberg, Architects

A. Y. Owan Photos

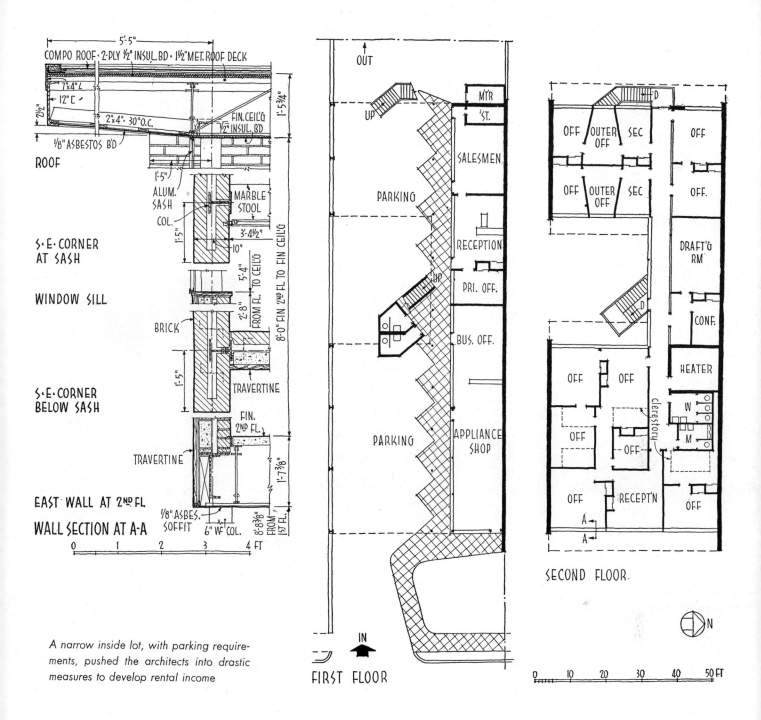

ROOF

COMPO ROOF · 2-PLY ½" INSUL. BD · 1½" MET. ROOF DECK

5'-5"

7"×4" ∠
12" C
2'×4". 30" O.C.
FIN. CEIL'G
½" INSUL. BD
⅛" ASBESTOS B'D
1'-5¾"
2½"

S·E· CORNER AT SASH

WINDOW SILL

1'-5"
ALUM. SASH
MARBLE STOOL
COL.
3'-4½"
10"

5'-4" TO CEIL'G
8'-0" FIN 2ND FL TO FIN CEIL'G

S·E· CORNER BELOW SASH

BRICK
2'-8" FROM FL. TO CEIL'G

1'-5"
TRAVERTINE

TRAVERTINE
FIN. 2ND FL.

EAST WALL AT 2ND FL

WALL SECTION AT A-A

⅛" ASBES. SOFFIT
6" WF COL.
1'-7⅜"
8'-8⅜" FROM 1ST FL.

0   1   2   3   4 FT

*A narrow inside lot, with parking require-
ments, pushed the architects into drastic
measures to develop rental income*

OUT
UP

PARKING

PARKING

IN

FIRST FLOOR

MTR
ST.
SALESMEN
RECEPTION
UP
PRI. OFF.
BUS. OFF.
APPLIANCE SHOP

OFF OUTER OFF SEC OFF
OFF OUTER OFF SEC OFF.
DRAFT'G RM
CONF.
clerestory
HEATER
OFF OFF
W
OFF OFF M
A
OFF RECEPT'N OFF
A

SECOND FLOOR

N

0   10   20   30   40   50 FT

A RATHER unusual program was given to the architects of this speculative office building. The owner had an existing business site that he wanted to put to more lucrative use. His only requests were the provision of as large a building as possible, with minimum maintenance, operation and upkeep costs. Decisions as to the type of building to be built, its exact size and cost, and subsequently its management, were left entirely up to the architects.

The site was an inside lot on a busy traffic artery with no parking allowed. It was located about a mile north of the city proper, close to hospitals and a shopping center. Adjoining property could not be purchased. Zoning ordinances required a set amount of parking area for each square foot of rentable space. Three stories was the height limit allowed.

The program of requirements was drawn up by the architects after an analysis of office space requirements, property values and building costs, type of building needed in the area, leases and potential return on long term leases. It was finally decided to construct an office building to serve general businesses which must be close to the downtown area, but not necessarily in the heart of town. Provision for private automobiles therefore became a major factor. To assure maximum rental values, outside light and ventilation to all spaces was necessary.

The final size of the building was determined by the fact that a paying investment was required by the owner. Thus taxes, insurance, rate of return and the rental per sq ft of this type of office building determined its final size. A two story height was settled on after computing that the rentals from a third floor would not pay for its costs plus the cost of an elevator, which would then be necessary.

To obviate the feeling that any of the office spaces were at the rear of the building, a drive-through feature with parking spaces for each tenant was created on a large portion of the first floor area. The building above was made U shaped for maximum air and light on the inside lot. All automobile entries are made from the street and exits out the alley.

Court walls use as much glass as possible, to get maximum light into interior spaces, since the narrow lot affords no "light protection," and party line walls can have no windows. A few inside offices are given extra light by means of clerestory windows (right, below)

Wurster, Bernardi and Emmons, Architects

ELEVATED BUILDING PROVIDES PARKING

HERE we have an instance in which parking becomes perhaps the major determinant in the planning of an office building. Here presumably the sacrifice was less than in a later case (p. 150), since this is an office project for an industrial concern. In any case the now-familiar device of elevating the building works out nicely to provide covered parking and entrance ways, and at the same time to lift the working offices above the distractions of the street level, also to give them better daylight.

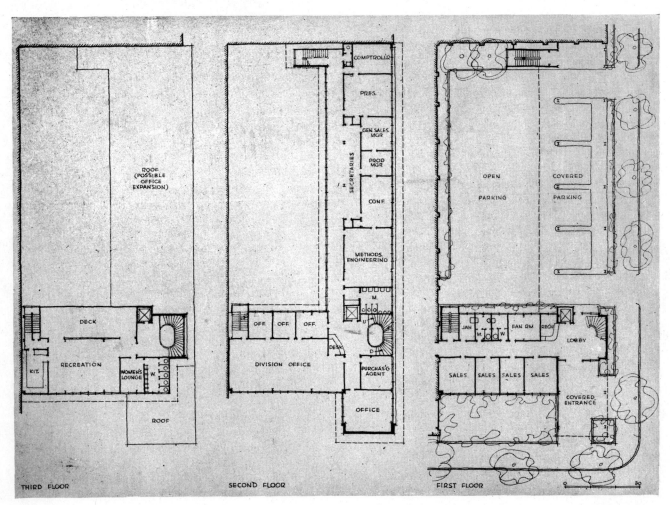

THIRD FLOOR   SECOND FLOOR   FIRST FLOOR

VERMONT ELECTRIC CO-OPERATIVE, INC.

JOHNSON, VERMONT

Whittier & Goodrich

Architects

Joseph Molitor Photos

*Display room is clearly visible
from walk leading to entrance*

THE Vermont Electric Co-operative building stresses modular construction almost as strongly as does the Caledonian Record plant shown next (on pages 96, 97 and 98). Foundations also are concrete block, but exterior walls are of patented hollow-core semi-modular cement brick. Interior plans again revolve around the 4-in. module established by selection of materials for exterior walls and framing.

Although the two buildings are alike in plan and elevation, each reflects its own particular purpose. The Caledonian Record plant is thoroughly businesslike, intended to attract a strictly business clientele; the Vermont Electric Co-operative building is planned to appeal to the consumer, and features a large display room opened to the street with plate glass display windows.

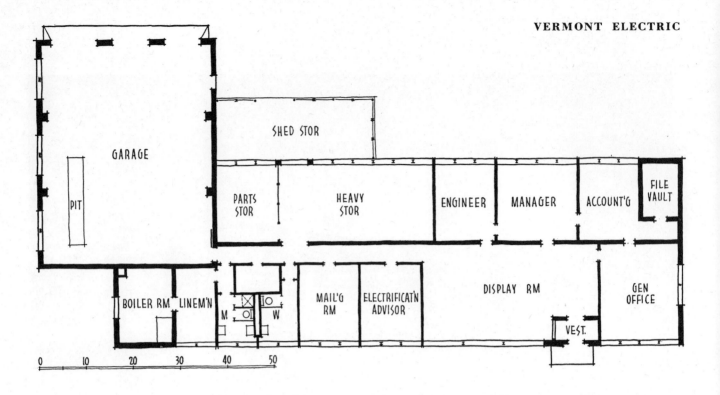

GARAGE

PIT

SHED STOR

PARTS STOR

HEAVY STOR

ENGINEER

MANAGER

ACCOUNT'G

FILE VAULT

BOILER RM   LINEM'N

M   O   W

MAIL'G RM

ELECTRIFICAT'N ADVISOR

DISPLAY RM

GEN OFFICE

VEST.

0   10   20   30   40   50

Building is so planned that each of its functions is segregated. Linemen's quarters are handy to both garage and storage rooms. Offices are at opposite end of building, opening to display room which serves also as a lobby. Floors throughout are asphalt tile, ceilings are acoustic tile. Both incandescent and fluorescent lighting are used; fixtures are mostly recessed

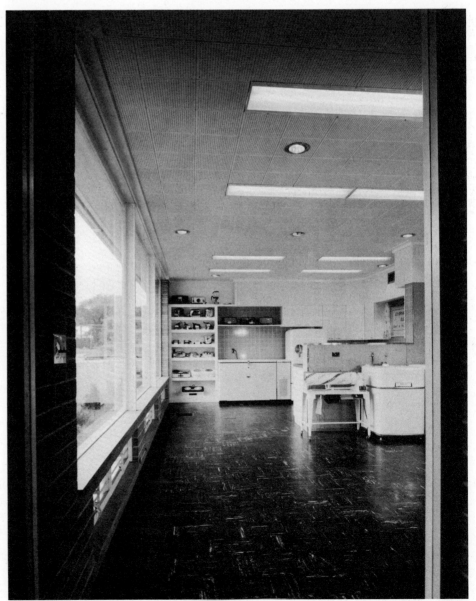

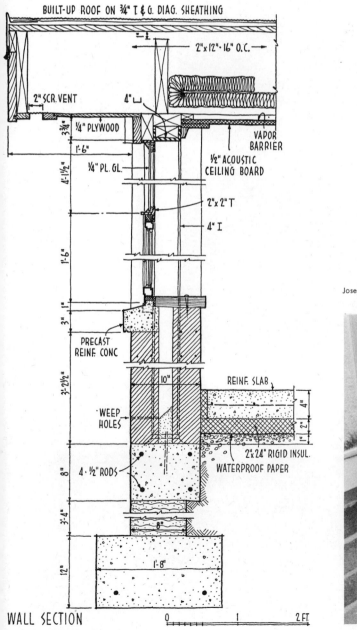

BUILT-UP ROOF ON ¾" T & G. DIAG. SHEATHING

2" x 12" - 16" O.C.

2" SCR. VENT

4"

¼" PLYWOOD

3¾"

1'-6"

VAPOR BARRIER

½" ACOUSTIC CEILING BOARD

4'-1½"

¼" PL. GL.

2" x 2" T

4" I

1'-6"

3"

PRECAST REINF. CONC

3'-2½"

10"

REINF. SLAB

4"

2"

1"

WEEP HOLES

8"

4 - ½" RODS

2" x 24" RIGID INSUL.
WATERPROOF PAPER

3'-4"

8"

12"

1'-8"

WALL SECTION   0   1   2 FT

Above: *manager's office; door at extreme right leads to display room, center door to accounting department. Ventilation in display room is provided by stock louvers beneath the plate glass windows (detail below)*

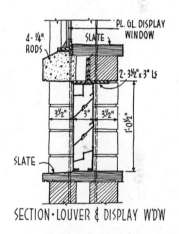

4 - ¼" RODS

SLATE

PL. GL. DISPLAY WINDOW

2 - 3½" x 3" Ls

3½"   3"   3½"

1'-0½"

SLATE

SECTION · LOUVER & DISPLAY W'D'W

Joseph Molitor Photos

Joseph Molitor Photos

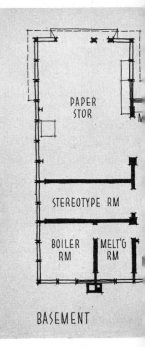

PAPER
STOR

STEREOTYPE RM

BOILER
RM

MELT'G
RM

BASEMENT

CALEDONIAN RECORD PUBLISHING CO., INC.

ST. JOHNSBURY, VERMONT

Whittier & Goodrich

Architects

IN THE DESIGN of this small newspaper plant and of the Vermont Electric Co-operative building (page 93), the architects were frankly experimenting with the use of modular coordination and inexpensive materials and detailing to hold down construction costs. The two buildings, erected almost concurrently, are therefore very much alike both in simplicity of plan and in exterior appearance.

The newspaper plant shown on these three pages is completely self-sufficient, providing every facility re-

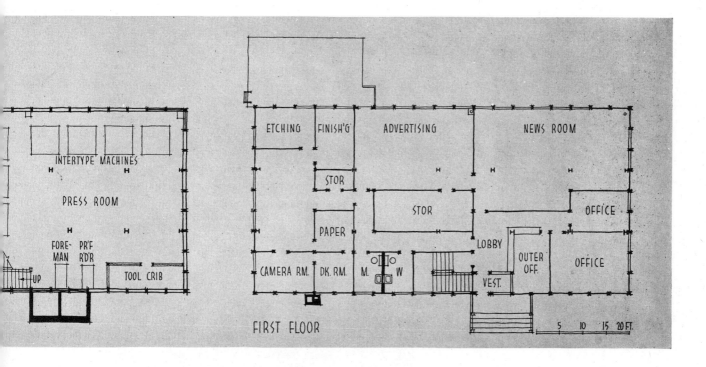

FIRST FLOOR

Opposite page: a sloping site was used to give building a seemingly one-story front (top) and two-story rear (bottom). The press room (center) is on lower level, handy to mailing room and paper storage, well lighted and well organized

quired not only for the printing and mailing of the paper itself, but for income-augmenting job printing as well. Within the economical rectangle of its exterior walls is ample room for the many departments required by a newspaper. Yet the building has no pretense about it; it blends happily with the surrounding Vermont countryside; and it gives unmistakable evidence of economic planning.

Foundations are concrete block, framing is steel with wood joists. Exterior walls and all interior partitions are cement fiber panels in modular sizes, which were used in conjunction with 4-by-4 verticals to achieve virtually complete modular construction. Floors are asphalt tile, ceilings are acoustic tile.

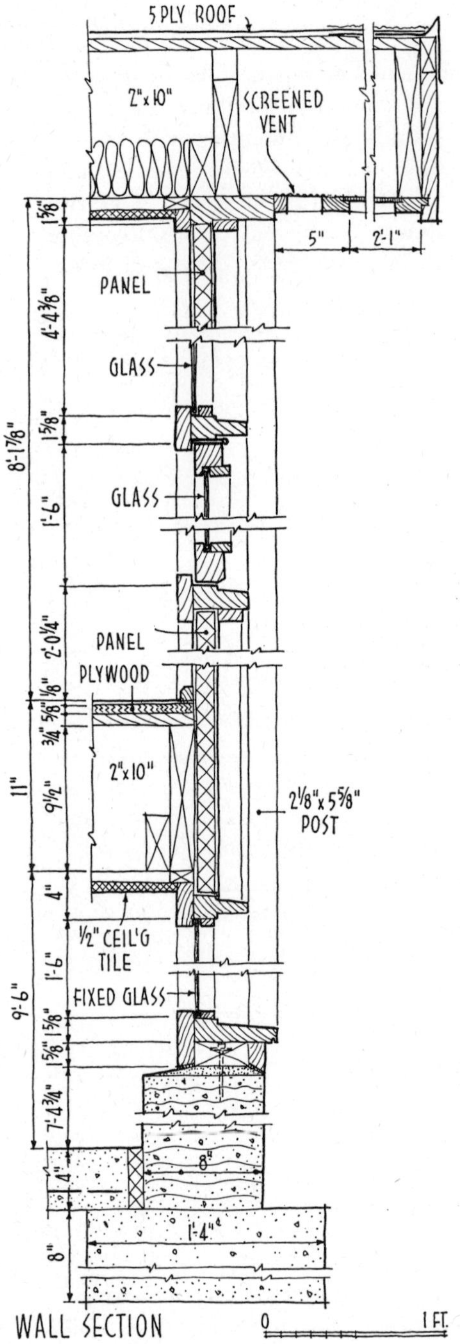
5 PLY ROOF
2"x10"
SCREENED VENT
5"
2'-1"
1⅝"
4'-4⅞"
PANEL
GLASS
8'-1⅞"
1⅝"
GLASS
1'-6"
2'-0¼"
PANEL
PLYWOOD
⅛"
¾" ⅝"
2"x10"
11"
9½"
2⅛"x5⅝" POST
4"
½" CEIL'G TILE
1'-6"
FIXED GLASS
9'-6"
1⅝"
1⅝"
7'-4¾"
8"
4"
1'-4"
8"
WALL SECTION
0
1 FT.

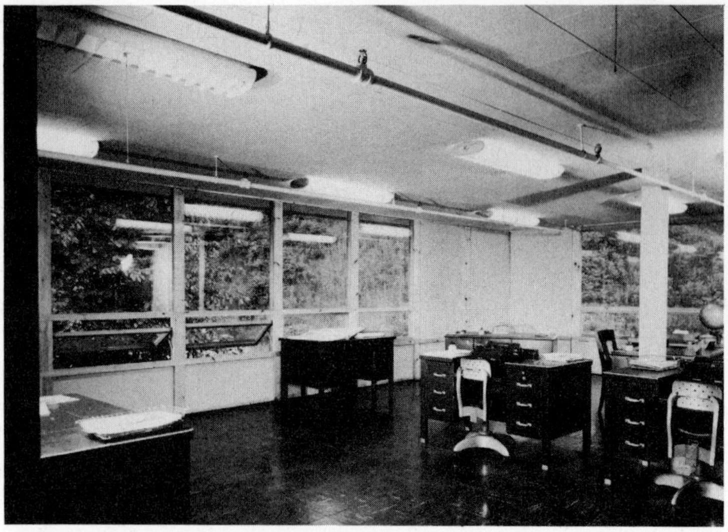

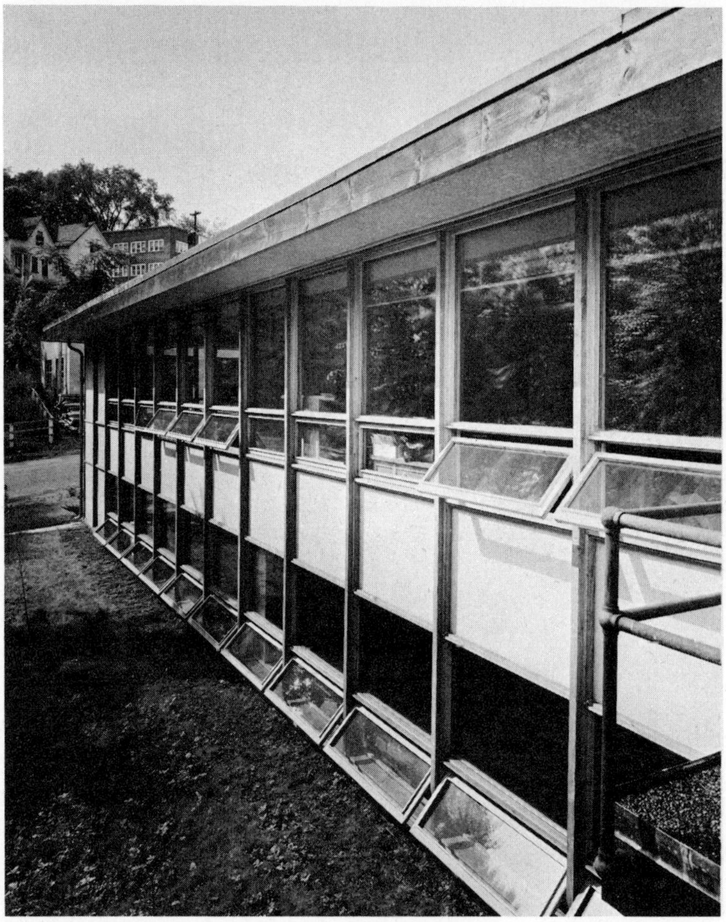

Careful attention to detail is evident in wall and window sections above and right. Use of modular wall panels, standard posts and windows cut down on construction costs without in any way detracting from efficiency and comfort of the building

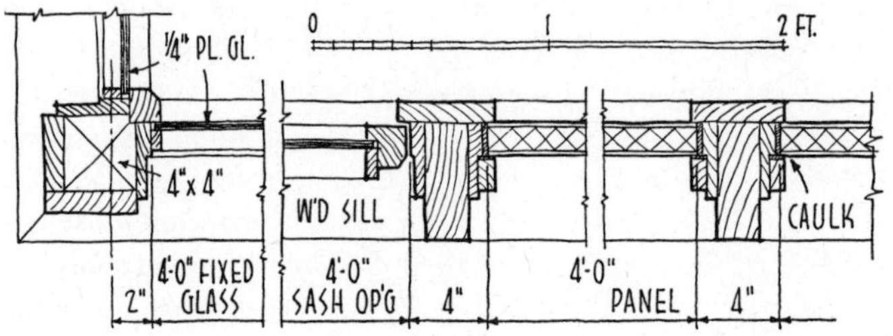
¼" PL. GL.
0
1
2 FT.
4"x 4"
W'D SILL
CAULK
2"
4'-0" FIXED GLASS
4'-0" SASH OP'G
4"
4'-0" PANEL
4"

TWO NEW ARCHITECTS'
OFFICE BUILDINGS

JAMES A. BRITTON, A.I.A.

JESSEN JESSEN MILLHOUSE & GREEVEN

Wʜᴇɴ ᴀɴ ᴀʀᴄʜɪᴛᴇᴄᴛ designs and builds for himself — his own offices or his own home — he is, consciously or not, designing and building a promotion piece for the whole architectural profession. No matter what he says, what he does for himself is bound to be taken, in his own community at least, as the best and most advanced thinking of his profession. The same is true whether he remodels an existing structure (a happy solution in many cases) or builds from the ground up. His clients — past, present and possible future — will look it over and judge him accordingly. He cannot afford to put anything but his best into his designs for his own use.

Yet all too often an architect is content with rented office space which he adapts sketchily to his particular needs. He is reluctant to take on the financial burden of his own building and closes his eyes to the effect his crowded, cluttered and often musty quarters may have on his clients. Fortunately, his clients usually close their eyes, too, to his surroundings and concentrate on the work he turns out.

It doesn't make sense, of course. If he designs and builds his own offices he stands to gain on three separate and specific counts:

1. His building will be good advertising.
2. It will show his clients what he can do.
3. It will give him more efficient production and a far happier staff.

The experience, of the two firms whose offices are shown above and on the next eight pages are typical. In Greenfield, Mass., James A. Britton, A.I.A., had been looking forward for some time to a building of his own. He had bought a large lot in a semi-residential area rather far out on the main street, and had sketched various plans for a building which would house his offices and would also bring in rental revenue. Then one Sunday noon he needed a certain plan in a hurry. Completely exasperated when he could not find it (his storage facilities were like those of most architects), he decided then and there to forget about a possible tenant and to

build solely for his own use. He sat down at a drafting table, made a few rough sketches — and that was that. By three o'clock the next afternoon both contracts and sub-contracts had been let. The bulldozer moved in at nine o'clock the following morning.

In Austin, Texas, the architectural firm of Jessen Jessen Millhouse and Greeven decided at about the same time to put up no longer with makeshift quarters. Like Mr. Britton, they designed a one-story building exclusively for their own use. They chose a site in a residential area and obtained the required zoning waiver. By a curious coincidence both firms elected to open their reception areas to the public with generously proportioned windows along the main thoroughfare, and both angled their buildings to give the public the best possible view of their activities. Far apart as they are geographically, the two buildings thus have a lot in common.

Both firms report uniformly favorable reactions to their new quarters. Mr. Britton credits several sizable commissions directly to the impression his present offices made on prospective clients. Jessen Jessen Millhouse and Greeven report that their new building was a traffic hazard for months because so many Austin motorists stopped for a look. Both firms stress the promotion advantages noticed to date.

But what would happen to these two buildings if their owners vacated them? Are they so "special" that they could be used by no one but architects? The answer is emphatically no. Either building could be converted almost without alteration to doctors' or dentists' offices, a small clinic, perhaps a nursery school. Each has two large rooms — reception and drafting — plus smaller offices and what amounts to a frank store front. No matter what happens to the firms now occupying them, these two buildings have a long and useful life ahead of them. Meanwhile they are adding materially to the prestige of the architectural profession and are bringing to their owners innumerable unexpected benefits.

OFFICES OF JAMES A. BRITTON, A.I.A.

Greenfield, Massachusetts

Color plays an important part in the effectiveness of Mr. Britton's new building. Exterior is red brick and white stucco. Reception room (right and opposite) has one wall of lime yellow corrugated transite, one of natural redwood; drapes are lime yellow and garnet. An aquarium filled with colorful tropical fish stands in the window just behind the secretaries' desks; it fascinates waiting clients. Lighting here and in Mr. Britton's office is fluorescent, a combination of warm white and daylight blue, which can be used alone or together to change the lighting mood

UNDERLYING MR. BRITTON'S DESIGN for his new offices
is a strong understanding of public relations. The
building is planned to make the citizens of Greenfield
constantly aware of what is going on inside: passersby
approaching from either direction get a clear view of
the reception room, even at night. The large site is
landscaped to permit seasonal displays along the front
and a "working garden" in the rear to supply cut flowers
for the reception room and private offices. Prospective
clients are led through the drafting room to the conference room.

Joseph W. Molitor Photos

The building impresses the visitor instantly as compact and orderly. There is no clutter anywhere. Not a
single file cabinet juts out from the wall. Blueprint
files, book shelves, storage cabinets, all are built in.
Not an inch of space is wasted. Even the garage, below
the drafting room wing, serves a multiple purpose—
it doubles as an exhibition hall, as a model workshop
(the firm builds all of its own models), and as a gar-
dener's toolshed.

Exterior walls are brick, stucco and redwood siding.
Framing is wood and steel on a foundation of 12-in.
cinder concrete units on 8-in. reinforced concrete slab.
Ceilings throughout are acoustic tile.

*Filing cabinets and supplies in the
combination reception room-office are
hidden in a closet (barely visible at
extreme left of photo above) just
opposite the secretaries' desks*

Because Greenfield is close to no large city, Mr. Britton has planned his offices to be as self-sufficient as possible. He makes his own blueprints, photostats and models, and plans to add a decorator's service later on. Decorator's office would be an extension at south end of reception room, with own entrance

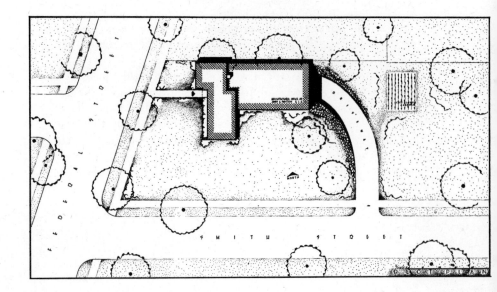

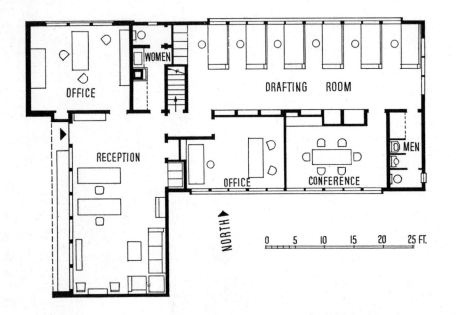

Mr. Britton's own office (below, left) has one wall in gray, one in henna brown corrugated transite; the third is Southern pine, sand-blasted to remove soft winter wood, lacquered and sprayed with white lead; window trim is orange geranium, drapes are Pegasus print in white and geranium; carpet is soft green over an inch-thick padding of sponge rubber. Conference room (below, right) is in deep green with one brown cork wall for display; accents are deep henna red; lighting fixtures are Finnish spun brass

Joseph W. Molitor Photos

Drafting room (right and below) has lobster red storage wall against background color of blue-green. Built-in units are a warm tan-gray. Almost all furniture for entire building was designed by the staff and made on the premises; table and desk tops are flush-type birch veneer doors. Display frames take standard 30 by 40 mounts, can be remounted in seconds

Chief designer's office (right) has one brown dubonnet wall, other walls in kid gray. Interior of cabinets is dubonnet. Brass rings are used as handles on cabinets and drawers throughout the office

OFFICES OF
JESSEN JESSEN MILLHOUSE & GREEVEN

Austin, Texas

Mears Studio Photos

Exterior of the building is grayish-pink stone with warm gray stucco panels under windows. Strong color accents of dark brown, yellow, blue and terra cotta red are used on beams, posts, window trim. Conference room opens to a terrace (right)

As its name implies, the Austin firm of Jessen Jessen Millhouse & Greeven consists of four partners who work together as a team. This is reflected in the plan of their new building: instead of four private offices there is one large reception and office area flowing into the conference room. The whole plan centers on the drafting room which is large enough to accommodate the architects' own four tables and up to six others for draftsmen. The adjoining work room has a snack bar; a sample room and two machine rooms are readily accessible.

The building is located in a residential section about a mile and a half from the center of town, in a section adjoining the University of Texas campus. It fronts on a one-way street not over-burdened with traffic; parking is no problem. The shape and rather small size of the lot, however, called for careful placing of the building, and resulted in a plan (see next page) angled to give the conference room complete privacy while at the same time opening the reception room to passersby.

In the year since they moved in, the owners have become more convinced than ever that pleasant surroundings add much to business in general. They are increasingly enthusiastic about their new location, and very pleased with the reaction of their neighbors.

Both drafting and reception rooms face the street and give passersby a glimpse of the activities within. Except for north wall (above) the general character of the building is residential to fit the neighborhood

JESSEN JESSEN MILLHOUSE & GREEVEN

Some architects tend to look on their drafting room as a strict working area to which the general public is not admitted. Others consider it the *raison d'être* for the whole building and plan it to be seen and inspected by all visitors. Jessen Jessen Millhouse & Greeven chose a middle path: their drafting room is clearly visible from the street but is completely shut off from interior traffic.

Ceilings throughout the building are acoustically treated — with fiber matting in the reception room and acoustic board elsewhere. Floors are sandstone or asphalt tile. The building is air conditioned, and insulated in walls, ceilings and roof deck.

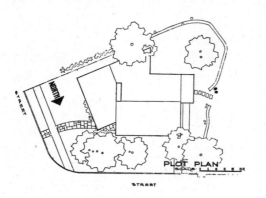

PLOT PLAN

STREET

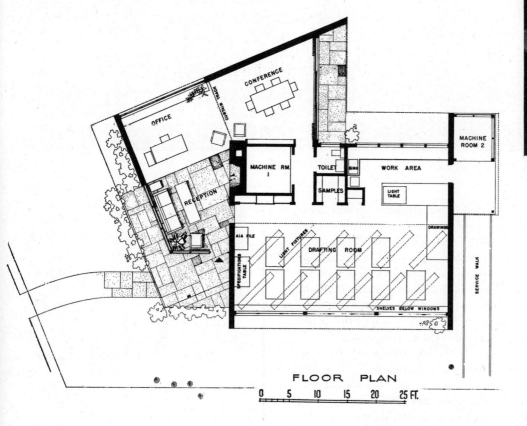

FLOOR PLAN

0   5   10   15   20   25 FT.

Many of the materials used on the exterior carry through to the interior, notably the ledge stone of the fireplace wall. Carpeting in conference room and office is beige, drapes are a blue figure on a natural gray background

Drafting room walls are a grayish-yellow; ceiling is white. Fluorescent fixtures are mounted obliquely over the tables, giving the maximum possible intensity just where it is wanted. Book shelves are installed below the windows, files are convenient

1. *Page, Southerland & Page Building, Austin, Texas*

2. *Thornhill-Craver Office Building, Houston, Texas*

3. *Technical Instrument Co., Houston, Texas*

4. *Remington-Rand Building, Dallas, Texas*

1

2

3

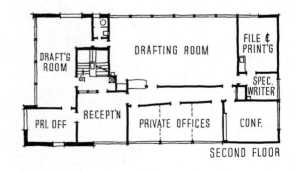

4

These four Texas buildings were cited briefly in the January, 1950, Building Types Study. Because of the excellence of their design, it was felt that they deserved a fuller coverage than was possible in the previous article.

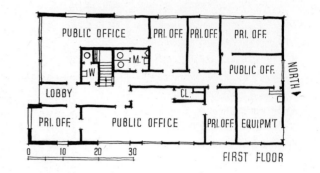

PUBLIC OFFICE | PRI. OFF. | PRI. OFF. | PRI. OFF.

M.

W

PUBLIC OFF.

NORTH

LOBBY

CL.

PRI. OFF. | PUBLIC OFFICE | PRI. OFF. | EQUIPM'T

0   10   20   30

FIRST FLOOR

Mears Studio Photo

PAGE, SOUTHERLAND & PAGE BUILDING

Austin, Texas

Page, Southerland & Page, Architects

DRAFT'G ROOM | DRAFTING ROOM | FILE & PRINT'G

SPEC. WRITER

dn

PRI. OFF | RECEPT'N | PRIVATE OFFICES | CONF.

SECOND FLOOR

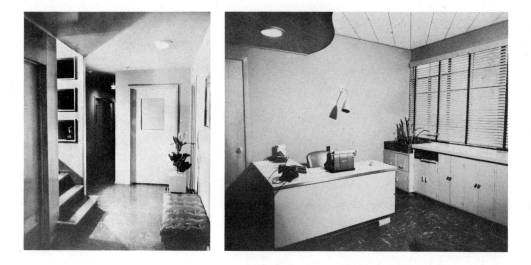

Interiors are finished for ease of upkeep. Entrance hall (right) is staggered behind stairs to avoid shot gun effect. Dropped ceiling in reception room (far right) houses ducts, lights

THE four buildings presented here represent varying solutions to the problem of housing office and light manufacturing space in less expensive, low density building areas. Planned occupancy varies from a single company to an assemblage of individual offices. Each of the structures is an outgrowth of the principles of planning small office buildings, as given in the study on pp. 166-185 of this book. Land values were paramount in determining building heights, site coverage and exterior exposure for offices; rental values served to determine location of tenant office spaces. All these buildings have certain features in common: low to moderate cost; ease of maintenance; some use of native materials; and deference to the climate, with air conditioning, insulation and sun shades or blinds. Advertising values for each occupant were carefully considered in the designs. Decorative effects have been achieved in a

logical fashion by contrast in building masses and materials.

The Page, Southerland & Page Building was specifically planned to provide quarters adapted to the needs of the architects, which could be amortized for the amount of rent normally paid for a similar space. For economy, the plan was based on a central corridor, flanked by exterior offices. The more rentable first floor was allocated to manufacturers' sales offices and an insurance agency, the second to the designers and an engineering firm with whom they have frequent business. An exterior sign, integrated as a design feature, lists all occupants of the building. The structure is wood frame with ledgestone and stucco exterior, cotton batt' insulation. Interiors have acoustical tile and fiberboard ceilings, textured plaster-board walls, asphalt tile on oak floors. Parking space at rear allows future addition.

Three private offices are divided by curtains for flexibility: they can be used as extra drafting room, or partitioned for renting. Conference room (right) doubles as completely private work space

Mears Studio Photos

THORNHILL-CRAVER BUILDING

Houston, Texas

MacKie and Kamrath, Architects

THE simplest problem of the four is typified by this building: that of providing offices for a single company in a semi-residential neighborhood. It has been handled in an honest and straightforward manner. Plywood walled offices flank a corridor in a long, narrow plan. Each has ample daylight and sun protection with wide overhangs. The straight, wood frame and brick veneer facade is relieved by planting and a break emphasizing the entrance.

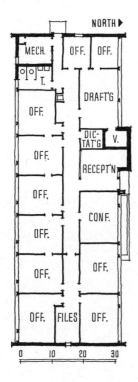

Domestic character has been imparted to the design by small scale and low, pitched roof. Projecting fins of the end walls give unity with roof, serve as decorative elements

TECHNICAL INSTRUMENT COMPANY

Houston, Texas

MacKie and Kamrath, Architects

DESIGNED to house shop and testing rooms for light precision manufacturing, as well as company offices, this building employs an L-shaped plan with services grouped in the center. Offices are given choicer front areas, shops are relegated to the rear. The structure has concrete block and brick veneer bearing walls, interior pipe columns, bar joists and built-up tar and gravel roof. Interior walls are sand-finished plaster.

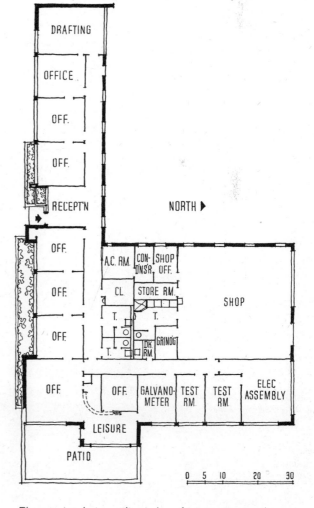

The exterior design utilizes play of intersecting overhangs, building projections, patio walls and unified planting

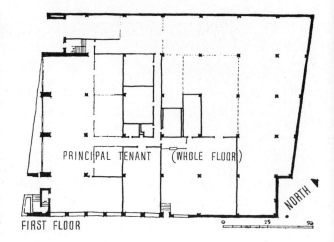

Location of the building in a semi-residential neighborhood permits use of planting and indoor-outdoor relationships suitable to the semi-tropical climate. Reception lobby (above) has plant box continuing on the interior. The office below adjoins lounge space and patio for entertaining clients. The bar can be closed off by a sliding partition

Lindenthal Photo

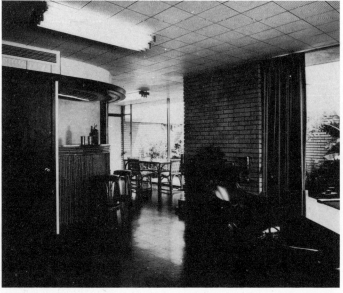

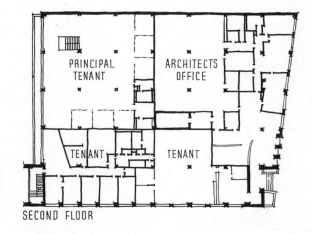

REMINGTON-RAND BUILDING

Dallas, Texas

George L. Dahl, Architects & Engineers

INGENIOUS use of a sloping site gives individuality, separation and private entrances to owner, architects and tenants of this building. The lot faces two important streets, permits entrances at two levels. Remington-Rand occupies the two-story portion of the facade shown. The large glazed block points up stairs leading to upper floor offices of the Music Corp. of America. On the next street (refer to photograph on page 181 of present volume) are entrances to the Associates Investment Co. and the architects' quarters. Reception room, library and drafting room of the latter are shown here. Office spaces are mostly interior, and make use of clear glass and folding partitions; controlled air, light and sound. Exterior walls contrast brick, cordova shell stone and ledgestone.

EDIFICIO ESSO

CARACAS, VENEZUELA

Lathrop Douglass, Architect

Fred N. Severud, Structural Engineer

For Creole Petroleum Corporation

Guy B. Panero, Mechanical Engineer

THE architect for this building is one of those who have called attention to some new criteria for office building design.* The project here presented is unusually fortunate for demonstration of new standards as applied to a specific case, for here the site and circumstances allowed virtually complete freedom in design. The project has been approved and the drawings completed, but construction has been voluntarily postponed by Creole. With a limited supply of steel and other critical items available for export, Creole has elected in the national interest to devote all of its allocations to actual oil production, even though its office employees must continue under unsatisfactory conditions.

Although the final design is quite happy with respect

to clean lines and imposing masses, these esthetic considerations waited upon the realization of more utilitarian objectives. In this case they did flow very naturally from the working out of functional solutions.

The long narrow form resulted from several factors: orientation in a hot and sunny climate, planning for the most direct circulation and greatest flexibility, and integration of specific office needs of the company that will occupy the building. (These are analyzed in detail as separate items on succeeding pages.) The wide, heavy base came from massing several large departments on two lower floors. The neatly closed ends grew out of the sun problem, as did also the long horizontal lines formed by sun visors. And the projection of the elevator core was by no means whimsical; it came directly out of the engineers' earthquake design. The separation of cafe-

*"New Departures in Office Building Design," by Lathrop Douglass (see pp. 161-164 of this volume).

Louis H. Dreyer Photo

teria and other employee facilities as a separate structure was also a logical development of the local problems — in Caracas recreational and similar employee provisions are exceptional, and the separate building permits a longer and more relaxed use than if these were in the main building. In general, then, this whole building project represents a from-the-ground-up study of office building functions, applied first to the individual company and then to the special considerations of its locality, everything falling into place nicely in an unusually handsome building.

It is interesting to note that in another building (page 120), done by the same architect, for the same company, from the same criteria, but for another location, the final design differs in important respects, but is also visually pleasant.

The Caracas climate, which hovered so constantly over the architect's drawing boards (even though they were in New York), was important in two major respects. The year-round temperature is almost ideal — it was necessary to provide neither heating nor cooling. Always, provided, of course, that the almost tropical sun can be prevented from making the interior of a building act like a solar heater. In other words, control the sun and one need never worry about temperature. On the other hand, there are very humid days; thus ventilation is important on this count also, and thus it was necessary to air condition the I.B.M. rooms to keep the cards from curling limply. This is another reason, by the way, for the deep interior spaces of the first and second floors.

These same conditions also led the architect to use a light, hollow exterior wall of prefabricated panels, in line with the current trend. The outer surface is sheet aluminum, backed by steel cellular panel (like the floor panel); then there is insulation, against solar heat only

(temperature differences are so slight that there is no problem of condensation); then an air space; and the interior surface is merely a finished steel panel (wall section on page 117).

Views are inspiring from this plateau high in the mountains. While the long narrow disposition is otherwise explained, the building does make the most of the mountains lined up at the rear and the open views to the front. The site is about half way between the business district of Caracas, a congestion of small buildings,

Louis H. Dreyer Photo

and the better residential districts. It was large enough to permit placing the buildings as desired, and to permit plenty of room for parking and recreation; and it is open enough so that the visual impressiveness of the building is completely unrestricted.

Of many criteria set up, these were selected as outstanding:

1. Flexibility, through standardized office sizes based on practical and efficient office layouts;

2. Direct, foolproof circulation, vertical and horizontal;

3. Conditions of occupancy as ideal as possible for efficient work by humans — involving temperature, light, ventilation, and acoustics especially, but not forgetting more incidental facilities;

4. Planning for individual departments and for departmental integration, and for expansion, also on a departmental basis;

5. Economy in both final cost and maintenance.

As for circulation, it was decided that a straight-line approach would work best, provided that the distances were not too long. Rockefeller Center experience seemed to set 175 ft. as thoroughly acceptable walking distance from elevators if the route were straight. Twice that, or 350 ft., might be taken then as an empirical maximum building length. This, tested here as to departmental divisions of space, worked out well, and checked also with other factors tending toward the long narrow building.

Maintenance as a planning factor also needs a special mention. It was considered worth extra attention for a building where normal sources of supplies were not at hand and where skilled maintenance labor might not be readily available. First cost then was studied with maintenance cost as the first test.

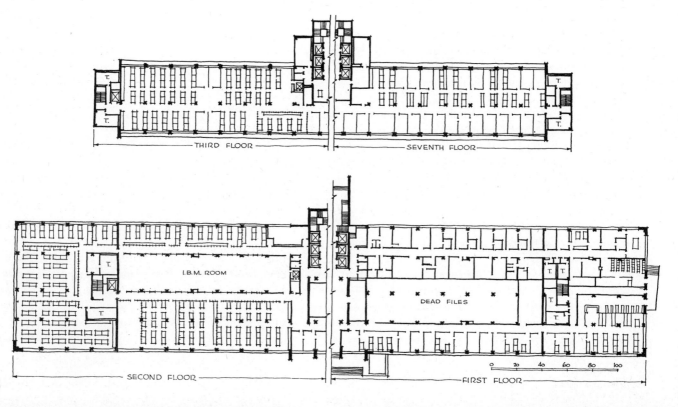

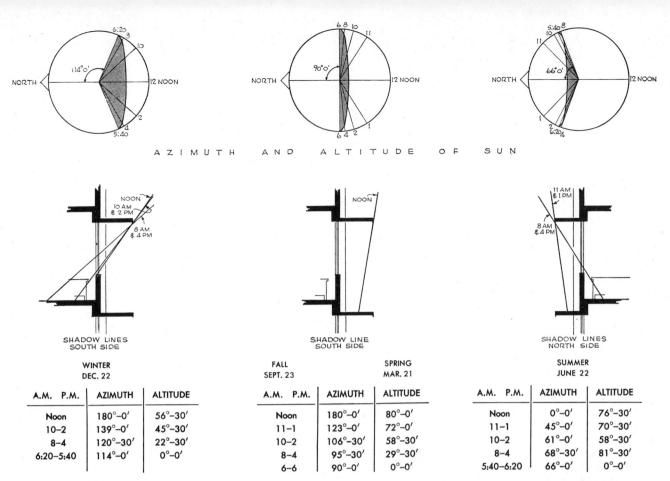

AZIMUTH AND ALTITUDE OF SUN

SHADOW LINES
SOUTH SIDE

SHADOW LINE
SOUTH SIDE

SHADOW LINES
NORTH SIDE

WINTER DEC. 22			
A.M. P.M.	AZIMUTH	ALTITUDE	
Noon	180°–0'	56°–30'	
10–2	139°–0'	45°–30'	
8–4	120°–30'	22°–30'	
6:20–5:40	114°–0'	0°–0'	

FALL SEPT. 23 — SPRING MAR. 21		
A.M. P.M.	AZIMUTH	ALTITUDE
Noon	180°–0'	80°–0'
11–1	123°–0'	72°–0'
10–2	106°–30'	58°–30'
8–4	95°–30'	29°–30'
6–6	90°–0'	0°–0'

SUMMER JUNE 22		
A.M. P.M.	AZIMUTH	ALTITUDE
Noon	0°–0'	76°–30'
11–1	45°–0'	70°–30'
10–2	61°–0'	58°–30'
8–4	68°–30'	81°–30'
5:40–6:20	66°–0'	0°–0'

SUN DICTATES FORM

Here the sun was considered first from the standpoint of its heat — air temperature is almost ideal the year 'round, but a building can become a solar hot-bed. As the charts indicate, the sun in Caracas is high as well as hot. It shines from the south in winter, from the north in summer. On north and south sides it is easily screened off with fairly narrow visors. But on east and west ends, sun protection would be all but impossible.

The answer was obvious — a long, narrow building running east and west, with all offices facing north or south. And an extension of this idea was to block off both east and west ends with toilet rooms and stairs. Then no working space ever need have sun-heat troubles. As the sections (above) show, not even the desk nearest the window is ever touched by sunlight, and only rarely does any window glass get any sun. On the lower floors, the sun protection is by outside aluminum louvers, not overhanging visors, but the result is the same.

For maximum daylight, under such shading it is possible for the windows to be continuous, and inside shades or venetian blinds are not needed. A factor in this is that the glare of the sun is also avoided, yet normally glare would be such a consideration as to rule out such building forms as H or U plans, for the glare from one interior wall to another would be very disturbing. Fortunately the open site obviates glare from surrounding surfaces.

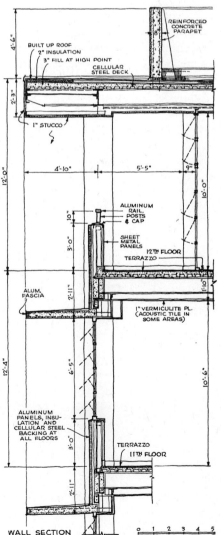

WALL SECTION

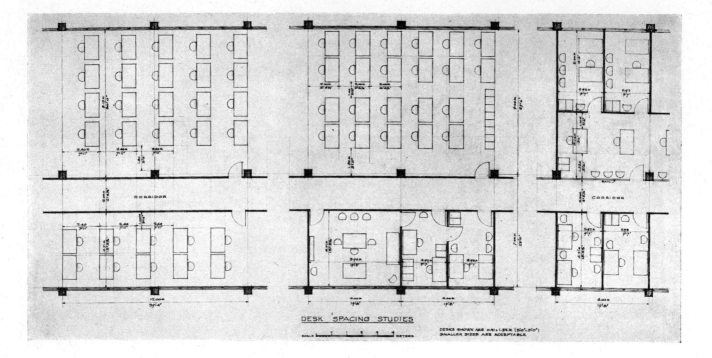

DESK SPACING STUDIES

DESKS SHOWN ARE 0.91 x 1.52M (3'0"x5'0")
SMALLER SIZES ARE ACCEPTABLE

DESK ARRANGEMENTS DICTATE DIMENSIONS

The width of the building was determined by much diagramming of desk placing, of which the studies here shown are typical. Most of these diagrams are the early studies, made before some other considerations had their say as to width and column spacing, but they did set the pattern. It was these that suggested the off-setting of the center row of columns — while column spacing along the outside wall is uniform, the depth from the windows differs on the two sides of the building. The 29 ft. 6 in. depth permits five 3 by 5 desks in an open office, as shown, while the shallower depth is better for partitioned offices.

The horizontal column spacing started out to be 6 meters (18 ft. 6 in.), with a module of 1½ m for partitioning at the mullions. It was later decided to do the plans in feet, so the column spacing went to 20 ft., with 5 ft. modules.

Columns outside the building wall was an early objective to keep the interior free of any obstruction to desk placing or partitioning. A slight contretemps developed when it was later found that earthquake bracing would block this idea. More studies were made (lower

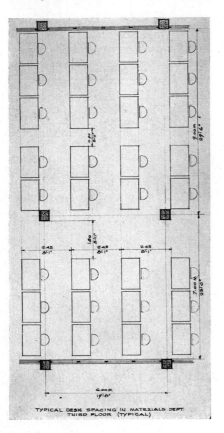

TYPICAL DESK SPACING IN MATERIALS DEPT.
THIRD FLOOR (TYPICAL)

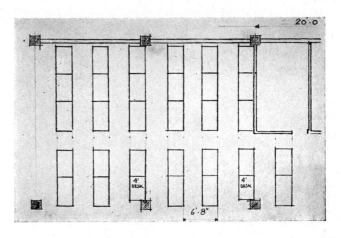

AND EARTHQUAKE ENGINEERING CROSSES THE FINAL T

right-hand corner) to see what the sacrifice would amount to, and whether the building ought to be widened enough to keep the same clear space. It was found, however, that the five-desk case was the only one much affected, and that a cheaper answer was to substitute a 4-ft. desk in every third row, and that widening the building might be carrying the desk theory a bit too far.

Although there has not been an earthquake in Caracas in 100 years, it is considered to be in an earthquake zone, and the resulting structural design had two important effects on planning. One has just been mentioned — it was necessary to keep the columns in line with outside walls. This came about through the angle bracing required, as shown in the detail in the lower right-hand corner. Note that the braces are concealed in the spandrels. The other effect was the lateral bracing required — the heavy masonry walls at the ends and

at the center. At the ends these walls fell right in with the sun-protection scheme, and in the center they shoved the elevator core out the rear of the building (for additional stiffness). But this worked out nicely too, for they are well placed for any future extension of the building, which would logically be done from this central core.

DETAILS OF EARTHQUAKE BRACING

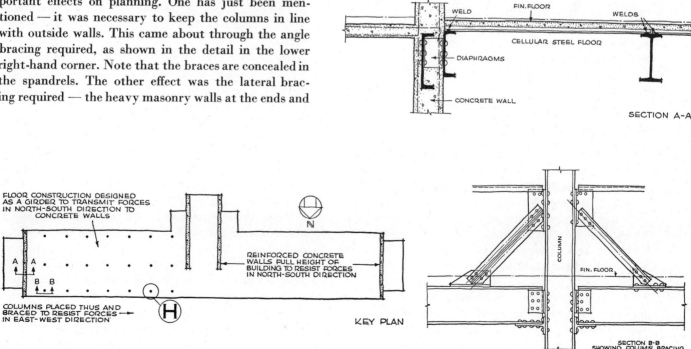

ESSO BUILDING, BATON ROUGE, LOUISIANA

For Esso Standard Oil Company

IN PLANNING this office building the architect — the same architect who designed the Esso Building for Caracas (page 114)—started with the same basic criteria, for the same client. But the fact that the location was quite different introduced many different design factors. While the two buildings have a superficial resemblance, in the long, clean horizontal lines, and the same simple, effective masses, the general route to this result was not the same.

Climate was the outstanding difference. Here in Baton Rouge the summer temperature is plain hot, and it is also humid, and air conditioning became a necessity. And while the sun introduced the usual problems of heat and glare, in this instance there was not the opportunity for its control by static devices. Here, too, there were surrounding buildings and street patterns, which fixed not only the orientation but also the exterior brick finish. And, last but not least, in place of an earthquake condition as a determinant for structural design there was a special soil problem which had an equally strong effect.

In the interior the resemblance between the two buildings is even stronger, and the functional reasons therefor parallel each other more closely, though here too there are some differences. Here are the basic criteria

at work — direct and easy circulation, the utmost in flexibility of space use, the best possible provisions for effective office work. Economy in maintenance was not quite as important as first cost, for in Baton Rouge supplies could be had and skilled labor was readily available.

Because the orientation was really predetermined by the site, it was necessary here to control solar heat and glare by a combination of devices. The sun visors help, but since the main exposures had to be east and west, they could not possibly keep sun off the windows; therefore the 3-ft. overhang is purely arbitrary. For the rest, venetian blinds were used, and the air conditioning load was calculated to take out what solar heat was inevitable. Since air conditioning was necessary in any case, this was relatively easy.

With these provisions, the continuous windows utilize daylight to the full, but it was not so practical as in Caracas to keep the building narrow. Here the main portion of the building is 72 ft. deep; layout studies showed this to be desirable and economical. Outer space makes excellent private offices, in any desired multiple of a 4-ft. module, and the deeper air conditioned space balances out well for services, files and storage.

The flexibility of partitioning is not hampered by any

Model photograph below shows original scheme calling for six stories. When one story was cut out, photograph on opposite page was corrected.

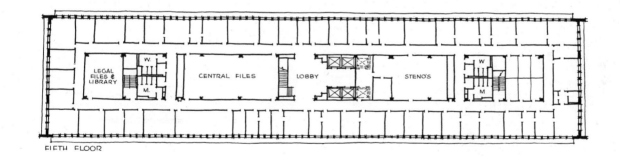

John W. Harris Associates, Construction Management

Lathrop Douglass, Architect

Carson & Lundin, Associate Architects

Guy B. Panero, Mechanical Engineers

Strobel and Salzman, Structural Engineers

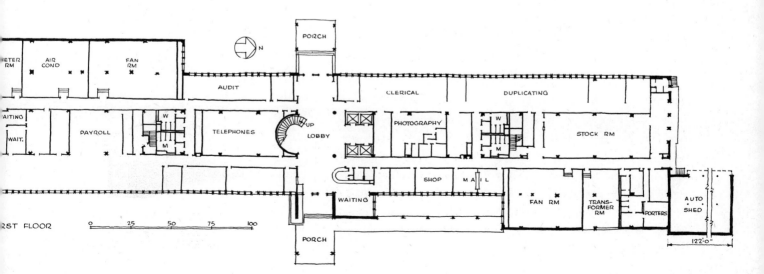

FIFTH FLOOR

LEGAL FILES & LIBRARY | W. | M.
CENTRAL FILES | LOBBY | STENO'S | W | M

FIRST FLOOR

METER RM | AIR COND | FAN RM
AUDIT | PORCH | N
CLERICAL | DUPLICATING
AITING | WAIT. | PAYROLL | W | M | TELEPHONES | UP | LOBBY | PHOTOGRAPHY | W | M | STOCK RM
WAITING | SHOP | MAIL | FAN RM | TRANSFORMER RM | PORTERS | AUTO SHED
PORCH
0 25 50 75 100
122'-0"

columns at the outside wall; here it was possible to keep the columns within the depth of the wall, and within 8 in. in width. Several ideas for light columns were studied; the final one (detail page 123) is a channel and a plate shop welded, fireproofed with vermiculite plaster. These columns alternate with a simple T-section mullion similarly fireproofed.

To add to the flexibility from unbroken walls, the ceiling is also unbroken, and the cellular steel floor provides continuous ducts for bringing wiring to any desired location. Air conditioning and lighting are also placed so that partitions can be changed at will.

The light weight of this floor and column system was quite necessary on another count — the ground is a deep silt with no hard pan under it. The designers were limited to one ton per sq. ft. — the building had to be

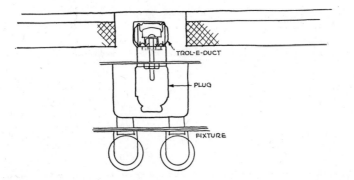

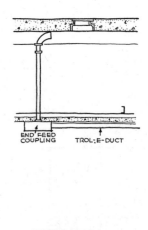

In their desire for the utmost in flexibility the architects made use of a continuous bus system of connections for overhead lights, which was developed really for industrial building. The light fixture is connected to the duct by merely inserting a plug and giving it a twist. Thus fixtures can be placed anywhere and moved as desired in a moment. In adapting this for the office building the architect was able, in most places to recess the duct in the acoustic tile, keeping a reasonably smooth ceiling and minimizing the effect of long horizontal lines

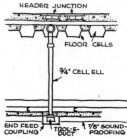

light, also horizontal. Moreover, the continual dampness virtually made a basement impossible; this accounts for the extended first floor for mechanical equipment (penthouse superstructure houses cooling tower and fan rooms).

The building, which will have a total of 170,000 sq. ft. of floor space, is now under construction, as is also a separate cafeteria building.

Here is a wall with no projecting columns to interfere with furniture arrangements or with partitioning. After trying various combinations of normal steel sections, the designers settled on the one shown below as the simplest to erect, with channel and plate welded in the shop

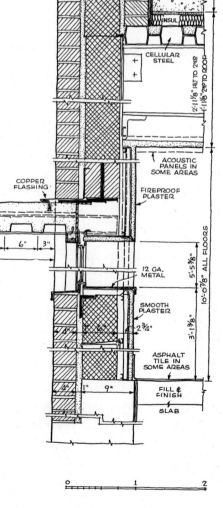

TYPICAL WALL SECTION

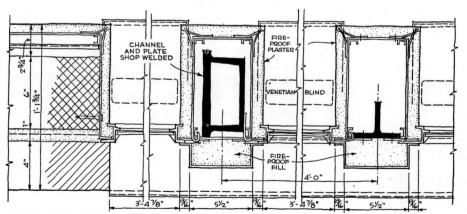

TYPICAL WINDOW PLAN SHOWING COLUMN

WATERMAN BUILDING, MOBILE, ALABAMA

For Waterman Steamship Corporation

Platt Roberts, Architect

O. W. Long, Jr., and A. B. Benson, Associate Architects

As the office building breaks farther away from the almost frozen pattern of the late Twenties, there is bound to be some fairly bold experimentation with "functionalism." Here the designers tackled with particular vigor the once-ignored problems of sun and heat in a very warm climate. Because they were limited to a restricted downtown site, there was no relief to be found in natural orientation (as in the case of the Caracas building, page 114). The west exposure, coming on a property-line, was the natural place to group elevators and services, thus avoiding heat on the worst exposure. But that left three sides exposed to the hot sun (the south side has a 36-ft. light-protection site; the north exposure gets sunlight in the late summer afternoons).

The architects adopted external controls for the sunlight, and went "all out" with them. All office windows are protected with vertical fins of stone to control rays from the side, and with external sunshades for the direct rays. On the south and east sides the shades are horizontal, and are movable through an arc of 180°. On the north side, the rays are all from the low afternoon or early morning sun, so here the shades are vertical and are fixed (they supplement at the center of the window the vertical stone fins). All windows are double-glazed with ¼-in. plate, with a ½-in. sealed air space between, for maximum insulation against heat (or cold). The architects report that these measures, while costly, saved many tons of refrigeration in the air conditioning system, and point to an operation saving continuing through the life of the building.

All shades (horizontal) in one window operate together, but each window has individual control. Normal position would be horizontal; on bright days shades would be turned down slightly until lighting desired was obtained. On dull days they would be turned up to gather all light possible and reflect it inward. No solar heat need be directed into the building, something which venetian blinds could not accomplish. The Universal Corporation assisted the architects in the design of external shades.

Flexibility in space was another principal objective. The whole building will be occupied by the Waterman

On three sides, north, south and east, all windows are shaded from the hot Alabama sun by projecting stone mullions (the west wall, on a property line, is blank). On the south and east sides (shown above) adjustable outside shades of lacquered aluminum provide the final control of sunshine. On the north side, there are vertical outside shades

Wm. Lavendar Photos

Steamship Corp., and heavy partitioning changes are anticipated. Also the limitations of the site did not give any natural flexibility to the floors. Air conditioning at the windows is by means of individual window units, for flexibility in control; interior zones are air conditioned by a conventional duct system through ceiling diffusers. Lighting and windows were designed on a 4-ft. module system, so that partitioning can be put at any mullion without disturbance to either natural or artificial lighting. And the steel cellular floor provided maximum flexibility for telephone and service wiring.

The entire building (except for the brick panels on the west side) is faced with architectural stone, using granite and silica for aggregate and matrix with white portland cement. The basic color is deep buff. Vertical mullions are coral in color and have a honed finish. The rear or service shaft on north and south is a combination of blacks, reds and browns with a high polish finish.

Sunshades on the north side (left) are fixed in vertical position half way between stone mullions — they protect against early morning and late afternoon sunlight. Horizontal shades (above) rotate through 180° — those for each window can be controlled separately, but all for that window are controlled in unison

First floor elevator lobby has floor of pink marble, walls of Appalachian Fluri and Antique Rose marble. Ceiling is acoustic plaster

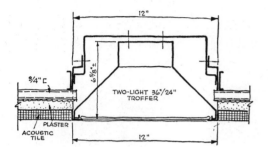

Besides the still unpacked new furniture shown, office space will have acoustic tile ceiling, with recessed fluorescent lighting, and a combination of individual and zone system air conditioning. Sub floor is cellular steel deck for flexibility in wiring. Everything is done on a 4-ft. module; partitioning can be installed at any mullion

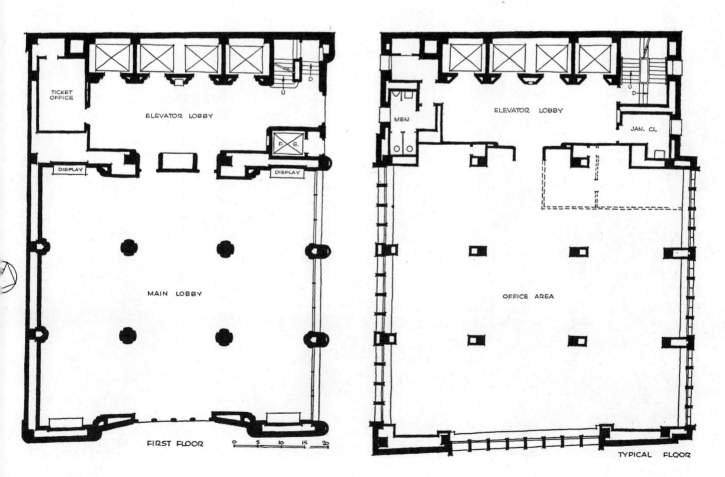

SMALL OFFICE BUILDING, NEW APPROACH

American Osteopathic Association Building, Chicago   **Perkins & Will, Architects and Engineers**

IF the office buildings of another generation seemed to ignore sunshine and solar heat as factors in design, the current generation seems to have exactly reversed the process of design. Today many façades take their form largely from various devices for controlling and utilizing sunlight.

This building, which faces south on an interior lot in the near North Side section of Chicago, is well surrounded by taller buildings. Its façade gets sun only in the warmer months. The architects sought the maximum utilization of the rather limited natural light with continuous windows, shading them with sun visors and drapes, and using glass which filters out much of the solar heat. In the main these same measures are useful in keeping winter heat inside, and the drapes are frequently useful in acoustic control.

The set-back of the façade is not explained, however, by these sun measures. The building is semi-commercial in character, being the home of a professional society, the American Osteopathic Association. The architects felt that a small set-back would imply this semi-commercial aspect, and would give the building some sense of reserve.

The set-back, coupled with the horizontality of the sun shades, serves also to frame the building and give it some distinction among its taller neighbors. Not being able to compete in height, it asserts its own position with some emphasis.

The side-winding entrance is a natural result of its location, which is east of the principal traffic from which its visitors will come, Chicago's proposed "Magnificent Mile." The entrance opens naturally to approaching callers. Its visitors will not be the general public, but members of the professional association.

In color, the exterior is cool and fresh, the frame surrounding the building being of limestone, columns silver, terra cotta a soft grey green, and the glass the green heat absorbing plate. The large granite block marking the entrance and identifying the building is basically grey with some black and red markings.

In the large executive-conference room, the front wall of glass block achieves an interesting textural pattern, as well as admitting maximum daylight while preserving the privacy of the room and shielding the occupants against both the noise and the distractions of the sidewalk just outside. Note the flexible partition

Hedrich-Blessing Photos

General office and reception room occupies the center of the first floor, and is made inviting and warm with light and color. One wall is painted rust, set off by grey on adjacent walls

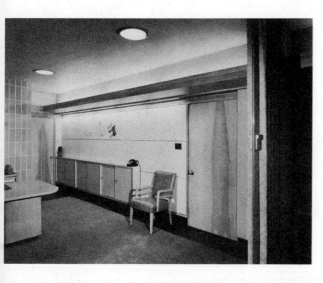

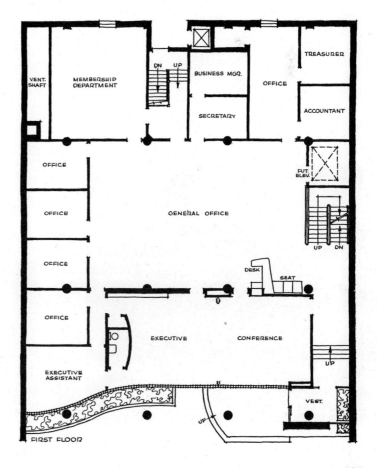

Hedrich-Blessing Photos

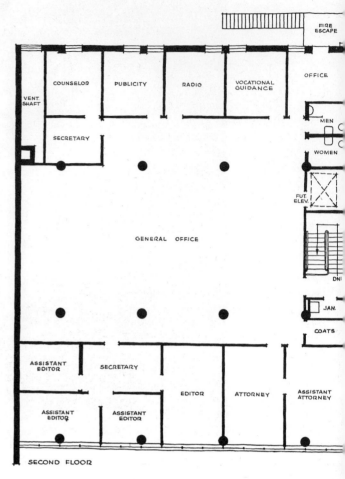

SECOND FLOOR

Private offices on second floor, front, have full width windows, acoustic ceiling, air conditioning. The drapes, which are beige with a small gay figure, are useful in controlling noise as well as daylight. At present only first two floors and basement are used for the Association office. There is a third floor, however, for expected expansion, now used for storage

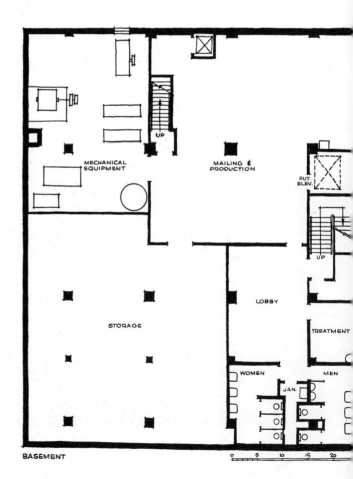

BASEMENT

ESSO OFFICE BUILDING, BATON ROUGE

Esso Standard Oil Company of Louisiana

John W. Harris Associates, Inc., Construction Management; Lathrop Douglass, Architect

WHEN office buildings escape the arbitrary patterns of downtown sites, architects find increasing opportunities to make them both utilitarian and expressive. Here is one that finds its expression in a highly functional floor plan, though the architects are quick to assert that some of the details of the final design are purely arbitrary.

This apparent paradox springs from a complex set of circumstances, which were detailed in an earlier study of this building (pp. 120 through 123 of this book). Briefly, the long, narrow site permitted a disposition of office space with all advantages of direct and easy circulation, utmost in space flexibility, full use of daylight, idea space proportions. Planning for these resulted in the long, clean lines, the simple, pleasing masses. But the site also prescribed certain other conditions affecting design. The orientation was fixed on a north-south axis, the soil has no hardpan, the climate is hot and humid. Thus the sun-control eye-brows are purely

Carson & Lundin, Associate Architects

Guy B. Panero, Mechanical Engineers

Strobel & Salzman, Structural Engineers

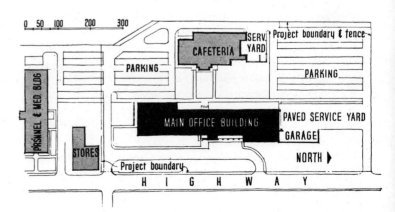

arbitrary — they do help protect against glare and solar heat, but it would be impossible for any static devices to do the whole job. In any case, the climate demanded full air conditioning, not merely sun control.

The soil condition made necessary a low, light building; also made a basement virtually impossible. Air conditioning and other machinery is therefore accommodated in various spaces appurtenant to the building, at first floor and penthouse, with a slightly cluttering effect. There was one happy result, however — the necessity for lightness fitted in with the desire to eliminate columns at exterior walls. A simple combination of a channel and a plate welded together (detail opposite page), makes a fireproofed column less than eight inches wide overall and completely contained within the depth of the wall. These alternate with light T-section columns in the same width, on four-foot centers. There is, then, a four-foot module for office space which is maintained continuously. Interior design keeps the module intact in air conditioning outlets, lighting and controls. Also floors and ceilings are continuously finished, so partitioning can be done at will.

Interior furnishings were also specified by Architect Lathrop Douglass, so that the promise of the exterior is maintained throughout the building.

Main lobby, looking toward front entrance

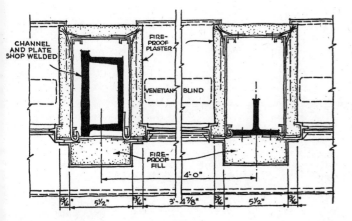

CHANNEL AND PLATE SHOP WELDED

FIRE-PROOF PLASTER

VENETIAN BLIND

FIRE-PROOF FILL

4'-0"

5½"   3'-4⅞"   5½"

View from waiting room toward lobby

View directly into waiting room

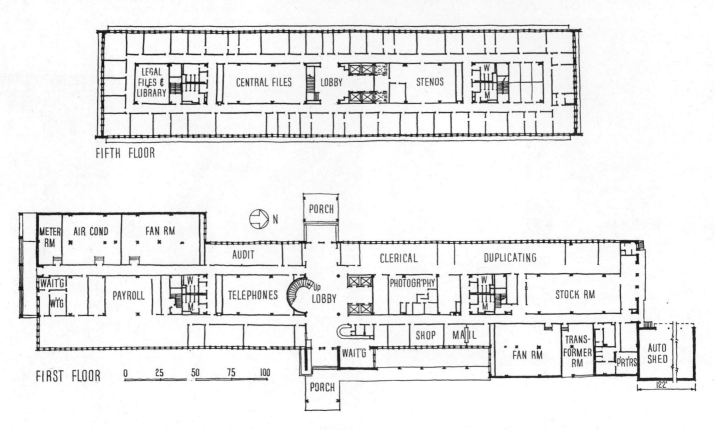

FIFTH FLOOR

FIRST FLOOR 0 25 50 75 100

Main portion of building is 336 ft long, 72 ft deep. Length is figured at just about the maximum for acceptable walking distance. Depth gives exterior private offices 15 ft deep, and a good allowance of interior space for utilities, files and "bull pen" space

Gottscho-Schleisner Photos

Photograph shows appearance of exterior wall unbroken by projecting columns. Space along outside walls can be used to full effectiveness, whether the area is partitioned or open

Though this photograph does not show full use of space, office layouts were intensively studied, for open as well as private offices, before depth of building was set

Interior design for private offices as well as special rooms was done by the architect; uses, with some restraint, the style, color and efficiency of modern furnishings

Rear of Esso Building looks almost exactly like the front, but has covered walks leading to the cafeteria and other accessory buildings, also to parking areas. Since, as explained in the text, the sunshade design was arbitrary anyway, it was kept uniform on all sides

Gottscho-Schleisner Photos

Laughead Photo

EMPLOYERS INSURANCE BUILDING

Dallas, Texas

George L. Dahl, Architects & Engineers

WHEN this new Dallas building opened its doors recently it was
greeted with much local fanfare. The Dallas Morning News
for July 10th devoted a special 10-page section to it, hailing it as
a "gleaming jewel in the diadem of expanding downtown development," and describing it in the most minute detail.

The 13-story building, owned and occupied by the Employers

Casualty Company and the Texas Employers Insurance Association, is a striking one. Rising high above its neighbors, it presents on three sides, for most of its height, a solid expanse of aluminum and glass. On the street sides of the ground floor (the lot is a corner one, bounded to the north by an alley and to the west by an adjoining building) the facing is polished Texas pink granite; the large windows are plate glass in extruded aluminum store front sash. The windowless second floor is faced with Indiana limestone on the street sides, and ornamented with terra cotta plaques. From the third floor through the 11th the walls on three sides consist of alternating aluminum pilasters and aluminum windows interspersed with cast aluminum spandrels. Light face brick is used entirely around the top two floors and for the wall facing the adjoining property.

The vertical aluminum fins are not mere ornament, but house the air conditioning pipes serving the exterior zones of the office floors. The building contains many innovations, chief among them the handling of air conditioning and lighting (ARCHITECTURAL RECORD, Jan. 1950, pp. 112–114). Because the owners required maximum flexibility of office space, both air conditioning ducts and lighting conduits were installed in a perforated metal tile ceiling so constructed that the position of outlets may be changed easily without altering the appearance of the ceiling. For the same reason, cellular steel floors were used, allowing electric and telephone

High pressure air conditioning conduit and piping run down exterior in insulated aluminum pilasters, connect with window units and ducts to interior zones. First floor (below) also has access to basement parking garage

Main entrance

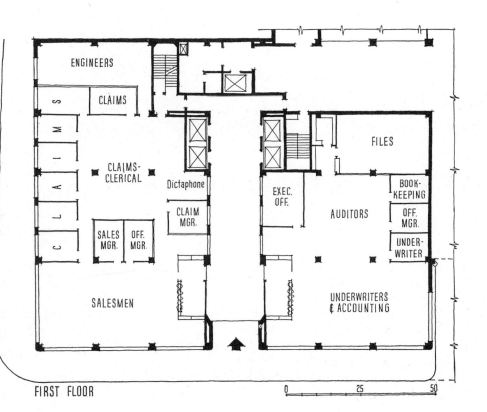

FIRST FLOOR

Dallas agency offices, first floor

Typical partitions, first floor

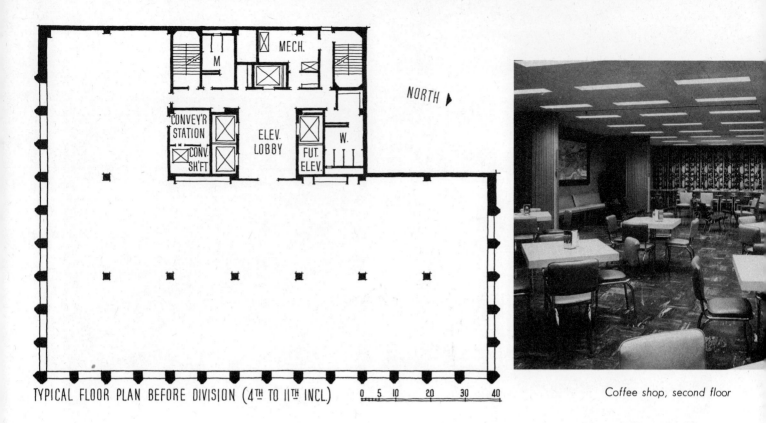

TYPICAL FLOOR PLAN BEFORE DIVISION (4TH TO 11TH INCL.)   0 5 10   20   30   40

Coffee shop, second floor

Typical plans above and below show unusual openness and flexibility of office space. Plan below is the 11th, or executive floor, but partitioning is typical of all floors

outlets to be located at any desired point. Mechanical equipment is concentrated on the top of the building, increasing the rentable area on typical floors by minimizing the space required for pipes, air shafts and flues, and permitting the use of the entire basement level for a 110-car garage.

The first floor of the building, occupied largely by the Dallas agency offices of the two insurance companies, has an automobile entrance accommodating truck

TYPICAL FLOOR PLAN AFTER DIVISION (4TH TO 11TH INCL)   0 5 10   20   30   40

Board room, 11th floor (left) and typical office space, sixth floor (right)

service, and access to the basement garage via a spiral ramp. General employee facilities such as recreation room, coffee shop, conference rooms, etc., are on the second floor; the first aid department and personnel offices are on the third. The equipment room, two stories high, takes about a third of the area of the top two floors, the rest of which is given over to record files and supplies. A vertical electric conveyor connects storage and office areas.

Floors throughout are of cellular steel covered with lightweight concrete fill and rubber tile with the exception of executive offices on 11th floor, which are carpeted

Opposite and below: elevator lobby and general executive offices, 11th floor

Roger Sturtevant Photos

HEADQUARTERS AND "FRONT" FOR FOOD PROCESSING

Richmond Chase Office Building, San Jose, California

Wurster, Bernardi and Emmons, Architects

Landscaping by Thomas D. Church

SITUATED on the main street of San Jose, this head-quarters office building for one of the largest canning companies of the area, with packing plants spotted throughout the fruit growing district, was intended as a "front" and something of a trademark. It has a capacity of a hundred or more office staff, and the possibility of further expansion in the center toward the north. The garden area in back is for employee recreation, and a cafeteria will eventually be built here. The same architects once designed an office building for another canning company with striking use of horizontal wooden barge-boards as "shutters." The use of tan awnings here is equally gay and perhaps more direct and colorful under the copper facing of the roof overhang.

In the two small top views, the awnings may be seen pulled down — the architects say this saves expense of air conditioning. At right they are seen rolled up into the soffit of the overhang. Awnings are tan, pipe columns vermilion, overhang band copper-faced. Walled-in front gardens (right) give executives a pleasant outlook; chain link fences at ends let breezes through. For planting plan, back garden, see p. 148

Starting with the view at the upper right corner (the lobby), the photographer has led us back into the building. The second view reveals a second glass screen, opening a view into the spacious skylit interior. In the third (lefthand page), there is seen an adjoining row of outer offices occupied by executives, and, finally, in the two bottom views, the large central office room. Sash and doors are painted dark green, interior walls blue-gray (darker in outer offices). Lighting is fluorescent except for incandescent light in monitor coves. Floors are asphalt tile, ceilings acoustic tile on wood strips (4 in. of rock-wool insulation). Lobby walls and counters in general offices are finished in oak plywood; the sampling room (see plan overleaf) is in natural-finish vertical grain Douglas fir and has stainless steel counter tops. The broken planes of the skylight ceiling absorb noise

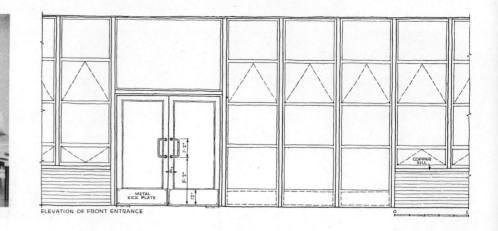

ELEVATION OF FRONT ENTRANCE

METAL
KICK PLATE

COPPER
SILL

0   5

6"
4"
1" ⌀ METAL
14 GA. METAL DOOR
4"

PLAN OF DOOR PULLS

Above: Details of front curtain wall, seen in photo opposite page

Below: Building plan and plot plan. Building plan shows possibility of expansion in the center section. Points on this plan give a clear impression of the fact that the pipe columns are the only vertical elements in the building. Landscaping was by Thomas D. Church, whose planting plan is indicated in the right hand drawing

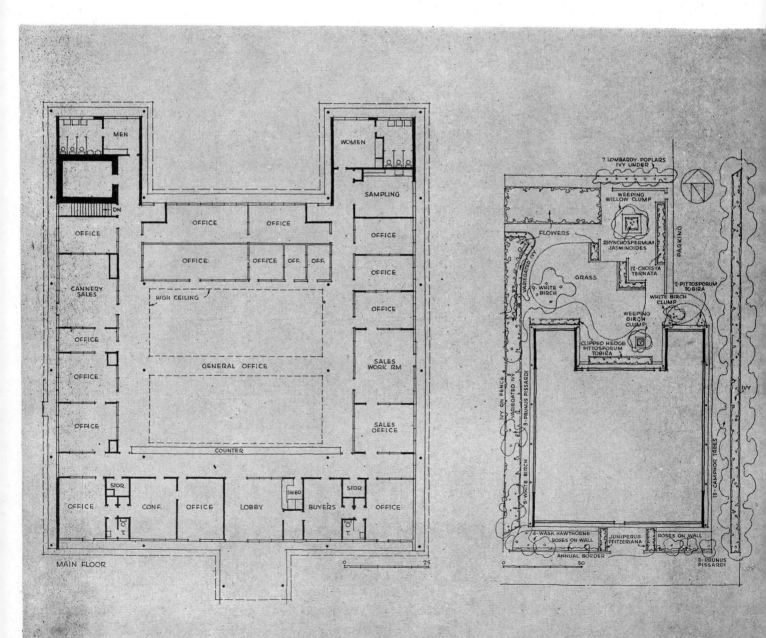

MEN

WOMEN

SAMPLING

OFFICE   OFFICE

OFFICE

OFFICE

OFFICE   OFFICE   OFF.   OFF.

OFFICE

CANNERY
SALES

HIGH CEILING

OFFICE

SALES
WORK RM

OFFICE

GENERAL OFFICE

OFFICE

SALES
OFFICE

COUNTER

STOR.   SWBD   STOR.

OFFICE   CONF.   OFFICE   LOBBY   BUYERS   OFFICE

MAIN FLOOR   0   25

7 LOMBARDY POPLARS
IVY UNDER

WEEPING
WILLOW CLUMP

FLOWERS

RHYNCHOSPERMUM
JASMINOIDES

PARKING

GRASS   12 CHOISYA
TERNATA

9 WHITE
BIRCH   2 PITTOSPORUM
TOBIRA

WHITE BIRCH
CLUMP

WEEPING
BIRCH
CLUMP

CLIPPED HEDGE
PITTOSPORUM
TOBIRA

4 WASH. HAWTHORNE
ROSES ON WALL   JUNIPERUS
PFITZERIANA   ROSES ON WALL

ANNUAL BORDER   3 PRUNUS
PISSARDI

0   50

13 CAMPHOR TREES

IVY

IVY ON FENCE

VARIEGATED IVY

3 PRUNUS PISSARDI

5 WHITE BIRCH

What with the awning above and the parapet wall below, to look at, the executive is given a pleasant view and no sky-glare to contend with. Vines to be added

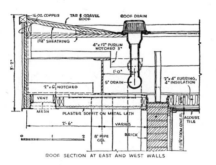

ROOF SECTION AT EAST AND WEST WALLS

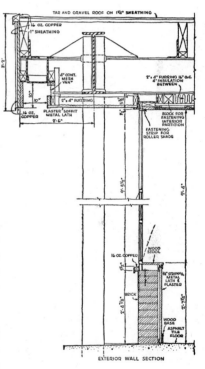

EXTERIOR WALL SECTION

Sawtooth monitor details have been carefully worked out so as to carry heating ducts for the forced warm-air (gas-fired) system and also to provide light-coves for the fluorescent lighting. The structural engineer was A. V. Saph, Jr., the mechanical engineer, James Gayner. The exterior pipe columns are firmly anchored in the concrete base — not only are pipe columns the only vertical supports but the long center span is a partial cantilever

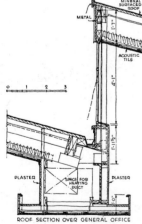

ROOF SECTION OVER GENERAL OFFICE

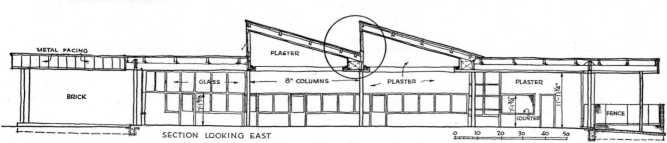

SECTION LOOKING EAST

Eugene Weston, Jr., Architect

HAS THE AUTOMOBILE MADE THE SKYSCRAPER OBSOLETE?

SOME interesting questions on planning insistently hover about this nice little "drive-in" office building. Here is a fairly large site in downtown Los Angeles developed with a two-story building, with its private parking area occupying most of the plot (plan on page 152). For example, has the parking problem become so compelling that it has overridden the old rules of economical site development? Is the skyscraper to fall victim of the automobile? Or have past financial difficulties of large office buildings made them unpopular? Or maybe the so-called "amenity values" of parking space and garden proved so attractive that a large building for this site

never was seriously considered. The architect contents himself with the simple statement that "in view of the already crowded adjacent automobile parking facilities, it was decided to provide ample parking space at the new location." The building is completely air-conditoined, the equipment being housed in an insulated machine room on the roof. The small vents in the windows were not required for the functioning of the system, but were included as a psychological hedge against a completely closed building. The building has a concrete frame, floor system and exterior walls, with a wood roof system and wood windows and frames.

Parking provisions led naturally to a particularly nice feature — the informal, recessed entrance combined with the covered driveway

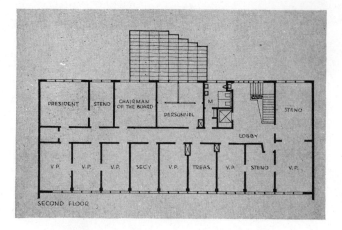

SECOND FLOOR

Public lobbies and corridors have grayed ochre walls, and all offices have grayed yellow-green walls. Conference room (opposite page, below) has blue-green walls, wine colored upholstered furniture and a white ceiling. Woodwork is painted to match the walls

First floor, shortened by the two driveways, houses only general offices, lobby and conference room. This last, opening into the garden, has a small kitchenette, as this company makes a point of daily conferences, at which a cup of coffee brightens the morning

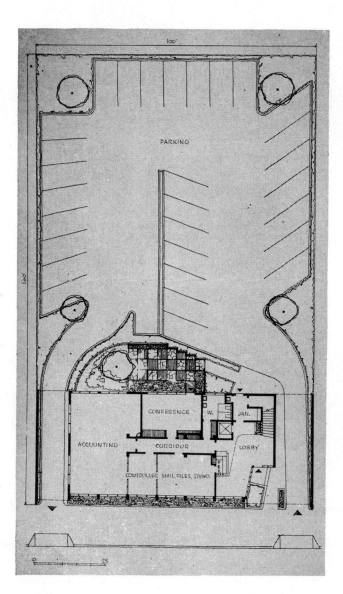

PARKING

CONFERENCE

ACCOUNTING

CORRIDOR

LOBBY

COMTROLLER MAIL FILES STENO

Street frontage is planted with boxwood myrtle and Pfitzer juniper. In the parking area the ground cover between bumper curbs and property lines is English ivy, and Maderian ivy is planted against the building walls, with Canary Island ivy at the north property line. Other areas have ironbark Eucalyptus, ricepaper plants and wax-leaved Privet, Ospedistra and Philodendron in boxes

Walter Wurdeman and Welton Becket, Architects

GENERAL PETROLEUM BUILDING, LOS ANGELES

WITH calm modesty the architects write: "this building does not radically differ in concept from office buildings of the past except that it features thin aluminum fins for sunshades, removable office partitions, and an extremely light steel frame, considering our earthquake ordinances. Because of high land values the problem was to condense the plan to obtain maximum floor area in the height allotted, 150 ft. For this height, set-back is impractical and unnecessary. The plan is laid out in 7-ft. modules, interior office partitions are movable so that offices can be laid out in any multiple of 7 ft., and a window is provided in each module." With all this, parking is not neglected: a separate garage is to be constructed near the building, on a site already owned by the company.

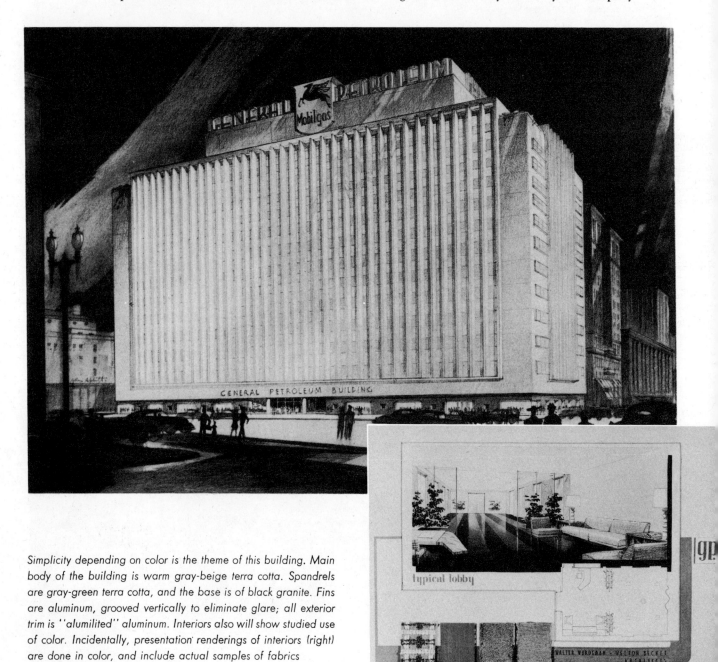

Simplicity depending on color is the theme of this building. Main body of the building is warm gray-beige terra cotta. Spandrels are gray-green terra cotta, and the base is of black granite. Fins are aluminum, grooved vertically to eliminate glare; all exterior trim is "alumilited" aluminum. Interiors also will show studied use of color. Incidentally, presentation renderings of interiors (right) are done in color, and include actual samples of fabrics

typical lobby

Otis Rothschild Pho

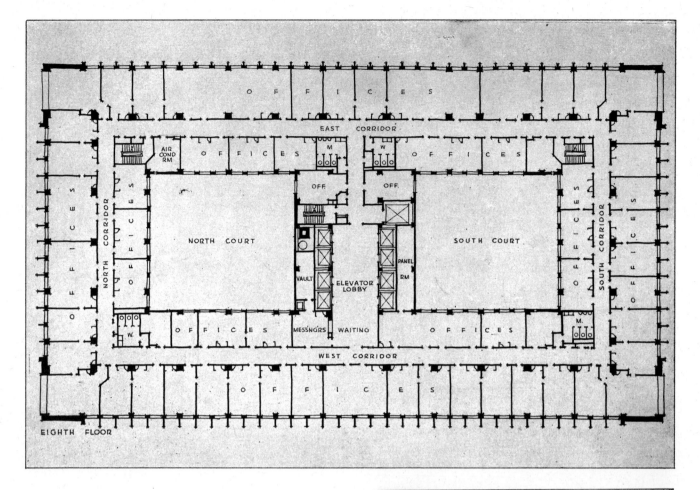

EIGHTH FLOOR

"The building is oriented so the main façade faces west and slightly north. As our sun problem in California is mainly on the west and south, a grid system of fins was devised to keep sun off the glass. A fin at each 7-ft. module, or at each window mullion, provides shade on the west façade through the hot period so as to save 300 tons of refrigeration by limiting impingement of direct sun on glass"

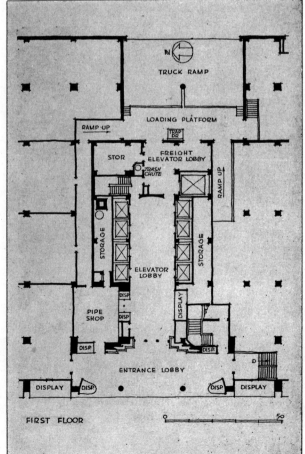

FIRST FLOOR

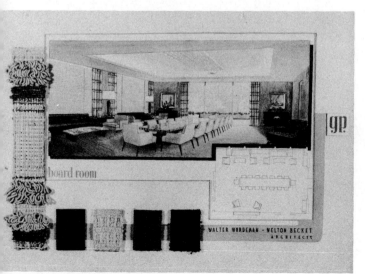

board room

WALTER WURDEMAN - WELTON BECKET
ARCHITECTS

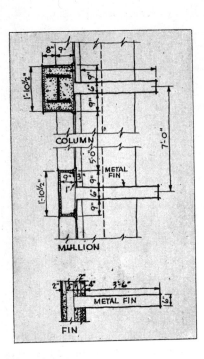

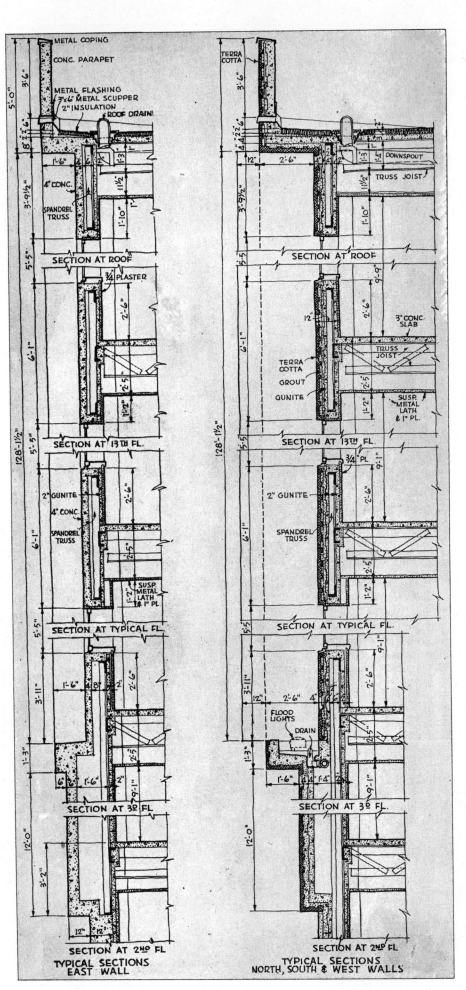

"The structural frame system," writes Walter Wurdeman, one of the architects for the General Petroleum Building, "is unique in that all concrete above the first floor, is lightweight concrete, using rocklite, pumice or similar aggregate. The exterior walls are hollow, a combination of lightweight concrete inner walls and lightweight gunite exterior walls. Material savings in dead weight of construction and tonnage of structural steel result from the use of the lightweight concrete. We have taken advantage of the recently-enacted ruling of the Board of Building and Safety Commissioners regarding fireproofing requirements of Type 1 buildings. The floor panel systems are steel joists and concrete slab constructions, a type which heretofore has been prohibited in California. The structural spandrels are fabricated steel trusses which use the hollow exterior walls for fire protection. Fins will be of aluminum encasing vertical structural steel trusses."

BUILT-IN AIR CONDITIONING

New York's newest office building boasts central and controlled system for air cooling in summer, air tempering in winter

News accounts of the Universal Pictures Building attribute to its air conditioning system "the cooling effect of a column of ice six miles high and 1 ft. square, melting every day." No one will find a solid core of ice running upward through the 22-story building, but the statement gives an idea of the cooling capacity of its 1000-ton refrigerating system that circulates chilled water to fan rooms on each floor, from which cooled and dehumidified air is circulated to offices by ceiling ducts. In winter, warm tempered air is circulated through the same system of ducts for good ventilation and to augment the heating effect of convectors, by preventing indrafts at windows.

This is the first fully air conditioned office skyscraper in New York, and the first large office building completed there since the war, occupying an entire block frontage on the east side of Park Avenue between 56th and 57th streets. During construction, it was known as the Tishman Building.

The cooling effect is produced by two carrier centrifugal refrigeration compressors powered by two steam-driven condensing turbines. The air conditioning system has a separate control station on each of the 22 floors. Each station contains its own system of fans, cooling coils, heating coils, and filters through which the air is circulated.

Although a few of the tenants presented special problems — restaurant, beauty shop, etc. — the air conditioning system was designed primarily for offices following a general pattern of private

The recently completed Universal Pictures Building on Park Avenue in New York (formerly called the Tishman Building): Kahn and Jacobs, Architects; Jaros, Baum, and Bolles, Consulting Engineers; Fred N. Severud, Structural Engineer; Tishman Realty and Construction Co., owner-builder; Kerby Saunders, Inc., contractors for air conditioning equipment, Atlas Sheet Metal Co., ductwork

Seidman Photo

offices around three sides of the building and large open office space in the interior areas. Elevators, fan room and services occupy most of the fourth side of the building.

Preliminary studies by Jaros, Baum, and Bolles, mechanical engineers, considered a "peripheral" system of ducts rising inside the exterior walls (from refrigeration and fan rooms in the basement). This idea was discarded, however, because of (1) too great extent of interior areas, which would require separate inside ducts; (2) varying office layouts and requirements on separate floors; (3) the effect of sun and shadow on different levels of the same building face; and (4) inadequate space for vertical ducts at exterior walls and offsets. It was decided therefore that each floor should have its own fan room; and that the several parts of each floor should be zoned separately, instead of zoning the building vertically.

For reasons of overall economy in design and materials, fan rooms for all floors have the same type of equipment and layout, and identical connections for steam and chilled water, although the systems on the smaller upper floors have smaller fans, coils, and ducts to suit the reduced cooling and ventilating requirements.

Each floor is divided into five zones: (1) north periphery (north is actually northeast, so receives early morning sun); (2) west periphery (receives direct afternoon sun); (3) south periphery (receives mid-day sun); (4) and (5) interior areas on the north and south sides.

Separate ducts lead from the fan room to each of these zones. In many cases, an entire floor is leased to a single tenant with special requirements for partitions and floor layout. While these variations required minor modifications in duct design and changes in location of grilles, major duct layout and zoning remain the same.

A modular system of grilles is provided on ducts supplying peripheral zones (1 grille to every two windows) so that partitions may be relocated without affecting the air conditioning.

Three types of controls are provided to prevent over-cooling. Ducts supplying interior zones have volume control only, in the form of dampers operating fully open to two-thirds open. Ducts supplying north and south zones have volume control and a reheat coil in zone ducts. The duct supplying the west zone has volume control, reheat coil, and also an after-cooling coil to give extra cooling effect required when sun is on that side of the building in late afternoon.

Air temperatures are regulated by indoor thermostats that respond to the thermal effect of increased sunshine, lighting, or increased number of people in the zones they control. These thermostats are automatically reset by an outdoor thermostat, to give comfort and operating economy under changing weather conditions.

Air cooling goes into effect when outside temperature exceeds 70°. Then, for every 2½° rise in outside temperature, inside temperature is raised 1°. At 95°, considered the maximum practical de-

sign temperature for New York City, temperature within the building is maintained at 80°.

Dehumidification of circulated air keeps relative humidity at 50 per cent or below in the summer. There is no humidification of tempered air in the winter because windows have only a single thickness of glass, with danger of frosting.

Refrigeration Room

It was considered impractical to install individual refrigeration rooms on each floor in conjunction with the fan rooms. Not only would space requirements and structural loads be increased, but also initial cost and maintenance problems. Then, too, economical steam-driven machines could not have been used.

The refrigeration room in the basement is equipped with two 500-ton refrigerating machines (compressors), each capable of maintaining one-half of the maximum refrigerating load. They are designed to be driven by steam supplied from an outside source at 125 lb. per sq. in. pressure (or by a boiler plant in the building, if later installed).

During spring and fall, one of the machines will suffice, operating well loaded at a cost materially below that of a single larger machine only partially loaded.

As an economy factor, water from the cooling tower, after condensing the refrigerant, is used to condense steam from the turbines. This reduces steam consumption by about one half.

Ceiling ducts which supply cool dehumidified air in summer and tempered air in winter, from fan rooms on each floor, generally follow this pattern on all floors, with minor modifications to suit individual requirements (floor shown will be occupied by Monsanto Chemical Co.). Floor area is divided into five zones: three peripheral zones and two interior zones. North side of building is at left

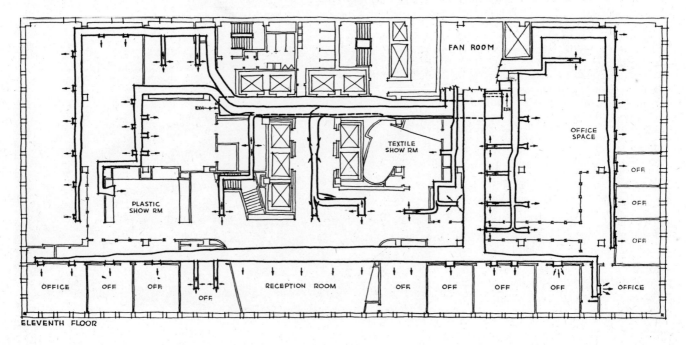

ELEVENTH FLOOR

Skidmore, Owings & Merrill, Architects

INSURANCE OFFICES AVOID THE COLONIAL

THE tradition that an office building for a life insurance company must be in Colonial style was one of the last to go. But here is evidence that an insurance office building can violate the tradition. This one is now under construction in Indianapolis for the Standard Life Insurance Company of Indiana. If there is some suggestion of classicism in the deep reveals on the west façade, nobody need make any false assumptions about styling intentions. The deep piers shade the huge windows through much of the day, and make it unnecessary to use the venetian blinds except for the worst hours of western sunshine.

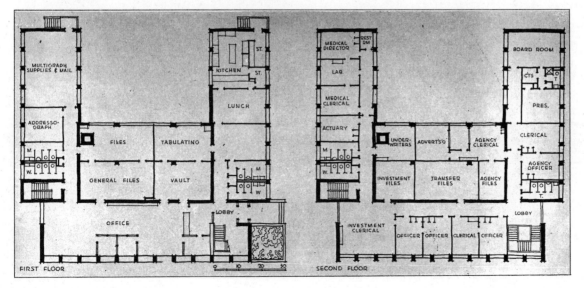

BY, OF and FOR ARCHITECTS

A club and office building in São Paulo, Brazil

Forte, Ruchti, Ciampaglia, Architects

MANY an American group of architects will envy the new building Brazilian architects have planned for themselves as a combined club, exhibition hall and office building. The ground or street floor is devoted to exhibition space, handy and inviting to the general public. Below is the meeting room or auditorium which can be used for many different occasions as there is ample storage space for chairs and other paraphernalia when the floor must be kept clear. The restaurant and bar on the second floor is bound to be popular. The floors above should be ideal for architects' offices — rentable space to make the project self-supporting. Construction is of reinforced concrete, brick and glass, resting on pile foundations under the columns.

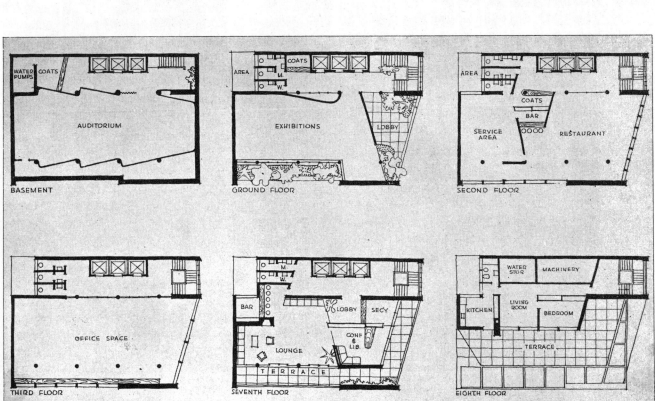

160

NEW DEPARTURES IN OFFICE BUILDING DESIGN

By Lathrop Douglass, Architect

THE pitfalls of façade-first design have long been apparent to architects, but I think office buildings particularly require that we forego the sketch-drawing until a thorough study has been given to what goes on inside the building.

It is perfectly true, of course, that between the Twenties and the Forties we should expect progress in matters of exterior design, but I insist that there is equal room for improvement in matters of function. These advances we must assimilate or develop before we can find anything but superficial words in such phrases as "horizontal or vertical treatment," "revealing the skeleton," "all-glass walls," etc.

As for the great American skyscraper, perhaps there is a temptation to think that it reached a high state of functional efficiency in the late Twenties. At least some of the few that have been built since then seem to repeat the pattern. I cannot agree that the old ones were so good. Some of them — Rockefeller Center, for example — provided good office space, with a notable quantity of that all-important ingredient, flexibility. But many of them were just façade-first designs. They did not provide that *sine qua non* of an office building: comfortable, efficient, flexible, standardized, economically operable office space. Certainly we can do better today, as this article will attempt to show.

FLEXIBILITY

Flexibility is the most important criterion of all. Corporations grow large, or small, or they move, or change their lines of business. The president of a large concern in Louisiana told me the other day that when they at last moved into their carefully-planned new building they thought nothing ever would have to be changed. In six years 50 per cent of the partition work has been changed.

Flexibility for future changes is not achieved without good planning of many different elements. First, the space must be standardized as far as possible for the largest possible number of uses. Modular locations must be developed for all such things as lighting fixtures, air conditioning grilles or radiators, or other service items, so that partitions can be moved overnight without tearing out important pieces of equipment. Fenestration must be designed in such a way that office widths can be varied to suit changing needs, to provide minimal

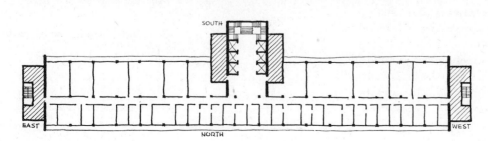

Office building plan, by the author, for a latitude of 10 degrees north, with good year-round air temperatures but intense radiant heat from the sun. Long axis is east-west. Continuous horizontal sunshades anticipate sun's angles in winter and summer. Sun never strikes any window, summer or winter. Result: no glare, no blinds, no radiant heat; also rain protection. Stairs and utilities protect ends of building from the sun

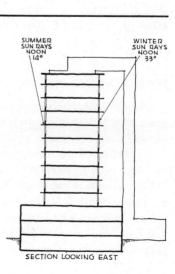

private offices or larger ones without waste of space.

The building managers who struggle with profit and loss figures in the old-time skyscrapers talk a great deal about depth of space from the windows. In an air conditioned, well-lighted building, the problem naturally is not so critical. Any reasonable depth would seem

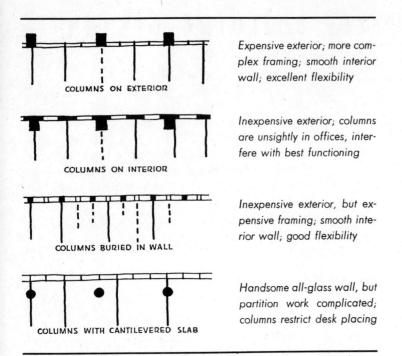

Expensive exterior; more complex framing; smooth interior wall; excellent flexibility

COLUMNS ON EXTERIOR

Inexpensive exterior; columns are unsightly in offices, interfere with best functioning

COLUMNS ON INTERIOR

Inexpensive exterior, but expensive framing; smooth interior wall; good flexibility

COLUMNS BURIED IN WALL

Handsome all-glass wall, but partition work complicated; columns restrict desk placing

COLUMNS WITH CANTILEVERED SLAB

satisfactory, so long as people generally can see somewhere in the distance a patch of sky. Nevertheless, I am inclined to side with the building managers in their contention that excessive depth of space is a waste of money. Where the requirements include a large number of small private offices — for engineers, copy-writers, etc. — the exterior wall space is at a premium, while there may be little use for interior space. It seems poor economy, then, to create undesirable space simply because it can be done cheaply. The number of square feet of usable space per man is the criterion.

I know of two buildings, in different locations, owned by the same company. One has 12 ft. as the standard office width module (and this is far from economical); in this building the space per man is 140 sq. ft. The other building has 9 ft. as the standard width (much more economical), yet the space per man is 200, because of excessive depth.

FENESTRATION MODULES

The most heartfelt speech of the building managers deals with fenestration. Indeed the most serious charge against the skyscrapers of the Twenties is that usually the fenestration was designed for appearance and froze office space in uneconomical units.

For example, a handsome well-appointed office building in the South has windows 6 ft. 6 in. c-c. The result is that offices cannot be narrower than 13 ft. Six-and-a-half feet is too narrow for a private office, even for an engineer's cubicle. But 13 ft. is much too wide.

Rockefeller Center, on the other hand, stands out in my opinion as far ahead of practically all of our modern skyscrapers. Perhaps the simple alternating rhythm of 4½ ft. windows and 4½ ft. piers is not revolutionary enough in "design" for armchair commentators, but there is an almost unrivaled flexibility. Such buildings are functional in the true sense of the word.

The Tishman Building, newly completed in New York, has taken a different approach, but one that also is truly functional. There is a continuous row of windows separated from each other by a 12-in. mullion. Partitions can be placed anywhere on a 4½ ft. module, allowing offices of 9, 13½ and 18 ft. There are no columns projecting into the rooms, and the windows are virtually a continuous band of glass. The partitions, however, have to be on this exact module, whereas in Rockefeller Center the 4½ ft. masonry pier permits an infinite variety of widths.

Architectural magazines are showing more and more buildings with all-glass walls. Superficially the all-glass wall seems highly functional. It may be, in many cases. In others it may simply be creating a problem in order to solve it.

Glass walls with their maximum daylight are obviously desirable, provided we solve the problems of radiant heat of the sun and of sun glare. Otherwise our glass wall will be nullified by venetian blinds, or the occupants will be scorched, even if we specify special glass to cut the actinic rays by 50 per cent. And what if the sun keeps playing hide and seek behind the clouds?

Early installations frequently were not adequately calculated in this respect. For example: I visited a very nicely-planned air conditioned office building on one of the Caribbean Islands. Large areas of the walls were in glass block, with a small clear-glass window every so many feet, through which one could feel contact with the world. The glass block was carefully checked for its heat transmission coefficients and the air conditioning designed accordingly. But nobody had considered the problem of direct radiant heat rays of the sun which went right through the glass. The occupants were almost blistered when the sun came around their way, and a tremendous added load was put on the air conditioning.

Bad enough to guess wrong with glass block. Think of the problem with ¼-in. plate glass, even double glass

Continuous fenestration on 4-ft. module; offices of 8, 12 or 16 ft., but no fractional variants

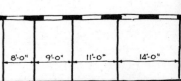

| EXEC | SECY | TYPICAL | TYPICAL |

CONTINUOUS FENESTRATION · 4' MODULE SPACING

Alternating 4½-ft. windows and piers give exceptional flexibility; office widths can be as desired

| 8'-0" | 9'-0" | 11'-0" | 14'-0" |

ROCKEFELLER CENTER SPACING

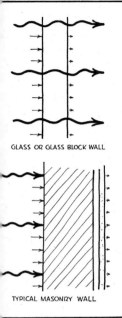

With glass or glass block walls, heat transmission is partly by conduction and convection, partly by radiation through the glass. Unless fins shield glass, air conditioning must meet this load

GLASS OR GLASS BLOCK WALL

In the typical masonry wall transmission of heat is by conduction and convection. Radiant rays from the sun tend to heat up wall and increase conduction, but do not of themselves penetrate the building

TYPICAL MASONRY WALL

with air space. The air space doesn't mean a thing to those heat rays.

I should make it clear that I am not criticizing glass or its manufacturers. The heat problem, both ways, is carefully stated; you can look in Sweet's and find tables for both heat transmission and radiant heat for different kinds of glass or glass block. What I am trying to bring out is that the designer cannot blithely assume that the all-glass wall is wonderful without designing his building very carefully.

As an example of the design problem, I am planning a building for a tropical location at a high altitude. We worked out a long narrow building, with plenty of glass: all offices have continuous windows. The long axis is placed east and west, offices facing either north or south. Only utilities are on the sun-baked east and west ends. Fins or sunshades along north and south walls anticipate the varying angle of the sun, to the north in summer, to the south in winter. The sun never gets into any window at any season. With this protection against radiant heat of the sun, we need no air conditioning, for the air temperature is ideal the year around. Nor is there any need for venetian blinds.

COLUMNS AND FRAMING

Exterior columns are a definite problem. They tend to interfere with partitions, upset modular spacing of windows and may have an unpleasant appearance. The system of cantilevered floors with columns set back a few feet from the exterior seems in actuality to be but a *post facto* rationalization of the desire for the all-glass wall. For loft buildings or small offices, where changes will not occur, this system may be all right, but partition locations are a serious matter for a large building requiring many types and sizes of offices. There is reduced flexibility of partition work, and desk spacing is handicapped unless columns are some 6 ft. away from the wall. Should flexibility and interior planning economy be sacrificed just for a "smart" exterior? Perhaps in some

cases this should be done for the advertising value of good appearance, but it is not functional architecture.

Columns outside the building proper seem a better solution, not because they "reveal the skeleton" (which they do), but because they give a smooth, uninterrupted interior surface to the exterior building wall, so that partition work can be standardized and simplified. This system has been used on the Savings Fund Building in Philadelphia, and appears slated for a number of projected buildings. It seems like a very practical idea, except for the higher cost of exterior masonry and the more complicated column connections.

A still better solution under certain circumstances seems to be the use of angles or T's at frequent intervals imbedded entirely within the wall. They are less complicated than exterior columns; interiors are smooth; spacing of windows can be absolutely uniform, so that any module system can work. This system is ideal for continuous windows.

The Tishman Building seems to be pioneering this idea in New York, though building code requirements have resulted in very heavy mullions.

Following along this line, I am currently planning, with Carson & Lundin as associates, a long six-story office building for which the owners have very intelligently insisted on a 4-ft. module, in order to provide

When occupant has nearly all small offices for such employees as engineers or copy writers, interior space would be largely wasted

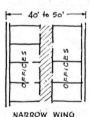

NARROW WING

When there is a good balance between private and "bull pen" offices, or where windows are desired for all, try the off-set corridor

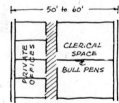

OFFSET CORRIDOR

For a commercial office building with many small tenants, clerical areas are usually inside; depth from window not much over 25 ft.

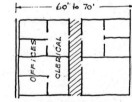

TYPICAL OFFICES

For large offices inside space may be used for open offices, with partitions only for private offices. Double corridors set off by railings

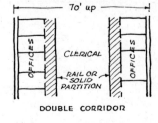

DOUBLE CORRIDOR

8-ft. secretary offices or engineer cubicles, 12-ft. standard offices for one to two people, and 16-ft. executive offices. This would be impossible without an absolutely uniform spacing of windows on the 4-ft. module; i.e., you must be able to place a partition equally well at any mullion and still have exactly 8, 12 or 16 ft. c-c. partitions. We have been able to cut the exterior steel down to a box of two 6 by 3½-in. angles welded and placed every 8 ft.; i.e., every other mullion is structural.

This scheme may have an added advantage in uniformity. To illustrate: I remember once showing a sketch of a proposed plan to a former official of this same company. An over-zealous draftsman had very accurately scaled off the areas of the various offices on the sketch. The office assigned to the man in question showed 296 sq. ft., whereas his equal-ranking neighbor had an office marked 300 sq. ft. In all seriousness he called me up and asked why he had been discrimi-nated against in the matter of the size of his office.

Cost of maintenance (operating cost) seems too frequently ignored. It is inescapable that every maintenance dollar spent in a year is the equivalent of $15 to $20 in first cost (depending, of course, on interest rates). If a company is planning an office building which is expected to last a score or more of years, it scarcely seems intelligent, unless there is difficulty in financing, to save $100,000 on first cost by cheap material or poor planning, and then have for the life of the building a maintenance bill every year whose capitalized value might be $200,000. The upward spiral of inflation underlines this argument even more forcefully. Annual charges on the capital investment do not increase as inflation proceeds, but maintenance costs go steadily upward; in fact have doubled in the last few years. The prudent man who insisted on cutting maintenance and operation costs to the minimum should be reaping his reward.

PERHAPS THE BEST IS ACTUALLY THE CHEAPEST

By Lathrop Douglass, Architect

IF this really is a new era for office buildings, with improved functional designs and better styling, let it also be a new era as regards costs. And not a penurious era.

In making this special plea for a new type of realism on costs, I am not going to dwell upon the high building costs that have been making headlines. Certainly costs are high, but the *level of costs* does not greatly affect the *comparative costs*. This message deals with relative costs of the buildings and the operations that go on inside them. I think I can show that in the past we have been building offices too cheaply.

It seems reasonable to say that "first costs" fall into three fairly obvious classifications:

1. The cost of space; that is, the structure itself.

2. The cost of "plush," or the advertising value of a handsome show — the marble, the 100-story tower.

3. The cost of such features as partitions, lighting, air conditioning, acoustical treatment, etc., which are all a means of improving the efficiency of the office employees.

To repeat once again, an office building is a means of providing, on a proper site, the most comfortable, efficient, flexible space for housing the activities of employees; whether for one firm or for many. The important and very interesting question is: to what extent do these features affect the employee? Does a man turn out more work in a cool, dehumidified building, a well-lighted building with a private, sound-proofed office for himself? How much more work does he turn out in these surroundings than in a humid, hot, ill-lighted bull pen amidst the clatter of typewriters and the time-wasting gabble of his fellow employees?

During the early part of the war I worked in a room with two other people, no acoustical material, hard floors and ceiling, poor lighting, drafty, no air treatment. When I wasn't wasting time talking to my office mates I was going crazy listening to the racket of their talking to each other. When people came in to see me I was apologetic. In the summer the office had to be closed every so often because the heat made work an impossibility. Yet this was structurally and in appearance one of the best office buildings in New York. I used to try to calculate the average amount of time I lost every day over a long period of time. From all causes combined, the best guess I could make, and of course it was only a guess, was about 20 per cent. I understand actual controlled experiments have been made on this subject. Anyway at that time I had a salary of around $8000 a year. Twenty per cent of $8000 is $1600 — a possible $1600 worth of lost time every year. The capitalized value of $1600 should be around $25,000. On the other

SALARIES OF ALL EMPLOYEES ████████████
CHARGES:
  STRUCTURE (Walls, Floors, etc.) ▮
  "PLUSH" (Marble facades, etc.) ▮
  FACILITIES (Acoust, Air cond, etc.) ▮

MAINTENANCE ▮

CHARGES ON LAND, REAL ESTATE TAXES, ETC.▮

FIRST COSTS VS. SALARIES

hand, how much would it have cost to give me a first-class, private, air conditioned office all to myself, with a good acoustical ceiling and good office furniture — i.e., space and equipment that would for the most part eliminate that estimated 20 per cent loss in efficiency?

Curious as to the answer, I worked out not long ago the following series of tables. Different interest rates, salary averages and other cost units can be substituted for those I have used, but the results will be much the same. To me they are amazing. Why should millions of perfectly good dollars be literally thrown away through inefficient working conditions, year after year, by the false notion that bare minimum standards save money? Actually the most perfect, efficient, attractive working conditions are literally cheap compared with the loss in efficiency from the unsatisfactory conditions.*

An engineer, or a bookkeeper, earning (with all benefits), say $6000 a year occupies a portion of a badly-planned bull pen, hot and humid in summer, incorrectly lighted, reverberating with the noise of conversation and typewriters. He occupies a certain area of rentable space. He has a certain average daily output of work which is directly affected by the heat, the noise, the idle conversation, the general office morale.

Should his firm consider either an entirely new building, or modernization and expansion of existing space, in order to secure greater output per man, what percentage of this average employee's annual salary will these improved conditions cost? If it costs 1 per cent or 2 per cent, and his efficiency is improved by 10 per cent or 20 per cent or perhaps 50 per cent, why, the profit is 1000 per cent or maybe much more. The annual payroll in any average office is so very much greater than the annual charges for modern improvements that it seems almost an axiom that improving the employees' efficiency is what counts — the cost of space and improvements is negligible.

To make a common ground for comparisons, we can assume certain figures, which of course could be easily adjusted to fit any given set of conditions:

Assume 150 sq. ft. of net rentable space per employee (this figure is intentionally liberal and would include a share in the corridors, etc.). Assume $6000 average salary (any other figure would serve just as well). Interest and amortization @ 6 per cent.

1. *Acoustic tile* to reduce the distraction from noise:
   Cost per employee @ 50¢ per sq. ft. $75.00
   Annual charges per employee @ 6 per cent. 4.50
   Percentage of salary 075

This is the equivalent in cost of only *19 seconds* of the hypothetical employee's working day. And there is no added maintenance cost.

2. *Office partitions* to provide privacy and space to concentrate, reduce idle conversation and build morale:

   Good quality movable metal; assume $20 per lineal ft. allowing 25 ft. per man

   Total cost per employee. $500.00
   Annual charges @ 6 per cent 30.00
   Percentage of salary 5

* This thesis has been forcibly presented by C. F. Braun in his pamphlet, "White Collars and Tools."

This is the equivalent of only *2 minutes* of daily time (assuming of course no increase in allotted floor space). And here again there is normally little maintenance to be considered.

As a matter of interest in this connection, charges for masonry partitions would be only about $12 annually, but there is scarcely a firm that does not continuously change its office layout, and in comparing the cost of movable versus masonry partitions one should take into account the fact that movable partitions can be changed at will even overnight, whereas a plastered and painted masonry partition, if changed, will cost a lot more than the contract cost because of the large amount of employees' time lost from dust and noise and confusion, while existing walls are torn down and new ones built up, plastered and painted.

3. *Air conditioning*
   Total cost per employee @ $3.00. . . . . $450.00
   Annual charges per employee @ 6 per cent. 27.00
   Annual operating costs (a guess). 40.00
   TOTAL ANNUAL COSTS 67.00
   Per cent of employees' salary. 1.17

This is equivalent of only 4½ *minutes* of the hypothetical employee's day. Think of this in terms of afternoons off because of 90° up temperatures, of lackadaisical work, of sleepiness from stuffy rooms in winter, to say nothing of the continuous dirt and the cost of janitors.

Until I worked out these figures I had been recommending omission of air conditioning in the New York area as an unnecessary expense. These figures have changed my mind.

The above are of course only a few of the more obvious items that could vastly improve employee efficiency and save payroll expenditures. A similar tabulation could easily be made for furnishing or other little extras which might improve working conditions.

As a final example let us assume an entirely new building, modern, complete with every common-sense item of good planning and worthwhile detail and equipment practicable.

If it cost in the neighborhood, let us say as a broad guess, of $16 per sq. ft., the total cost per employee would be $2400. Inclusion of $600 more for land value would bring this to $3000. Charges on this investment @ 6 per cent would be but $180. Adding in taxes @ $90 and operating expenses @ $150, the entire operation would come to an annual cost of $420.

However, for the poorest kind of crowded unsatisfactory space one would be paying in today's rental market, let us say $300 per year per man.

So your new well-planned modern building with its enormous payoff in increased efficiency and morale would actually cost only the difference between $420 and the $300 rental for existing space. That is, all the improvements of the new building would actually cost but $120 more per year per employee.

This is 2 per cent of our hypothetical employee's salary - the equivalent of less than *9 minutes* of his day.

Is this argument sound? If it is, why then, what are we waiting for?

SMALL BUSINESS BUILDINGS

Frederic Arden Pawley, Architect

The RECORD has published annually many studies of tall office buildings.* This year we decided to examine smaller types of more general interest to architectural offices located outside major metropolitan areas. Potential volume of new buildings for the country as a whole will be greater in this class of structure in the multi-story class. Six stories, through an arbitrary limit, seem appropriate and the range downward includes the one-story taxpayer.

OCCUPANCY types vary enormously in general-purpose buildings. There are few design and planning factors common to them all. The appended bibliography shows an extensive literature on office-planning space standards which will be reviewed briefly herein. Perhaps this intrinsic variety suggests a primary design principle — flexibility is mandatory. Ground floor space will usually house retail, showroom or other occupancies requiring easy public access. Rear areas may possibly provide public commercial recreation or entertainment facilities. Each of these is regularly treated as a sub-

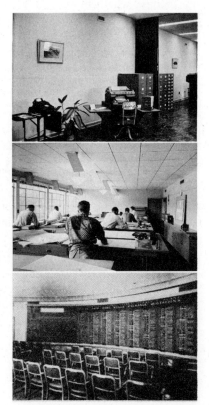

Left, Remington-Rand Bldg., Philadelphia; Thalheimer & Weitz, Archts.; C. V. D. Hubbard photo. Above, American Home Bldg., Queens, N. Y. (S. Minskoff, owner-builder), Boak & Raad, Archts. Facing page, Technical Instrument Co., Houston, Tex.; Mackie & Kamrath, Archts.; Mears Studio photo. Interiors, top to bottom: office, Remington-Rand, Dallas, Tex., G. L. Dahl, Archt.; own drafting room, Page, Southerland & Page, Archts., Austin, Tex.; board room, Merrill Lynch, Pierce, Fenner & Beane, Orlando, Fla., James Gamble Rogers III, Archt.

(*See Bibliography references: 44-51)

ject for a Building Types Study in itself. Consequently, in this article, emphasis will be on the building as a whole.

The architect must coordinate, in a commercial building project, many correlative and often divergent points of view. To sell his own services he must be acquainted with preliminary and operating procedures. To this end we have consulted experienced real estate men, lenders of construction and permanent funds, building managers, maintenance experts and corporations who are tenants with national experience in leasing office space. They have generously contributed data for the following pages.

It is equally important for these factors in the building industry to understand the architect's point of view and to recognize the financial as well as esthetic benefits of his function of comprehensive coordination. The essential fact is that commercial buildings are not well designed unless they are continuously profitable.

This ideal result, a continuously profitable building, is a complex product of intelligence applied to the following problems:

PROBLEMS:			
location	rentable areas		ARCHITECT PLUS
climate	(including shapes)		owner
orientation	flexibility		financier
local conditions	services & equipment		realtor
& regulations	fenestration	STUDIED	consultants
site selection	materials & workmanship	BY	contractors & labor
parking	types of occupancy		code officials
plot size & shape	construction costs		insurance organizations
height	management, personnel		tenants
structure	& operating costs		operating staff
	financing		

A successful commercial building project, perhaps more than any other building type, implies the solution of a giant equation including all the above-tabulated known, unknown and variable factors. Accurate resolution of all these contributory forces into a structure meeting the needs of its population, owners and community — including esthetic needs — is the especial function of the architect. To perform this function properly he must be retained at the beginning of the project and to be of most use at this stage he must know a few fundamentals of real estate, finance and insurance practice.

SMALL BUSINESS BUILDINGS
Finance and Real Estate Viewpoint

Rental return or income from a proposed building, usually measured in dollars per square foot of rental space, is naturally a primary concern of lenders and real estate managers. Type, area and cube of building are studied by them in preliminary financial set-ups devised to show a profit above an adequate income to defray costs of financing, construction, taxes, depreciation and operation and to arrive at a reasonable rent per square foot. Decision on whether a project goes ahead must be based on such "adequacy of improvement."

Preservation of income in bad times is more difficult in some types of buildings than in others. Experience has shown need for flexibility of space arrangement (and for ease of re-subdivision, particularly into smaller units) to provide for changes in tenancy. Low operation and maintenance costs are essential. It is second nature (or perhaps first) for a building manager to consider "eventual tenants" more than original or current occupants. This influences managerial attitudes toward tenant alteration practices, approvals and expenditures, even in the cases where alterations are paid for by the tenant.

Kind of occupancy for specific buildings affects lenders' viewpoint. Even a 20 to 25 ft retail frontage can secure an adequate institutional loan provided the tenant can develop the required income from the property. It would be impossible space for a variety chain store but quite acceptable for a specialty shop with concentrated selling of high-margin-of-profit goods. A 50 ft six-story building may be an unsound investment in bad times. Major tenants may move out leaving larger spaces which are expensive to alter for small tenants. Rents will be lower due to competition, particularly those paid by such smaller tenants because they can move easily. Increased partitioning reduces rentable area (additional non-revenue corridor, etc., required). Operating costs increase with number of tenants and even if parts of building are closed off there may be spotty tenancy requiring uneconomic service for partly vacant areas. Under depressed conditions managers often cannot afford to maintain premises as well as in normal times; and a building which, because of poor plan, materials or equipment, is difficult (i.e. expensive) to maintain, will be neglected. Rents obtainable from a shabby building are depressed and the situation becomes a pernicious downward spiral of blight.

Multi-occupancy is by some authorities considered not as desirable as larger unit leases. Professional offices, doctors, dentists, etc., although traffic producers

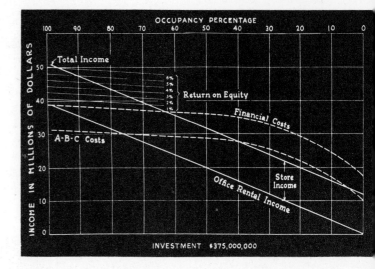

This graph illustrates how quickly most buildings would begin to lose money at present rental rates were their occupancy to drop sharply. It was prepared by the National Association of Building Owners and Managers (11), and is based upon a spotcheck survey of rental incomes and operating expenses for more than 100 buildings at the end of the year 1947. Net income disappears at about 65% occupancy, and is only about 5% at 90% occupancy. "A-B-C costs" are three categories of operating and fixed costs periodically reported to the N.A.B.O.M. by members throughout the country

profitable for some locations, create special problems such as increased operating expenses and maintenance (special utilities) and baby-carriage parking!

On the other hand, a New York City savings bank president, whose mortgage department made more loans in August 1949 than any other lender reported for that month, points out that higher rents can be obtained from small offices. They may be priced on a unit basis rather than on the square-foot basis used for larger space. As an example he compared one floor bringing $10,000, rented as a whole, with another floor of same area in same building which brought $14,000, rented as many small offices.

The architect may be in the position of establishing floor development plans for buildings before rental and he must balance such differing viewpoints against local demand.

Left: Deep space—controlled conditions: *air, light, sound, for efficient operation.* George L. Dahl, Architects & Engineers, Dallas, Texas

Right: Multi-occupancy: *Architects, consulting engineers, manufacturers' sales offices, insurance agency.* Page, Southerland & Page, Architects & Engineers, Austin, Texas. *Photo: Studtman Photo Service*

The usability of upper-floor rental space for a variety of occupancies is often a matter of depth of space from window walls to corridors. Some tenants, such as insurance offices or others with large clerical, filing and storage requirements, may need deep space. Lathrop Douglass, A.I.A., has pointed out in an excellent article (45) a number of office-planning fallacies and showed the actual economies of furnishing air conditioning, superior lighting, acoustic treatment, etc., to provide Class A space anywhere in a building. The old rule of no space deeper than 27 ft from a window wall and the real estate aphorism that "people want to buy windows" is less true from a technological viewpoint in such conditioned space. It still holds from a psychological viewpoint, however, especially where large-area leases are not concerned. This will be referred to again under planning.

There are other amenities which increase the desirability of a building for tenants and which will act to preserve income in competitive periods. Adequate nearby parking facilities are extremely important. A decentralized location, if appropriate for proposed occupancy, may bring other attractive advantages of light, air, space, landscaping and less expensive land.

Certain tenants will welcome provision of facilities for joint use: conference rooms, telephone answering service and low-cost storage areas in basement. The latter recommendation is based on current policies of record retention. There is no reason why a tenant should pay premium rents for inactive file and storage space and in competitive times the smaller tenant cannot afford to do so.

An attractive, convenient entrance, lobby and public spaces will also help to hold tenants. Tortuous access

SMALL BUSINESS BUILDINGS
Finance and Real Estate Viewpoint

Decentralized offices

Thornhill Craver Co., Houston, Texas, Mackie & Kamrath, Architects. Photo: Mears Studio

Lobbies and public spaces

Left: Citizens' National Trust & Saving Bank, Los Angeles, Stiles Clements Associates, Architects. Photo: Shulman. Right: Costello Bldg., Los Angeles, McFarland & Bonsall, Architects. Photo: Knowles

Conference rooms

Top photo: Own offices. Page, Southerland & Page, Architects. Photo: Studtman Photo Service Lower two photos: Esso Headquarters, Richmond, Va. Carneal & Johnston, Architects. Photo: Dements' Studio

to offices makes a poor impression and often indicates wasteful use of space. The ratio of rentable area to total building area possible to develop on the plot, particularly on high-cost land, must be watched in planning a building for profit. If a building develops vacancies when exit, elevator and service area is excessive this factor alone may alter financial relationships sufficiently to cause distress.

Some operative builders and experienced building owners develop tenants and secure commitments from them before breaking ground for a new building. Lenders naturally prefer this situation; money is more easily available if at least one strong tenant is signed up. Favorable terms of financing will depend largely on the location of the project in relation to the business district and the demand for its proposed occupancy. No hesitation is usually found on loans for projects in a 100% business district since resale is rarely difficult. One insurance company making "building and permanent" loans currently quotes $3\frac{1}{2}\%$ to 4% interest on one or two-story buildings in 100% districts with short term leases. In an 80% district the interest rate would be $4\frac{1}{4}\%$ to $4\frac{1}{2}\%$ and longer term leases would be required (10 to 20 years maximum, permitting determination of and adjustment to district trends). To these rates must be added amortization of 1% to 3% per year. A popular method is the constant payment plan whereby the proportions of payments on principal and interest vary as the principal is reduced.

Determination of rental rates

In office building financial analyses a vacancy allowance is now normally set at 10%. A postwar article on Philadelphia conditions (11) pointed out that that city had had an average vacancy of 18% for 25 years previous to the war. Averaging this with 5 years of 100% occupancy the author recommended use of a 15% allowance. Actual 1949 Manhattan vacancy is about 2%. These figures are given to show that local conditions must govern such estimating allowances.

Entrance establishes character

Left: Sill Bldg., Bakersfield, Calif., Kump & Falk, Architects. Photo: Roger Sturtevant. Center: Costello Bldg., Los Angeles, McFarland & Bonsall, Architects. Photo: Ralph E. Knowles. Right: Remington-Rand Bldg., Phila., Thalheimer & Weitz, Architects. Photo: Hubbard

SMALL BUSINESS BUILDINGS
Finance and Real Estate Viewpoint

Sixty per cent is the normal operating ratio for tall office buildings (based on total rental areas — operating ratios based on rentable office areas were 75% for 1947 and 72.7% for 1948) (7). This means that 60% of total income is normally required for operating expenses. Sixty per cent of operating expenses is required for labor, not including management, with little hope of reducton. It is concluded, therefore, that any substantial improvements in operating ratio must come through increases in rental rates.

An editorial by Charles A. McCaleb of *Buildings & Building Management* (15) says in part: "Devised originally as a measuring stick to aid building operators in comparing operating costs, the square-foot unit soon found its way into renting, when renting men discovered that it provided a quick and easy means of obscuring physical differences between good offices and bad in comparing competitive offerings."

The Sheridan-Karkow rental rate formula (explained on page 174) is derived by reference to a standard unit office 18 x 25 ft (deep) facing street frontage of building on the 8th floor. Since its formulation a number of refinements have been proposed. These are reviewed by B. L. Lefler (17) who points out that there are difficulties in applying such criteria rigidly because space variables are not fixed. Technological changes with increased use of air conditioning and better lighting have improved deep space. Tenants with more than 5000 sf may need considerable deep space. The variety of tenant installations makes great differences in maintenance and service. Doctors and dentists cost more than large fire insurance agencies. Small tenants generally cost more than large ones and shallow space more than deep. A plan with many private offices increases costs. Small law firms cost more than average business tenants.

COMPANY BRANCH OFFICES IN

Firms with 100–200 branch offices throughout the country vary in leasing and location requirements. One prefers 10-year maximum leases near but not in the 100% districts. A competitor wants 5-year maximum leases, preserving more mobility for offices similarly located, and may move to get into a better market area or away from an expensive location or to provide for expansion. One insurance company insists on 5-year maximum leases although its average tenancy has been about 20 years for hundreds of offices. Length of lease has direct effect on extent of alterations and make-ready expenses tenant is willing to assume.

An architect may become vitally interested in such details of loans and leases if he is retained at the outset of a project or if he becomes architect or consultant for a company with a multi-branch office organization

26	Acme Steel Co.
14	Ahlberg Bearing Co.
27	Airetool Mfg. Co.
62	Air Reduction Sales Co.
27	Ajax Flexible Coupling Co.
23	Aldrich Pump Co.
20	Allegheny Ludlum Steel Corp.
16	Allen-Bradley Co.
59	Allied Chemical & Dye Corp.
99	Allis-Chalmers Mfg. Co.
54	Aluminum Company of America
14	Aluminum Cooking Utensil Co.
27	American Brass Co.
26	American Cabinet Hardware Co.
65	American Chain & Cable Co., Inc.
25	American Cyanamid Co.
13	American Emblem Co.
21	American La-France Foamite Corp.
15	American Manganese Steel Div. American Brake Shoe
19	American Mineral Spirits Co.
15	American Nickeloid Co.
264	American Optical Company
21	American Phenolic Corp.
10	American Tobacco Co.
32	Anchor-Hocking Glass Corp.
41	Anchor Post Fence Div., Anchor Post Products Co.
26	Armco Steel Corp.
39	Armstrong Cork Co.
26	Atlas Powder Corp.

48	Automatic Sprinkler Corp. of America
18	Automatic Temperature Control Co., Inc.
39	Babcock & Wilcox Co.
18	Bailey Meter Co.
15	Bemis Bros. Bag Co.
13	Bentley-Harris Mfg. Co.
37	Bethlehem Steel Corp.
17	Binks Mfg. Co.
15	Black Mfg. Co.
41	Black, Sivalls & Bryson, Inc.
32	Blackmer Pump Co.
22	Bowser, Inc.
14	Bridgeport Brass Co.
15	Brockway Glass Co., Inc.
14	Brown-Brockmeyer Co.
29	Brown Instrument Co.
15	Charles Bruning Co., Inc.
22	Buckeye Tools Corp.
26	Bull Co.
9	Carboloy Co., Inc.
14	Philip Carey Mfg. Co.
34	Carnegie-Illinois Steel Co.
19	Carrier Corp.
15	Celotex Corp.
25	Chain Belt Co.
16	Chapman Valve Mfg. Co.
24	Chicago Pneumatic Tool Co.
18	Cincinnati Electric Tool Co.
20	Clark Equipment Co.
18	Clary Multiplier Corp.

Another formula approach (18) to pricing office space, which can be applied also to modernization projects, is more arithmetic than criteria:

$$\text{Average rental psf} = \frac{\text{Capital investment} \times \text{Interest return desired}}{\text{Total rental area} \times \begin{array}{c}\text{Retainable profit} \\ \text{from rental dollar} \\ (= \% \text{ oper. profit})\end{array}}$$

EXAMPLE:

Assume:

Capital investment	$1,000,000.
Interest return desired	.06
Total rentable area	50,000 sf
Retainable profit (from each dollar of rent)	.03

$$\begin{array}{c}\text{Avg} \\ \text{Rental} \\ \text{rate}\end{array} \quad \frac{1,000,000 \times .06}{50,000 \times .03} = \frac{60,000}{15,000} = \$4.00 \text{ psf}$$

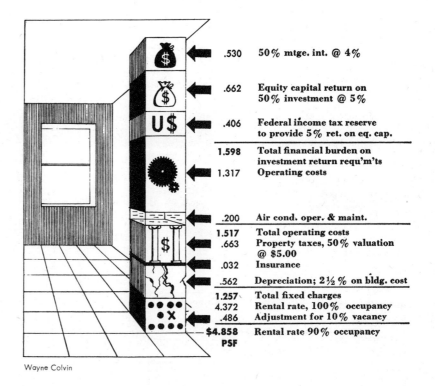

.530	50% mtge. int. @ 4%
.662	Equity capital return on 50% investment @ 5%
.406	Federal income tax reserve to provide 5% ret. on eq. cap.
1.598	Total financial burden on investment return requ'm'ts
1.317	Operating costs
.200	Air cond. oper. & maint.
1.517	Total operating costs
.663	Property taxes, 50% valuation @ $5.00
.032	Insurance
.562	Depreciation; 2½% on bldg. cost
1.257	Total fixed charges
4.372	Rental rate, 100% occupancy
.486	Adjustment for 10% vacancy
$4.858 PSF	Rental rate 90% occupancy

Wayne Colvin

THE UNITED STATES

Approximate totals including major subsidiaries and divisions. Agents, sales representatives, etc., omitted.

38	Cochrane Corp.	28	Foxboro Corp.	35	Oliver Corp.
28	Colson Corp.	223	General Electric	20	Oliver Iron & Steel Corp.
15	Commercial Solvents Corp.	29	B. F. Goodrich Co.	268	Otis Elevator Co.
54	Continental Can Co., Inc.	98	Graybar Electric Co., Inc.	26	Owens-Corning Fiberglas Corp.
22.	Continental-Diamond Fibre Co.	24	Hercules Powder Co., Inc.	22	Permanente Metals Corp.
17	Continental Electric Co.	31	Homelite Corp.	11	Pittsburgh Plate Glass Co.
25	Continental Rubber Works	24	A. C. Horn Co., Inc.	1200	Prudential Insurance Co.
126	Crane Co.	18	Howe Scale Co.	200	Remington Rand
31	Cutler-Hammer, Inc.	34	Ingersoll-Rand Co.	48	Republic Steel Corp.
43	Cyclone Fence Div. American Steel & Wire Co.	46	Inland Steel	37	Revere Copper & Brass Co.
		70	Interchemical Corp.	42	Reynolds Metals Co.
16	Deere & Co.	200	International Business Machines	19	Rheem Mfg. Co.
44	Diamond Alkali Co.	84	International Harvester Co.	16	Scovill Mfg. Co.
19	Diamond Mfg. Co.	18	Bryon Jackson Co.	37	Signode Steel Strapping Co.
21	Dings Magnetic Separator Co.	28	D. O. James Gear Mfg. Co.	74	Simplex Time Recorder Co.
18	Dodge Mfg. Corp.	55	Johns-Manville Corp.	46	Square D Co.
12	Dow Chemical Co.	23	Kelley-Koett Mfg. Co.	21	Sterling Electric Motors, Inc.
134	E. I. Du Pont de Nemours & Co., Inc.	28	Kennametal, Inc.	37	Sun Chemical Corp.
		22	Libbey-Owens-Ford Glass Co.	18	Sylvania Electric Products, Inc.
16	Economy Fuse & Mfg. Co.	40	Link-Belt Co.	26	Syntron Co.
19	Electric Storage Battery Co.	48	Liquid Carbonic Corp.	42	Timken Roller Bearing Co.
21	Elliott Co.	100	Merrill Lynch, Pierce, Fenner & Beane	82	Union Carbide & Carbon Corp.
28	Erie City Iron Works			30	Union Iron Works
20	Exact Weight Scale Co.	1000	Metropolitan Life Insurance Co.	36	United States Rubber Co.
18	Fafnir Bearing Co.	64	Minneapolis-Honeywell Regulator Co.	135	United States Steel Corp.
38	Fairbanks-Morse & Co.			48	West Disinfecting Co.
30	Federal Electric Products Co.	20	Monsanto Chemical Co.	263	Westinghouse Electric Corp.
18	Federal Products Co.	28	Mueller Brass Co.	28	Wheelco Instruments Co.
25	Federated Metals Div. American Smelting & Refining Co.	51	National Cylinder Gas Co.	42	Worthington Pump & Machinery Corp.
		28	National Steel Corp.		
28	Fibre Specialty Mfg. Co.	19	National Vulcanized Fibre Co.	22	Wyckoff Steel Co.
14	Flintkote Co.	21	Okonite Co.	41	York Corp.

SMALL BUSINESS BUILDINGS

Finance and Real Estate Viewpoint

One rather elaborate attempt to arrive at fair rent for office space is known as the Sheridan-Karkow formula. Its interest to architects is not in results for any particular case but in the criteria it sets up to define good space from user's point of view. Diagrams and photos compare criteria of this nature.

FACTORS WHICH AFFECT REAL ESTATE VALUE

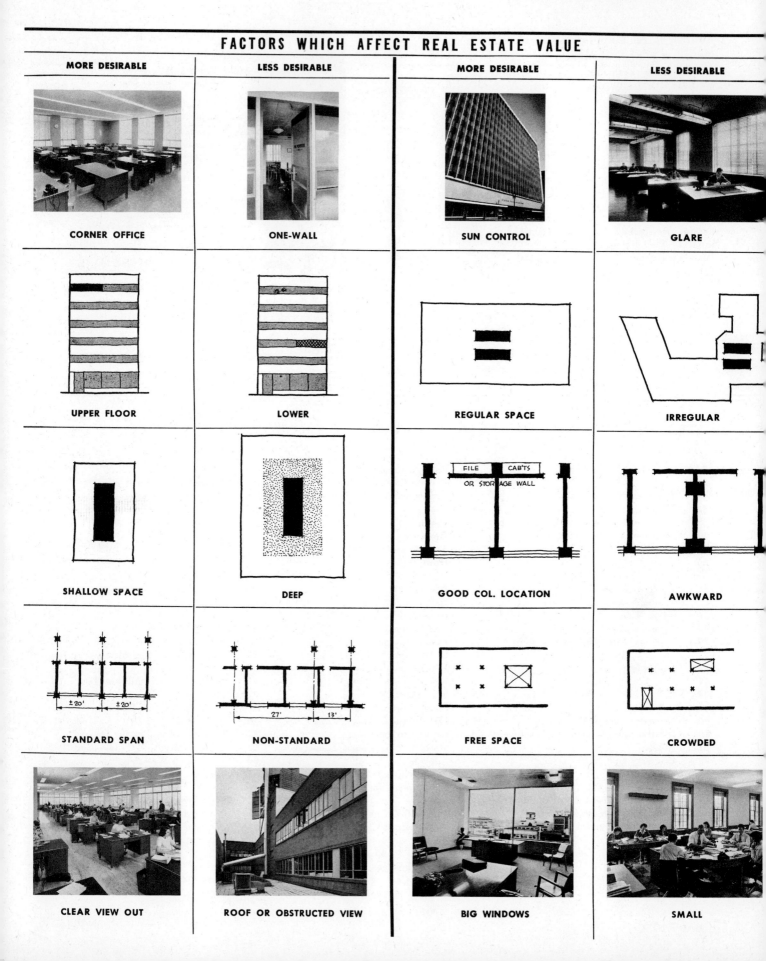

MORE DESIRABLE	LESS DESIRABLE	MORE DESIRABLE	LESS DESIRABLE
CORNER OFFICE	ONE-WALL	SUN CONTROL	GLARE
UPPER FLOOR	LOWER	REGULAR SPACE	IRREGULAR
SHALLOW SPACE	DEEP	GOOD COL. LOCATION	AWKWARD
STANDARD SPAN	NON-STANDARD	FREE SPACE	CROWDED
CLEAR VIEW OUT	ROOF OR OBSTRUCTED VIEW	BIG WINDOWS	SMALL

LOCATION FACTORS:

DECENTRALIZATION, ZONING, PARKING

Decentralization has resulted in an increase of office building construction in smaller cities. Reasons are various; defensive dispersal is only one. The financial advantage which may determine whether manufacturing administrative offices should be located at a plant or in an office building is only the difference between the capitalization of the two projects. The operating expenses and taxes will be approximately the same and contemporary communication facilities avoid most inconveniences due to separation. A recent article by a life insurance official (9) points out several reasons for reduction of new general office building construction in central areas:

(1) Industrial office space (at plants)
(2) "Home of their own" tendency
(3) Medical arts buildings
(4) Decentralization of merchandising

Lower interest rates are available to large organizations with national credit such as telephone and oil companies. This permits them to pay off on new construction years before private owners and consequently "high building costs alone will not stop new office building where large space users feel they need it." (9) An insurance or other sales branch office should be located to serve its territory with least travel by salesmen. This results in a two-sided location concept — *decentralization* of company as a whole and *centralization* of branch in its territory. Often no particular survey methods are used. Variety and food chains and other public-access services are usually established first and define a neighborhood or suburban shopping center based on their own careful surveys. "Many large companies make and keep current such studies on communities in a number of cities in which the location of a store might be desirable in the future. . . . No population center remains constant. Whatever type of area is selected for a store, it is important to select one that is not declining — and it is preferable to select one that is growing now and will continue to do so. . . . A market area is a dynamic thing, constantly adjusting to the economic and social forces which determine its pattern. . . . A good location of today may, in a few years, become a poor one." (33)

Real estate analysis or appraisal techniques for retail or office building sites include preparation of occupancy or strip maps showing location of all business and other occupancies in a city district. Realtors who specialize in chain-store locations prepare these for many cities as a basis for site selection in that highly competitive market.

Cities with "pin-wheel" or radial access highways often lack adequate circumferential connections. For satisfactory office building sites, a city plan should have what one location executive calls "criss-cross" transportation. The usual unplanned suburban development lacks these crossways and building locations remote from main intersections or "hubs" will not properly serve the area. Insurance offices must consider ease of access to parking, transit, post office and banks. Security and commodity brokerage offices must be in financial districts, near banks, unless they are local branches decentralized for some special area near a concentration of customers. "It is preferable to be situated as closely as possible to organizations with which the greatest volume of business is done." (38)

"It has become evident that there is no dependable relationship between the quantity of pedestrian traffic and the value of a site as measured by retail sales. The Bureau of Foreign & Domestic Commerce made a study of traffic-trade relationships for drug stores and concluded that traffic volume when unrelated to character of the traffic is an unreliable measure of potential business of a site. . . . Corners having the heaviest traffic are not always the best business addresses . . . frequently traffic is too congested. . . ." (33) "The value of an office location from the standpoint of advertisement cannot be overlooked. It may be financially impossible to secure comparable advertising value through other mediums." (38)

"Vacant buildings are regarded as bad neighbors, thus vacancies nearby should be carefully investigated. It is possible that the buildings are old and untenantable. On the other hand, perhaps a small amount of face-lifting on several old buildings for which the rent is relatively low would improve the entire block. One store might be able to start a low-cost but very effective renovating program, to the advantage of a group of stores. . . . A great deal can be learned from studying the occupancy history of the site under consideration." (33)

Zoning: A review of existing and proposed zoning regulations throughout the country indicates a definite trend toward mixed use. A number of cities for years have permitted retail and service shops on ground floors of multi-family dwellings. Progressive zoning proposals indicate still more intimate relationships between residence and employment. These may be effected by increased residential use of space above commercial occupancies in closely-built districts and by offices and very light or precision manufacturing in residential areas, with attractive lawns and landscaping. Offices and laboratories are already found in some low-

SMALL BUSINESS BUILDINGS

Location Factors

Below left: Brokerage office attached to bank building. Merrill Lynch, Pierce, Fenner & Beane; Phoenix, Arizona; Lescher & Mahoney, Architects
Below: Good design is best advertising. Sill Bldg., Bakersfield, Cal.; Kump & Falk, Architects

Left: Great Southwest Photography (Olchvary). Above: Roger Sturtevant

density residential areas and offices in high-density residential districts.

"One side or end of the (best retail) block is usually better than the other . . . normally, the better side or end is in the direction of the town's growth. Usually such growth is towards the town's best residential area. . . . In many of the larger cities, a majority of the volume of a city's retail business is conducted outside the central shopping district." (33)

Clinics or medical arts buildings belong near the centers of their tributary populations. If a small city develops an industrial area residential sections will grow elsewhere and groups of doctors' offices belong nearer the homes. Retail store "proximity to offices of professional men is desirable especially in outlying shopping centers. People having appointments with doctors, dentists, lawyers, etc., quite often will become shoppers if stores are conveniently accessible." (33)

Office buildings or office space to accommodate any sizable office organization, according to the Urban Land Institute, however, are "not desirable as a rule in outlying centers, increase trade very little, and unless rigidly controlled, will usurp all day parking space which should be reserved for shoppers. . . . Professional offices, particularly doctors and dentists where

they occur in any number, are in the same category. They are expensive tenants, janitor service alone running about two times that of other tenants. Where they cannot be accommodated in second floor locations, the provision of a semi-residential type of building located to act as a buffer between the center and adjacent residential development is a satisfactory solution." (30)

The general purpose buildings with which we are mainly concerned, therefore, belong still nearer the business centers or in local retail districts. Cleveland has a regulation limiting to five persons the number of employees in business offices in such local retail business districts.

A buffer area is provided by transition zoning regulations in some cities to avoid undesirable use-district relationships. These may occur between residential and local retail or residential and industrial districts.

There are a number of zoning techniques for controlling bulk of buildings and density of population. Height, cubage and lot coverage limits are familiar to most urban architects. A more recently developed measure which has somewhat more critical value is the so-called "Floor Area Ratio" (ratio between total floor space — out-to-out dimensions all floors except ground floor — and total area of lot measured to street lines).

Mears Studio Photos

Application of this to a tall building may result in a ratio of 25 to 30. A two-story taxpayer will show a ratio of less than unity. Between such limits zoning classifications may be established in any city to regulate building bulk and population much more satisfactorily than cubage and height, for instance; these because of variation in story heights, have less relation to occupancy.

Complete zoning control, of course, must also include regulations to assure light and air and amortization of non-conforming uses.

Parking: There is considerable national variety in existing zoning controls of parking facilities. A 1947 study (36) of 70 cities from 50,000–100,000 population showed 21% required parking for office buildings and, of 22 cities reporting loading, 24% required loading areas for office buildings. Some other larger city rules and proposals are tabulated below:

Detroit. . . . . .1 space/400sf for office buildings
Los Angeles. . . . . .1 space/100sf business & commercial over 7500sf
Minneapolis. . . . . .1 space/100sf business & (proposed) commercial over 500sf

San Francisco. . . . . .1 space/450sf banks, business (proposed) or professional offices
South Central Connecticut regional zoning. . . . . . .1 space/250sf ground floor (proposed) 1 space/500sf upper floors less than 500 ft. distant

The Urban Land Institute reports favorably on a parking solution for large cities consisting of fringe or marginal parking areas served by shuttle buses traveling from one parking area to another across a city.

One of the best studies of all phases of the parking problem is the 181-page Parking Manual issued in 1946 by the American Automobile Association's Traffic Engineering & Safety Department. "The trend for parking to be considered as a public use is reflected in the fact that 33 states have passed legislation permitting municipalities to undertake the provision of off-street parking . . . as a municipal function." (35)

The Urban Land Institute further recommends that "All leases should prohibit employers or employees from parking their cars in 100% business parking stations. . . . Employees' parking should be in the (more remote) locations even if a walk of two to three blocks is required." (30)

SMALL BUSINESS BUILDINGS

Planning (See Bibliography references 38–63)

Branch Office Procedure

Large organizations with many branch offices often have their own locations, field office planning, or branch office layout departments. These establish planning, equipment, materials and finish standards, make surveys of existing space being considered, prepare layouts, schedule and supervise the work. Local architects are retained when the alteration is of sufficient size, or for new buildings. The accompanying data indicate the approach of such company planning departments which is largely concerned, as far as appearances go, with identification of the branch office as a unit of the parent company. There are also obvious advantages of mass purchasing and standardized planning.

Such organizations usually have Branch Office Manuals or Inspection Checklists for selection of location and assembly of data on proposed offices in new or existing structures.

Stockbrokers are another desirable tenant for a small business building. Merrill Lynch, Pierce, Fenner & Beane, securities and commodities brokers, for example, have approximately 100 branch offices which are usually in ground or second floor locations for the convenience of clients. Their essential policies are clear identification as a Merrill Lynch operation and insistence on privacy of the customer's business.

Identification is effected by simple standardized equipment, uniform arrangement, decoration and services. Privacy is assured by a plan arrangement which always permits a customer to go to the Manager's office, to the cashier and to visit the investment department without passing through the crowded boardroom. The wire operators are also placed in a private location adjacent to the cage.

Standard partitions of two heights have been carefully designed for company use. Private offices and cages are enclosed by 66 in. walnut and glass partitions. Account-executive booths, which must permit vision of the board and yet give privacy to conversation and papers, are 36 in. walnut plus 9 in. glass. The booths are approximately 6 x 6 ft (single) and 6 x 12 ft (double).

Branch offices of this organization range from about 1000 sf to 5000 sf in area. The standardized quotation board of silicate slate sections has approximately 36 lf of arc set on varying radii (22–35 ft) and requires considerable ingenuity in planning for vision. Where Tele-register automatic quotation service is available it is replacing these chalkboards.

Each account-executive must have quick access to the wire operator. In larger installations message conveyor-belts are provided; in most cases an ample and direct passage is essential.

It is company policy to provide complete air conditioning, acoustic treatment and usually fluorescent lighting. The Locations Executive sums up this policy as follows: "Our design of offices is intended to provide the maximum convenience, efficiency and comfort for the account-executives who are the producers and also for the operating employees, the cashier and his staff and the wire operators. Although all our customers visit the offices at some time or other, taken by and large, over 90% of our business originates over the telephone and we must be set up to handle it rapidly and above all things, accurately."

Problem Space

Some characteristics of undesirable space are shown on page 174. Branch office experience in renting offices all over the country yields some additional items.

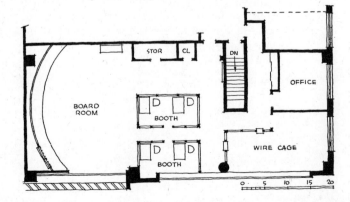

Standard equipment, brokerage office, Merrill Lynch, Pierce, Fenner & Beane; left, office in Orlando, Fla.; James Gamble Rogers III, Archt. Below, office, Phoenix, Ariz.

BOARD ROOM

STOR   CL

DN

OFFICE

BOOTH

WIRE CAGE

BOOTH

0   5   10   15   20

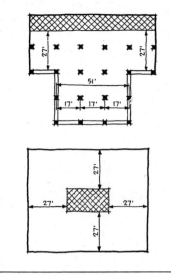

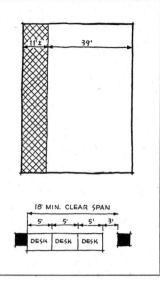

Left:

Depth and span dimensions proposed by a real estate and office layout specialist

Right:

Actual plan, 6-story Remington-Rand Building, Philadelphia; Thalheimer & Weitz, architects; completely free for any partition arrangement desired

Left:

Optimum space for general offices suggested by a business man; the tenant's point of view

Right:

Clear span recommendations made by office layout division of an office equipment manufacturer

Shape of space and location of services

A major insurance company finds a tendency for the type of building they occupy as second floor tenants to be designed primarily for the first floor. Public stairs located at one side of a wide building and similar locations of toilets increase travel distances and complicate office planning. Long narrow space is equally bad since it is impossible to plan for group meetings. They favor a plan which permits rental of an end of a floor or a wing incorporating corridor space. This occasionally involves access to a fire exit but some codes permit locking such access if the office doors have large glazed areas. Elevators and utility stacks should be located so as not to crowd or make rentable space irregular.

Space planning and flexibility

The architect must reconcile many points of view on office space. Each project will have its own special conditions but the accompanying diagrams indicate some span and depth recommendations by various authorities.

Flexibility of office arrangements is important for the commercial office building because of changing requirements of both present and new tenants. For office purposes flexibility is often measured by spacing of window mullions which permits subdivision into various office widths. Mullions spacing recommendations vary from 3 ft 6 in. to 4 ft and 4 ft 6 in., giving multiples of:

7, 10–6, 14, 17–6, 21
8, 12, 16, 20, 24
9, 12–6, 18, 22–6, 27

(Note: 18 ft clear spans imply approximately 20 ft column center spans which work out for 4 ft 0 in. mullion spacing.)

Use of stock 6 ft linoleum and 9 ft and 12 ft carpet widths for determination of office widths has been considered an economy factor by some planners.

The Sill Building, designed by Kump & Falk, has an arrangement of corridors on top of window sun-screens which results in increased flexibility. A climate in which

Section and view, exterior corridor, Sill Building, Bakersfield, Calif. (photo: Roger Sturtevant). All services in flush hung ceiling of removable tiles; partitions demountable — an invaluable aid to flexibility

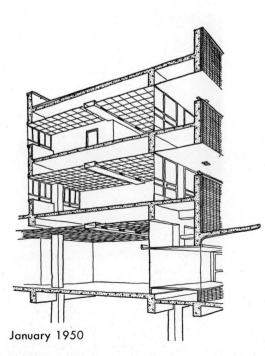

SMALL BUSINESS BUILDINGS

Planning

Delivery facilities: left, Esso Headquarters, Richmond, Va., Carneal & Johnston, Archts. (Photo: Dementi). Right, Sill Building, Bakersfield, Calif., Kump & Falk, Archts. (Photo: Roger Sturtevant)

exterior gallery-corridors of this type are appropriate gives this opportunity to free the plan of non-revenue space.

Facilities

An architect may help increase the rental values and tenant-holding ability of a commercial building by persuading the owner to consider certain additional equipment and amenities as a part of the basic building. Their cost is insignificant in relation to loss of revenue from vacancies.

Branch office experts all emphasize the importance of knowing who installs and who pays for utilities, lighting fixtures, water heaters, air conditioning, toilet room accessories, various maintenance services and alterations. Many buildings offered for use of companies of national scope are inadequately equipped and leases may provide that tenant-installed items become property of owner when lease expires. The following typical examples of inadequacy have resulted in selection of other buildings: Single and bare toilet rooms instead of separate and properly equipped facilities for men and women, no hot water, lack of freight elevators or hoisting facilities, no loading or large object access, insufficient security of rear windows, inadequate wiring for equipment loads.

Expansion and preplanned Growth

Expansion of a building obviously can be either horizontal or vertical. There are many examples of preplanning both varieties, by plot plan or structural provisions for the future space. Another method is to construct more space than needed for the major occupant and lease the extra area on a temporary basis, planning and earmarking it for expansion needs. A final type is internal — re-study of space for more efficient layout. This also may be preplanned by providing excessive areas for original occupancy, such as conference rooms for later conversion to private offices or loose arrangements of desks and equipment for eventual tighter planning. The private office is declining in favor among management experts and space-saving conversion of private office

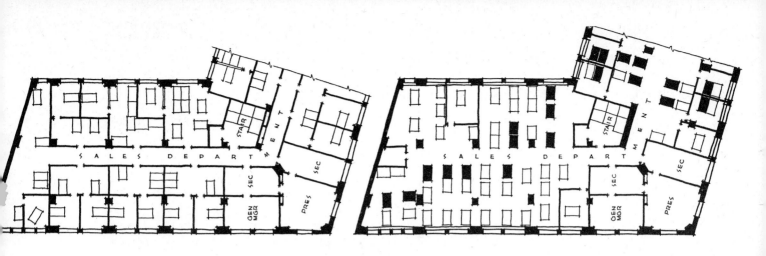

Plans above show economy of open office space; an actual office re-planning done by an office equipment company. Black squares are desks added after replanning. Photos (by William Langley) and plans below: office building in Dallas, Texas, takes advantage of sloping site; two story portion occupied by Remington-Rand, some space for other tenants, one-story portion entered from next street, occupied by the building's designers, George L. Dahl, architects and engineers

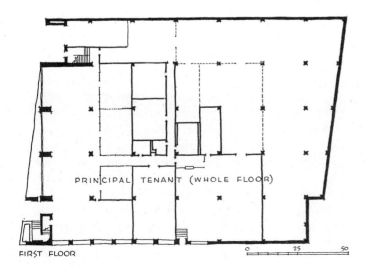

FIRST FLOOR

0   25   50

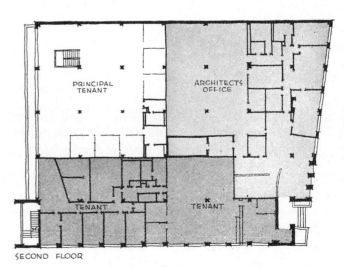

SECOND FLOOR

SMALL BUSINESS BUILDINGS

Planning

Top, general offices planned for growth; International Business Machines, Portland, Ore. (Photo: Photo-Art). Right, offices divided merely by curtains to permit expansion (can be thrown into one) or to simplify permanent subdivision if that should become necessary; own office, Page, Southerland & Page, Architects, Austin, Tex.

space to pools and general office areas has been accepted by many institutions.

Planning which eliminates the double-circulation of connecting doors between private offices will also save space. Departments which are expected to expand should be placed next to available or easily altered space.

Features — Equipment — Materials

There has been much written in recent years about "integrated design," perhaps without any full realization of what the words mean and imply. The term involves completeness of parts and relationships, clearly defined functional expression; and is closely related to that other catchword, integrity or honesty. It implies an esthetic and practical marriage of architecture and engineering throughout the job. This so works that it is impossible to draw a line and proclaim: this is architecture, this is engineering. It is design in three-dimensions, completely conditioned for use and appearance. In addition to space and circulation such conditioning includes:

> Atmosphere (air conditioning, etc.)
> Orientation (sun screens)
> Light (natural & artificial)
> Color (bibliography 81–83)
> Sound control (machine areas, general space)
> Finish materials (bibliography 72–80)
> Maintenance facility (including window cleaning, accessibility of mechanical equipment)
> Utility availability (wiring for business machines, telephone ducts)
> Ease of alteration (smooth ceilings for uniform partition heights, re-usable partitions, etc.)
> Structural fitness (appropriate floor load capacities)

Air Conditioning

"It has long been our opinion that Architects in this locality could not afford to work in a building that was not air conditioned and the improvement in the performance of our force since occupying this building has strengthened this opinion" (Page, Southerland and Page, Texas architects).

A tendency to provide complete air conditioning results in increased floor-to-floor heights often with ducts above removable ceiling installations. This affects relationship between cubage and square feet of space in such manner as to change former valuation standards. In some large buildings air conditioning is available on a rental basis and can be a most profitable business.

Increased use of business machines results in heavier air conditioning loads, particularly where operation requires 100% duty. Typical outputs:

Card-punching machine . . . . 150 btu/hr
Accounting machine . . . . 4000 btu/hr

Heavy electronic equipment used in some home office installations may require several tons of refrigeration.

Fire Insurance (Bibliography references 84–92)

Conformance to local building code is not enough for the commercial building. Construction system, selection of materials, equipment, plan and proposed occupancy must also be reviewed to obtain lower insurance rates. The accompanying hypothetical case comparison illustrates the importance of this factor of operating budgets. Experienced building owners expect architects to submit insurance data along with plans and specifications.

A change in occupancy may cause a greatly increased rate. Rate schedules are further subdivided for contents insurance. Naturally these kinds of insurance are not under the architect's control and we have highlighted only the subject of building insurance rate.

Insurance rate schedules which apply to 90% of the examples of this building type are established in each state by a state-wide fire insurance rating organization

EXAMPLE OF FIRE INSURANCE COMPARISON FOR TYPICAL SMALL BUSINESS BUILDING

Assume area 20,000 sf

	Area	Height floor-to-floor	Occupancy
basement	20,000 sf	11 ft	retail storage heating plant
1st floor	20,000 sf	15 ft	retail
2nd floor	20,000 sf	12 ft	offices & light occupancy

CASE A: FIRE-RESISTIVE; rate per $100 is .035

basement	20,000 x 11 = 220,000 cf @ $ .50 =	$110,000.
1st–2nd	20,000 x 27 = 540,000 cf @ 1.12 =	604,000.

Fire-resistive total construction estimate $714,800.

CASE B: NON-FIRE-RESISTIVE; rate is .560

basement	220,000 cf @ $ .50 =	$110,000.
1st–2nd	540,000 cf @ .94 =	507,600.
Non-fire-resistive total construction est.		$617,600.
Difference in construction estimates		$ 97,200.

CASE A: yearly ins. cost = $\dfrac{714,800 \times .035}{100.}$ = $ 250.18 per year

CASE B: $\dfrac{617,600 \times .560}{100.}$ = $ 3,458.56 per year at 100% valuation

In 20 years on annual renewals (can be bettered on term privileges):

(Note: Interest, taxes, maintenance, etc., disregarded)

(Estimating data from Murphy Brinkworth Construction Corporation)

CASE B: $ 69,171.20
CASE A: $ 5,003.60
SAVING $ 64,167.60
71% of construction difference

---

supported by the fire insurance stock companies (although a few mutual companies participate) under state government supervision. Separate schedules are developed for each class of occupancy (mercantile, manufacturing, etc.) and for fire-resistive and non-fire-resistive construction.

An architect may save his client thousands of dollars over the life of a building by an insurance review and plan revision before construction. The National Building Code recommended by the National Board of Fire Underwriters (84) (which also considers general safety provisions) will serve as a guide to approved practice. The 1949 edition is in form appropriate for adoption as a local municipal building code. Previous editions have been so adopted by over 100 cities. When practical difficulties arise in a specific job a recommendation may be obtained from the nearest office of the state fire insurance rating organization.

Decisions on fire protection and safety features will depend on a comparison of construction costs of alternate plans and corresponding insurance rates. Protection of vertical openings, exposure to and "communications" with adjacent hazards are important factors in determining rates. The schedules also provide protectional credits for the following items:

> automatic fire alarms
> standpipes
> automatic sprinklers
> watchmen, clock and special
> building signals
> fire pumps
> fire pails and extinguishers

It will be found uneconomic to provide elaborate protection for ordinary light occupancies. As in any other analysis such a study can be prepared only for a specific building. In usual projects it need not require a formal or lengthy review.

To sum up, fire insurance rates are predicted on construction, protection, occupancy and exposure. The building valuation to which rates are applied is entirely the responsibility of the insured party. The schedules list items, to be added or deducted in order to arrive at the rate, in cents per $100 valuation per year.

ANNOTATED BIBLIOGRAPHY

After each reference one or more code letters indicates the content of the article according to the following key:
b bibliography   **m** maps
d details or diagrams   **p** plans
f forms   **s** sketches
g graphs or charts   **t** tables
              v photo views
Several specialized periodicals are listed at the end of the main body of references.

REAL ESTATE, FINANCE & OPERATION

1. Lench, Charles H. *The promotion of commercial buildings.* Architectural Economics Press, N. Y., 1932. 253 pp. Chapter XVI: Financial set-up pp. 141–156. Chapter XXII: Office Buildings pp. 206–211.

2. Holmes, Lawrence G., Editor. *The real estate handbook.* Prentice-Hall, N. Y., 1948. 783 pp. Comprehensive real estate reference data. **dfptv**

3. McMichael, Stanley L. *How to operate a real estate business.* Prentice-Hall, N. Y., 1947. 455 pp., Site selection: (1) Outlying neighborhoods; (2) Satellite towns; (3) Natural traffic intersections. **dftv**

4. *Real estate business* (Basic information sources). U. S. Department of Commerce, Office of Domestic Commerce. GPO 1949. 8 pp. Governmental & non-governmental books, periodicals, bibliographies, lists of associations, directories & services. **b**

5. "How inside space can earn outside rates." By George R. Bailey. *Buildings,* Aug., 49:44. Top grade space throughout building by use of air conditioning, lighting, decoration, acoustic treatment, furnishing. **d**

6. "New buildings may have metal walls." By R. L. Davison. *Buildings,* July 44:45–46. Additions to rentable area & increased total rent due to decreased wall thicknesses now approved.

7. "What is a fair rental rate?" By Le G. Moore. *Buildings,* July 49:30–31 (Part I), Aug. 49:30–31 (Part II). Examples & calculations for existing & new building financial set-ups.

8. "Three ways to cut your operating costs." By K. A. Wing. *Buildings*, Mar. 49:24. Economies through study of lighting, heating & elevator costs & controls.

9. "Who will build them this time?" By Glenn McHugh, VP Equitable Life. *Skyscraper Management*, Aug. 49:5–7, 31–34. Trend toward reduction of office building construction in central areas.

10. "Commercial real estate market for 1949." By Leo J. Sheridan. *Skyscraper Mgt.*, Mar. 49:3–5, 32–34. Address before Mortgage Bankers Assoc. Dangers of new construction for existing rentals. **g**

11. "How high can office rentals go?" By Sterling H. Bigler. *Buildings*, Mar. 48:38–41. Report to Middle Atlantic Conference of Building Owners & Managers. Opposition to new construction. **g** Same material in *Skyscraper Mgt.*, Feb. 48:8–9. **g**

12. "Building construction under present conditions." By Charles M. Chuckrow. *Buildings*, Mar. 48:27–28. Financial analysis: 23-story building built in N.Y.C. in 1946. Same material in *Skyscraper Mgt.*, Mar. 48:3–5, 27–28. **g**

13. "Case study of present construction costs." By George R. Bailey. *Buildings*, Dec. 47:28–30. Tall building cost & rental income analysis.

14. "Allocation of costs." *Buildings*, Aug. 47:49. Rule of thumb for apportionment of costs to ground & upper floors.

15. "Sell function, not footage." Editorial by Charles A. McCaleb. *Buildings & Building Management*, Mar. 46:23.

16. "Chart aids in analyzing office building operation." By G. M. Lewis. *Buildings & Building Mgt.*, Jan. 46:28–29. **g**

17. "A critique of fixed formula methods of pricing office space." By B. L. Lefler. *Journal of Property Mgt.*, Dec. 45:97–104. Refinements of Sheridan-Karkow formula.

18. "Planned profit-timing for office buildings." By W. Earl Martin. *Buildings & Building Mgt.*, May 45:31–33. Formula for office space financial analysis.

19. "Occupancy decline less than expected." By Dale R. Cowen. *Skyscraper Mgt.*, June 49:3–6. Semi-annual summary of office building operations. **gt**

20. "Slight decline again registered in office building occupancy." By Dale R. Cowen. *Skyscraper Mgt.*, Nov. 48:3–6. 2495 buildings, occupancy av. 98.88%. **gt**

21. "Occupancy trend continuing down." By Roy J. Johnson. *Skyscraper Mgt.*, June 48:3–6. 2445 buildings, occupancy av. 98.99%. **gt**

22. "Income & operating expenses in office buildings." *Buildings & Building Mgt.*, Feb. 45:20–21. Charts of income, expense & operating ratios for 1924–1943.

Year	Income	Operating ratio
1924	$2.27 psf	57.9% ("normal")
1934	1.45	(low)
1941		80.7% (high)
1943	1.66	76.9%

23. "1948 operating costs in 96 San Francisco buildings." *Buildings*. Total $1.8048 psf rental area. **gt**

24. "1947 operating costs in 93 San Francisco buildings." *Buildings*, Oct. 48: 42. Total $1.6404 psf rental area. **gt**

25. "1947 operating costs in 35 Philadelphia office buildings." *Buildings*, Aug. 48:30–31. Totals: Over 100,000 sf, $1.919 psf; under 100,000 sf, $2.077 psf. **gt**

26. "1946 operating costs in 37 Philadelphia office buildings." *Buildings*, Nov. 47:38–39. Totals: Over 100,000 sf, $1.843 psf; under 100,000 sf, $1.774 psf. **gt**

27. "1945 operating costs in 35 Philadelphia office buildings." *Buildings & Building Mgt.*, Dec. 46:30–31. Totals: Over 100,000 sf, $1.255 psf rental area; under 100,000 sf, $1.345. **gt**

28. "1945 operating costs in 70 San Francisco buildings." *Buildings & Building Mgt.*, Oct. 46: 30–31. Total: $1.4939 psf rental area. **gt**

29. "1940 operating costs in 35 Philadelphia office buildings." *Buildings & Building Mgt.*, Nov. 41:20. Total: $1.39 psf rental area. **gt**

LOCATION, DECENTRALIZATION, ZONING & PARKING

30. Urban Land Institute, Community Builders' Council. *The community builder's handbook.* Urban Land Institute, Washington, D.C., 1947. 205 pp. Preliminary steps, planning, protecting future of development, shopping centers (308 types of business classified in 4 lists for location), statistical appendices. **gptv**

31. Urban Land Institute. *Technical Bulletins:*
 #1. Mistakes in community development. By J. C. Nichols. 1945.
 #2. Urban redevelopment enabling acts.
 #3. Trends: Urban development & redevelopment.
 #4. Mistakes in developing shopping centers. By J. C. Nichols.
 #5. City planning bibliography. 1946.
 #6. Auto parking in central business districts. 1946.
 #7. Slums — "Improved land" value. 1947.
 #8. Subdivision regulations. 1947.
 #9. Commercial parking in residential areas (transitional). 1948.
 #10. Prohibition of residences in industrial districts.
 #11. Shopping centers (19 examples). 1949.

32. Armstrong, Robert H. & Homer Hoyt. *Decentralization in New York City.* A preliminary report to Urban Land Institute, Jan. 1941. Excellent survey of N.Y.C. population & other statistics. **gt**

33. Canoyer, Helen G. *Selecting a store location* (Economic Series #56). U. S. Department of Commerce, Office of Domestic Commerce, Marketing Division GPO 1946. 68 pp. Selection of town, community & site. Practices in seven selected retail lines. Appendices: Distribution & operating expense ratios. Excellent bibliography on location. **bdt**

34. *Picking a location for a small business* (Small Business Series #3). N. Y. State Department of Commerce. Elementary location techniques. **st**

35. *Parking Manual.* American Automobile Association, Traffic Engineering & Safety Department, Washington, D. C. 1946. 181 pp. The parking problem — Causes & effects of parking difficulties — Factual studies — Improving curb parking conditions — Off-street parking facilities — Educating the public — Other community activities affecting parking — Appendices — Review of zoning regulations in 40 cities. **bdfgptv**

36. *Zoning applied to parking.* Eno Foundation for Highway Traffic Control. Saugatuck, Conn., 1947. Survey (586 returns) of cities of 50,000–100,000 pop.

37. "A new solution for parking." By P. M. Rea. *Journal of Property Mgt.* Sept. 47:33–43. Electro-Park, an automatic elevator parking system. **dgm**

PLANNING & GENERAL REFERENCES

38. Maze, Coleman L. (NOMA) *Office management, a handbook.* Ronald Press Co. N. Y., 1947. 870 pp. Chapter 11: *Office environment:* pp. 299–331. Location & setting — Building characteristics — Construction — Maintenance & operation — Appearance. Data on color & insurance (39 types outlined). **dfpv**

39. Ripnen, Kenneth H. *Office space administration — Streamlining office methods & layouts* (Office Management Series #114). American Management Association, N. Y., 1946. pp. 15–24. Report of lecture & discussion on basic office plans, organization elements, standards, compartmented organization, flexibility, office planning tools, steps, maintenance & control.

40. Pennicke, H. C. *Office layout for effective operations — Standards for measuring office efficiency* (Office Management Series #110). American Management Association, N. Y., 1946. pp. 28–47. Report of lecture & discussion on layout, site, private offices, lighting, clerical areas, space standards, layout suggestions, reception space, washrooms & wardrobes. **pt**

41. *Cost of industrial moves.* By R. H. McCarthy. American Management Association, N. Y., 1950. Successive moves of large organizations because of inadequate space or poor planning may cost as much as new construction. Urges more careful recording of moving costs.

42. *Office planning & layout.* Report issued by Policyholders Service Bureau of Metropolitan Life Insurance Company, N. Y. Rev. 1945. 26 pp. Surveys, area allocation, rough layout, partitions, heating & ventilating, lighting, acoustic treatment, decoration, finished layout, furniture, moving, small office layouts, references. **bp** Reprinted by Remington-Rand and in *The Office*, Feb. 46:70. *Buildings & Building Mgt.* Mar. 46:30–33 **p** Apr. 46:33–36 **pt**

43. *Washroom & locker-room facilities.* Report issued by Policyholders Service Bureau of Metropolitan Life Insurance Company, N. Y. Rev. 1948. 28 pp., Planning, special requirements, materials, fixtures & equipment. **ptv**

44. "Office buildings." Building Types Study #145. *Architectural Record*, Jan. 49:97–116. Esso buildings in Caracas & Baton Rouge, office buildings in Mobile and Chicago. Solar & earthquake problems. **dmpv**

45. "Office buildings." Building Types Study #130. *Architectural Record*, Oct. 47:119–146. New departures in office building design (Lathrop Douglass): Flexibility, fenestration, columns & framing, modules, economics. Examples. **dpsv** Same material in *Buildings* Jan. 48:36.

46. "Modern offices." *Architectural Record*, Mar. 45:99–116. New trends, patterns in office planning, examples. **pstv**

47. "Office & loft buildings." Building

Types Study #73. *Architectural Record*, Apr. 43:73–82. Article by Ely J. Kahn. Time-saver Standards on office building flexibility, space distribution, rentable area, construction, utilities. **dmpv**

48. "Office & commercial buildings." Building Types Study. *Architectural Record*, Dec. 41:81–91. Shopping center at Belmont, Mass. & several smaller office buildings. **dpv**

49. "Office buildings 1891–1941." *Architectural Record*, Feb. 41:43–49. Examples. **pv**

50. "Buildings for business." *Architectural Record*, Dec. 40:73–94. Examples & Time-saver Standards for telephone installations & flashings. **dpv**

51. "Design reference on office buildings." *Architectural Record*, Dec. 38:86–118. Planning, layout, clearances, summer air conditioning, acoustic control, lighting, color, rentability, examples. **bdptv**

52. "Physicosocial environment of the office." By A. H. Stricker. *The Office*, Aug. 49:29–44, 110–117. Adequate seeing conditions, noise control, ventilation, checklist for working conditions. **tv**

53. "When you build your own office building." By Harold C. Pennicke. *The Office*, Oct. 49:56–60, 151–161. Comprehensive article. See also "Layout standards for modern offices" by same author published in *The Office* for Mar. & Apr. 45 & to be republished soon. **dv**

54. "Principles of office space planning." By Ralph Tabakin. *The Office*, Sept. 48:48–51, 153–157. **v**

55. "Space allotment & control." By Kenneth H. Ripnen. *Office Management & Equipment*, Feb. 48:31–32. Report form for preliminary design projects. **f**

56. "Modern office layout will pave the way for more profitable renting." *Buildings & Building Mgt.*, Aug. 45:27–30; Sept., 45:40–42. Typical offices for accountants, lawyers, insurance & general use. **p**

57. "Planning the new office building." By I. A. Herrmann. *The Office*, May, 45:37–40. **dpt**

58. "Layout standards for modern offices." By Harold C. Pennicke. *The Office*, Mar. 45:37–42; **dpt**; Apr. 45:38–44, 74, 76. **dv**

59. U. S. Post Office Department. *Leaflets giving regulations for mailing equipment & installations*:

(1) Mailing chute rules, regulations & specifications.

(2) Apartment-house mail receptacles. Regulations & instructions (used also for business flats in residential areas).

(3) Instruction sheets listing approved manufacturers of apartment mail receptacles.

60. Two office buildings (MacKie & Kamrath). *Progressive Architecture*, Dec. 48:50–55. One-story, stone & wood construction. **pv**

61. Two-story office building (Raphael Soriano). *Arts & Architecture*, Nov. 48:38–39. **v**

62. Office building for 5 business agents (Ain). *Arts & Architecture*, Aug. 48:30–31. One-story project. **ps**

63. Projects: Lawyers' office building (Ain). *Arts & Architecture*, May 47:26; **ps**; Oct. 48:36. **ps**

LIGHTING

64. *Recommended practice of office lighting.* Illuminating Engineering Society, N. Y., 1947. 47 pp. Office tasks, influence of lighting on seeing, environmental factors, office lighting (daylight & artificial), specific areas, brightness ratios, nomenclature, wiring. **dtv**

65. "Proper maintenance — antidote for light loss." By W. R. Wilson. *Buildings*, May 49:36–39. Wiring, line voltage, access to lighting equipment, painting. **gtv**

66. "Light, eyesight, environment & their influence on production." *Office Management & Equipment*, Mar. 48:19–22 **v**; *The Office*, Dec. 47:68–72, 110–114. **v** Reports of two-year study by Public Buildings Administration in Washington in punchcard subsection of Bureau of Internal Revenue.

67. "Office lighting — a cost study." By R. L. Oetting. *Buildings*, Aug. 47:21–23, 48. Annual costs psf of office space illumination using: enclosing globes; deep bowl indirect; silver-bowl lamp indirect; fluorescent direct-indirect; fluorescent single-lamp troffer. **t**

68. "Light finishes improve office performance." By R. L. Oetting. *Office Management & Equipment*, July 47:33–36. **v**

69. "Influence of lighting on office production." By R. L. Oetting. *Office Management & Equipment*. Oct. 47:62–66, 106.

70. "Improving office seeing." By W. S. Greenwood. *The Office*, Dec. 46:44–52. **tv**

71. "Basic standards for good lighting." By LeRoy E. Varner. *Buildings & Building Mgt.*, Mar. 46:38–41. Lighting levels, lamp characteristics, brightness & glare, chart for lighting stores & offices. **dt**

MAINTENANCE

72. *Profitable building operation & maintenance.* Stamats Publishing Co. Cedar Rapids, Iowa. Book of reprints from *Buildings & Building Management* magazine.

73. "Outline of building maintenance." By Boyles & Farquhar. *Buildings & Building Mgt.*, May 46:28–30. I, Structure: II, Elevators; III, Equipment.

74. "A building manager's outline of modern cleaning methods." By Boyles & Farquhar. *Buildings & Building Mgt.*, Apr. 46:46–49. I, Public areas; II, Offices; III, Window washing; IV, Blinds & shades; V, Service calls.

75. "Here's why city air is so dirty." Chicago Association of Commerce, Smoke Abatement Committee. *Buildings & Building Mgt.*, Sept. 46:38. Weather & atmospheric conditions related to smoke, coal consumption & dustfall. Dustfall found to measure weather conditions, not a measure of fuel consumption. **g**

76. "Background for floor maintenance." By C. A. March. *Buildings*, Sept. 47:48–53. Safety measures, materials & methods for floor maintenance. **t**

77. "Background for floor selection." By C. A. March. *Buildings*, July 47:38–40. Cement-concrete, cork, asphalt & mastic tile, hard tile & terrazzo. *Buildings*, Aug. 47:39–43. Linoleum, magnesite, marble, travertine, wood.

78. "Longer life for resilient floors." By D. E. Smalley. *Buildings & Building Mgt.*, Jan. 47:13–15. Maintenance for linoleum, cork, rubber, asphalt tile flooring.

79. "How to select floor treatments." By D. E. Smalley. *Buildings & Building*

Mgt., Oct. 46:19–20, 39. Waxes, cleaners, sealers, paints.

80. "What every manager should know about techniques in decorating." *Buildings*, Aug. 48:47–51. Article on painting. **gt**

81. "Color schemes for offices." By C. E. Seghers. *The Office*, Nov. 46:60–66. Talk at National Business Show. Chart showing physical characteristics of spectrum colors, reactions, associations, etc. **g**

82. "Use of color for office painting." By W. W. Krug. *The Office*, Mar. 46:37–41, 54–60. DuPont recommendations. **v**

83. Color under foot. *Buildings*, Oct. 49:35. Benefits of dark, colored sidewalks: reduction of reflections, glare and surface cracking. **v**

FIRE PROTECTION & SAFETY

84. *National Building Code.* National Board of Fire Underwriters, N. Y., 1949. 258 pp. **dt**

85. *Building code standards for installation of heat producing appliances, heating, ventilating, air conditioning, blower & exhaust systems.* National Board of Fire Underwriters, N. Y., 1949. 40 pp. **dt**

86. *Standards . . . for installation of air conditioning, warm air heating, air cooling & ventilating systems.* National Board of Fire Underwriters, N. Y., 1946. (NBFU Pamphlet #90). Includes appendix dated Aug. 1948.

87. *National Board of Fire Underwriters Bulletins.*
#10. Jan. 22 '35: Hazard of combustible lining in airducts.
#35. Apr. 15 '37: Hazard of air conditioning systems.
#68. Dec. 15 '38: Life safety in buildings.
#121. May 15 '41: Automatic devices for heating equipment.
#165. Apr. 2 '43: Acoustic materials.
#168. May 15 '43: Fire-resistant floor & ceiling constructions.
#239. Sept. 2 '46: Oil burner fire causes.

88. *List of inspected fire protection equipment and materials.* Underwriters' Laboratories, Inc., Chicago, N. Y., San Francisco. Jan., 1949. 200 pp.

89. "Tough category — Tough spot — Action needed." By Rex E. Hieronymous. *Skyscraper Mgt.*, Jan. 48:10–11. **g**

90. "Fire causes." *Buildings & Building Mgt.*, Jan. 45:36.

91. "The day our office burned." By Mary J. Scott. *The Office*, Apr. 47:48–52, 72–73. Graphic story of fire salvage. **v**

92. *Office hazards.* Report issued by Safety Bureau of Metropolitan Life Insurance Company, N. Y., 10 pp. Checklist.

PERIODICALS

In addition to the regular architectural periodicals the following will be of interest to office building planners:

93. *Buildings* (Monthly). Stamats Publishing Company, 427 Sixth Ave., SE, Cedar Rapids, Iowa. $3.00/yr. (Formerly Buildings & Building Management).

94. *Skyscraper Management* (Monthly). National Association of Building Owners & Managers, 134 South Lasalle St. Chicago 3, Ill. $3.00/yr.

95. *Journal of Property Management* (Quarterly). National Association of Real Estate Boards, 72 West Monroe St. Chicago 3, Ill. $5.00/yr.; $1.25/copy.

96. *Urban Land* (Monthly). Urban Land Institute, 1727 K St., NW, Washington 6, D.C. $10.00/yr.

ARCHITECT-ENGINEER OFFICES, PEORIA, ILLINOIS

WHEN this architectural firm expanded to the point of designing its own building, it chose an outlying site, about a mile from the center of the city, on a fairly prominent hillside. The building is placed to be seen from a considerable distance, and is floodlighted at night. The building was designed to provide exceptionally good working conditions for a total personnel of 36; besides 8 architects, there are 5 licensed engineers, 18 draftsmen and superintendents, a delineator and 4 stenographers or accountants, including as a not-unimportant part of the facilities, parking space for the employees' cars. Scruggs and Hammond were the landscape architects. The heating and air conditioning system includes several innovations, some experimental. Heating combines radiant heating with forced warm air, permitting a large volume of ventilating air to be circulated. The duct work is divided into two zones, so that different exposures may be separately heated or cooled. To reduce water consumption in the cooling period, an evaporative condenser was installed with the compressor. Dehumidification is exceptionally important for hot Illinois weather, especially in a drafting room, where humidity hampers drawing. Air handling equipment can supply 100 per cent fresh air, when weather conditions are propitious. A tri-ethylolene vaporizer is installed in the ventilation system on an experimental basis, in the belief that it may cut down absenteeism due to colds. The architects point out that it frequently has had this result. So far, however, no definite conclusions have been reached regarding its effectiveness in this particular office.

Office Building of J. Fletcher Lankton

John N. Ziegele and Associates

Architects and Engineers

Exterior is of Indiana limestone, backed with insulating concrete block. Large pieces of stone are shot sawed: ashlar is of long pieces of two different thicknesses

Drafting room walls are the concrete blocks, painted with two coats of resin emulsion paint: in other rooms the block is plastered and painted. All ceilings are acoustic tile; floors are rubber tile, except in executive offices where carpet is used. The basement contains, besides air conditioning equipment, a model shop, dead files, and an employees' lunch room, where the coffee making equipment is always much appreciated

Above: view of reception room, looking toward entrance. Right: conference room. Below: general office, looking toward receptionist's desk and waiting room Indirect lighting of the display renderings is effectively arranged in connection with the cabinets

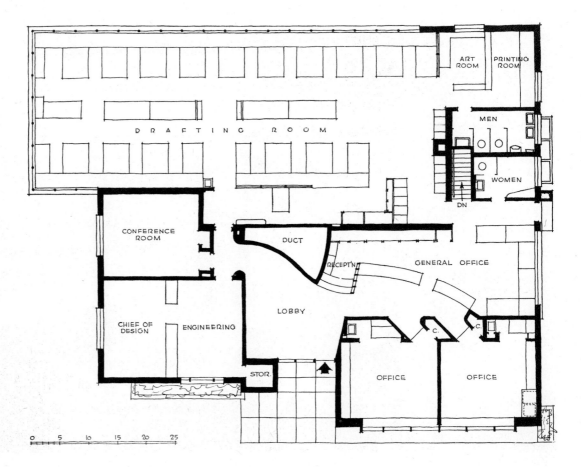

OFFICE FOR A PLUMBING & HEATING CONTRACTOR

Dixon-Christopher Office, Greensboro, N. C.

Edward Loewenstein, Architect

BUILT FOR A FIRM which engages in engineering and contracting, this attractive office building is located in a rapidly growing commercial area formerly an army base. The old warehouse at the rear has recently been replaced by storage and work sheds.

The wood frame and brick structure contains interior partitions of striated plywood or pine planks on studs; asphalt tile floors; acoustical tile ceilings.

The sunshade at the southwest office windows has proved effective in reducing the air conditioning load.

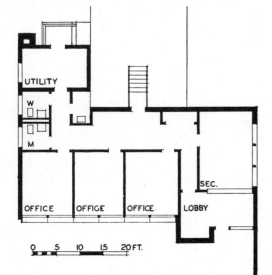

Joseph W. Molitor

CL
CLARKE
&
COURTS
113
115

5"WF

4" ALUM. LOUVERS

1/4" Ø PIN

CLARKE & COURTS BUILDING, HARLINGEN, TEXAS

Cocke, Bowman & York, Architects

IN TEXAS, the blazing southern sun must (as the architects put it) be "broken down" — and this building's most intriguing feature stems from that need. It consists of aluminum louvers in a cantilevered framework which serves also as construction for indirect sidewalk lighting. The 6-ft. spacing of the verticals is repeated in the façade proper, resulting in an interesting interplay of glass versus void versus louver in three dimensions. Both visitors to and tenants of the offices above, pass through a glass enclosed lobby and stair, thus view the owner's tempting display of office equipment each time they enter and leave.

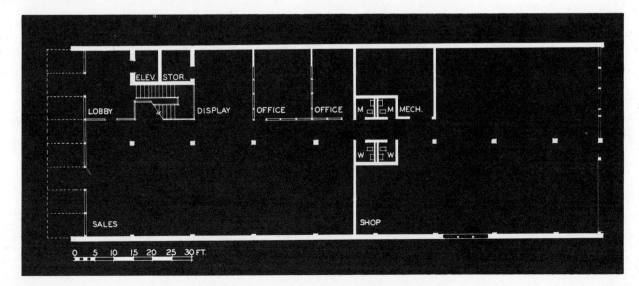

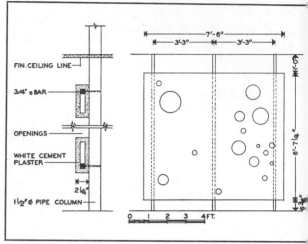

FIN. CEILING LINE

3/4" □ BAR

OPENINGS

WHITE CEMENT PLASTER

2½"

1½" ∅ PIPE COLUMN

7'-6"
3'-3"   3'-3"
6'-7¼"
6'-3"

0 1 2 3 4 FT.

Offices for the Marquette Cement Company

Jackson, Mississippi

OFFICE INVITES PUBLIC VIEW

The conversion of approximately 1420 sq ft of typical office building space into the kind of offices the Marquette Company wanted for its Jackson headquarters won the architect a well-earned Award of Merit at last October's convention of the Gulf States Region, A.I.A. The problem was complicated by Marquette's major requirement: the office must attract public attention and be visible in part from the elevator lobby even though the space leased was on an upper floor and at the far end of the public corridor. The area provided, furthermore, was barely adequate to accommodate the required reception room, general office, and three private offices — one of the latter large enough to double as a conference room and to be equipped with a bar for use in client entertaining. *And* — there was a large concrete column, load-bearing and non-removable, in almost the exact center of the rented area.

Since the reception room was the only part of the office which logically could be exposed to public view, its position at the end of the corridor was inevitable. An entrance wall of clear glass extending the full width of the

James T. Canizaro, Architect — Engineer

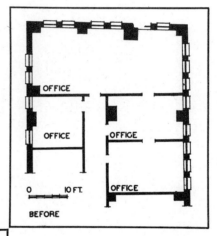

BEFORE

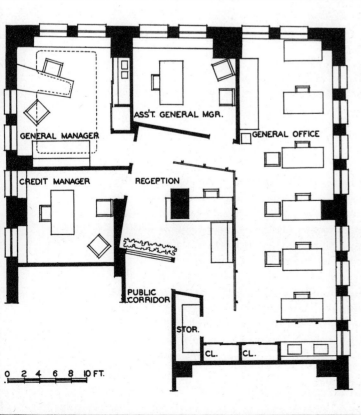

Floors in reception room and general office are covered in green and white rubber tile; walls are light green, ceilings bright yellow. Corrugated cement-asbestos board covering column in reception room is dark green, columns of general office partition are rust-colored, as is reception room couch. Decorative panel of cement plaster (detail opposite) behind desk advertises company's product, increases privacy of executive offices. Desk and couch in reception room were designed by architect, most other furniture selected by him

193

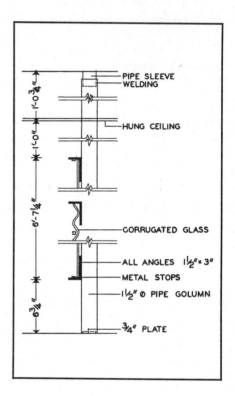

PIPE SLEEVE
WELDING

HUNG CEILING

CORRUGATED GLASS

ALL ANGLES 1½" x 3"
METAL STOPS
1½" ⌀ PIPE COLUMN

¾" PLATE

*Behind corrugated glass partition at end of general office is a
cabinet containing two lavatories and individual storage space
for each employee's toilet articles; clothes closets are adjacent*

corridor allows roughly half of this area to be seen from the elevator lobby.
The receptionist, however, is no goldfish-in-a-bowl; she is protected by the
awkwardly placed structural column, now covered with corrugated cement-
asbestos board and incorporated into the design of the reception desk. A
decorative panel of cement plaster behind the desk advertises the company's
product and at the same time increases the privacy of the offices at the rear
of the reception area.

Since not one inch of floor space could be wasted, the partitions separating
the private offices and the reception room were angled to give each office
as much room as possible. The partition between the general office and the
reception room is of corrugated glass, with a foot of open space at top and
bottom, providing the central area with natural light and ventilation.

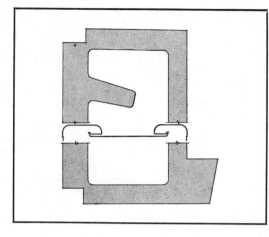

Walls of general manager's office (right and below) are light oak plywood; suspended acoustical plaster ceiling contains light cove, is painted a dark blue-green. Oak desk was designed by architect. Carpet is beige, chairs are upholstered in red. Office has built-in bar complete with refrigerator, sink, work counter, storage cabinets

Joseph W. Molitor

Assistant manager's office (below) and credit manager's office have green and white rubber tile floors, light yellow walls, rust-colored acoustical plaster ceilings. Desks and chairs, selected by architect, are walnut, as are cabinets below windows

DESIGNED TO BE FUNCTIONAL IN PLAN

Home Office Building for Phoenix Insurance Co., Hartford, Conn.

Seelye, Stevenson & Value, Structural Engineers

Meyer, Strong & Jones, Mechanical Engineers
A. F. Brinckerhoff, Landscape Architect

P ERHAPS it should be assumed that every important office building would be thoughtfully planned, functional to a high degree, beautiful and inspiring as may be. These are normal objectives. But this one, new home office building for a large insurance company, seems distinguished for the assiduous analysis of purposes, the detailed study of many factors frequently taken for granted. Naturally in a special-occupancy building these matters are possible of positive determination. But there was also a special reason here, in that the decision for a new building was not made without a long study of the company's old building, to check in detail its inadequacies, to set against these the specific possibilities of a fresh start.

For example, take space use in an insurance building. What is the basic space unit for large occupancy? Has it changed? How can units best be combined?

Or, what is the exact purpose of a window?

How exactly can a building contribute to better employee relations? How far to go? How evaluate good lighting, air conditioning, social and recreational facilities, a pleasant site or general "atmosphere"?

As to fenestration, a client group with the architects visited a great many buildings with widely different fenestration. The windows seen here, then, were a deliberate decision, specifically a vote against the strip window fad. Reasons cited were: cold areas near windows, windows found largely shielded by drapes, unbalanced light (especially in deep space as here contemplated), a sense of "special privilege" near windows. Windows — this is the group decision — should not be relied on for lighting, should give a normal sense of unconfined outlook, should not be glare spots, should not be designed for striking esthetic effect.

Recreational facilities for the use of the employees have been very liberally provided, again a firm determination, based on company policy.

QUIET IN EXPRESSION

R. B. O'Connor and W. H. Kilham, Jr., Architects

Teresa Kilham, Color Consultant

Joseph W. Molitor

Joseph W. Molitor

Space needs were the subject of much paper work. Total space requirements were questionnaired by departments, with expansion estimated for ten years ahead. It all sifted down to a space module, for a man at a large desk (34 by 60 in.), of 6 ft 3 in. by 7 ft 6 in. This was later increased to 6.6 by 7.8 to allow a bit more for passages and partitioning. This latter unit became the basis for column spacing, which is 46 ft by 19 ft 6 in. The architects say that this might be splitting hairs — maybe the shorter dimension should be an even 20 ft, to give a bit more freedom where, say, tile walls might tend to squeeze interiors an inch or so.

As for architectural esthetics, the decision was to be neither sentimentally old-hat nor doctrinaire modern, but to have the building fit pleasantly into a residential area of a New England city, with familiar materials and with reliance on good taste and good proportions.

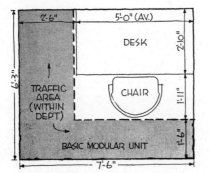

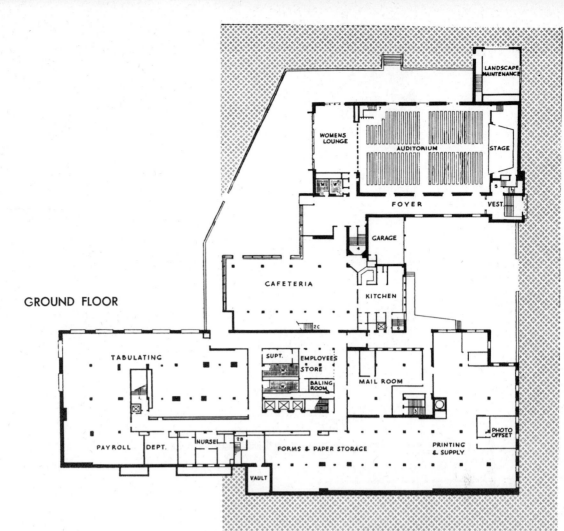

GROUND FLOOR

LANDSCAPE MAINTENANCE

WOMENS LOUNGE

AUDITORIUM

STAGE

FOYER

VEST.

GARAGE

CAFETERIA

KITCHEN

SUPT.

EMPLOYEES STORE

BALING ROOM

MAIL ROOM

TABULATING

PHOTO OFFSET

PAYROLL DEPT.

NURSE

FORMS & PAPER STORAGE

PRINTING & SUPPLY

VAULT

Ground floor is at ground level in rear only, due to slope of site. There are actually three levels below first floor

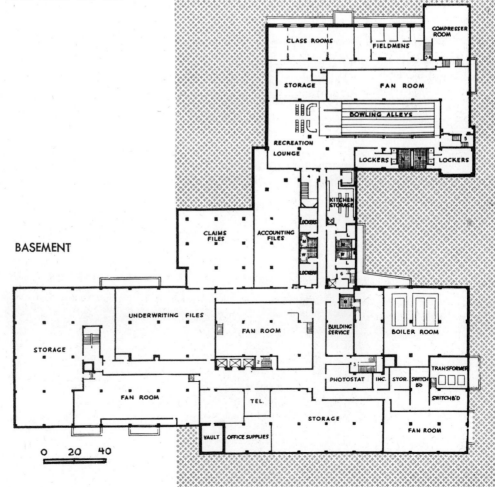

BASEMENT

CLASS ROOMS

FIELDMENS

COMPRESSER ROOM

STORAGE

FAN ROOM

BOWLING ALLEYS

RECREATION LOUNGE

LOCKERS

LOCKERS

KITCHEN STORAGE

LOCKERS

CLAIMS FILES

ACCOUNTING FILES

LOCKERS

UNDERWRITING FILES

FAN ROOM

BUILDING SERVICE

BOILER ROOM

STORAGE

FAN ROOM

TEL.

PHOTOSTAT INC.

STOR.

SWITCH B'D

TRANSFORMER

SWITCHB'D

VAULT

OFFICE SUPPLIES

STORAGE

FAN ROOM

0   20   40

December 1952

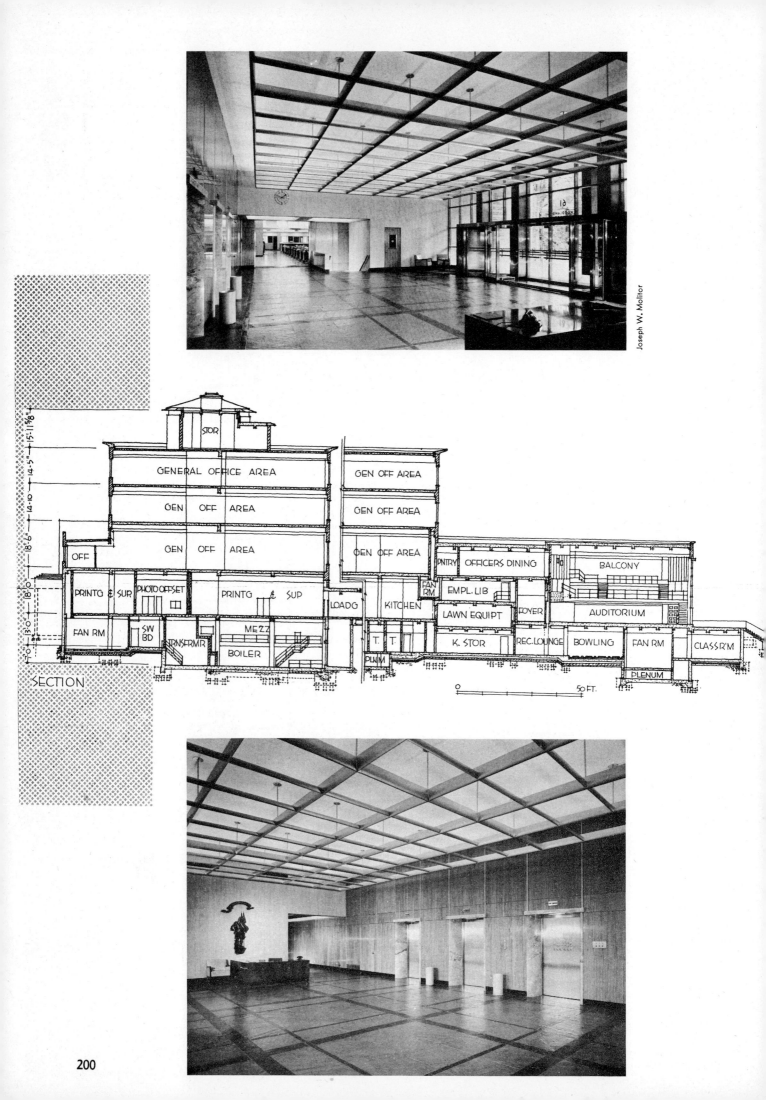

Joseph W. Molitor

SECTION

STOR

GENERAL OFFICE AREA   GEN OFF AREA

GEN OFF AREA   GEN OFF AREA

OFF

GEN OFF AREA   GEN OFF AREA

PNTRY   OFFICERS DINING   BALCONY

PRINTG & SUR   PHOTO OFFSET   PRINTG & SUP   LOADG   KITCHEN   FAN RM   EMPL. LIB   AUDITORIUM

FAN RM   LAWN EQUIPT   FOYER

FAN RM   SW BD   TRNSFRMR   MEZZ   T. T.   K. STOR   REC. LOUNGE   BOWLING   FAN RM   CLASS R'M

BOILER   PLNM   PLENUM

0   50 FT.

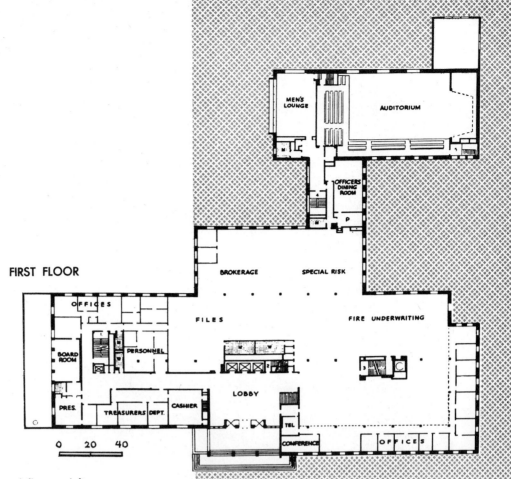

FIRST FLOOR

MEN'S LOUNGE

AUDITORIUM

OFFICERS DINING ROOM

BROKERAGE   SPECIAL RISK

OFFICES

FILES   FIRE UNDERWRITING

BOARD ROOM

PERSONNEL

PRES.

TREASURERS DEPT.   CASHIER   LOBBY

CONFERENCE   OFFICES

TEL

0   20   40

*Mezzanine comes between ground floor and first.
Lower floors are largely occupied by heavy operations, of which there are many like tabulating and printing, and for extensive employee facilities*

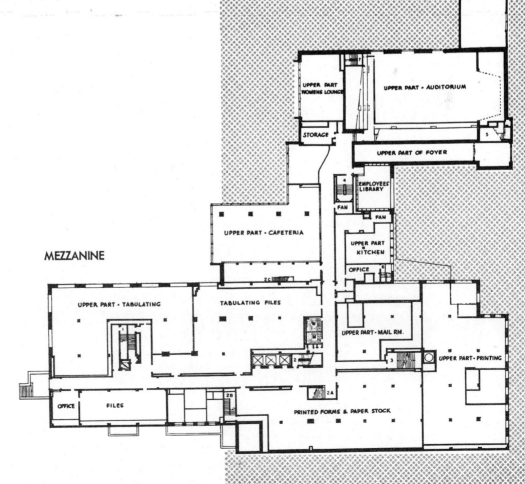

UPPER PART WOMENS LOUNGE

UPPER PART - AUDITORIUM

STORAGE

UPPER PART OF FOYER

EMPLOYEES LIBRARY

FAN

FAN

UPPER PART CAFETERIA

UPPER PART KITCHEN

OFFICE

MEZZANINE

UPPER PART - TABULATING   TABULATING FILES

UPPER PART - MAIL RM.

UPPER PART - PRINTING

OFFICE   FILES

PRINTED FORMS & PAPER STOCK

Second floor (and third) becomes the typical insurance company office space, mostly open with few partitioned offices. Lighting, acoustic treatment, air conditioning are important

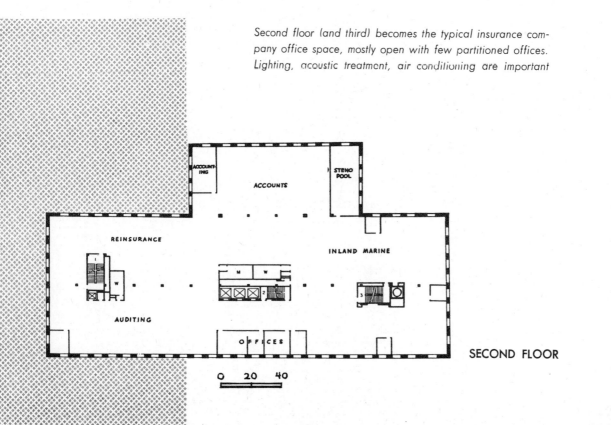

SECOND FLOOR

0   20   40

Joseph W. Molitor

Typical office partitioning is metal and glass, for flexibility. Only executive offices, above and below, have plastered partitions

Bowling alleys, employees' cafeteria and lounges are part of extensive installations many insurance companies make to brighten the working and evening hours of their workers. Indeed these things are among the important reasons-for-being for this new building vs. converting the old

Joseph W. Molitor

Auditorium, also part of employee facilities, has its acoustic design done frankly and expressively. The curved panels in the hung ceiling are smooth surfaces to reflect sound properly to back of auditorium. Other ceiling surfaces are acoustic treated to soften unwanted reverberations

Section II

BANKS

Julius Shulman Photos

BOLD DEPARTURE FROM TRADITIONAL BANK DESIGN

Citizens National Trust and Savings Bank, Los Angeles

Stiles Clements Associated Architects & Engineers

REPRESENTING a distinct departure from traditional bank architecture, the new branch of the Citizens National Trust and Savings Bank on Wilshire Boulevard, Los Angeles, features an impressive façade of plate and corrugated glass panels, aluminum and limestone. The west side of the building (right in photo above) is of architectural concrete finished with mica flakes; ground floor windows here have dark green louvers to minimize the glare of the afternoon sun.

The exterior stone flows through into the interior to add interest to the plaster and bleached mahogany veneer wall treatment. Floors are terrazzo in the entrance areas, carpeted in soft green elsewhere. Fixtures are of bleached mahogany and corrugated glass; railings are plate glass. Drapery and corrugated glass baffles screen the tellers' area from the noise of the work space.

The bank itself occupies only the first floor and mezzanine. The second floor contains a rental area totaling about 10,000 sq. ft., lounges, and future escrow room for the bank. Additional rental space is provided by a store to the east of the main entrance.

The main entrance (above) looks across Wilshire Boulevard to Hancock Park and the Hollywood Hills. Doors are tempered glass with aluminum metal finish. The parking lot entrance to the rear is similarly treated (see page 210).

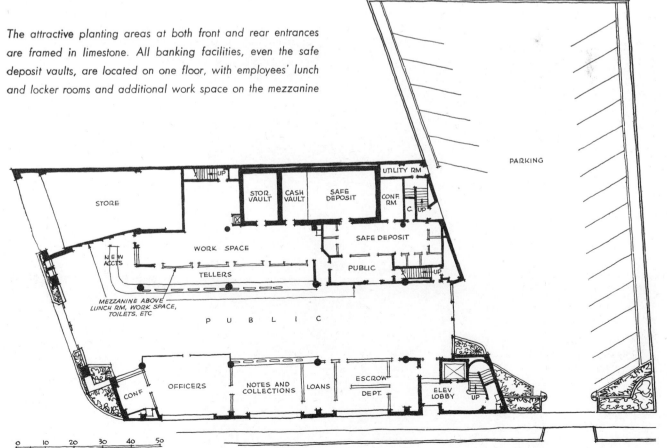

The attractive planting areas at both front and rear entrances are framed in limestone. All banking facilities, even the safe deposit vaults, are located on one floor, with employees' lunch and locker rooms and additional work space on the mezzanine

Above: view through the bank from main entrance to parking lot. Columns are green Verde Antique marble. Ceiling is sprayed asbestos to increase acoustical absorption; center portion is 2 ft. lower than side panels, permitting continuous longitudinal fluorescent light troughs. The drop ceiling also has rectangular light troughs, and flush floods are widely used

The officers' section (left) is separated from the public area by a plate glass railing. Corrugated glass screens the conference room

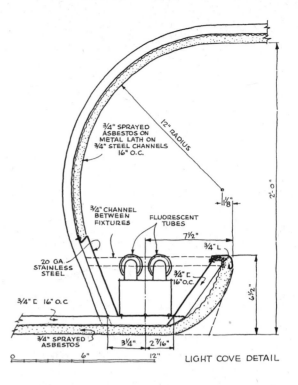

Lighting has been carefully worked out to maintain approximately 35 footcandles at counter height for the critical areas such as desks, counters and tellers' cages. Detail of light cove at right

The area behind the corrugated glass panel at right houses the general accounting offices, vaults and safe deposit department. Light is admitted through panel and through the corrugated glass walls immediately behind the tellers

Philip Fein Photo
Joseph W. Molitor Photo

Sigurd Fischer Photo

A COMPARATIVE GLANCE AT THREE NEW BANKS

1. *People's Savings Bank*
Providence, Rhode Island
Cram & Ferguson, Architects-Engineers

2. *Central Branch, Continental Bank & Trust Co.*
Salt Lake City, Utah
Snedaker & Macdonald, Architects

3. *Broadway Savings Bank*
New York City
Harold R. Sleeper, Architect
Ackerman & Ramsey, Associates

NOT SO LONG AGO the emphasis in bank design was on the monumental facade and the lofty interior considered essential to impress the general public with the institution's solidity. Banks were cold, unfriendly, over-ornamental, and quite frequently impractical from the public's point of view.

In recent years there has been a strong trend away from that old tradition. The banks being built today are straightforward expressions of their function; they are out not to impress the public but to attract it.

The three banks shown above and on the following six pages are far apart geographically. They are quite different in shape and size. Yet all three have treated their public areas, safe deposit facilities, and general working arrangements in much the same way. For purposes of comparison, they are shown here as a unit.

PLAN 3

FIRST FLOOR

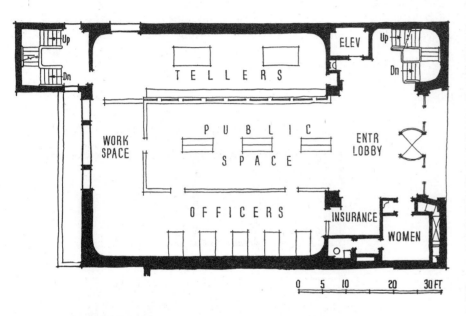

ELEV

Up

Dn

Up

T E L L E R S

WORK SPACE

P U B L I C
S P A C E

ENTR LOBBY

O F F I C E R S

INSURANCE

WOMEN

0 5 10 20 30 FT

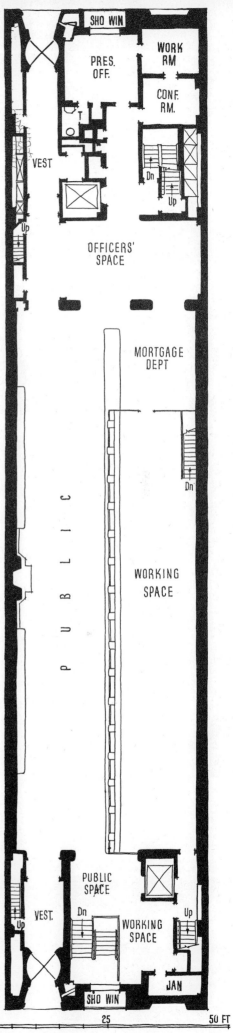

SHO WIN

PRES. OFF.

WORK RM

CONF. RM.

VEST

Up

Dn

Up

OFFICERS' SPACE

MORTGAGE DEPT

P U B L I C

Dn

WORKING SPACE

PUBLIC SPACE

VEST.

Up

Dn

WORKING SPACE

Up

WORK

JAN

SHO WIN

0 25 50 FT

FIRST FLOOR

PLAN 1

THREE NEW BANKS: PUBLIC SPACE

Despite the difference in overall shape of these three banks, each has a more-or-less rectangular public area, visible in its entirety from the main entrance. There is no island of tellers' cages around which the customer must play hide-and-seek, but instead a neat row of tellers' windows ranged along one side. Grille work is happily missing. Lighting is good, public desk and waiting space is convenient, ceilings are acoustically treated. Access to all facilities is obvious and easy. Of particular note are the skylighted ceiling of the People's Savings Bank (1) and the angled tellers' desks of the Continental Bank & Trust Co. (2).

1. *People's Savings Bank*

2. *Continental Bank & Trust Co.*

3. *Broadway Savings Bank*

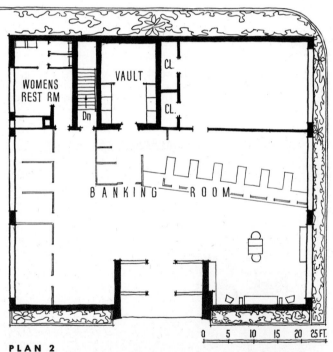

PLAN 2

Because Providence has had several severe floods in the past (the 1938 hurricane caused a great deal of flood damage), special precautions were taken in the design of the People's Savings Bank (1). The architects describe the lower portion of the building as a heavy waterproof concrete box extending well above flood level. The four openings in the walls of the "box" — a show window and a door on each street front — are equipped with water-tight doors which are closed after banking hours or in case of flood. Each entrance doorway also has a low portable metal dam for use in case of shallow street floods, to protect the building and still permit access to it.

Should water seep in despite all these precautions, it would drain into a pit in the sub-basement and be removed by a waterproof electric pump capable of handling 250 gpm. A larger pump, with a capacity of 600 gpm, would go into action automatically if the smaller one should be overtaxed. The building has an emergency power plant on the 6th floor to provide power if the usual sources should fail.

Sigurd Fischer Photo

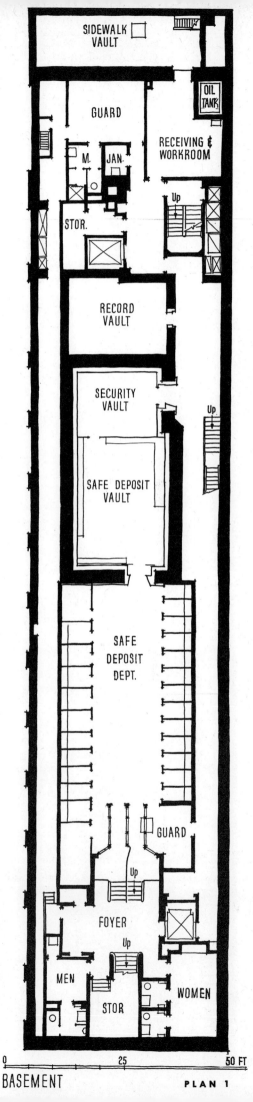

BASEMENT   PLAN 1

Space allotted to bank employees has been carefully worked out in all three plans. Both of the larger buildings (1, 3) have well-lighted and pleasantly decorated employee dining rooms and kitchens on upper floors. All three banks have easy access from public to working areas, and conveniently placed officers' platforms. The smallest of the trio (2) has a compact built-in tellers' area.

1. *People's Savings Bank*

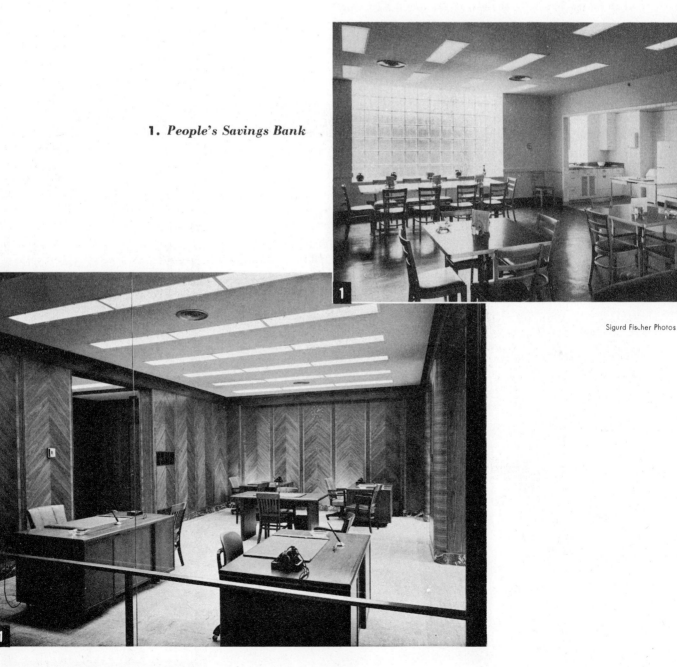

Sigurd Fischer Photos

THREE NEW BANKS:

SAFE DEPOSIT FACILITIES

1. *People's Savings Bank*

2. *Continental Bank & Trust Co.*

3. *Broadway Savings Bank*

Philip Fein Photo

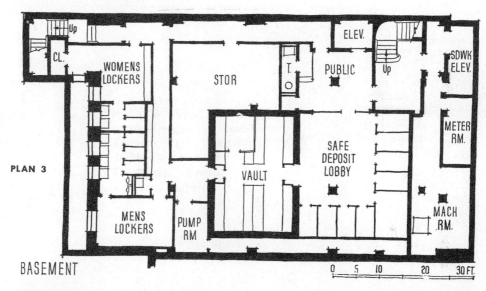

PLAN 3

BASEMENT

WOMENS LOCKERS · MENS LOCKERS · PUMP RM · VAULT · STOR · SAFE DEPOSIT LOBBY · PUBLIC · ELEV. · SDWK ELEV. · METER RM. · MACH RM. · CL. · Up

0 5 10 20 30 FT.

3

3. *Broadway Savings Bank*

Joseph W. Molitor Photos

2. *Continental Bank & Trust Co.*

Philip Fein Photo

PENNSYLVANIA COMPANY
FOR BANKING AND TRUSTS

Philadelphia, Pa.

Howell Lewis Shay, Architects

IN PHILADELPHIA, a city of history and tradition, a 23-year-old office building is practically a youngster, but start to bring it up to today's standards and you soon find how seriously obsolescence and depreciation have affected it. This was the case when the Pennsylvania Company for Banking and Trusts acquired the strategically located 1500 Chestnut St. Building for its new banking headquarters.

Back of the obvious matter of appearances, the architects found, in their survey, that while the basic structure was sound, all piping, generators, pumps, electrical system were in poor condition and needed complete renovation. Add virtually complete change of occupancy in 21 stories and complete air conditioning for the building, and the project becomes extensive.

Altogether the remodeling consisted of removal of all existing partitions and installation of complete new plumbing and electrical services, installation of year-round air conditioning, a new two-story facade on the Chestnut and 15th St. fronts, a new kitchen and cafeteria in the basement, a banking room and vault on the first floor, and interior refinishing of the rest of the building. The bank occupies the first ten stories for banking room and offices of a "shop" nature, upper floors being retenanted.

The new facade is of buff limestone and stainless steel with windows of double insulating glass. The "windows" virtually amount to full glass walls from floor to first floor ceiling line, a full open front. The visual effect, however, is that of huge windows in massive frames of stainless steel. The base is a low course of granite.

The banking room is characterized by soft colors, indirect lighting, open areas for free circulation, and curving forms. Tellers' desks are combined in one long curving counter, which winds around a prominent splayed column marking the officers' space. The counter is covered with plastic of a rich brown color and trimmed with two bands of stainless steel. The curve of the counter is matched above by a lighting cove combining direct and indirect light. The lighting installation won a first prize award in General Electric's 1949 planned lighting competition.

The terrazzo floor picks up some of the brown tones of the counter and check desks across the room, using in rather bold fashion a considerable variety of marble colors and chip sizes. The building columns occurring in the banking room were given the minimum fireproofing, taking a frankly H form.

To find space for air conditioning equipment required strong shoehorn methods, to the point where the building's boiler plant was removed in favor of purchasing steam from the local utility. Cooling compressors and pumps are in the sub-basement, cooling tower on the roof. Actual air heating, cooling and dehumidifying equipment is divided into two parts, one in sub-basement, one on 21st floor, each serving half of the building. Office radiators are orificed to maintain 70 deg. against window and wall losses; air conditioning supplies heated ventilation air. In summer the system will cool to 80 for an outside temperature of 95.

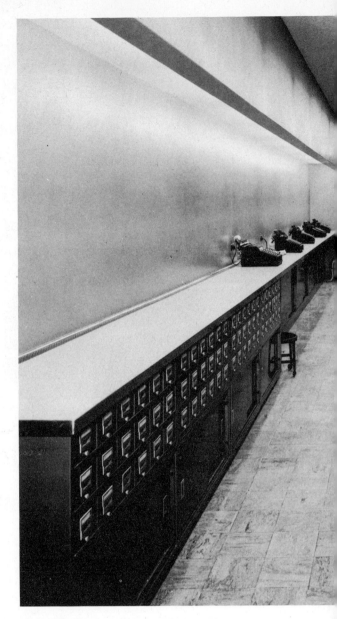

Condax Studios Photo

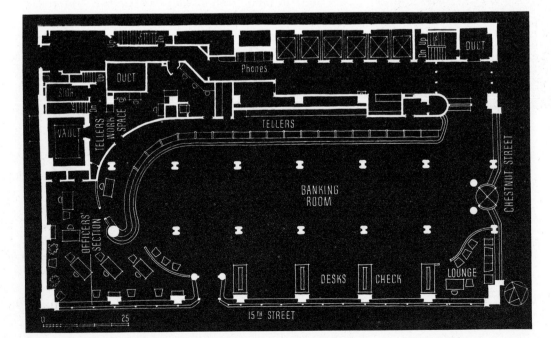

Condax Studios Photo

Universal Photo Service

August 1950

WESTERN SAVING FUND SOCIETY   Philadelphia, Pa.

Harbeson, Hough, Livingston & Larson, Architects

Willing, Sims & Talbutt, Associate Architects

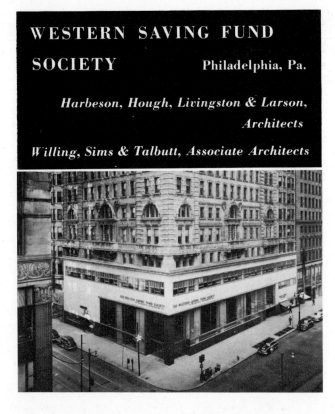

Extensive remodeling was limited to quarters for bank occupancy

THE DECISION to remodel this 50-year-old building was a sort of double-take. In 1945, when the bank bought it to obtain a new location, there was careful discussion of whether to remove the upper stories and remodel space for the banking quarters or raze it and start over. The decision then was to raze it, and the architects drew plans for a new building, but construction costs rose so precipitously that the plans were later set aside in favor of remodeling.

Two principal considerations influenced the design of the new banking room. One was a wish to remove the monumental granite and deeply inset windows which spread a gloom over this important business corner — Broad and Chestnut. Also contemporary design was wanted for itself, to brighten up dealings with the bank's clientele. The bank's officers were at first willing, then "increasingly enthusiastic . . ."

The bank exterior uses great glass panels above a granite base, and above the glass a wide course of pink marble adds a desirable note of color, and one which establishes a harmony with the older facade.

The dominant color inside the banking room is the brown of teak paneling covering the walls, along with the natural travertine on the piers, and blue green with which columns are painted. Floor is terrazzo, the marble chips black and buff.

The architects explain that the bronze panel on vesti-

bule walls does not represent anything. It serves as enclosure for ventilating and heating ducts, and, of course, as a separation of the vestibule from the banking room, and metal seemed more frank than would marble or granite masonry.

The third and fourth floors were completely rebuilt also, to house bank offices and officers' rooms. The second floor was included in this remodeling; it is now tenanted until such time as the bank may need it for expansion. Certain officers' rooms were fitted into the fifth floor. Alterations to the rest of the building were relatively minor.

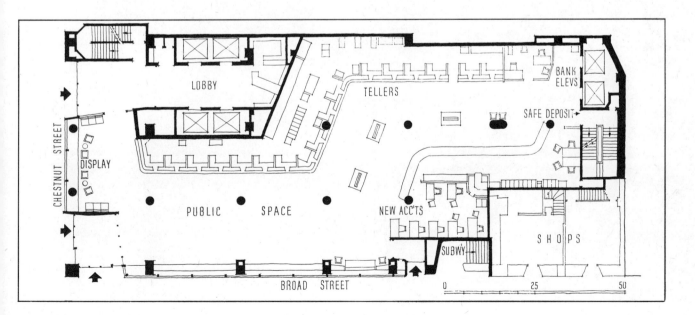

Though the photographs show the curtains drawn, the tall windows usually flood the interior with daylight, and the pleasant aspect has been one of the features most commented on by customers of the Western Saving Fund Society. The architects won full support from officers in the avoidance of unnecessary symbolism and meaningless decoration. Dominant colors in banking room are soft brown of unstained teakwood and the buff of natural travertine

Cortlandt V. D. Hubbard photos, courtesy Armco Steel Corporation

THE OLD theory that a busy corner was always a good business location is accepted today with great reservation. It has become increasingly difficult for would-be customers to find places to park. Passenger car registrations in the U. S. have risen from 26 million to over 33 million in the past five years. Establishments of all kinds are finding it necessary to urge greater public facilities for this increase in automobiles, and to seek methods of providing private services of their own. Drive-in concerns are rapidly coming to the fore to fill this need. Motels, restaurants, theaters, banks, shopping centers, even a church, have been planned for the use of motorists.

Most drive-in types were started in depression days as novelties to lure customers. Questionable connotations arose during this period — the drive-in restaurant was often considered a drink stand, or a honky-tonk; some banks used a rigged-up affair for drive-in service; and theaters were often regarded as rather slip-shod concerns playing third rate movies. They are all now developing into solidly housed, sound businesses, and are acquiring a permanent status in our social habits.

Families are being won over by the drive-in sales slogans — "No parking problems! Fast service! Convenience, comfort! No need to dress up! No standing in line!" Perhaps the most convincing argument for many is that small children may be brought along, kept out of harm's way in the car.

This is all reflected in current building figures. Drive-in theaters have increased from less than 100 in 1947, with a capacity of 5000 cars, to more than 2000 at the present time. The capacity exceeds 775,000 cars. The growth of restaurants has closely paralleled that of theaters. The U. S. Dept. of Commerce Bulletin, *Restaurants and Other Eating Places*, states ". . . mass feeding in a wide variety of types is now an integral part of American life and is likely to assume an increasing role." The popularity of the drive-in restaurant makes its importance obvious. The American Bankers Association estimates that there are about 800 to 1000 drive-in banks in the country, with two or three new ones being reported almost every day.

The Editors wish to thank the following contributors to this study: BANKS (p. 226) W. S. Bucklin, Pres., National Shawmut Bank, Boston; Mosler-Duplex Co.; Diebold, Inc. THEATERS (p. 394) William Glenn Balch, Architect; Jack Corgan, Architect; Motion Picture Herald; Jay Emanuel Publications.

The First National Bank Drive-in Facility, St. Petersburg, Florida, William B. Harvard, Architect, and John B. Dodd, Associate

Florida Photo

SUPPLEMENTARY banking facilities for motorists are being incorporated in all types of banks, all over the country. Aside from helping to alleviate street congestion and parking dilemmas, exterior tellers' windows and parking areas are used to ease crowded banking floors, develop new business, and improve customer service. They have been used in every type of neighborhood from business and industrial to residential sections. The convenience offered is said to have caused success even where parking is not a problem. Most banks where units have been installed feel that the investment and maintenance was worth while and developed new business for their concerns.

TYPES AND EXTENT OF SERVICES

Facilities offered range from parking lots adjoining banks to installations of one to four tellers' windows with overhanging canopies or completely enclosed drives. Variants include walk-up windows for pedestrians, and curb tellers. The latter are remote control units with tellers' booths located under the sidewalk. Although a reasonable traffic turnover by a drive-in window will cut down on need for parking areas, some provision must be made for motorists who have business to transact in the bank itself. Precise needs of an individual bank are best indicated by a poll of its customers on services desired.

Many banks offer complete teller services at drive-in windows. Others limit them to commercial account transactions, deposits, check cashing, or special deposits and payrolls. Some require advance notice of an hour or more to prepare payrolls. In some localities, early morning and evening services are offered on special days.

By properly training tellers serving drive-in windows and educating customers to their use, transactions can be handled with considerable speed. This is increased where services are limited. The customer is expected to have checks and forms filled out and signed on arrival; some banks provide booths off the parking lot for customers who have failed to do so. Where a large number of transactions are handled, additional windows are often used. If two windows are placed in line on a

Desert Bank, Inc., Cathedral City, Calif., Clark & Frey, archts. Bank has parking lot and single drive-in window for both interior and exterior service, car transactions sheltered by roof

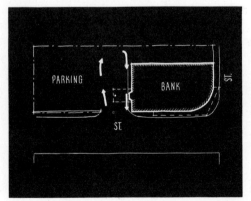

Julius Shulman Photo

single wall, the number of transactions cannot be doubled, as there is always a period of delay or interference by the first car in line. Business usually increases at the windows on stormy days. Peak loads in general coincide with lobby traffic loads.

If the volume of business is sufficient, a full-time teller may be kept at a drive-in window, with extra duties for slack periods. In other banks it may be advisable to have any teller free at the time perform the duties. The location of some parking lots will necessitate a part- or full-time guard. His duties will consist of directing customers to open parking spaces, and seeing that they do not overstay the privilege of free parking. Such policing also discourages attempted robbery. Most banks make no security provisions for the customers other than possibly providing a gun port at the window. Some patrons feel that there is, even so, an added safety in handling transactions in the car.

The use of regular drive-in windows by pedestrians can be hazardous, as well as slow up traffic. Many banks fill the customer's first request, but suggest that he use the regular facilities in the future. Walk-up windows offer a safe alternative.

Civil authorities in general are very favorable toward drive-in banking service. Some communities object to the curb-teller units, however, on the basis of city codes against sidewalk vending.

LOCATION, CONNECTION WITH BANK

In main bank: Permission may sometimes be obtained to use an inset section of sidewalk or window traffic and parking on a main thoroughfare. A unit might also be placed on a public alley at the rear of a bank building. Care must be taken in such a case that there are no truck loading docks in that section which would block the drive-in window from traffic. In some cases use might be made of a basement for drive-in and parking facilities. In new construction roof areas might be used for parking.

Island units: Small booths could be placed in parking lots or garages adjacent to, or across the street from the bank. They could be entirely separate or connected by a tunnel or overpass to the main building. Legal restrictions may require a physical connection. Such a set-up could have its own ledger and signature cards, or be

---

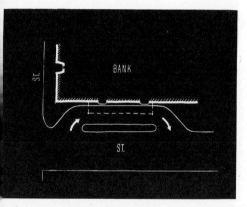

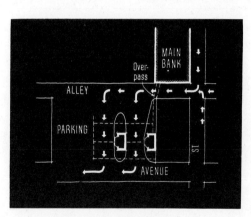

The First National Bank of Boston, Boston, Mass., Cram & Ferguson, archts. Two windows, but no parking, at main bank. Difficult approach used to place window on car's left

First National Bank Drive-in Facility, St. Petersburg, Fla., Wm. B. Harvard, archt., John B. Dodd, assoc. Double units adjoin main bank; limited parking provided on lot

Courtesy of Mosler-Duplex

Florida Photo

connected to bank facilities by pneumatic tubes or conveyor belt.

In branch banks: Growth of local shopping areas in lower cost suburban zones has caused the establishment of many small branch banks in their environs. Location of teller units and parking lots is generally a lesser problem in such a case, due to the availability of more space. Completely separate records and personnel are required.

Below: Bank of Passaic & Trust Co., Passaic, N. J. An island type drive-in is housed in portion of ground floor, connects with two streets for dual approach. Walk-up window serves pedestrians and patrons from adjacent parking lot

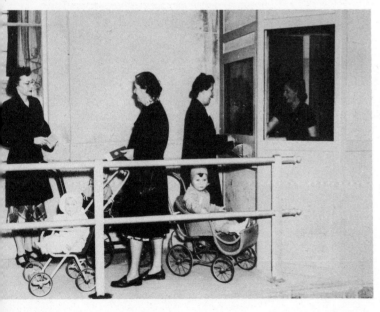

Above: Bayside National Bank, Bayside, N. Y. Walk-up window for pedestrians and shoppers. Wide walk permits passage of baby carriages. Guard rails prevent customers from stepping into traffic. Standard drive-in window unit is used for this service

PLOT LAYOUT

Entrances: Where there is a separate exit, entrances should be a minimum of 10 ft in width. When both parking lot and drive-in window are served by a common entrance, 20 ft width minimum should be provided if possible. It is common practice to provide gate posts and a chain to close off the parking area after hours. Such posts should be of solid masonry to ward off damage if hit by an automobile. Fences around lots should be durable and protected by some type of buffer on the parking lot side. The grade of sidewalk ramps should be low enough to prevent scraping of cars.

Approaches and drives: A straight approach to a window is best, and should allow sufficient space for several cars to line up off the street. Where a "U" turn is required, about 50 ft should be allowed, with the window far enough away for the car to be out of the turning stage on arrival.

The window transaction requires less effort on the part of the driver when located to his left. Often, however, the advantages of allowing extra line-up space, or the utilization of both sides of an island unit, will

Below, left: Union National Bank, Ventura, Calif. Lot adjoining bank treated as patio-like drive for auto service. Location of window places it on drivers' right, but permits nine cars to line up off the street to avoid traffic congestion

Photos Courtesy Mosler-Duplex

justify the placing of a window unit to the driver's right.

If two windows are in line, enough room should be left between them so that the second car in line can pull out and depart after being served. Where possible, the second window should be so located that it may be approached by a separate line of cars. An electric-eye indicator is often used to tell customer which window to use.

Painted stripes or bumpers are used to guide cars into position at the windows. A curb should be provided below the window to protect it from collision.

Guard rails should be placed around any building

exits opening on driveways.

Several types of devices are used for signaling the teller, during slack periods, of a customer's arrival at the window. These include: a compression hose on the drive, push-button buzzer on the window, mirrors and photo-electric cells.

Parking lots and paving: Wide variation in the size and shape of lots, and their relation to streets and buildings prevent the forming of any standard layout for parking areas. In general, ease of maneuvering automobiles, and a maximum capacity for the lot are prime factors.

Security Trust Co. Auto Bank, Rochester, N. Y., A. Charles Pioch, archt., Edgar N. Phillips, dsnr. Integrated roof shelters approach to drive-in window. Placement towards rear permits car line-up, easy access by all tellers

Joseph Molitor Photos

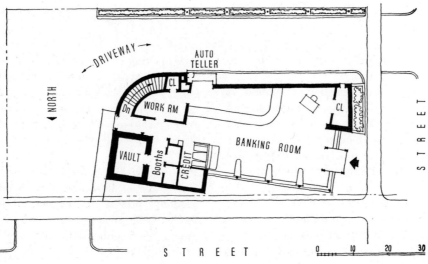

First National Bank Drive-in Facility, St. Petersburg, Fla., Wm. B. Harvard, archt., John B. Dodd, assoc. Right: adequate lighting gives safety at night for money handling and traffic. Second floor houses storage room. Below center: an overpass connects drive-in unit with main bank. Banking laws would have required separate charter for drive-in if it were not physically connected with bank. Bottom: detail of teller's cage. Work counters and opening provided for manufactured window unit

Florida Photo

Concrete or asphalt are generally preferred for paving. The usual precautions should be taken for foundations and drainage. Radiant coils are sometimes used in concrete slabs for snow removal.

GENERAL PLANNING

Window location: A location centered behind banking room tellers' cages is usually best for a drive-in window. This permits any of the tellers to perform the service, and dispenses with the need of an extra full time teller for the average bank.

Use of the windows is expected to increase; it would be advisable to provide for future expansion if possible.

All enclosed units should be air conditioned and draft-proof. Inside pressure should be slightly above that of the exterior to prevent entry of exhaust fumes.

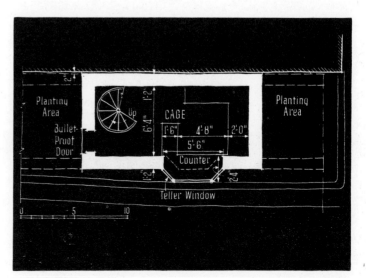

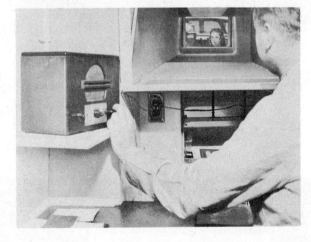

Above: Mercantile-Commerce Bank & Trust Co., St. Louis, Mo. Curb teller gives drive-up service where space is unavailable for window. Deposit placed in unit is lowered to teller's booth below sidewalk. Mirror system and two-way speaker permit customer and teller to see and converse with each other

Weather shelter: In all cases, windows should be provided with some form of shelter to protect the area where the customer will be reaching to the teller's unit. This may be a completely covered drive, or just a 6 ft square marquee. Height of marquees should be clearly marked to warn trucks using the service. Although few banks provide after hour service at present, it would be well to wire marquees for future lighting installations.

EQUIPMENT, INSTALLATION

Window selection: Manufactured window units are available to fit most types of bank design. The units vary chiefly in the operation mechanism of the pass door or tray. Each system permits only one side of the pass to be open at a time. Some types also incorporate such items as package receivers, night depositories and gun ports. Care should be taken to select one with a durable finish, and with safety features preventing mashed fingers as the pass door is shut. The glazing should be bullet-proof glass. Metal enclosing the unit should be armor plate.

University National Bank Parking Lot Branch, Seattle, Wash., Smith, Carroll & Johanson, archts.: designed for inside service

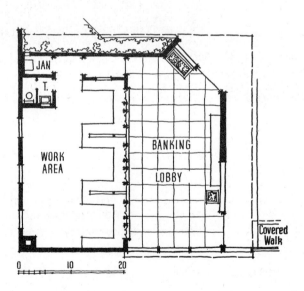

Window installation: A wall opening should be provided as specified by the manufacturer of the unit selected. The units are usually installed directly into the space. The different window types require different mounting heights; the manufacturer's advice should also be followed on this. The average height of the bottom edge of the driver's window in a car is between 43 and 47 in. On some of the older models it is more; some of the more modern are as low as 38 in.

The window should be of sufficient width to permit full teller service. A minimum of 42 to 60 in. should provide counter space for such change machines, adding machines, etc., as might be needed.

Speaker units: Two-way speakers are generally found to be the most satisfactory means of communication between the teller and the customer. A switch permits the teller to check accounts without being overheard by the driver. The unit may also be used to amplify instructions over the parking lot.

PROMOTIONAL FEATURES

A drive-in service should be introduced to customers and the public through statement stuffers, direct mail, newspapers and other advertising. They should be fully informed on the methods of its proper use, and the directions of traffic flow. A large sign at the site is helpful to acquaint customers with the service.

It has been found by many banks that without

Julius Shulman Photos

Dual facilities lessen banking floor traffic, permit more informal relations. Open tellers' booths and lounge are used

Desert Bank Inc., Cathedral City, Calif., Clark & Frey, archts. Drive-in window and parking lot for interior service provided

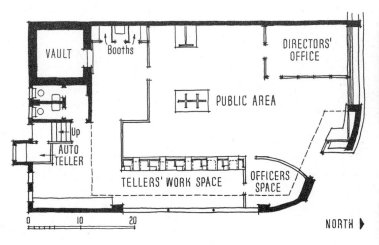

sufficient advertising, full use has not been made of the drive-in facilities offered to customers.

Landscaping of plots can be used to advantage for securing good will in residential areas. It should, however, be kept as simple as possible to avoid high maintenance and replacement costs.

Edward L. Varney, Associates

Architects and Engineers

DRIVE-IN BANK STRESSES ROADSIDE ADVERTISING

Six Points Branch

First National Bank of Arizona

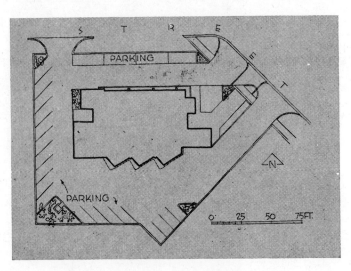

DRIVE-IN BANKS are still in the experimental stage, as the architect of this one in Phoenix points out. Like the motel and the retail store, they require a site on an important traffic artery and a plot large enough to accommodate driveways and parking areas; unlike their predecessors, however, they need special security facilities and must overcome the traditional conservatism of their owners if they are to be successful.

This new bank in Phoenix was planned to serve an expanding industrial district on the edge of the city. The site is on the principal East-West highway, well suited to a silent advertising campaign stemming from an attention-calling building. The exterior was designed with this advertising potential in mind: hence the bold canopies over the entrances, the towering un-bank-like sign, the native field stone, redwood and precast concrete selected to reflect a "desert feeling."

A saw-tooth arrangement of three drive-in windows was adopted to permit quick servicing at all hours; the windows were placed on the south side of the building at a 90 deg angle to the main thoroughfare in anticipation of the probable traffic flow.

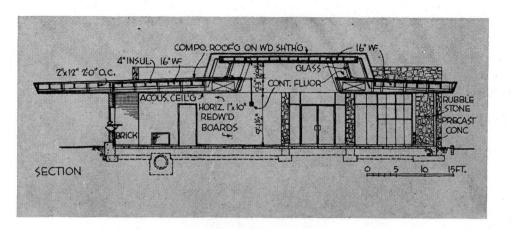

SECTION

COMPO. ROOF'G ON WD SHTH'G
2"x12" 2'0" O.C.   4" INSUL.   16" WF   16" WF
GLASS
CONT. FLUOR
ACOUS. CEIL'G
HORIZ. 1"x10" REDW'D BOARDS
BRICK
RUBBLE STONE
PRECAST CONC

0   5   10   15 FT.

Stuart A. Weiner

April 1953

Stuart A. Weiner

Main entrance (opposite), at eastern end of building, is marked by huge sign typical of drive-ins; night depository is at right of doors. Public space runs straight through building from east to west, with an entrance at each end, tellers' "windows" along one side and officers' platform along other. Owner's requirement that no glass be used on either side wall resulted in clerestory; main banking area was kept free of columns by use of rigid steel frames for clerestory, carrying moment over to the outside walls. All materials used on exterior are repeated on interior: redwood in ceiling over public area, field stone and precast concrete in walls. Clerestory windows are heat-absorbing

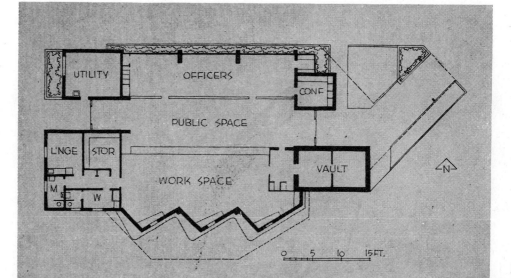

Officers' platform (left and below) is separated from public space by long counter containing storage cabinets. Ceiling here and in work area on opposite side is acoustic tile; lighting is fluorescent

Stuart A. Weiner

At one end of officers' platform is wall of closets and cabinets, plus built-in steel filing cabinets. At other end (above) doors lead to small storage room and staff conference room

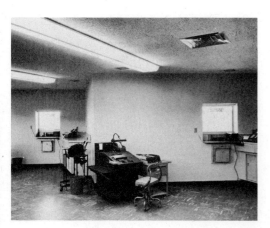

Above: drive-in windows are served from built-in counters directly across work area from tellers' "windows." Below: canopy over western entrance is 18 ft deep; louvers in wall are redwood, ventilate utility room. Note pavement markings directing traffic to the three drive-in windows

Ph. B. Wallace Photo

George Howe, writing from the American Academy in Rome—a post he is soon to relinquish, says: ". . . As the president of the Society at the time of building made me guarantee on my word of honor that we had designed the building in the interests of the bank and not of our personal reputations among the ivory tower boys, I take a personal and particular interest in its success. . . ." Photographs, left: construction nearly complete in 1932. Below, street façades show little change; note modern automobiles in 1949 view. Facing page, main banking room shows greatest change, in lighting and counters, required by tremendous growth in bank's business

1932 **1949**

Joseph Molitor Photo

Howe and Lescaze, Architects

SAVING FUND SOCIETY BUILDING:

A RE-APPRAISAL

In August, 1932, the Philadelphia Saving Fund Society opened its new branch bank and office building at 12th and Market Streets. Almost immediately the building won national and international acclaim; it has been pointed to as a thorough fusing of structure, materials and equipment; hundreds of high school and college students still visit it annually. Does the building live up to this succes d'estime? The seventeen years since its completion afford time enough for an honest re-evaluation based on the experience of owner and tenants as well as our own more mature critical attitude toward non-traditional architecture.

THE OLD BEAUTY

By Frederick Gutheim

FROM along the Schuylkill, through the web of overhead wires, you can see it, still the biggest and proudest thing in Philadelphia, now almost twenty years since it was born on the drafting table in the office of Howe and Lescaze. A fretted white tower announces with authority **PSFS**, spelled out at night in red neon, still commanding the skyline.

A cynic might very well say that the last thing built always commands the skyline, and nothing much of consequence, admittedly, has been built in downtown Philadelphia since the Society erected its skyscraper in the depression days of 1932. But hold! Have the last twenty years produced anything in the way of a tall building — except for the United Nations secretariat, now a promise in steel — that provides the same functional satisfaction or as much eye food? If you had to pick the one American skyscraper, this would have to be it.

When people have finished talking about verticals in the Daily News Building, horizontals in the McGraw-Hill Building, the planning virtues of Rockefeller Center, or the simple height of the Empire State — when all this has been done, and you come down to the fundamentals of good building and design — there is PSFS. Today it is still a satisfying building, to its occupants,

to the public, and to the architecturally aware visitor. It does not invite comparison. It still has an excitement to communicate, a few surprises one has forgotten since the last visit, against a pleasant sense of finding things as satisfactory as one remembered them. Most of all, the building has that unique combination of boldness, of rugged strength approaching ugliness that was Lescaze's polytechnic contribution, and of richness, luxury and refinement approaching over-refinement that was Howe's.

You admire it still, although the building belongs in the awkward age. Not new enough to be contemporary, but not old enough to have become a readily placed historical monument, it is aging gracefully. That fascinating miraculous preservation is part of its charm. There was an architectural wisecrack contemporary with the building of PSFS, calculated to jar the exponent of pure functionalism: "Yes, but will it make a good ruin?" It has become almost possible to answer that one. We can see that a modern building does not age in the same way a traditional building does. Modern materials — and double entry bookkeeping, perhaps — assure that in age the modern building will have a special charm of its own that we have not known before.

At first you think that jaunty ageless, frightening atmosphere, a little on the embalmed side, is due chiefly

1932   1949

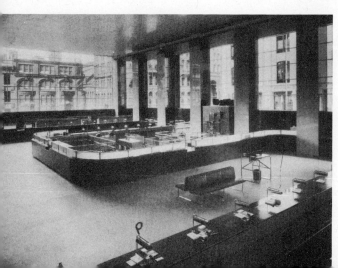

Entrance to second-floor bank: the simple doorway hardly prepares one for the monumental stair hall. Stairs begin so close to entrance that incoming customers automatically hurry up. Facing page, top and bottom: comparisons, main banking room. Number of customers' desks substantially increased; tellers' windows doubled; and local lamps eliminated from counters to make room for the machines required to accommodate increased business

to the extraordinarily good maintenance the building receives. Then you think it derives from the marble, glass, stainless steel, copper and bronze, the whole battery of ageless, and nothing but ageless, materials that have gone into it. The building, piece by piece, might just as well have been built yesterday. But obviously, it wasn't.

What has aged is not the building but the style. With-

Entire building is air-conditioned; to this, plus efficient maintenance, is attributed low cost of upkeep. Above, duct supplies conditioned air to vault, pivots out of way so door can be locked at night. Air-conditioning and good office-floor design have consistently attracted tenants although building is not in Philadelphia's financial district. Right, remote control board for electrical system, (C. D. Fawcett, designer). Incoming high voltage is stepped down for separate light and power circuits, so interconnected that one may take both loads if the other fails

Richard Dooner Photo   **1932**

1949   Joseph Molitor Photo

out even entering you see the enormous curved corner, the building's principal label of association with the modern movement of the late twenties and early thirties. Critics were not lacking, even at that time, to point out that the corner destroyed the sense of volume, but it took subsequent excesses and corruptions to kill off this cliché simply by making it tiresome. Anyhow, there it is, unarguable evidence of the period.

Inside, it is still what Frank Lloyd Wright denounced as "the cardboard box;" inside you are even more conscious of style. The monochrome interior emphasizes what must have been, twenty years ago, new and daring structural forms; the design proclaims its affinity with the T-square and the layout artist's pad. There is a strong flavor of typography. And there is a faint formaldehyde reminiscence of buildings and sketches

1932   **1949**   Joseph Molitor Photo

October 1949

Philadelphia's skyline shows little change except for television masts, one of them atop PSFS. Though not in the financial district, PSFS office spac

of buildings seen in books, not of buildings seen as buildings. Was this, perhaps, a paper architecture expressing a wistfulness ingrained in the modern movement, with its many unbuilt projects and its emphasis on theory?

These characteristics, not unique in PSFS, are difficulties of that right-angled age into which it was born; nor are these stylistic details of cubism obtrusive. You think of them only when you find the building eluding criticism by explaining politely that it was not born yesterday. You could even say that no building twenty years old can with decency seem to have been born yesterday.

From the time a building is completed its destruction begins. This change the unadulterated functionalists of the twenties denied. They could not see that closely reasoned designs would grow out of date as there came change in the human needs they were designed to meet. Consider, for example, that the PSFS building, first

1949. *Building originally provided for growth in nearly every department: of the more-than-enough coupon booths (left) initially installed one row was dismantled and later re-installed. Vault (right) had room for greatly increased number of safe deposit boxes*

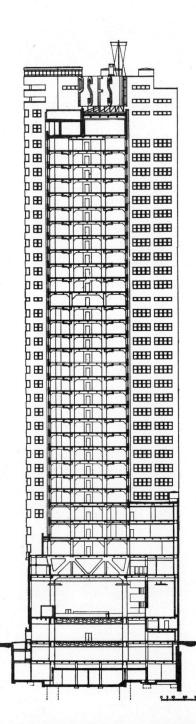

Twentieth floor: mechanical equipment, including air-conditioning for offices.

Third floor truss space air-conditioners for bank. Store conditione are in basement.

...een fully rented for years, thanks to management, equipment, planning, "style"

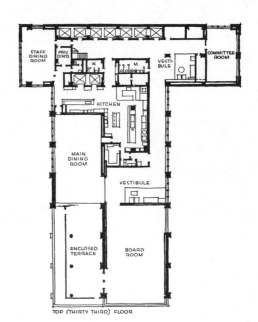

TOP (THIRTY THIRD) FLOOR

thought of as a branch, is now the headquarters of the bank; that since 1933 traffic through the main banking rooms has about doubled. It would have been astonishing if these changes had not made necessary corresponding changes in the design of the building, invalidating the doctrine of extreme functionalism, urging a greater flexibility and more recognition of changing needs.

Yes, a series of changes, undertaken in the names of progress and of maintenance, begins to take place in a building from the moment it is occupied. The process begins most easily with decoration and other elusive details. In older buildings it spreads to store fronts, lighting fixtures, elevator cabs, lobbies, corridors, and their very facades. Advanced stages are signalized by major reconstructions. Hardly one of these individual changes can be objected to with any force, but their cumulative effect leads to anonymity.

In PSFS the process starts with the main banking room, which originally took the appearance of a cube,

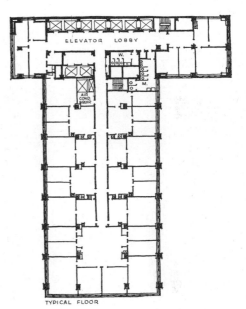

TYPICAL FLOOR

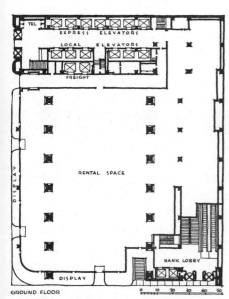

GROUND FLOOR

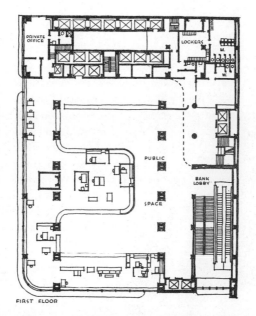

FIRST FLOOR

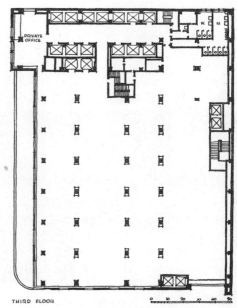

THIRD FLOOR

1932

1949

Office building elevator lobby: directory at left caused traffic jam; moving it to alcove at right eliminated crowding. Typical upper floor corridor (right) has black marble wainscot, reducing maintenance. Thanks partly to air-conditioning, plaster above marble has required repainting only at infrequent intervals

each side with its own character: now glass, now marble, now white, now black, now hard, now soft. The recently installed lighting changes that conception. So does the substitution for the original white nubbly textured curtain that covered nearly the whole of the room's east wall of a new curtain in a color called burgundy.

The catalog of change might be expanded. It leads squarely into questions which deserve full exploration, for which there unfortunately is not space here: How far may the architect go in translating into rigid form the fluid function at the moment of design? What is the responsibility of an owner for his work of art?

The PSFS building is our most charming skyscraper. It has, I insist, style. That style, integral throughout the building, can be tampered with only at the risk of destroying the building's chief distinguishing features. Its handsome directors' rooms on the top floor, with their views over the city and its two rivers that took the breath of the United Nations Headquarters Site Commission when they visited Philadelphia, are designed, if you please, in browns. Its chief room is a study in black and white. Its corridors are cleanly designed, sharply developed in light and shadow, boldly composed in squares and primary colors. These are the details that decide everything in the building's appearance.

If I may borrow for the heading of this article the title of Miss Willa Cather's last slim volume of stories, without her suggestion that in a gentler day it was enough to be beautiful, it may serve to express some conclusions we may draw from our experience with PSFS. When functionalism in the United States was raw, red, and steamy-new, it found few more devoted followers than Howe and Lescaze. Theirs was the pure dogma. Up with pure function and to hell with good looks; at best, it was claimed, good looks would take care of themselves.

Yet today what remains is not function but beauty.

It is a curious, haunting, and distinctive kind of beauty, this palette of black and white, these textures of stainless steel, polished marble, and plate glass, these forms so purely cubistic. The effect may not have been calculated, although one doubts the assertion, but it is

Joseph Molitor Photo

1949   *Typical rentable office space*   **1932**

consistent beyond accident. It is not what one would aspire to today, but it is what one is glad someone once aspired to and succeeded in creating.

PLANNING, STRUCTURE, MATERIALS, EQUIPMENT

Inevitably the building has undergone the changes of which Frederick Gutheim writes, many of them because the bank's business has grown; since 1933 daily

Office floors: location of columns, plumbing, etc. is such that an average tenant can be accommodated in 15 to 25% less space than in other Philadelphia buildings. Stainless steel window sills and radiator covers have right-angled profile and square corners for durability and to simplify the work of fitting partitions for tenant changes. Due to air conditioning, windows are locked except when being cleaned. Tenants have always accepted this without protest.

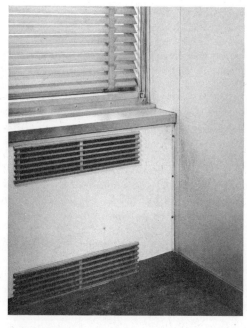

Joseph Molitor Photo

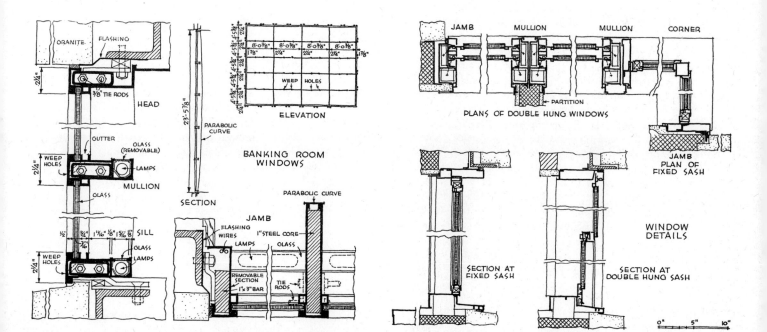

traffic through the main banking room has increased from 1250 persons to about 2500. Fortunately there was space for much of the increase. The Society is not certain but suspects with gratitude that the architects provided a series of corner offices, one above another and connected by a private elevator, for the precise purpose of housing the chief officers when the change from branch to head office should be made. When the demand for safety deposit boxes increased, room for more was found waiting in the vault. Doubled banking traffic doubled the number of tellers' windows required and more than doubled the work, entailing the use of numerous machines. Some time after the building's opening, George Howe says, a scheme of U-shaped teller spaces, following the original counter outline and in plan much like the arrangement whose installation has just been completed, was developed in collaboration with Louis McAllister (who ran the Howe & Lescaze office in 1932 and now has his own Philadelphia office). That scheme was never detailed. As now rebuilt, the counters were designed by the building's own competent tenant architect, Alexander Hazell, using unframed plate glass and, surmounting the original black counter, some of the light gray marble left over from 1932.

In the original banking room design, general lighting was indirect, coming entirely from incandescent lamps concealed above the long air conditioning baffles just beneath the ceiling. This supplied relatively few foot candles at counter levels; intentionally, there were individual counter lamps for local high-intensity lighting. Also, in accord with then accepted technical theory, the heat load of the general lighting sources was to be overcome by the air conditioning system. Today such a theory is questioned; operating costs usually force minimizing of the lighting heat load. Because the local lamps occupied valuable counter space and to reduce the air conditioning load by an appreciable number of tons of refrigeration, then,

the owners have disconnected the original general lighting, removed the counter lamps, and installed recessed, lensed downlights which, sparkling in the high ceiling and reflected in the polished marble walls, supply 30 or more foot candles at counter height. Neither Howe nor Lescaze was consulted on this

Second-guessing the structural (Purdy and Henderson) or mechanical (R. Berkeley Hackett) engineers on PSFS is difficult. The great difference in column spacing between lower and upper floors is a logical solution of the differing requirements of stores and bank vs. rentable office space. The great load of the tower on the trusses above the banking room ceiling and on the columns below entailed massive construction which was considered as a series of rigid frames in designing the tower wind bracing. For this purpose kneebraces were used at every girder-to-column connection, to develop full continuity in the girders. Possibly a different form of haunch, perhaps welded, might be used today; the detail is mentioned, however, because it is an instance of recognition of the structural principle of continuity at a time when that was not common practice.

Utilizing continuity gave practical benefits. Office stories are only 12 ft. floor-to-floor. While the knee-braces cut down considerably on the headroom around columns, column spacing (17 ft. 8 in.) is such that a bay accommodates a pair of average-sized private offices or one larger office; in these instances braces are in the plane of partitions. In large general office space, it is true, headroom appears to be low (1932 office photo shows one condition, 1949 photo the other). To gain every possible inch of headroom, the ceiling is not furred; beams, the underside of the floor slab, and air conditioning ducts, all plastered, are exposed. All this results in a minimum cubage for the total rentable area. Without air conditioning and ample daylighting the relatively low ceilings might be oppressive; with them —

and the scheme included both from the beginning, at least in the architects' minds — this is not much of a problem.

Although air conditioning for the entire building was not accepted until construction of the steel frame was almost complete, space was found without much difficulty for the ducts and equipment — another instance of advance planning? — which has all functioned perfectly for 17 years. In 1949, one unit broke down and was out of service for a few days; to obviate further difficulties, an additional standby unit is to be installed shortly.

The cooling towers on the roof are concealed by the sign whose huge neon initials, PSFS, have become a landmark. The owners were at first dubious (this was in pre-alphabetical-agency days) of the dignity of such a sign; but when they saw that the Society's full name was undecipherable from any distance they acceded. Since, PSFS has become the name by which the bank is generally identified.

As to materials, there have been two instances only in which today's knowledge might have been of benefit. All the large panes of glass at bank level have been reset; some time ago one fell out and others cracked. The cause, determined to be hardening of the setting material, has been remedied. At another time some brick joints were observed to be powdering; though the condition was not serious, as a part of their policy of preventive maintenance the owners decided to repoint all brickwork. In some places the hard surface glaze of the tower brick appears to be weathering. Interior surface finishes — marble, sheet bronze and stainless steel, rubber tile flooring, painted plaster in rented offices, even the plywood panels surfaced with rare woods which line the directors' suite on the top floor, all have a record of relatively easy maintenance and, for items such as the sheet metal, of thorough polishing required at extremely infrequent intervals. In part, air conditioning is credited for this.

Section III

TRANSPORTATION BUILDINGS

Airports ·

Railroad Buildings ·

Service Station ·

Bus Terminal ·

ENTIRELY ARCHITECT-DESIGNED

Municipal Airport, Shreveport, La.

Samuel G. Wiener, E. M. Freeman & Associates
Architects and Engineers

Shreveport's new airport was designed in its entirety—including runway layout and all buildings—by one firm of architects and engineers. Old airfield could not be expanded, was dangerously close to a military field; increasing commercial traffic necessitated move to a safer field where facilities could grow. Photograph shows present stage; black lines are relocated highway (bottom of photo), co-axial cable (across center of field), and service roads. Cross-hatching indicates next stage; hatching, final stage; potential hangar sites at upper left and right.

Sʜʀᴇᴠᴇᴘᴏʀᴛ's ᴍᴜɴɪᴄɪᴘᴀʟ ᴀɪʀᴘᴏʀᴛ, built under the authority of the city's Department of Public Works, of which H. Lane Mitchell is Commissioner, cost approximately five million dollars. Financed by a municipal bond issue and by a grant from the Civil Aeronautics Administration, it was entirely designed by one architect-engineer firm. Between its conception and its recent opening there were not only many months of work; it was also somewhat of a *cause célèbre* locally, though discussion has now given way to pride in the city's new transportation facility.

Due to increasing air traffic at Shreveport, it became necessary to either enlarge the old airport or build a new one. The old one had a decided advantage; it was within one mile of the city's business center. But it was also on the concave side of a curve in the Red River, which made expansion somewhat of a problem, and military traffic at Barksdale Air Force Base only 3 miles away was a source of annoyance if not of danger. Enlargement versus building anew became a heated issue, involving civic societies, newspapers and individuals. At a referendum, Shreveport voted to build a new airport; a bond issue was passed; and a more distant 1600-acre site, mostly hilly wooded land with some cultivated fields, in several privately owned parcels, was purchased.

As terminal building looks to arriving passengers: facing page, from air; above, when taxiing up; below, from concourse after de-planing

Ulric Meisel

Main Entrance

Inside Lobby

Airline Counters

252

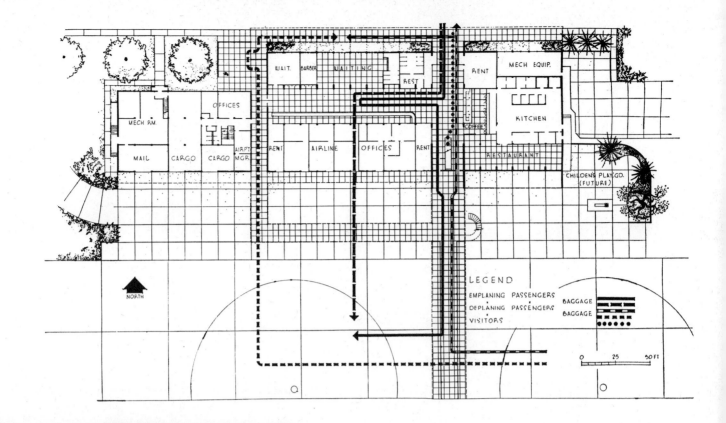

NORTH

LEGEND
EMPLANING PASSENGERS
DEPLANING PASSENGERS
VISITORS

BAGGAGE
BAGGAGE

0   25   50 FT

*Passengers use lower doors to field;
visitors, stairs to observation level above*

Site preparation consisted of a substantial amount of clearing, grading, filling and compacting. A highway was re-routed; a co-axial cable had to be protected; some pipelines and utilities were relocated. Roads were extended, water wells drilled, power and gas brought in, and subsurface drainage installed. Now built are two runways, one, instrument-controlled, 6400 by 200 ft; the other 4800 by 150 ft. Locations for two more runways have been determined. Taxiways are 175 ft wide. Concrete runways and plane parking areas are 8 to 10 in. thick. In addition to the Terminal Building there are buildings for Maintenance, Remote Communications, Gasoline Fueling facilities and Water Pump House. Spots for future buildings and hangars have been determined. The entire airport and its facilities can grow in orderly fashion as needs arise.

The Terminal Building is primarily a transportation

Pedestrian and baggage traffic are not mixed

Ulric Meisel

depot, with circulation of passengers, personnel, visitors, baggage and service equipment carefully organized on a one-level scheme to minimize interference. The architects decided to separate the administration and operation unit from the passenger unit by a breezeway. It was early decided not to bring deplaned baggage into the building or to handle it unnecessarily; the breezeway facilitates this. The structure, of reinforced concrete and steel frame faced with brick, has no basement; a crawl space continuous under both units and breezeway will permit future changes in wiring and services as tenants and equipment change. Public, rental and office spaces are air conditioned; the two mechanical rooms are at a slightly lower floor level.

Special features, some now completed, include the 350-ft-long "finger" concourse, 200-ft-long observation deck, and space reserved between building and ramp for a future planted, equipped children's playground. The project was conceived as a show-place for the city as well as a smoothly functioning airport.

Left, observation platform on south (field) side of structure; center

ELASTIC CORD
FABRIC
UPHOLSTERY DET.

1" FOAM RUBBER

WD ARM REST

2" FOAM RUBBER

3/4" □ RODS - ALL
JOINTS WELDED

·SIDE ELEVATION·

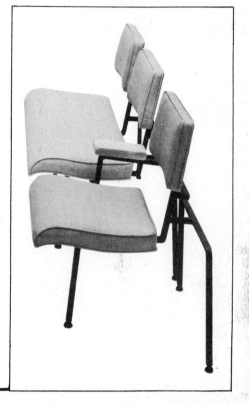

Furniture in main waiting room, specially designed by architect-designer James R. Lamantia of New Orleans, is of height suitable for waiting passengers but not comfortable enough to encourage lounging. Benches are convenient height for depositing baggage. All pieces are heavier than strength alone demands, to prevent pushing them around. Removable plywood panels permit taking off fabric for cleaning. Floor is terrazzo, walls marble, ceiling acoustical tile

Furniture photos: Frank L. Miller

. . . stair to concourse level; right, restaurant

Ulric Meisel

SHREVEPORT AIRPORT

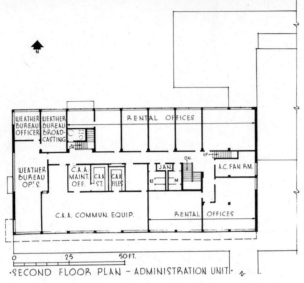

·SECOND FLOOR PLAN – ADMINISTRATION UNIT·

Second floor of administration unit (plan at left) contains weather bureau, CAA offices, rental space. As in all air terminals, official spaces here and in control tower floors (controller offices, radar room, control cab) contain much special equipment required by regulations, with provision for more and different future **equipment**

H. O. Wiseman

H. O. Wiseman

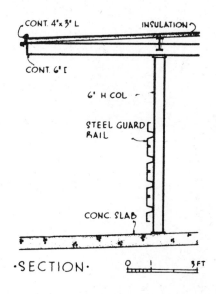

CONT. 4" x 3" L   INSULATION

CONT. 6" I

6" H COL

STEEL GUARD RAIL

CONC. SLAB

·SECTION·   0   1   3 FT

*Steel guard rail at concourse and stair to observa-
tion deck are painted fire-engine red; copings and
signs are porcelain enamel. Below: de-planed passengers and baggage meet under cover on north side*

Ulric Meisel

Of all types of facilities built to serve the needs of modern man, the airport probably demands a higher degree of collaboration among the design professions than any other. There was a time when an airport was primarily a facility for handling airplanes. Under such a premise the engineering aspects of airports dominated their design. However, with the growth of civil air transportation airports have become primarily facilities for handling people — that is, the emphasis has shifted from "planes flying" to "people flying." If airborne freight increases in volume, another shift in emphasis is to be expected. Under such an appraisal, the architectural aspects of airport design have an importance at least equal to the engineering considerations.

We are using the term *architectural* in its broadest sense to connote the designing and planning activities that determine the organization of space so as to fulfill the human and functional requirements that bring a project into being. This ap-

AIRPORT DESIGN:

WHAT constitutes an airport, which renders it susceptible to study by the architect? Every airport, from the smallest to the most complex, from civilian to military, is very much akin to a town plan or neighborhood development. A complex of structures has to be organized in relation to each other as well as with relationship to the runway pattern. A system of streets must be laid out — frequently with separation of high-speed and local traffic; separation of trucks from passenger vehicles. Vehicular parking lots must be laid out in relation to the various buildings they will serve, and sized to accommodate the volume of traffic which each building will generate. Many of the problems confronting the designer of a shopping center will be found since considerable attention must be paid to development of non-aviation revenues. A firehouse and police station must be planned to serve both the building groups and the airfield area. Many airports have, as part of their program, the development of recreational areas to serve both the visiting public and the working population — which will number from one hundred or so upwards to many thousand people. In many cases, the areas sur-

proach affords the sharpest distinction between architecture and engineering. Although the runways may have a ground area many times larger than that of the terminal, administrative and maintenance portions, the latter facilities return several times as much revenue to the airport. A scheme which unduly compresses the terminal area so as to hamper design, limit future expansion, or hinder the flow of passenger and cargo traffic (all *architectural* considerations) will also limit airport income disproportionately and increase the dependence upon subsidy.

The interrelation of functional requirements, engineering considerations, operational procedures, and economic practicability demands the highest degree of collaboration and understanding among the various design professions involved. The study which follows emphasizes the architectural aspects of design of the airport as a whole, a phase of the problem which has not received sufficient consideration in the past.

— THE EDITORS

Avro Jetliner; photo courtesy Society of Automotive Engineers

ITS ARCHITECTURAL ASPECTS

*By Walther Prokosch, A.I.A.**

rounding airports are well suited for development for industry, or parks, or housing, or commerce, or a combination of all of these. All these facilities and many more, including water and sanitary systems, electric power distribution and communications, must be related to the topography and local climate; to the population center which the airport serves; to the neighborhood developments which surround it.

The foregoing remarks apply primarily to civilian airports. For military airbases city planning talents are called for to an even greater extent; here, in addition, provision must be made for housing, community facilities, schools, transportation — in short, every component of a town plan.

Truly, the well conceived airport calls for the intimate collaboration of architect and engineer; for the highest degree of professional service which each can offer. Although the original determination of the runway pattern will result from the studies of the specialist in this field, the inclusion of the architect in the original team will insure that the areas allocated for development of facilities will be adequate and suitable.

THE PROGRAM

The evolution of a program for the various facilities needed on an airport consists of a complex series of calculations which are generally prepared by the airport specialist. However, the steps which are taken in this process should be of interest to the architect since an understanding of them will permit him to be of greater service when the detailed design of structures gets underway. Also, the basic problem is one of circulation, human and vehicular, and hence of coordination of the various parts of the scheme, a problem with which the architect is familiar since this is fundamental to the design of almost every structure. Thus, his participation during this phase can become a healthy stimulant to the thinking of the specialist.

Every study must begin with preparation of traffic forecasts for passenger, airmail and cargo volumes. Forecasts are compounded from a study of the economic character of the community to be served, indications of future economic and industrial growth or stability together with past history of air traffic. Recent compre-

* *Associate, Knappen Tippetts Abbett Engineering Co.; formerly Architect, Engineering Division, Eastern Air Lines*

hensive national traffic estimates have been prepared by the staff of the Port of New York Authority. These indicate an upward trend in air traffic through 1980 based on (1) a continued rise in population, (2) an increase in national income exceeding the rate of growth of population, and (3) progressive improvements in the technological and service characteristics of aircraft which will serve to increase the airline share of total inter-city travel. Thus, it would appear that for all communities, except those which have reached a definite level of stability in population and economic vigor, an air traffic growth rate roughly proportionate to the national average may be anticipated for at least the next thirty years.

Annual traffic estimates are then reduced to estimates of peak hour traffic since the design must be able to accommodate a normal peak period's traffic. An evalua-

analyzing the space requirements of each of the users of the airport. These include air carriers, governmental agencies, local flying establishments (fixed-base operators), concessionaires and the public-passengers and visitors.

The air carriers will furnish their space requirements for various categories such as ticket counters, operations, cargo areas, maintenance shop and overhaul space. The government agencies (Civil Aeronautics Administration, Weather Bureau and others) will, likewise, give their requirements. As a rule, these figures will apply only to the immediate future — for a five- to ten-year period. The designer will have to project these figures to a 20-year requirement so that the Master Plan may provide for future growth. He should evaluate independently the figures given him, to make sure they do not reflect a potential user's possibly undue optimism.

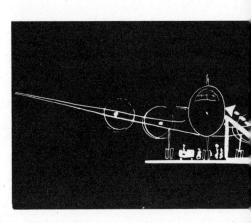

Must the passenger puddle-hop from waiting room to plane,

tion is then made of typical aircraft types which may serve the airport during the period under consideration. A further study is made of the efficiency of utilization of loading positions which may be anticipated.

The division of the peak-hourly traffic by the airplane size (at a given load-factor), and by the utilization factor, will determine the number of airplane loading positions required at the terminal building. This figure is the key to later planning since it determines the size of both the building and the loading apron. The traffic estimates will furnish an indication as to whether the community will be able to support cargo operations in a separate cargo terminal or whether this traffic can be accommodated in the passenger building. If future volume appears sizable and a separate building becomes a part of the program, the steps outlined previously for passenger traffic will be taken in modified form to determine the number of loading positions required for the cargo building.

The next step in building the program consists of

Facilities and structures to be built immediately cannot be designed for this ultimate growth for obvious reasons. It becomes necessary, therefore, for the planner to prepare at least two sets of space requirements: those upon which design for immediate construction will be based; and a set which will indicate the probable limits of expansion.

For every terminal or service area, then, a Master Plan should be prepared. Even though the traffic figures may vary from those predicted when the next stage of construction is required, the Master Plan will have provided space for expansion. Lack of such space has been one of the most serious problems confronting airport management in the past.

In preparing the Master Plan, the designer must examine each component in sufficient detail to permit expansion to be effected economically and with the least possible interference with airport operations. The ultimate pattern of air routes has not been established. Nor has the ultimate in aircraft design — passenger or cargo — been detailed. The extent and timing of the plateau of air traffic volumes can be predicted only within general limits. Thus, the most important consideration, as the planner tackles detailed design of the various buildings and services, becomes flexibility, to be applied to interior arrangement, to increase in overall size and to changes in shape.

NEW TRENDS IN TERMINAL DESIGNS

Most of the following suggestions are oriented toward the terminal which is designed to accommodate a larger volume of traffic, and may not be directly applicable to the more numerous intermediate or smaller stations.

Mechanical Docking

For many years the bane of passenger handling — at least from the passengers' viewpoint — has been the fact

The longitudinal spacing of *airplane loading positions* can be reduced by some 35 ft per position with an attendant reduction in terminal extent and walking distance;

B. A number of movable pieces of *airplane servicing equipment* can be eliminated with attendant reduction in service personnel and increase in working safety;

C. *Service facilities* such as fueling and cabin air-conditioning can be installed and operated with greater economy;

D. A *two-level* plan of *circulation* can be effected with passengers on the upper level, operations on the lower (this is described in greater detail below);

E. Mechanical means of *handling baggage and cargo* can be introduced, reducing manpower and handling time;

F. *The entire cycle of airplane docking, unloading,*

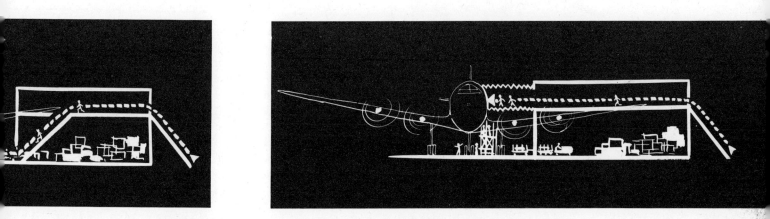

or climb to an exalted upper level only to descend again and mix ingloriously with the baggage? Oh, for some way to get him directly from upper level to plane!

that loading an airplane cannot be accomplished with protection from the elements. Extensible canvas awnings were used at a few airports with meager success. The ubiquitous umbrella almost lent a touch of comedy to the loading process as passenger and agent leaped among the puddles in a dash toward the cabin door.

Recently a device has been developed with the intent of alleviating the loading problem; it is similar to the locomotive transfer table in general use in railroad repair shops. It consists of a pair of tracks each of which supports a dolly. The airplane taxis onto a dolly with each of its main tires, and is then brought toward the loading gate by means of electric-powered cables. Projecting from the terminal is a fixed two-story "finger" with, at its outer end, a short ramp which can be adjusted to varying cabin sill heights.

In addition to permitting the loading of passengers or cargo to proceed on a level and under cover, use of this device permits a number of changes which should increase the efficiency of terminal operation:

loading and departure can be speeded up. (Here lies the key to efficient terminal organization. The investment in terminal facilities is so great that every device must be pressed into service to effect the maximum usefulness of all parts of the terminal.)

G. The estimated *cost of mechanical docking* equipment is such that it will almost be balanced by savings in loading apron paving, such as placing certain service facilities above ground rather than in pits, and other economies.

Two-Level Circulation

A number of existing airport terminal buildings have some form of two-level circulation. The best known example is at Washington National Airport. However, the full measure of planning efficiency has not been explored or attained; at some point the passenger must still go from the upper level down to the ground, and then up to cabin level again. The development of a practical method of loading passengers directly from an upper level onto an airplane gives designers the opportunity to explore and take full advantage of improvements in plan which can result. The fact that many larger railroad terminals have been organized on this basis has caused the normal passenger to expect to be subjected to the operational aspects of a transportation terminal as little as possible. One really cannot assume that a form of transportation has reached maturity until the passenger makes the transition from terra firma to vehicle smoothly and at no personal hazard. The point at issue is that although a number of two-

Illustration courtesy Whiting Corp., New York

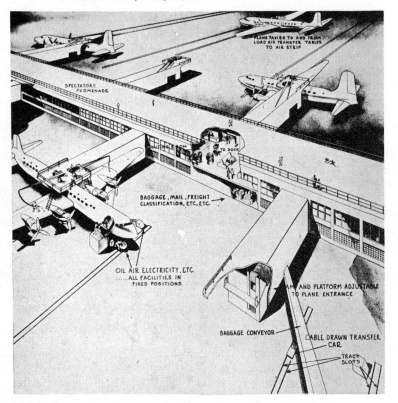

Whiting "Loadair", the loading device discussed in the text, draws planes into position on dollies running on sunken tracks

level schemes exist, there remains a real challenge to develop a plan which will carry this parti to a higher stage of efficiency.

Arrival and Departure Areas

The study of traffic trends, discussed previously, should also give an indication of the type of passenger traffic which will be encountered, i.e. whether preponderantly in-transit or terminating. If the latter predominates, loading positions may be organized on the basis of arrival gates segregated from departure gates. This will result in a number of possible improve-

ments. Actual airplane processing can be speeded up if only one type of operation is handled at a designated gate. The entire terminal plan can be organized around two principal passenger areas — a departure lobby and an arrival lobby. This, in turn, will simplify public circulation; will make it easier for departing passengers to find their way; will make it easier for friends to meet arriving passengers. Concessions can be grouped in a manner which will enhance their effectiveness by making them more accessible to those passengers who have the time and inclination to patronize them. Other advantages will become readily apparent as the problem is studied.

Almost every airport will have some in-transit operation even if the preponderant volume is terminating. The loading gates designated for in-transit traffic can be located between arrival and departure positions so that access for connecting flights can be provided as well as access to departure and arrival lobbies.

Apron Service Facilities

While not an immediate part of the building program, the facilities provided for servicing an airplane at a loading gate should be understood and considered by the designer. The approach in the past has consisted of providing many forms of airplane servicing at each position, including fueling, air-conditioning, water, compressed air, electric power, communications and others. Obviously, the capital outlay entailed is great. Further, this practice implies that a loading position is not only a place for loading the aircraft with its cargo, animate or inanimate, but also a convenient service station.

For the smaller terminal, which caters predominately to in-transit traffic, such an approach will probably continue; it would be uneconomical to unload a few passengers, move the aircraft to another location for servicing and then move it back again to take on more passengers for the next leg of the flight. However, for the "terminating" terminal, serious consideration and analysis must be devoted to determining whether the overall function of the terminal may not be increased and the capital cost reduced by designing the loading gates exclusively for loading (or unloading), and by providing separate service positions within reasonable proximity of, but removed from, the terminal. Again, the objective is to increase the rate of "turn-over" at the loading gates, as it is in every other form of transportation.

Cargo Terminals

Forecasting cargo potential is even more difficult and surrounded with more mystery than forecasting passenger traffic. That a sizable potential does exist is generally admitted, but a precise definition of "sizable" is hard to come by. It is probably safe to say that at smaller terminals the necessity for segregation of cargo from passenger traffic does not present a serious problem. At the intermediate terminal a cargo wing will probably provide the necessary separation of activity. At larger stations, however, consideration should be given to a separate cargo terminal.

While simple in general outline, a cargo terminal will contain elements which require the consideration of competent designers, and again, pioneering effort to develop a new plan peculiarly suited to a new set of conditions. In addition to general warehouse space, the building will contain office space, refrigerated storage space, bonded warehouse space for international terminals, strong rooms for valuable cargo storage and other facilities. The relationship of cargo terminal to service areas must be carefully worked out to provide *good operating characteristics* for the air carrier.

Concessions

In recent years tremendous emphasis has been placed on the development of concessions at airports. In some cases more income is derived from these sources than from the strictly aeronautical sources, and "economic studies" of revenue potential are the order of the day. This, a serious phase of terminal design, must not be neglected; the taxpayer should be relieved of subsidizing airport expenditures as much as possible. For this phase of the work, the architect might be well advised to team up with a financial advisor to determine the types and sizes of concessions to be included.

However, caution must be exercised to preserve the terminal for its primary function: handling passengers. While concessions should be well located and convenient of access, they should not interfere with the direct flow of passenger traffic. In some circles the belief exists that concessions will be more heavily patronized if the passenger must wend his way through a labyrinth of coffee shops and branch banks to get from front door to ticket counter. Actually the reverse is true, as has been amply proved in better planned railroad terminals. The well designed terminal provides first for the most direct circulation of passengers, and then will afford a variety of auxiliary services commensurate with the volume of traffic flowing through the building.

Municipal Airport building, Ramsgate, England; D. Pleydell Bouverie, Architect. Below that, view of Washington, D. C., terminal building (Howard L. Cheney, Architect), showing possibility for future expansion as well as excellent location for concessions

Below, two views of New York's International Airport, Idlewild, which at present has temporary central terminal buildings. At bottom, interior of a recent addition. The transitory nature of this and many another air terminal accurately reflects the many changes within the aviation industry. These cause a confusion of planning ideas which the designer must resolve

POSSIBLE SOURCES of NON-AERONAUTICAL REVENUE		
Terminal Size: Large		
Moderate Sized		
Small		

News Stand / Parcel Check Lockers / Pay Phones / Snack Bar / Taxi Stand / Telegraph Counter / Vending Machines / Auto Service Station / Barber Shop / Coffee Shop / Drug Store / Florist / Gift Shop / Observation Deck / Space for Displays / Bar / Book Store / Branch Bank / Conference Rooms / Guided Tours / Haberdashery / Hairdresser / Hotel / Laundry / Newsreel Theater / Restaurant / Valet

Note: Specific concessions which a terminal can support must be determined for each project.

EAST
BOSTON

WINTHROP

MAIN

SHIP

CHANNEL

ANCHORAGE BASIN

NORTH

Existing
Bulkhead

WIND ROSE

8000

10,000

7000

ALT. 10,000

ALT. 8000

7000

1500'

1500'

7000

1500

ALT. 7000

GOVERNORS
IS.

0   1000   2000   3000   4000   5000

LOGAN INTERNATIONAL AIRPORT
EAST BOSTON, MASSACHUSETTS

Thompson & Lichtner Company, Inc., and
Coolidge, Shepley, Bulfinch & Abbott, Associated Engineers and Architects

---

Design and supervision of construction of facilities carried out under direction of State Airport Management Board, Department of Public Works, and Massachusetts Public Buildings Commission by the associated engineers and architects with special engineering features by Office of Hollis French (heating, ventilation), Thompson Engineering Co. (electrical), Hayden, Harding & Buchanan (drainage), Coffin & Richardson (water supply), Eugene Groden (field lighting).

Since 1922 there has been an airfield of some sort on the State-owned property, most of it recently filled land, now occupied by Logan International Airport. In 1923 the first plane landed there. In 1928 the City of Boston leased the airport; in 1941 the State took it back; in mid-1944 a committee was formed to select a firm to design the facilities shown in these pages. Coolidge, Shepley, Bulfinch & Abbott applied for the job on the basis that the design problem required architectural as much as engineering services. In applying they agreed to associate with the Thompson & Lichtner Co., consulting and management engineers, and when

this engineer-architect combination was awarded the job, Thompson & Lichtner Co. were made the principals. The design team has functioned well; the entire airport has been studied as an architectural problem; four of the six runways have been put in operation and recently the apron building, first of several public terminal structures, was opened.

Before any designing was undertaken the design team was commissioned to survey the terminal facilities required. They took as basic the following factors: 1, a dual, 4-directional runway pattern was already established; 2, minimum distance from the city, with good roads and transit; 3, minimum taxiing distance for planes; 4, continued use of airport during construction; 5, adequate eventual facilities for the type and volume of air traffic expected; 6, provision for future growth; 7, flexibility to permit minimum construction at first, together with adaptability of initial construction to future expansion.

Although the 4-directional runway pattern was well established, none of the six airlines using the airport was satisfied with it. After serious study a 3-directional pattern was unanimously recommended; it was estimated that this would save $2,000,000 in fill, paving, lighting and drainage, and that considering direction,

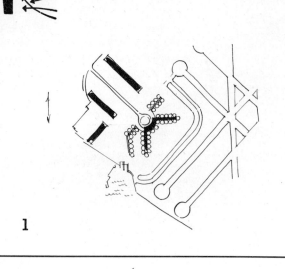

1

2

5

6

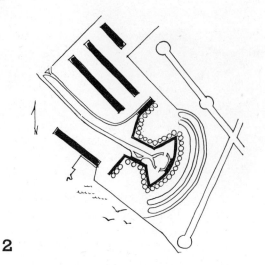

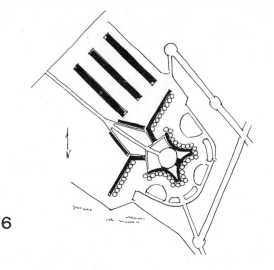

intensity and duration of prevailing winds, eliminating the fourth set of runways would not hamper operations more than ¼ of 1 per cent of the time. With the 3-directional scheme, also, terminal buildings and control tower could be placed closer to the runways. After much discussion the recommendation was adopted. It was subsequently found that the saving to the Commonwealth, based on actual runway construction costs, was $7,000,000.

A passenger traffic estimate was made by Thompson & Lichtner for the 5th, 10th and 20th post-war years. This, now proving of extraordinary accuracy, predicted 3,000,000 passengers per year in 1955, half arrivals and half departures. From these figures peak hourly traffic, the criterion for design, was arrived at from a survey of airport traffic throughout the world. For 1955 the peak hourly estimate was 1852 passengers,* which, in terms of known conventional types of aircraft, would require 84 plane movements (42 landings, 42 take-offs) per hour. A single-runway system can accommodate 60 plane movements per hour; therefore dual runways would be needed by 1955. These, CAA and the airlines agreed, would require a minimum of 30 plane positions on the apron. They also established the size of a plane position as a 150-ft circle on an apron 200 ft wide, or

Building development: Fig. 1, airlines proposed "finger" scheme with 2nd-floor passenger loading for which, at the time, devices had not been perfected; passengers would have to walk, baggage be carried, long distances (see text for discussion). Figs. 2 through 6, schemes for handling passenger, cargo, and international traffic (which must be segregated for customs reasons). Fig. 7, horse-shoe scheme, suggested to increase parking near apron, was found to lengthen walking distances. Figs. 8 and 9 provide parking for 2300 near central building and apron, separate the types of air traffic; and connect buildings to highways leading through Sumner Tunnel under main ship channel to downtown Boston, also to rapid transit system

4500 linear ft of apron for 30 positions. This set the minimum apron for the contemplated runway system.

Centralized vs. decentralized operation was another decision made only after thorough investigation. Washington, D. C., airport is centralized; emplaning passen-

The survey established the peak month as 1/10 of yearly traffic; peak day, 1/27 of monthly traffic; peak hour, 1/6 of daily traffic. Hence:

$$\frac{3,000,000}{10 \times 27 \times 6} = 1852$$

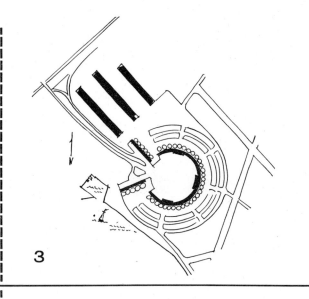

3

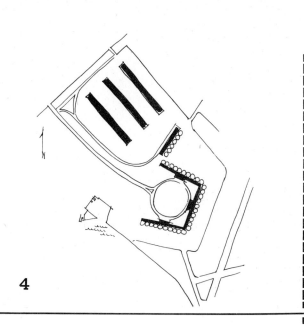

4

7

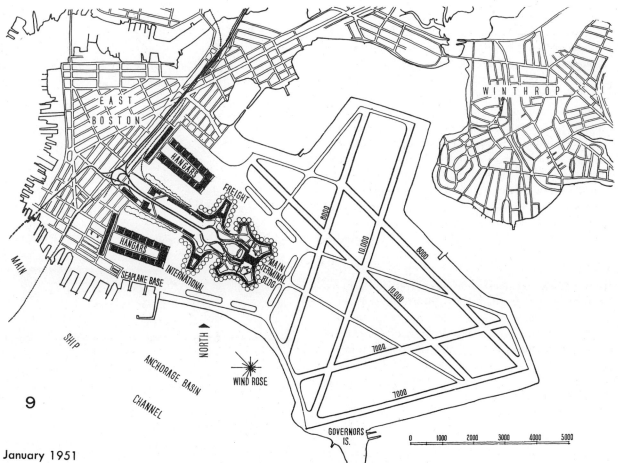

8

9

EAST BOSTON

WINTHROP

HANGARS

FREIGHT

HANGARS

INTERNATIONAL

SEAPLANE BASE

MAIN TERMINAL BLDG.

4,000

10,000

8000

10,000

7000

7000

MAIN

SHIP

ANCHORAGE BASIN

CHANNEL

NORTH

WIND ROSE

GOVERNORS IS.

0   1000   2000   3000   4000   5000

Fay Photo Service Photos

gers go through the central building to their plane; deplaning passengers likewise traverse the central building, going upstairs to the main entrance for a taxi or bus. Centralized baggage checking, both in- and out-bound, further complicates centralized operation; reclaiming baggage takes much too much time. At New York's La Guardia Airport, on the other hand, the apron building, detached, is in front of the central building; taxis and buses meet passengers and baggage close to the plane station. This speeds traffic, but since the central building is separated from the landing field by the apron building, La Guardia's concessions are diminished in value. At Logan, the aim has been to maintain the advantages of both, affording direct access by taxi or bus to the apron building yet preserving for the central building a fine view of the field.

To reach this goal numerous studies were made; several are shown in Figs. 1 through 9 (see page 266). The "finger" plan (1), a favorite of the airlines, was eventually discarded because it committed the airport to centralized operations, limited future development, caused congestion of passenger and plane traffic, increased hazards due to fire and snow, and for several other reasons. Figure 8 shows the scheme ultimately adopted, and 9 is a closely similar scheme shown in relation to the city, to vehicular travel via Sumner Tunnel under the harbor, and to the proposed rapid transit extension.

Requirements for a single airline station, checked with all lines using the airport, determined area (about 6000 sq ft) per station. Note direct access by bus or taxi. Section below shows provisions for second story, designed to permit second-floor loading when this becomes feasible

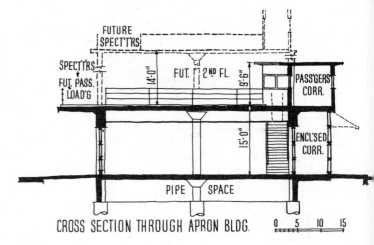

CROSS SECTION THROUGH APRON BLDG.

Ground floor of Apron Building has recently been completed. In it, permanent partitions are provided only around toilets and mechanical rooms. Remainder have been developed according to each airline's needs

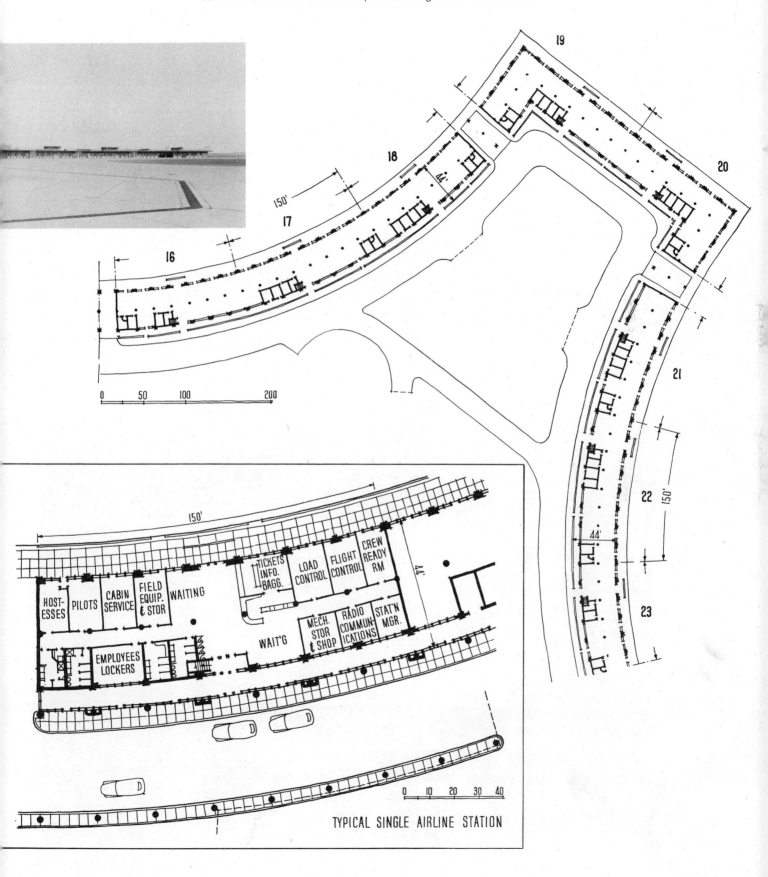

TYPICAL SINGLE AIRLINE STATION

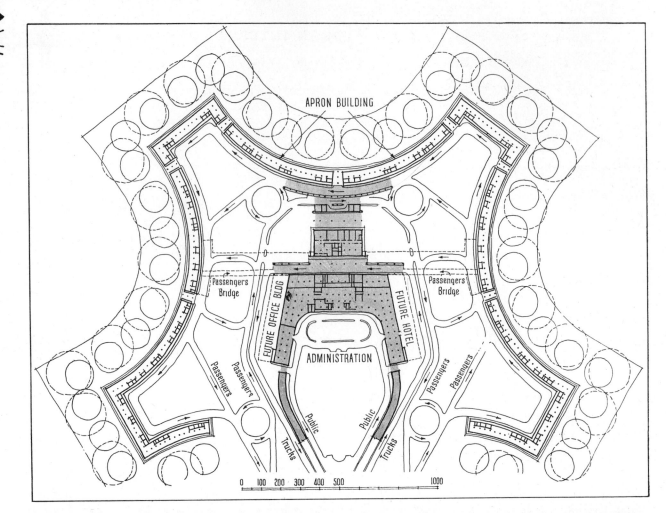

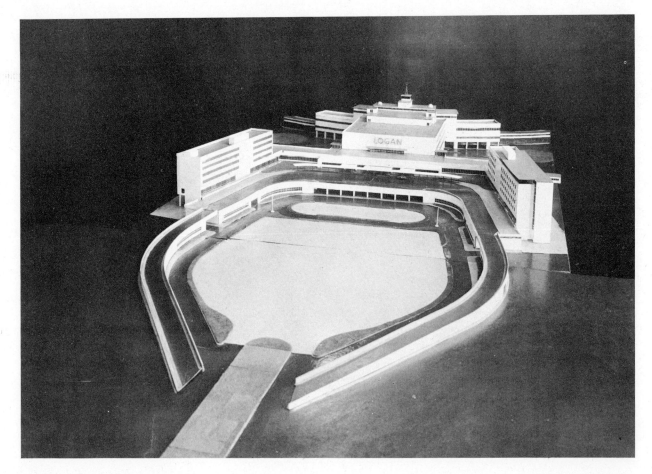

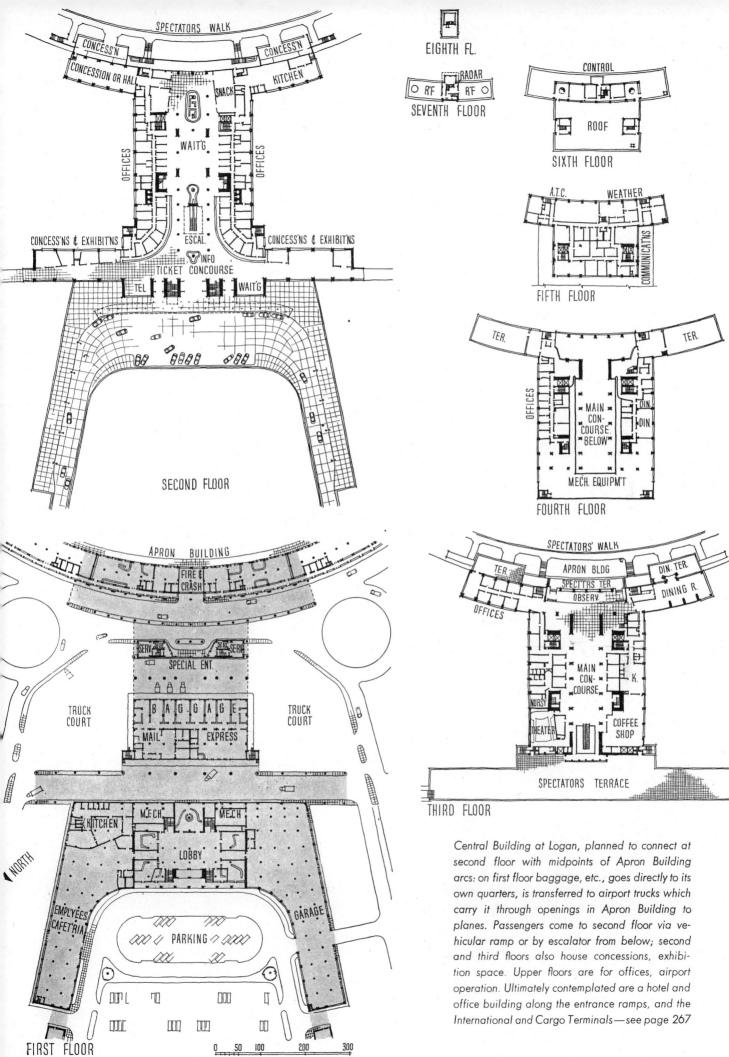

SPECTATORS WALK

CONCESS'N   CONCESS'N

CONCESSION OR HALL   KITCHEN

SNACK

OFFICES   WAIT'G   OFFICES

ESCAL.

CONCESS'NS & EXHIBIT'NS   CONCESS'NS & EXHIBIT'NS

INFO

TICKET CONCOURSE

TEL   WAIT'G

SECOND FLOOR

EIGHTH FL.

R'F   RADAR   R'F

SEVENTH FLOOR

CONTROL

ROOF

SIXTH FLOOR

A.T.C.   WEATHER

COMMUNICAT'NS

FIFTH FLOOR

TER.   TER.

OFFICES   MAIN CON-COURSE BELOW   DIN. DIN.

MECH. EQUIPM'T

FOURTH FLOOR

APRON BUILDING

FIRE & CRASH

SERV   SERV

SPECIAL ENT.

TRUCK COURT   B A G G A G E   TRUCK COURT

MAIL   EXPRESS

NORTH

KITCHEN   MECH   MECH

LOBBY

EMPL'YEES CAFET'RIA   GARAGE

PARKING

FIRST FLOOR

0   50   100   200   300

SPECTATORS' WALK

TER.   APRON BLDG   DIN. TER.

SPECT'RS TER

OFFICES   OBSERV.   DINING R.

MAIN CON-COURSE   K.

NURS'Y

THEATER   COFFEE SHOP

SPECTATORS TERRACE

THIRD FLOOR

Central Building at Logan, planned to connect at
second floor with midpoints of Apron Building
arcs: on first floor baggage, etc., goes directly to its
own quarters, is transferred to airport trucks which
carry it through openings in Apron Building to
planes. Passengers come to second floor via vehicular ramp or by escalator from below; second
and third floors also house concessions, exhibition space. Upper floors are for offices, airport
operation. Ultimately contemplated are a hotel and
office building along the entrance ramps, and the
International and Cargo Terminals—see page 267

STAPLETON AIRFIELD, DENVER,

G. Meredith Musick, Architect

THE design of Denver airport's terminal facilities, like those of most airports large and small throughout the country, has undergone many changes over a period of several years. Shifts in airline and municipal policies, changes in aircraft design, post-World-War-II conditions such as availability of materials, costs of construction, all affected the terminal's status. Complicating the problem further is the fact that one of the largest airlines, United, has selected Stapleton Airfield as the site for its Operating Base. Now it appears that the nearly three million dollar scheme shown in the rendering above will achieve substantial completion: its central portion (outlined in white), containing public spaces and restaurants, was completed early this year; a second unit, the airlines office building (at left of rendering) is out for bid as this is written.

The architectural firm of G. Meredith Musick was retained by the City of Denver in the winter of 1944–45 to work on the terminal buildings. In 1947, with average scheduled aircraft movements at just over 100 per day, Denver ranked 10th in air traffic in the country;

the situation is hardly less acute today. To relieve it, plans for the successive steps into which the entire project is divided are to be released as soon as possible for bidding. Of these, Schedule 1 is the office building referred to; it comes first to make way for succeeding steps. Schedule 1-A, one of the key steps, includes ticket offices, remodeling and material expansion of the present 3-story administration building (see following pages) and not only facilities for getting passengers to and from planes under cover, but also complete mechanical baggage-handling systems and other travel conveniences. Schedule 1-B comprises services: sanitary and storm sewers, and a new steam main. Schedule 2 includes the 5-level control tower (rendering at right) which, it is expected, will be built at the same time as the office building. Schedule 3, the detached building between the control tower and the completed structure, is to house the U. S. Post Office and to provide space for air cargo.

In arriving at this design, the architect had the advantage of being early appointed a member of an ad-

COLORADO

Rendering above shows ultimate building development being undertaken in stages: left, airlines office building; center unit, airport administration, passenger facilities and concessions; right, post office and cargo terminal; above that and detail at right, control tower

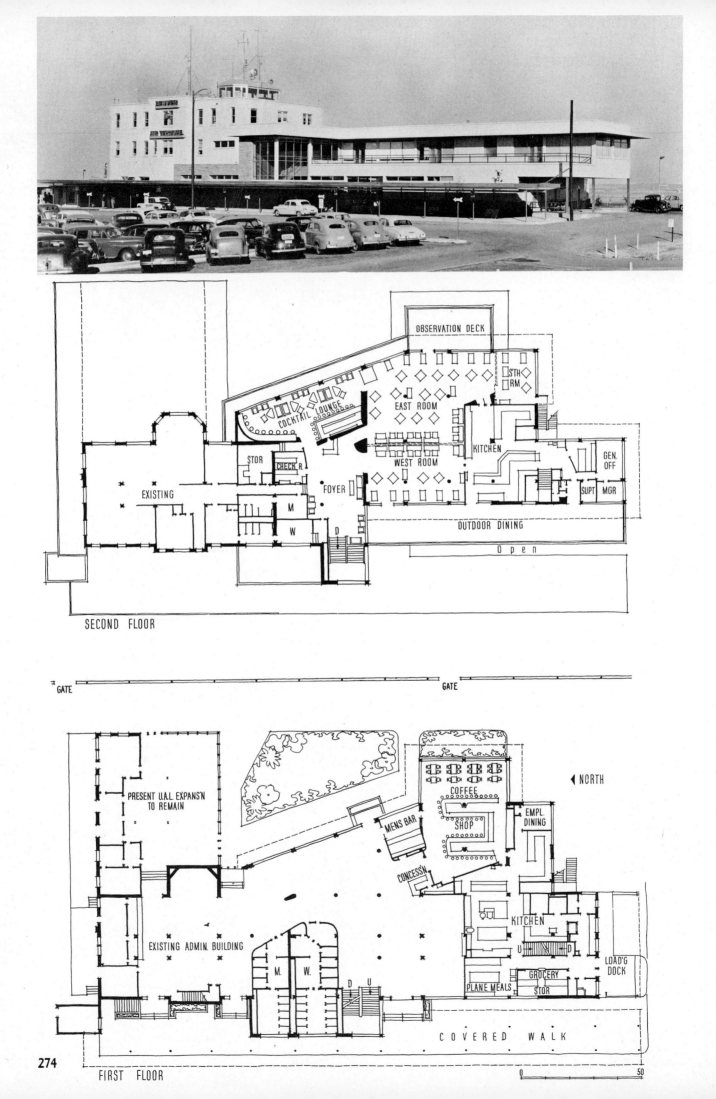

OBSERVATION DECK

STH RM

COCKTAIL LOUNGE

EAST ROOM

KITCHEN

GEN. OFF

STOR

CHECK R.

WEST ROOM

EXISTING

FOYER

SUPT MGR

M

W

D

OUTDOOR DINING

Open

SECOND FLOOR

GATE

GATE

NORTH

PRESENT U.A.L. EXPANS'N
TO REMAIN

COFFEE
SHOP

MENS BAR

EMPL.
DINING

CONCESS'N

KITCHEN

EXISTING ADMIN. BUILDING

M.

W.

D U

PLANE MEALS

GROCERY
STOR

LOAD'G
DOCK

COVERED WALK

274

FIRST FLOOR

0   50

STAPLETON AIRFIELD, DENVER

visory committee which was formed to study the terminal problem. Other members were representatives of the major airlines concerned; the committee's chairman was then Mr. George E. Cranmer, at that time Denver's Manager of Improvements and Parks. The committee was concerned with the over-all airport problem, including many phases beyond the architect's immediate concern, ranging from future runways to zoning of the surrounding area. Location of the passenger terminal building was thus determined with full knowledge of the other airport factors involved, including airport-to-city transportation and access roads.

One early solution for the terminal building placed public and other non-operating spaces to one side, in a reverse-curved plan; at first this was highly regarded, but thorough consideration brought the realization that such a scheme virtually prevented future expansion. Eventually the "unit" system, with units in a straight line and with no projecting "fingers", was adopted. (The architect, in discussing the scheme before the Chicago Chapter, A.I.A., in February 1947, deplored what was then an apparently insurmountable difficulty: getting passengers from terminal to plane without exposing them to the weather!)

It is estimated that the new Airlines Office Building, Schedule 1 of the project, will cost over $1,300,000 to build. It is to be

Portion of central building now completed is shown above on facing page, from parking area. Before the existing three-story office unit can be remodeled, the new airlines office building is to be built; after that, administrative and passenger facilities will be added to the present structure, much of which houses concessions. Photos show new Sky Chef areas: second floor foyer, bar and restaurant

D. L. Hopwood Photos

STAPLETON AIRFIELD, DENVER

460 ft long, 2 stories high, with part basement, and will contain 82,000 sq ft. It is to have an unusual, dual heating and ventilating system, using steam from a central boiler plant at Stapleton's Modification Center. Tempered ventilating air is to be supplemented by room convectors which will be connected to refrigerated water for summer cooling as well as to hot water for winter heating. There are to be under-floor ducts for all wiring, and, probably, thin-tube fluorescent lighting.

Below, rendering, Airlines Office Building on which bids have just been taken. Extensive space is needed because United Air Lines maintains its Operating Base at Stapleton

Rendering Courtesy United Air Lines

AIRPORT, YUMA COUNTY, ARIZONA

Edward L. Varney Associates, Architects and Engineers

Y UMA COUNTY'S airport is an example of the small "way station" type. Yuma is a town of about 10,000, located on the Arizona-California border. One air line now connects Yuma with Los Angeles, which means two planes a day. It is expected that another air line will soon connect it with Phoenix and the East; and since the surrounding truck farming region is growing rapidly as irrigation is extended, there are commercial possibilities.

These and other factors influenced the County authorities to provide more extensive facilities than present traffic justifies. The field, a former Army training field, has three excellent runways; the terminal building has been remodeled from an old World War II structure which cost the County nothing to acquire. The building was moved across the field, set on new concrete foundations and floors, and its interior was subdivided as indicated in plan. The fenestration was revamped and porches were added East and West to shield the new glass walls of the main portion. Construction cost was slightly over $52,300. Much of the contract cost went for mechanical services and electrical requirements of the Weather Bureau and C.A.A.

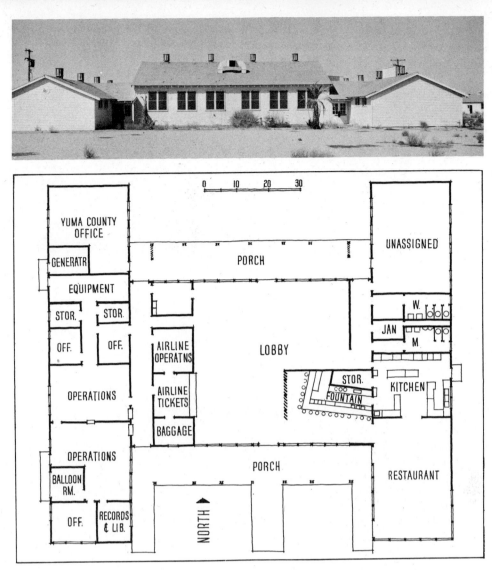

Top of page, old Army structure which was moved across Yuma Airport's field and remodeled into the pleasant terminal building shown below

Stuart Weiner Photo

Stuart Weiner Photos

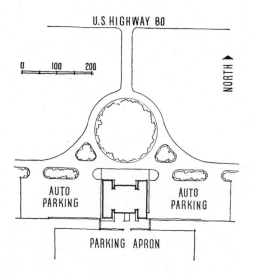

Wide porches shelter the glass walls of the lobby. Terminal, larger than present traffic requires, was economically converted from an existing disused military structure

Snack bar and fountain, below, are partially shielded from lobby by a louvered wood screen

STANDARD UNIT SCHEME VARIED TO SPEED

Hedrich-Blessing Studio Photo

Paul Gerhardt, Jr.

City Architect

Hedrich-Blessing Studio Photo

AIRPORT TRAFFIC

Chicago Municipal Airport Terminal

AN extended unit scheme helps allay confusion for some 2,500,000 passengers accommodated yearly in the Chicago Municipal Airport Terminal: each air line has individual facilities to serve its planes and passengers. Two lines share each waiting room. A corridor links units to the central block housing administration, operational space and concessions. The two major zones, air and ground transport, are bridged by a narrow plan, permitting short, direct flow of separated passenger and baggage traffic. Casual spectators have good observation posts, removed from operational activities, in a central public space and promenade roof deck.

The building was designed as low cost construction to be amortized within 10 years. Planning for a longer period was deemed unwise: perpetual change is expected in aviation requirements. For flexibility, the steel structure uses a module of 3 ft 4 in. longitudinally, six units to a bay. Exterior walls are buff-tinted concrete slabs, backed by concrete block; roof is poured gypsum.

CHICAGO AIRPORT

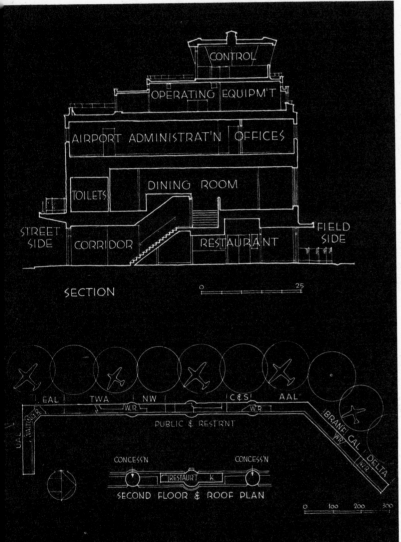

SECTION

SECOND FLOOR & ROOF PLAN

Hedrich-Blessing Studio Photo

Compact, private working space for airport operation and administration is provided on top floors of central tower. Glazed control room has remote controls for field lights, radar, radio and recording devices. Equipment is on floor below and in basement. Building is 40 ft wide, almost ⅓ mile long; has stations for 15 planes

Five waiting rooms (three shown below left) serve nine air lines. Each line has separate baggage rooms, ticket counters and offices. Design standards for furniture, signs, etc., set by air lines and architect. Counter design at top left provides extra baggage space, facilitates traffic. Floors are asphalt tile, ceilings acoustic plaster. Partitions are gypsum tile and plaster, built free of structure for easy change

Concessions help defray airport operating costs. Revenue is derived from parking meters, promenade deck, lockers, clocks and, above all, eating facilities. Main dining room overlooks field (above right), shares second floor of central tower with kitchens. Restaurant on first floor (below right) is served by dumbwaiters, remains open 24 hours a day. Refreshment stands are in flanking towers on promenade deck. Refrigerators and locker rooms are in basement

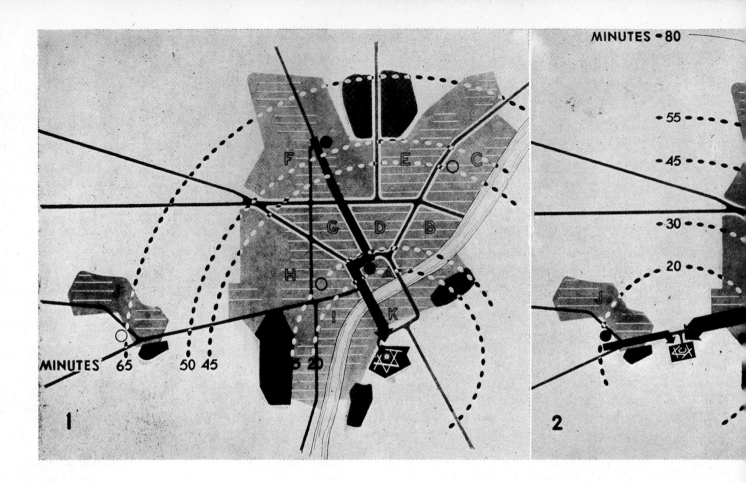

MINUTES 65 50 45

1

2

ESTABLISHING

LEGEND

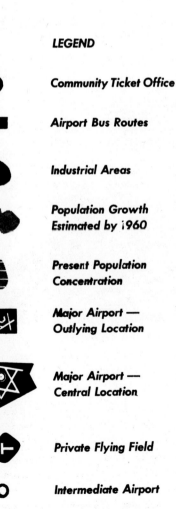

● **Community Ticket Office**

▬ **Airport Bus Routes**

◆ **Industrial Areas**

◆ **Population Growth Estimated by 1960**

▬ **Present Population Concentration**

⬛ **Major Airport — Outlying Location**

⬛ **Major Airport — Central Location**

⬢ **Private Flying Field**

○ **Intermediate Airport**

● **Private Flying Fields**

TYPICAL AIPRORT PLANNING SURVEY MAPS

1. **Driving Time. Major Airport. Central Location.** Map indicates that approximately 65 per cent of the air passengers will have a driving time of 45 minutes or less to an airport located directly across the river from the central business and hotel district. A central ticket office in area ''A'' and another in ''F'', with ground transportation between these and the airport will amply serve. Public attendance expected, 800,000 per year by 1960

2. **Driving Time. Major Airport. Outlying Location.** Map indicates that only approximately 40 per cent of all air passengers will have a driving time of 45 minutes or less to an airport located 20 miles west of the center of the city. In this case ticket offices are located at centers in areas ''A'', ''C'', ''F'', and ''H'' with ground transportation from each to the airport. Public attendance at this port would be chiefly in good driving weather, which in the northern states might be limited to less than 250 days per year and be further limited to summer evenings, weekends and holidays because of distance. Yearly attendance on this basis is expected to reach 300,000 by 1960 if good spectator facilities are provided

3. Map indicating the location of all airports in the region. The private flying field chosen for illustration is one of several serving area ''J'' with its population of 70,000 in 1950 and 90,000 in 1960. Area ''J'' has a college enrollment of approximately 20,000 students at present. Approximately 100 planes would be based at this point

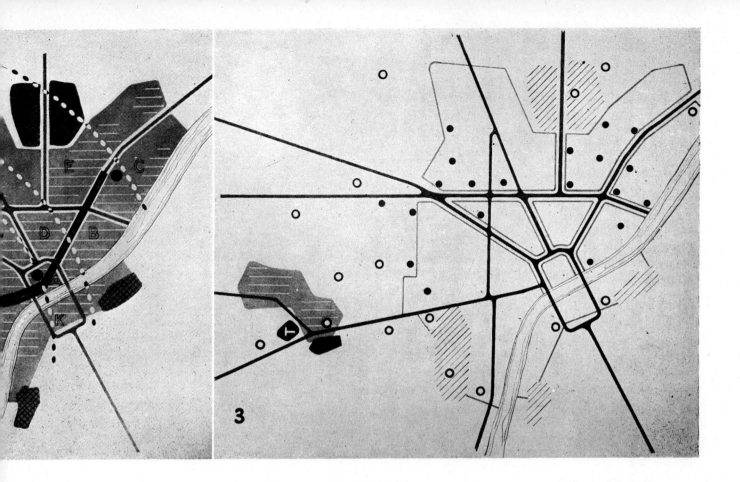

AN AIRPORT PLANNING PROGRAM

By Smith, Hinchman & Grylls, Inc.,

Architects and Engineers

IN a previous article entitled "Airport Programming Analyzed,"* we said: "Any competent airport survey sets up a master plan, not all of which can be built at once. The time factor is as important as the space pattern. An orderly sequence of development has advantages too obvious to require discussion."

Further, it should be said that a competent airport survey will provide the basic data necessary to establish an Airport Planning Program for any site within the region covered by the survey.

A program based on the needs of aircraft operations, maintenance and storage, as well as those of cargo, mail, passenger, private flier and spectator potential, should be established to meet the growing needs as set up in the survey and report. Only in this way can an economically sound base be laid for both present and future operations at any airport.

The tendency in the past has been to lay principal stress on the engineering factors of airport planning

* *Architectural Record*, April, 1947, pages 103–108.

with no program established to guide the engineer and architect in the long range requirements of an airport. Previously built airports have been used as guides to space-use patterns. These examples no longer serve that purpose.

No attempt is made in this article to deal with the everyday engineering encountered in airport design. These aspects have been treated at great length in handbooks, texts, and many publications.

Good engineering design of the paving, drainage, lighting and buildings will result in economical construction and lessen the annual maintenance costs. But the best engineering of these items will not make an ineffective layout effective, nor will the most beautiful buildings accommodate the efficient organization of the various functions to be performed therein unless the proper relationships between these functions is incorporated in the original plan.

The office of an architect-engineer staffed with personnel qualified to set up this program acts as the

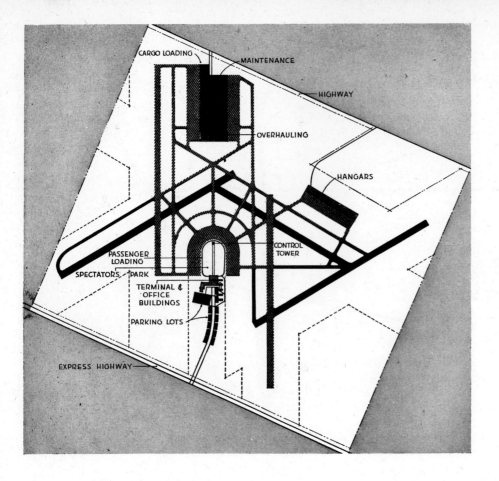

CARGO LOADING
MAINTENANCE
HIGHWAY
OVERHAULING
HANGARS
PASSENGER LOADING
CONTROL TOWER
SPECTATORS PARK
TERMINAL & OFFICE BUILDINGS
PARKING LOTS
EXPRESS HIGHWAY

The windrose analysis for each of the two major airport sites indicates that an open parallel 60° runway pattern will provide 99 per cent wind coverage and a field capacity of 120 plane movements per hour in contact operations. The survey indicates 50 plane movements per peak hour in 1950 and 90 in 1960. It is expected that with the successful development of swivel landing gear only two runways will be required to provide the necessary wind coverage at this airport. As indicated only two of the five runways shown would be required at such time as swivel landing gear is applied to all planes

owner's representative in the formative stages of each site development. Preliminary plans based on this program should be used in all lease negotiations.

Basic survey and report data to be used in the planning program should include:

1. **Air passenger potential**
2. **Air cargo potential**
3. **Air mail potential**
4. **Student flier potential**
5. **Private plane owner potential**
6. **Meteorological data**
7. **Market analysis**
8. **Land use**

Based on this data, supplemented by detail surveys and collaboration with designated airport authorities and the airline or fixed base operators, the development of an airport planning program can be accomplished.

SCOPE OF AIR OPERATIONS

The scope of air operations at any major scheduled service airport is determined primarily by the air passenger, mail and cargo potential and the extent of maintenance required to meet these needs. Similarly, the scope of air operations for the smaller or private flying and intermediate fields is determined by the volume of private flying, charter service and airline feeder service and the extent of ground service and storage necessary to meet these needs.

At major airports where provision must be made for scheduled passenger service ranging in distances from cross-country and international to the short feeder line distances, as well as mail and cargo service, the volume of peak hour and peak day plane movements will be determined by the type and capacity of planes used to develop schedules necessary to meet this volume of air travel.

At the private fields, provision must be made to operate and hangar the smaller planes necessary to meet the needs of private plane owner, student flier and charter service assigned to this field in the survey as well as ground service facilities for these aircraft.

The intermediate fields will require similar provisions as well as those necessary to meet the needs of feeder or local airlines operations and service.

RUNWAYS AND LANDING STRIPS

The wind rose has been and still is a prime factor in determining the alignment of runways and landing strips. However, there are several points which merit thorough analysis in using the wind rose information. First of all, an airport wind rose is an item of composite nature and should, if possible, be broken down to its velocity components and an analysis made of those velocities above 10 miles per hour. It is the high winds which should be used in determining the runway layout for an exclusive transport terminal or for a field which is to be used by both transport and personal flying.

Cross wind landing gear, which is now nearing a workable stage of development, when finally adopted for use

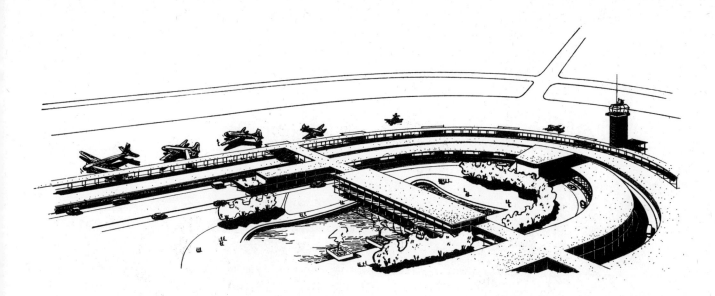

Terminal Plan — Major Airport — Central Location

At this site, considering the shorter driving time, it is entirely reasonable to expect that as many as 50 per cent of the region's air passengers may be ticketed at the airport terminal and that this same percentage may arrive in private cars or taxis, the remainder being ticketed at one of the city ticket offices and arriving in airline limousines or buses. The growth in air passenger potential from 1950 to 1960 requires the terminal area development to be flexible and if necessary expandable to meet growth and the changing needs. For example: the first stage of development in 1950 will require 14 plane spots and all weather loading from second level and 22 in 1960. All passenger handling, plane service and other ramp operations are on a consolidated operations basis. The enplaning passenger leaves his car or airline limousine at road level and point of baggage check-in and proceeds by escalator to second level ticketing, lounges, rest rooms, or directly to gate of plane departure. At this point he is checked in by a ticket agent and boards his plane by way of an all weather gangway. Guests of air passengers have access to air passenger lounge. The public has a separate entrance and a spectators' promenade at second level in common with shopping and recreational facilities

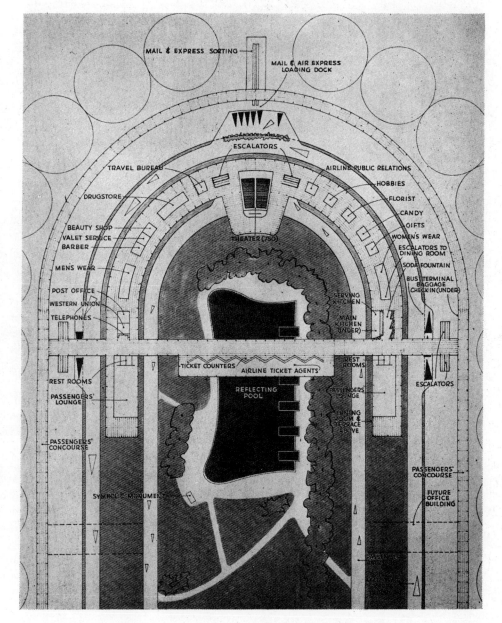

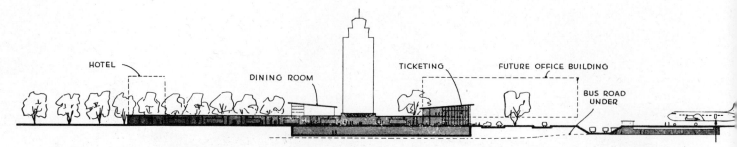

Section through terminal building

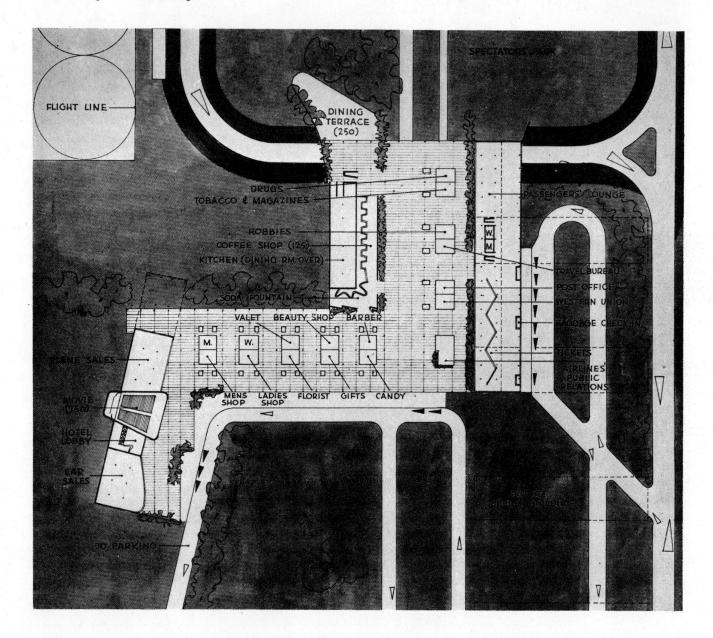

**Terminal Plan — Major Airport —
Outlying Location**

With 60 per cent of the air passengers in the region having a driving time of over 45 minutes it can be safely assumed that at least 75 per cent of these passengers will arrive, pre-ticketed, by airline bus or limousine. These passengers will go directly to their plane gates. The remaining passengers arriving in private cars, public bus or taxi will go to the ticket office and from there by an airport bus which serves all plane gates. A major airport in this location, we feel, will be a fair weather port as far as public attendance is concerned. For that reason the scheme illustrated indicates a spectators' park reached by passing through a shopping arcade

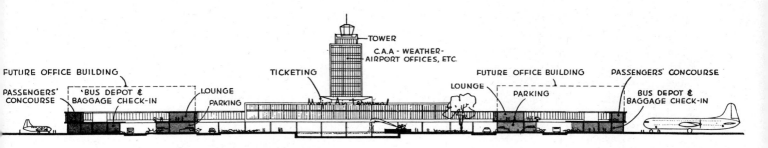

FUTURE OFFICE BUILDING

PASSENGERS' CONCOURSE

BUS DEPOT & BAGGAGE CHECK-IN

LOUNGE PARKING

TICKETING

TOWER

C.A.A - WEATHER- AIRPORT OFFICES, ETC.

FUTURE OFFICE BUILDING

LOUNGE PARKING

PASSENGERS' CONCOURSE

BUS DEPOT & BAGGAGE CHECK-IN

Section through Terminal Building at an airport centrally located

on all planes in scheduled, non-scheduled, and private flying, will require approximately one-third the area now needed to achieve the necessary wind coverage in airport planning. Full cognizance should be taken of this possibility in the development of a runway pattern for the ultimate or master plan.

While the wind rose analysis and the obstruction map will determine the alignment of runways and landing strips, their relative positions in the layout and their lateral positions will be determined by the ground traffic patterns. A study of the volume and the types of operations with respect to wind directions and frequencies will show which ground traffic pattern will be the most efficient compromise with the location of the terminal and building areas. Construction costs should not be the only criterion in developing the landing area design because the capital expenditure is a non-recurring expense, but excessive ground time is an ever increasing item of expense to operators.

TIME IS MONEY

Minutes can be added or subtracted from the plane movement time at this point of design. The importance of providing an efficient airport plan is emphasized by consideration of the cost of one additional minute of taxiing or waiting time based on an operating cost of $120 per hour, $90 per hour and $6 per hour, which are

comparable to the cost of operating four-engine transport, twin-engine transport and light aircraft. The number and position of taxiways will have an important effect on not only the cost of using the airport in excessive ground time, but also in the capacity of the airport. The *position* of taxiways is most important in the case of airports anticipating a large volume of transport type operations while the *number* of taxiways or taxilanes is most important in effectuating the capacity of a landing strip in light plane operations. This is particularly true where the ultimate expected volume of occupancy anticipates periods of use where simultaneous parallel landing will have to be permitted in order to reduce plane circling time during peak periods.

One of the most difficult problems facing the air transport industry is that of retaining airport capacities during instrument conditions up to the capacity in effect during contact conditions. Air navigation facilities designed to assist landings and take-offs under instrument conditions for the most part operate at frequencies which are influenced by moving or stationary objects in the field of the instrument. The planning program should include the installation of such equipment, especially at those airports anticipating either scheduled operations or an appreciable volume of cargo or other non-scheduled movements. This places additional limitations in planning, particularly in the location of buildings, including hangars, and the position of highways, railroads and

Perspective of Terminal Building at an outlying airport

electrical power transmission lines with respect to the runway ends and approach areas.

Whether a major airport is to be a terminal base for *all* of the airline operators (with provision for all line inspection and repairs, including motor and airframe overhaul, as well as hangar storage) or would include only a *portion* of these, depends upon the location of the port in relation to the scheduled air routes of the airlines using the port.

Resolving the peak-hour plane movements into plane positions on the ramp involves the analysis of the types of planes operating and the length of time and facilities required to service these ships. **Due consideration must be given to the advantages of consolidated ramp service and its consequent savings in personnel and equipment.**

PASSENGER TRAFFIC CONTROL

The method of handling on and off passengers and their baggage at all major airports (including line stops with low passenger potential and those with a high passenger potential as well as terminal ports, where the volume of transfer passengers becomes an important factor) will be determined by the distribution of this air passenger volume in the communities served by the airport. This will also be a factor in the determination of ground transportation and the ultimate location of airline ticket offices in relation to these community centers.

The method of passenger handling will determine to a large extent the number of passengers arriving at the airport pre-ticketed and the consequent extent of passenger facilities to be provided. At an outlying port where driving time is excessive and which is served by community ticket offices, passenger facilities may be reduced to a minimum. The same is true of a landing field which serves only as a ground to air transfer point. Public interest at such a port is at a minimum and will require a build-up of supplementary non-air facilities to encourage attendance and revenue from this source.

Whether the major airport has a central or an outlying location, all-weather protection for the passenger should be provided from point of ticketing to plane. Second level loading is favorably considered by most airlines, but the problem of all-weather protection from here to the plane remains unsolved chiefly because of the varying positions of plane loading doors and floor levels.

Segregation of air passengers from the general public is desirable to the extent that it will permit a free flow of passenger traffic from airline lounges and ticket offices to their planes and still provide supplementary facilities such as dining rooms, shops, Western Union, etc., which are easily accessible and visible to passenger and public alike.

The air passenger arriving at the terminal should be able to weigh and check in his baggage at the point of leaving the limousine, taxi or airline bus. For the convenience of the air passenger driving his own car, provision might be made to have an attendant take his car from the point of baggage check-in to a parking area.

Passengers departing from the air terminal should be able to pick up their baggage as their car is delivered to them.

Transfer passengers, as usual at present, would have no contact with their baggage at transfer points. Distribution of baggage would be handled to and from three points on the ramp: (1) point of entry and check-in; (2) point of exit and check-out and from a central transfer point by light motor trucks circulating free of passengers; and (3) terminal area service traffic.

At line stops and terminal airports provision should be made for airline public relations, ticket agents, airline communications and ramp offices for both plane servicing and passenger check-in as well as the general office space required by the airlines. Consolidation of ticketing and baggage handling now being considered by the airlines operating from the larger ports will result in a considerable saving of space as well as airline personnel.

OFFICES AND SUPPORTING FACILITIES

The flight control tower and office should be centrally located to afford an unobstructed view of the field and ramp. Space will be determined by CAA on the basis of volume of operations at the airport, as will be the general office space required by CAA.

Weather Bureau space should be provided as required. This space and CAA offices may be in isolated structures apart from the terminal building.

Post office and air express space requirements will be based on the volume established by the survey and collaboration with the Postal Authorities and the Air Express Company. This space should be located along the ramp in a position central to the ultimate number of plane positions.

Many supporting facilities necessary to the maintenance of field, ramp and terminal area service must be provided in the terminal area of a major airport, such as: space for a first aid station; ambulance and fire and crash trucks at central position on the ramp; kitchen service for meals aloft as well as for public dining rooms and coffee shop. Provision must be made for locker rooms and cafeteria service for terminal area employees, offices for the airport director and staff, and in some instances, offices for the regional airport authority.

The patterns of population distribution and transportation in relation to the airport site have a definite bearing on the number and extent of supplementary non-air facilities to be provided at any airport for the convenience and recreation of public, passengers, and private fliers. The population distribution as established in the report, when considered in relation to their driving, recreational and shopping habits will determine the kind and the extent of these facilities at the particular airport under consideration. A large per cent of the airport's revenue will be realized from this source and the kind and quality of these services must be carefully approximated to insure their successful operation. The location of these facilities in relation to each other and to the passenger handling program must be carefully studied, bearing in mind the desirability of passenger circulation segregation without isolating these facilities which must be available to passenger and public alike. The volume of business done by these facilities at a major port will be large and the careful selection of competent operators for each is of utmost importance to a continued high standard overall operation.

The airport plan as a whole, and in its many details of air and non-air operations, should fit into the projected land use patterns of the community with a minimum of inconvenience to these operations and become an integral part of the region's transportation system.

The balance sheet of land costs, land development

thority and responsibility for the development, operation, financing and management has been vested in a Metropolitan Airport Authority. This area, like many of our metropolitan centers of industry and business, is divided by a navigable river which is an important factor in the transportation of raw materials and finished manufactured products. The total population is at present 3,000,000 and is expected to reach 3,500,000 by 1960.

The report indicates a need for one major, 14 intermediate and 22 private-flying airports by 1960. Passenger distribution into areas of origin and termination is generally the resultant of population distribution by income, the volume of industry, and the travel habits of

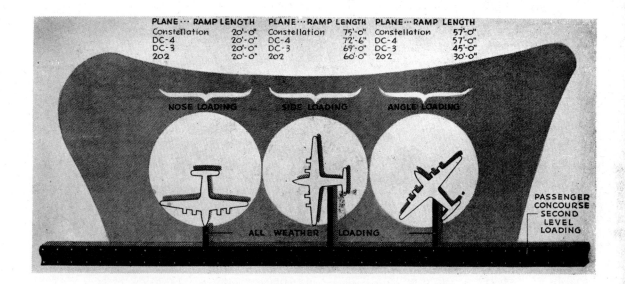

PLANE	RAMP LENGTH	PLANE	RAMP LENGTH	PLANE	RAMP LENGTH
Constellation	20'-0"	Constellation	75'-0"	Constellation	57'-0"
DC-4	20'-0"	DC-4	72'-6"	DC-4	57'-0"
DC-3	20'-0"	DC-3	69'-0"	DC-3	45'-0"
202	20'-0"	202	60'-0"	202	30'-0"

NOSE LOADING SIDE LOADING ANGLE LOADING

ALL WEATHER LOADING

PASSENGER CONCOURSE SECOND LEVEL LOADING

All weather passenger loading may soon be considered a must at major air terminals and at line stops along routes served by the larger ships. Its general acceptance will be dependent upon its flexibility, cost of construction and simplicity of operation. Nose loading forward of the inboard nacelle affords the shortest distance for a covered gangway between plane and second level loading. All weather loading at an outlying air terminal, as shown on page 288, might consist of passenger concourses under the ramp from the bus station to a hydraulic lift terminating at the plane entrance

costs, financing charges, maintenance costs, and operational costs, together with the revenues to be derived from all sources will determine the relative advantages of different sites under consideration and when considered with the operational aspects of each site will provide a basis for the selection and development of a sound "Airport Planning Program" for each stage of development.

THE EXAMPLE ILLUSTRATED

To illustrate some of the factors contributing to the preparation of an "Airport Planning Program" we assume that a survey and report have been completed for a region some sixty miles in diameter and that full au-

each. These can well be defined, as in illustrations No. 1 and 2, by major cross-city expressways. The areas shown are generally larger than any of the elementary junior or high school communities which are often used as a basis for planning the community life of a city, and represent a combination of these school communities defined by the expressway and transportation system of a metropolitan area.

The following data is then taken from the report to establish a close approximation of the air needs and the contributing non-air needs of the regional airports.

For scheduled passenger service the report indicates 340 plane movements per day in 1950 and 580 in 1960. For cargo service, 25 plane movements per day are indicated for 1950 and 60 for 1960. (See tabulation below.)

The economic characteristics of school communities, such as income, available shopping money and shopping habits, when combined in areas designated as passenger distribution areas, will indicate the dollar volume from which non-air revenue is to be drawn. This volume when considered in relation to the driving time to the airport and the driving habits of the area will indicate the revenue dollars in sales to be expected from the various concessions and services at specific airport sites.

Analysis of all air requirements, collaboration with the operators and airport authorities will likewise establish space use and functions for all areas including field and buildings at each stage of development.

The combined needs of air and non-air operations translated into area requirements in terms of square feet and development costs, then becomes a part of the region's financial program.

Area		Population	High School Communities	Air Passengers	Private & Rental Planes	Pilots
A	1950	370,000	7	350,000	250	500
	1960	325,000	7	650,000	450	1,000
B	1950	210,000	4	60,000	320	650
	1960	240,000	5	150,000	400	800
C	1950	110,000	2	250,000	1,550	3,100
	1960	160,000	3	800,000	1,850	3,700
D	1950	215,000	4	30,000	120	260
	1960	257,000	5	75,000	175	350
E	1950	90,000	2	135,000	80	150
	1960	175,000	3	300,000	150	300
F	1950	120,000	3	200,000	760	1,600
	1960	180,000	4	750,000	825	1,950
G	1950	350,000	7	350,000	2,200	4,600
	1960	375,000	8	900,000	2,500	5,450
H	1950	165,000	3	50,000	320	900
	1960	200,000	4	125,000	400	1,250
I	1950	190,000	4	85,000	100	260
	1960	220,000	4	270,000	150	375
J	1950	70,000	2	80,000	320	800
	1960	90,000	2	200,000	400	1,075
K	1950	70,000	2	20,000	80	150
	1960	80,000	2	80,000	100	200
Outlying Area						
	1950	1,040,000	20	390,000	700	1,500
	1960	1,198,000	24	700,000	900	1,900
Total						
	1950	3,000,000		2,000,000	6,800	1,500
	1960	3,500,000		5,000,000	8,300	18,350
Air Mail						
	1950	8,400 Tons				
	1960	12,000 Tons				
Air cargo						
	1950	37,000 Tons				
	1960	92,000 Tons				

Provision is made for complete maintenance and storage of 100 small planes at this post as well as classrooms for student fliers, overnight accommodations for transient fliers and airplane sales. To provide better facilities for the private flier and ensure successful operation at the field, a restaurant lounge and overnight facilities are located adjacent to the highway. This is also a means of creating public interest in the airport

292

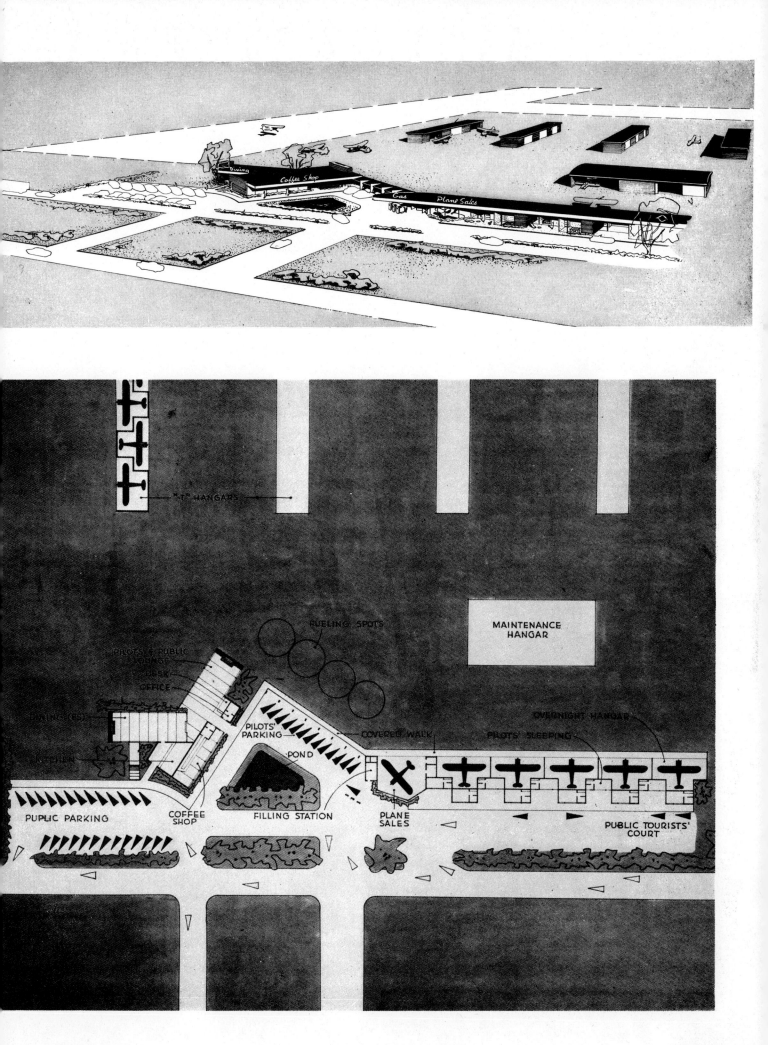

RAILROAD BUILDINGS

THE ARCHITECTURE

OF RAILROADS

EXPERIMENT · 1832

Courtesy New York Central System

"Come all you rounders, for I want you to hear,
The story of a brave engineer,
Casey Jones was the rounder's name,
On a big eight wheeler of a mighty fame. . ."

No country in the world owes as much to Casey Jones and his big eight wheeler as do the United States of America. And no architects in the world owe as much to the railroad as do the professional descendants of William LeBaron Jenney, whose early steel frame buildings, constructed of the structural steel sections first developed as railroad tracks, made possible the American skyscraper. The architecture of railroads — of stations, of engine sheds, and of railroad bridges — is, in America, a true and original part of our cultural heritage.

What has happened to this great tradition? Did it bog down in the economic depression of the thirties, that nearly broke American railroads? Are there signs of its revival in their startling and sudden economic recovery during the past few years? Is there any evidence that the shiny rail of steel, once the mainspring of our new architecture, will again help rejuvenate the art of building?

The Spirit of the Railroad

Ever since the first railroad train rattled through our land men have held romantic notions about this strangely unbeautiful thing. These notions held a very special quality of romance, for there was nothing pretty about the sooty, grimy steel monster; it was always gross, ugly, and endowed with an ear-splitting grind and a nerve-slitting squeak. But it was a thing of power, of grandeur, of all the crude glory of the vulgar age of the mechanical. And in America Walt Whitman, a connoisseur of vulgarity, wrote an ode to a locomotive: he knew that this monster, born in the Old World, held within it the passionate pulse of the New.

It is not strange, then, in looking back upon the hundred-odd years of railroad architecture that most of it has had about it a romantic streak. Some of this romanticism was Gothic; some of it Romanesque; some railroad stations were built to resemble medievel castles; others to invoke — probably to be on the safe side — the connivance of the Deity. In more recent times romanticists like Eric Mendelsohn have sketched railroad stations to resemble "frozen music." Only in the most recent past, when the smoky monster became a sleek, smokeless and often electric space machine, have architects produced neat and clean public buildings, pretending to be neither temples nor wind-tunnels, neither castles nor cathedrals, but, simply — stations.

The Architecture of Railroads

Basically there are only two types of railroad stations: the terminal, and the intermediate stop. Some of them may load passengers; others may load freight; still others may do both. Some will be small whistle stops — little more than a short concrete platform, with a stationmaster's house in the middle; others will consist of vast halls, spanned by daring steel and glass vaults, and harboring dozens of long platforms, waiting rooms,

A representative selection of engine shed types, from Wasmuth's Baulexikon. All dimensions are in meters

Bauen in Frankreich, Eisen, Eisenbeton—Giedion

1

(1) Hall of Machines, Paris, 1889; (2)
King's Cross Station, London, 1852; (3) &
(4) Grand Central Station, New York City,
1871; (5) Central Station, Milan, c. 1930

Country Life, London

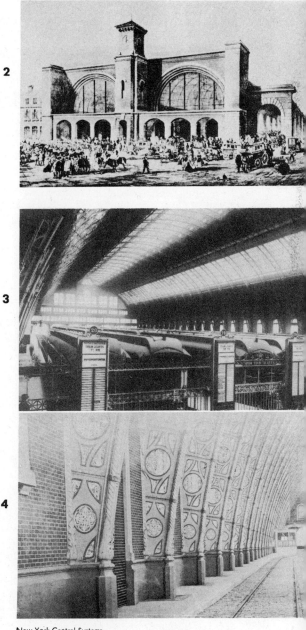

2

3

4

5

New York Central Systems

ticket offices and baggage rooms; all connected by
ramps, escalators, freight and passenger elevators;
all fed by subways, bus and trolley lines, taxi lanes,
truck convoys — and, possibly, even by airplanes. Such
vast traffic centers stretch out their tentacles over
many square miles of urban land, and decisively affect
the plans of cities, the spread of industries, and the
lives of those within their radius of influence.

Yet however complex a railroad station may become,
its planning will closely reflect the "flow diagram"
of its functions. Mart Stam's project for a station
at Geneva-Cornavin (page 299) shows this very clearly.
It is not here that the architecture of railroads presents
a problem to an able organizer. Rather, it is in the
esthetic expression of the essentially modern character
of rail-bound transport that the architects seem to
have hit a snag.

In most of the large stations, there is a clear architectural division into two building elements: one,
the large vaulted hall covering the many platforms;
and, two, the "architecturally treated" outer building,
containing waiting rooms, lobbies, ticket offices and
the like, and presenting a deceptive façade to the outside world. The first of these elements was generally
designed by engineers; the second, by deluded esthetes.
An exception — and a remarkable one — is London's
King's Cross Station designed, in 1852 (!) by Lewis

Architectura Moderna

297

Encyclopsédie de l'Architecture, Éditions Albert Morance, Paris

6

THE ROMANTIC IMPULSE

(6) Station at Noyon, France (date unknown); (7) Multi-level station, Antonio Sant'Elia, 1914; (8) Sketch for a Railroad Station, Eriç Mendelsohn, 1914; (9) Stuttgart Station, 1914–27; (10) Moscow Station, 1935

7

8

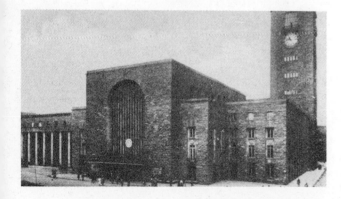

9

10

Cubitt who, being an engineer, felt free to design the entire station as one functional unit, whose façade is expressive of the large-scale vaulting behind it. But in most cases architects designed the outer portions of stations, while engineers designed the steel vaults. It is the latter aspect of station architecture that, today, seems to us to have had real architectural and esthetic merit.

The demand for these great spans to cover a number of parallel railroad tracks and engine sheds produced many beautiful examples of steel and concrete engineering. Depending largely upon the size of the spans required, arched trusses, two- or three-hinged, and rigid steel girder frames have been in extensive use from the middle of the last century to the present (see First Grand Central Station, 1871). Though many of the early arched trusses were unduly heavy — having been designed by people whose eye was still trained to the proportions of stone-arches — recent examples used extremely light bow-string trusses, whose tension members consist of thread-like wrought iron rods. The trend in very recent railroad architecture, however, has been altogether away from the large vaulted hall, toward individually covered, parallel platforms. These platforms are generally protected by cantilevered canopies, supported only at the center and constructed, more often than not, of reinforced concrete rather than steel.

Modern engineers, by and large, have been able to resist the romantic impulse and have — depending upon their individual ability — stuck fairly close to pure forms. However, some architects have been striving for a conscious railroad esthetic. whose outgrowths have occasionally been fantastic. In what seems to have been an uncommonly sustained stupor over Mr. Watt's little gadget, architects have tried, in various unfortunate ways, to blow off esthetic steam. An unidentified Frenchman evidently found himself reminded of wed-

Bauen in Frankreich Eisen Eisenbeton — Giedion

11

(11) Station Project, Tony Garnier, 1904; (12) & (13) Project for Station at Geneva-Cornavin, Mart Stam, 1924; (14) Project for Brussels International Station, Victor Bourgeois, (about) 1930; (15) Project for Central Station, Brussels, Victor Bourgeois, (about) 1930

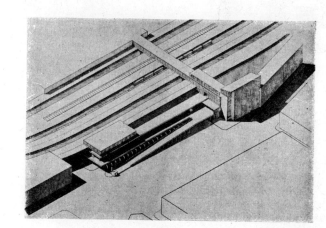

12

ding cakes; Antonio Sant' Elia, a futurist, was patently intent upon telling God about it — and upon getting within His earshot to do so; Eric Mendelsohn's sketch, though expressing a truly architectural concept, looks as aero-dynamic as the *Super Chief* — which, in stations (that ought, perhaps, to be stationary) suggests extreme confusion; the well-known, and now sadly blasted Stuttgart Station carries neo-Romanesque grandeur to the point of gloom likely to discourage pleasure travel; while the Moscow Subway Station, though presumably in the new "Stalin Style," does not seem to have made up its esthetic mind — a good thing for fun-loving architects in a land of switching party-lines.

Rational Esthetics for a Rational Industry

Despite some of these romantic tangents, clean, honest structural designs for railroad stations have been prepared by some architects from the start. One of the earliest 20th Century examples is the station designed in 1901–04 by Tony Garnier in reinforced concrete. It is remarkable not only for its clean appearance and its clear functional organization, but also for its daring use of thin reinforced concrete slabs, cantilevered over

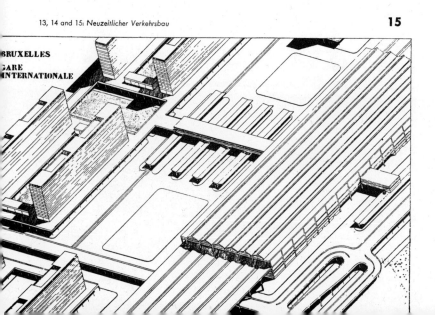

13, 14 and 15: Neuzeitlicher Verkehrsbau

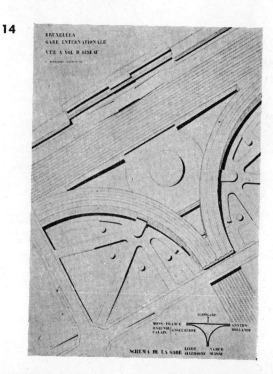

13

14

15

(16) Stratford, Conn., Station, 1867; (17) Wiesbaden-Biebrich Station, (about) 1928; (18) Trolley Car Shelter, Stockholm, Sweden, (about) 1934; (19) Covered Platform, Amstel Station, Amsterdam

16

17

Neuzeitlicher Verkehrsbau

platforms in a manner that only now, almost fifty years later, is becoming generally accepted. Though there are still a few minor Art Nouveau details, this project by Tony Garnier can hold its own against the best of the most recent crop of such designs. More than two decades later the Dutch architect Mart Stam designed his station for Geneva-Cornavin. Here again the emphasis is upon clean, reinforced concrete and glass, upon cantilevers that permit uninterrupted access to trains, and upon a functional expression of the station's flow diagram. Most interesting, perhaps, is the use of ramps to connect different levels, and the departure from the large, single-vaulted hall in favor of the parallel, individually covered railroad platforms. Around 1930 Victor Bourgeois designed two stations for Brussels: the Central Station shows certain organizational similarities to that of Mart Stam, though the massing of the principal units and their detailing seems more sophisticated; the scheme for the International Station introduces an interesting idea by joining rail and road transport to air traffic. To allow for separate access to all these facilities, Bourgeois used an intricate system of ramps and overhead passages, somewhat reminiscent of Antonio Sant' Elia's futuristic scheme (in 1914) for intersecting level traffic (see page 298). Thus the work of the romanticists, despite some of its aberrations, did make its valuable contribution to more realistic projects that followed.

G. E. Kidder Smith Photo

18   **19**

Rationalism and the Whistle Stop

It is a far cry from Victor Bourgeois' Rail-Motor-Air Terminal to the shed-like minimum facility of the whistle stop. But just as certain modern artists have returned to the simplest basic shapes in order to bring a new unity out of artistic chaos, some architects in recent years have concentrated upon the redesign of elementary structural units in order to progress, from these, to a new evaluation of larger structures. Edward Henry's painting of the Stratford, Conn., station in 1867 shows a simple wooden structure, conceived perhaps as just another house, but unpretentious in its expression of wood truss construction. The fact that such sheds were combustible soon led to the exclusive use of iron and concrete for railroad construction.

We have seen Tony Garnier's daring reinforced concrete canopies. In the Wiesbaden-Biebrich canopies the effect is still rather heavy, though a section reveals the roof slab to be very thin. Not until we get to the beautiful trolley-car shelter in Stockholm, built over thirty years after Tony Garnier's project was designed, is there any realization of the Frenchman's daring and prophetic idea. The canopies of the Amsterdam-Amstel station — which is covered in detail on pages 308-309—were designed in 1938; they show, perhaps, an even further refinement and the introduction of a simple decorative motif, typical of "new empiricist" architecture today.

In Great Britain, where the postwar nationalization of transport under the Labour Government has resulted in a flurry of excellent new railroad designs, a number of handsome little stations have been constructed recently. Similar in spirit to Lester Tichy's American prewar designs (see photo) are such fine island buildings as the one at Marsh Lane Station; these and other British examples show the logical next step in the hierarchy of railroad stations — i.e. the small intermediate stop.

20

"Topical" Press Agency, Ltd. Photo
(Copyright London Transport Executive)

21

Stewart Bale Ltd. Photo

22

(20) Oak Wood Station, London Passenger Transport Board; (21) Marsh Lane Station, British Railways; (22) Project for Prefabricated Station, Lester Tichy, Architect

RAILROAD ARCHITECTURE IN EUROPE

By J. L. Martin

THIS short article cannot pretend to deal with the subject in a comprehensive way. To do that it would have to refer to a far greater number of buildings. It would have to make some reference to those developments in design and esthetic theory which are stirring in so many European countries. It would also have to take into account all the differences of background, and the influences which give the railways of each particular country so distinctive a character.

To emphasize this point, it is only necessary to call to mind one or two outstanding contrasts. There is, for example, the sturdy regionalism of the early British Railways which showed such a marked influence on their architectural character. There is the typical French regard for the station as a *"monument publique."* There is the Swiss habit of using the station as rather a pleasant meeting place. Then there are all the differences of operation and detail — for example in Great Britain

the simple informality of taking a ticket or dealing with baggage, the traditional direct road-rail connection at terminal stations made possible by the collection of tickets *"en route,"* the overbridges, underpasses and fencing which contribute so much to the character of a British station, and serve to distinguish it so clearly from its counterpart in continental Europe or the U. S. A.

These contrasts, and their social and economic background, form part of a fascinating study. A short article of this kind cannot even touch upon such a broad treatment. It consists rather of a series of notes on one or two lines of development which are being followed up in connection with railway station designs in Europe — and more particularly with those types of development which may have interest for American designers.

Although the subject is a broad one, it can be divided conveniently into three main sections of work: first,

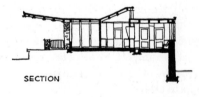

SECTION

Section, plan and perspective view show typical British station under the new program. Native materials are used to relieve possible monotony resulting from standardization

PLATFORM

PARCELS YARD AND PARKING

M.

WAITING

STATION MASTER   PORTERS

FUEL

HT'R

BOOKING OFFICE   PARCELS

TICKET WINDOWS

W.

BOOKING HALL   ENTRANCE

STATION APPROACH

DN

the smaller station building; second, the larger station; and, third, the remodeling and improvement of existing buildings.

I. SMALLER STATIONS

In two European countries at least, Great Britain and France, the problem of rebuilding smaller stations has become something more than the straightforward problem of individual buildings. The smaller buildings that are required in these countries are numerous.

In England the reason for this is a matter of history. The early, and unbelievably numerous competitive companies developed an intensive network of lines and stations which is without parallel. The stations differed widely from each other in architectural character; many of them have now reached a considerable age — some are too large for their present traffic, others too small. Most of them are difficult and uneconomical to maintain.

In France the need for remodeling and rebuilding stations has been increased by war damage. In both countries therefore, it is not a question of putting up one or two individual buildings. It is a question of dealing with programs. In both cases it is possible to obtain a total economy through some form of nationalization of requirements and construction.

This is a problem which does not appear to have presented itself in the U.S.A. The outstandingly satisfactory stations at Burlington and La Crosse by Holabird & Root, or Lester Tichy stations for the Pennsylvania Railroad are clearly and quite justifiably individual buildings. In England it is true we have before us the example of the London Passenger Transport Stations, built before the war, where a remarkable unity of treatment is maintained by a consistency of finish.

The L.P.T.B. (now London Transport Executive) with its program for opening up new electrified suburban lines was almost bound to consider buildings in series. Its fine policy and standards have incidentally made possible a rapid start on postwar schemes, and already the Central London line has been extended in both eastern and western directions. This extension program, which began immediately after the war in 1946, already has produced three new stations and a number of conversions to the east (designed by the Architect to the L.T.E., Mr. Bilbow) and two new stations below ground by Adams, Holden and Pearson, one of which, Gants Hill, achieves the considerable engineering feat of driving a large underground concourse between the two subway lines. To the west, three new stations, the work of Mr. Curtis, Architect to the Western Region, British Railways, are under construction.

But though these ranges of buildings in the London area form important programs in themselves they hardly can be taken as a guide to the methods that may have to be used in dealing with the large number of buildings with widely different requirements to be constructed in all parts of the country.

Several lines of approach to this problem are possible and can be justified by different conditions and circumstances. In France, for instance, the S.N.C.F.

Pleasant and clean design such as this is intended to turn British stations from grimy, unpopular stop-overs into real community buildings. Note how the plan permits easy circulation and free access to all services

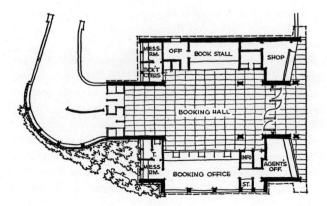

Experimental station building at Queen's Park is prefabricated in enameled iron panels. Interior walls are also assembled in section. The raised cantilever roof is an attractive tour de force

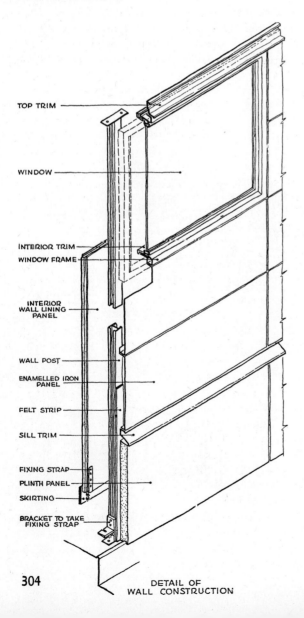

TOP TRIM

WINDOW

INTERIOR TRIM

WINDOW FRAME

INTERIOR WALL LINING PANEL

WALL POST

ENAMELLED IRON PANEL

FELT STRIP

SILL TRIM

FIXING STRAP

PLINTH PANEL

SKIRTING

BRACKET TO TAKE FIXING STRAP

DETAIL OF WALL CONSTRUCTION

has given consideration to the standardization of interior layout for all small and medium-size stations. This layout will vary only according to the size of station to be rebuilt, and although certain recommendations are made to avoid excessive cost the principal aim has been to leave the general architectural treatment as free as possible.

On the London Midland Region of British Railways, however (where the problem is different for several reasons), experiments in developing Unit Stations which began on the London Midland and Scottish Railway are being continued. These experiments follow the principle of coping with a number of buildings, and securing economy through the repetition of similar parts. Although the individual components of the building itself have been standardized, there has been no attempt to produce standard plans for the buildings themselves; in fact, the very opposite is being required, and the whole object of the experimental work is to produce a building which can use similar parts but which can be completely flexible from a planning point of view. As this experimental work has now achieved definite results, it is, perhaps, worth describing in some detail.

The former L.M.S. Railway Company several years ago set up a Building Research Committee which has made a special study of the problem of unit station buildings. The use of some form of unit construction was clearly indicated from the start. It was obviously desirable, for example, to have parts manufactured away from the site, and easily handled and quickly erected on the site itself. The problem was to produce such parts in materials which could meet the stringent requirements

This small island building—also prefabricated of enameled iron panels—
serves as a sheltered waiting room, with neatly designed wood-slat benches inside

of railway work. The wall required, for example, an impervious, easily cleaned and attractive finish above flow level; below flow level, a hard surface to resist damage from barrows was essential. It was desirable to obtain certain levels of insulation from the point of view of comfort and economy in heating. It was also desirable that the wall thickness should be cut down to a minimum.

These performance requirements were established after careful work on prototypes in the laboratory, and finally an experimental building was erected at Queen's Park near London. On this particular site it stood in a highly polluted atmosphere, and was adjacent to a fast traffic line and an electrified line so that its performance under severe conditions of vibration could be measured.

The experimental building designed in the office of the Architect to the Region, W. H. Hamlyn, has already been illustrated and described.[1] It is sufficient here to say that its main awning consists of steel columns which carry cranked beams running at right angles to the building. Between these cranked beams stressed skin plywood boxes form the awning, the roof being waterproofed by a felt membrane. Below this awning, wall posts are erected in the first instance, and the walling is then clipped into position. Externally, the building presents a flush surface which is easily washed down and in which bright color can be freely used in the areas covered with enameled iron.

The prototype building gave sufficiently satisfactory results to make further development worth while and since its erection a number of schemes have been worked

[1] Architectural Review, March, 1946.

out, and the first full-scale station now has been built at Marsh Lane near Liverpool. One of the most important single features arising out of this work has undoubtedly been the application of a system of dimensional coordination to the construction and planning. The materials used in the individual components may be changed — indeed, *should* be changed when they can be improved. The dimensional grid takes this possible variation of material into account, and will allow these changes to be easily incorporated as they are required without invalidating the flexibility allowed which is shown in the accompanying plans. It will be seen from these plans that they are all based on a grid. This grid has a module of 3 ft. 4 in., which proves to be the most convenient planning dimension.

From a planning point of view these schemes represent a considerable breakaway from the traditional station building, in which the platform acted as a kind of corridor from which the individual rooms of the building were approached. The number of rooms provided in traditional schemes was itself a reflection of a different social age: the segregation of ladies from the general waiting room was but a first step towards the further subdivisioning of first and third class. Separate rooms for all these various categories were commonly provided. This isolation of rooms is obviously unsatisfactory in present-day practice, and in the plans illustrated it will be seen that in various ways one single general waiting space replaces the independent waiting rooms.

This new freedom of planning leaves ample scope for the designer, and a considerable variety can be achieved.

This variety has again been deliberately emphasized by various means including the introduction of local walling materials. (See also Lester Tichy's designs in the U.S. — *Ed.*) It is realized that the widespread use of a single range of materials in areas and settings which differ widely in character leaves an opening for criticism that cannot be easily waved aside. One of the principal interests in the older station buildings in Great Britain is the wealth of variety in their regional character.[2] This is an interest which it would be a pity to lose, and there is no reason why it cannot be maintained in some degree at least in the design of unit stations. It is felt that by various means such as the color and use of local materials, the prefabricated components may be more effectively related to their different types of setting, and that a contrast of materials can be obtained which might well enhance the qualities of both the local and the imported components.

It now seems to have been proved that the smaller station can have the necessary freedom of planning and design in spite of the utilization of similar components. This means that the following advantages can be obtained:

1. It is possible to bulk-order the parts of a number of different stations, and so secure economy.

[2] Some of the reasons for this variety have been described elsewhere — see for instance J. M. Richards' article "Domesticating the Iron Horse" in the Architectural Review, June, 1942.

2. It is possible to rationalize the production of working drawings; in fact, component and assembly drawings for any number of stations have already been built up.

3. As a result of the scientific tests carried out on the prototype and its components, a definite standard and quality for future building work can be laid down.

4. It becomes possible to make an effective organization for the erection of these buildings on the site, and to develop a maximum speed for this operation.

It is not claimed that the system applies to every station building. But it is interesting to find that even in individual buildings, advantage can be taken of standardization of units in various ways.

II. THE LARGER STATION

If any adequate picture could be given of the amount of major station rebuilding which has been projected, there is no doubt that it would be impressive. In Great Britain alone, consideration has been given to the re-planning of many of the larger terminal stations. Although in France it has as yet been impossible to carry out any major station rebuilding, many studies have been made for the reconstruction of important stations destroyed or damaged during the war: thus at Amiens M. Pierani, Architect Head of the Estate Department of the French Railways, has collaborated with the

The prefabricated Marsh Lane Station again utilizes the raised cantilever canopy, which admits clerestory lighting to the platform. The lettering seems far too small for practical legibility—a common fault of British stations. Plans below show the flexibility of this prefabrication system

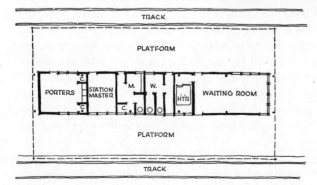

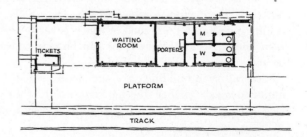

distinguished M. Perret, who is redesigning the Town Square; Calais Ville has also been designed by M. Pierani; Douai by MM. Mathon and Pierani; Lisieux by M. Camelot; Laon, M. Croize; Besançon, M. Madeline, and so on. Holland has fully developed rebuilding schemes for Leiden, Arnhem and Nijmegen. Belgium has a scheme for Brussels, and Switzerland provides the carefully studied 1946 project for the station at Zurich.[3]

The impetus behind the development of such schemes comes from various sources. In England, many of the terminal stations are old buildings, which, although still distinguished structures, can no longer cope with modern requirements. In addition to the need for rebuilding the older stations, war damage, as in the French stations and at Nijmegen or Arnhem, provides a further opportunity. Coincidentally, there is the influence of the awakening concern for town planning which has made itself so strongly felt throughout postwar Europe.

These factors have certainly engendered an activity in connection with station planning which is, perhaps, without parallel in opportunity since the days of extensive railway development. But although this activity has taken place, the plain fact of the situation (in France and England, at least) is that these schemes

[3]See Schweizerische Bauzeitung, May 1, 1948.

will, for some time to come, remain on paper. The shortages of both labor and materials, and the priority that must be given to housing have, for the time being, settled that issue.

There is, however, some point in paper work which establishes more clearly the actual requirements, and there is no doubt, from the point of view of the designer, that there has been an important development in the preliminary studies which have accompanied many of these schemes. An attempt has been made, for

The interior of Marsh Lane Station shows again the handsome seating units which have become standard in the new British stations. All interior surfaces were selected for ease of maintenance

Stewart Bale, Ltd. Photos

instance, to lay down standards for the provision of accommodation, and to state desirable sizes with some degree of accuracy. The exact requirements of a station are not easy to define in this way. The standards must allow, for instance, for widely varying numbers of travelers, and for the differing requirements of individual passengers. These studies of passenger movement and flow analysis have been considerably advanced by the work of the various Regions of British Railways. For instance, the work of the General Research Section of the London Midland Region has shown the proportion of passengers using the various parts of the station, and has demonstrated how this proportion varies with different types of station. The following comparison gives some idea of how the use of the parts of the station varies under different circumstances:

Proportion of Passengers using Facilities

	Ticket Office	Indicator	Bookstalls	Waiting Rooms	Toilets	Refreshment Rooms
Terminal Station	30%	62%	50%	10%	15%	20%
Interchange Station	4%	21%	16%	20%	19%	52%

A glance at these comparative figures will show just how important these studies are in establishing the planning of stations on a sound and economic basis. As a result of this type of work, it now seems possible to lay down diagrammatically the correct relationship of, for example, entrances, ticket offices, departure indicators; but in addition to this, the study of the movement of passengers has made it possible to relate peak numbers to the widths of passageways and staircases, areas of concourses, number of ticket windows, ticket barriers, number of lavatories, etc. There is no doubt that the application of this preliminary work, accompanied as it is by the development of prototypes for many of the separate items of the station will have a marked effect on the character and quality of future station building.

Some idea of what this character may be, can, however, be suggested. There are already in existence two stations in Amsterdam which are not, as yet, widely known, and which were guided in design by the careful preliminary study of detailed requirements. The two stations at Amsterdam (the Amstel Station and the Muiderpoort Station) were completed during the early part of the war by the Architect to the Dutch Railways, H. J. Schelling.

The Amstel Station perhaps illustrates best the main features of planning. An economically planned but

adequate concourse around which the main passenger requirements are centered forms the nucleus of the scheme. Passenger entrances are at one end of this concourse, which is enclosed by doors, and heated. Around the concourse between the entrances and the barriers to the platform subway are all the passenger requirements — ticket offices, timetable displays, shops, baggage rooms, telephones, lavatories, changing rooms, etc. The ticket barriers lead into the underpass from which there is a stairway connection to the platforms.

Architecturally, the concourse is a lofty glazed structure with adjoining single-story buildings. The strong Dutch tradition of the use of brickwork has influenced the external finishes. The Amstel Station exploits this in the use of light brick with raked joints (above a red Swedish granite plinth), and horizontal bands of glazed earthenware. The east façade is faced with French limestone. Internally, the main welded steel frames are left exposed, and are free standing from the roof plaster and glazed wall treatment. All underpasses are tiled.

A standard treatment is used for platform awnings, the main supports consisting of welded steel frames running at right angles to the track, and covered with purlins and narrow boarding.

The platform buildings themselves, as is the common practice on the Netherlands Railways, are faced with

The two Amsterdam stations shown here — the Muiderpoort Station (left) and the Amstel Station (above) — illustrate the current "new empiricist" trend in Western European architecture. Both emphasize a rather "human" touch, with pitched roofs, applied decoration inside and out, and with a somewhat casual architectural composition. Both stations were begun before the war, and completed during its early days

hard glazed materials which can be easily cleaned. At Amstel the platform buildings are tiled up to the sill level, and paneled above with structural glass.

One or two special features of this station should be mentioned. The first is the careful study that was given to the correct type of doorway for use of railway stations. Each door is separated from its neighbor by a glazed panel which allows for the sideways movement of the passenger passing through the partly opened door. The distance between outer and inner doors is carefully gauged, and laid down as a standard. A second feature is the development of the ticket window, in which the passenger speaks through a stretched membrane mounted in a circular frame in the glass of the ticket office front. The tickets and cash are exchanged between passenger and reservations clerk on a small sliding tray. The reservations office is a self-contained unit, cut off from all air movement from the concourse itself.

The station at Muiderpoort is a simpler, but equally striking version of the principles demonstrated in the Amstel Building, which together form not only important contributions to the fine architectural traditions of Holland, but also distinguished additions to the architecture of the Railways. In passing it should be mentioned that the Dutch Railways have also provided scope for Mr. Van Ravensteyn's personal experiments in architectural form.[4] The remodeling of Utrecht Station, carried out in stages and finally completed in 1940, and two signal boxes in particular illustrate the preferences for curvilinear forms and individual fantasy which are associated with the name of this architect.

III. RAILWAY IMPROVEMENTS

Probably one of the most important tasks that railway architects have to face is that of improving the appearance of all railway surroundings. This applies on a large scale in the railway sheds and incidental buildings of the railways.

The French review *Urbanisme* in September, 1943, devoted a special number to the railways and their relation to urbanism. In a series of articles, officials of the S.N.C.F. and others presented a brilliant statement of the problem and provided an impressive record of their own policy and achievements. The relation of the station to the town, the effect of the railways on landscape, the appearance of its bridges, its overhead electrification, in fact, the whole of its external aspect has received careful thought. The General Managers of the S.N.C.F. and particularly the two managers who were successively in charge of the technical department of Fixed Installations (MM. Porchez and Robert Levi) are to be congratulated on their efforts in this direction. Any travelers from Calais to Paris today can see the effect of this considered policy. They will also see the two great engine roundhouses at Longueau and that at Creil (at present under construction) which are part of a general program of some twenty schemes by

means of which the face of the French Railways is being changed.

The reconstruction of these engine sheds, which have not been widely illustrated, deserves some special mention on account of their distinguished character. Together with bridges and marshaling yards, reconstruction of engine sheds presented immediately after the war one of the most urgent problems which the French Railways (S.N.C.F.) had to face. The roundhouses themselves were designed by M. Paul Pierani (of the French Railways) in collaboration on the engineering side with M. Bernard Lafaille. Due to shortages of timber, steel and bricks, the buildings are largely constructed of reinforced concrete so that they continue the great tradition of experimental concrete work which the French Railways have so finely established.[5]

It was considered that the roundhouse with its exterior wall of glass, provided the most efficient means of housing locomotives. There remained, however, the problem of smoke extraction and the standardization of a constructional form to meet the different numbers of engines to be housed.

The second of these problems has been tackled by the standardization of two main types of building, one with a radius of 218 ft. for 44 engines, and the other taking 32 engines with a radius of 176 ft. A smaller number of engines can be housed by building a section of one of these roundhouses: this meets the immediate problem economically, and allows for easy extension.

The question of smoke extraction has been ably solved by vents in the main roof, and specially suspended smoke extractors over the smoke stacks of the locomotives themselves. By means of these roof vents and extractors, the smoke is carried away to a continuous ventilation around the top of the external wall.

Among the buildings to be reconstructed by the S.N.C.F. special mention should be made of the program of signal and point boxes and of the interesting study of railway workshop and shed roofs which M. Pierani has carried out in collaboration with the engineer M. Vallette, Head of the Department of Construction Work, S.N.C.F., and M. Mesnager, Consultant. The most recent of these sheds, outside the Gare du Nord, Paris, illustrates an important development of the concrete roof which enables a double-sided lighting to be arranged. M. Pierani has thus moved away from the restricted daylighting of the typical north light roof, and has ingeniously produced a type of lighting which is particularly suitable for railway work.

In addition to railway surroundings of this kind, there still remains the problem of remodeling many of the existing station buildings. It is to be remembered in these cases that remodeling work usually arises when the building structure is reasonably sound, but probably inadequate or uneconomical for use at the present day. From the designer's point of view this raises the

---

[4] *Architectural Review*, April, 1948, p. 56.

[5] The all-concrete station at Rheims (replacing the building badly damaged by shell fire in the 1914–18 war) with its ingenious overall roof, is now some 15 years old. Started in 1932 for the Chemins de Fer de l'Est and constructed from the designs of S. A. Enterprises Limousin, it was an outstanding though by no means the only fine experiment in concrete work.

difficult problem of bringing a sense of convenience and order into a large number of buildings in a way which can retain something of the individual character of the buildings themselves.

The principal advantages to be worked for are an improved layout of accommodation and equipment, improved economy by the removal of redundant areas and the substitution of materials involving a minimum of maintenance and an improved appearance.

The question of appearance is tied up with the design of innumerable details. Although each individual detail is small in itself, it may require, as it does in the case of the ticket window, an intensive study. The task of dealing with this type of problem consistently throughout the railway system is, from the point of view of the designer, just as exacting as the problem of the new station building, but it is far more widespread.

The S.N.C.F. in France, now a nationalized railway for more than a decade, has made considerable progress on this standardization of detail.[6] The coloring of station signs, the lettering, the types of ticket window are all the subject of type designs.

In England work on this study of detail and equipment was already well advanced before nationalization. The London Passenger Transport Board had already set a remarkably high standard in its equipment, its finishes and its advertising and information display. The London Midland Region, too, had developed a number of prototype models, for instance the ticket window, the ticket office front (which is worked out in relation to unit station planning), the screened platform seat and the standard waiting room seat. It is through the development of these new standards and by the adoption of annual programs of work that a consistent attack can be made on one of the largest and most difficult of the railway architect's problems — the transformation of railway environment.

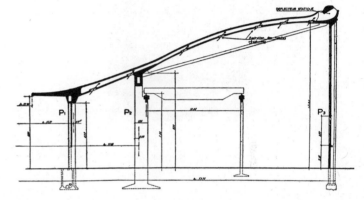

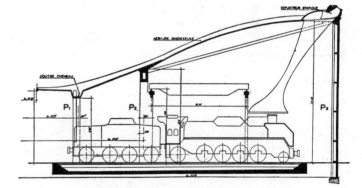

This fascinating roundhouse at Avignon, France, is remarkable for its ingenious and interesting structure, its functional architecture. The sections above show the special smoke-extraction system designed to remove smoke both from the building in general and from the engines in particular. The view at the top, left, shows the extraordinary lightness of reinforced concrete construction for which French engineers are so famous

[6] In England the Nationalization not more than a few months old, the principal visual evidences of unity have so far been confined to the "British Railways" which is appearing on rolling stock and the new colors which will shortly be seen. In these experimental schemes the locomotives have colors according to their class: powerful express passenger engines are blue; other express passenger engines, green; mixed traffic engines are black, but with lining; freight engines are all black. Chocolate and ivory or alternatively plum and cream are to be used for main line corridor trains. Local Suburban Stock will be maroon and multiple electric stock green.

Above and right: Raymond Loewy Associates. Below: Henry Dreyfuss

RAILROAD ARCHITECTURE IN

NORTH AMERICA TODAY

Back in Casey Jones's time, or Commodore Vander-bilt's, America's railroads were its pride and joy. They were also the apple of Uncle Sam's eye, and he found many ways to help them extend their lines across the country and build scores of new stations, in impressive if not very handsome architectural styles.

But that was a long time ago, and Uncle Sam has turned to younger, more exciting favorites. Now his largesse goes to highway systems and air lines, and autos and trucks and airplanes all take business from the railroads. Bus stations and airports have the new

and glamorous terminals, and the railroads are left to compete as best they can. All Uncle Sam does now is to tell them what they can and cannot do.

So railroad stations are still, as ARCHITECTURAL RECORD pointed out in December, 1943, a neglected architectural opportunity. There is no real program of station building in the United States, and it would seem that railroad executives are not convinced that architecture has anything to offer them in their current struggle for public favor and business.

The "opportunity" is nevertheless intriguing. There

These four stations, here anonymous, are all new. American railroads, which have streamlined and glamorized their trains, apparently have not given the same

Hedrich-Blessing Photo

are literally thousands of railroad stations in the land, virtually all of them at least 50 years old, obsolete, unsightly, expensive to heat and maintain. Once the pride of a growing community, they are now the eyesore of a city. Rail lines are under heavy pressure to modernize and rebuild them. They do something less than nothing to brighten a passenger's trip, or induce him to make a rail journey.

It is the apparent lack of appreciation for architectural design that warrants this article. In preparation for this Building Types Study, the RECORD contacted all of the major railroad companies, some 65 of them, to check on their plans and their current station building.

While it was not surprising that this effort showed that there was no real program of station building, it did turn up a considerable number of new or modernized stations. The distressing thing was the architecture of the current crop of stations, however small. There were, of course, a few excellent stations — Holabird and Root's station at Burlington (ARCHITECTURAL RECORD, October, 1944), some new ticket offices, a new station for an eastern line by Lester Tichy (see page 314). Against these there are a dozen or more nondescript imitation temples or imitation hot dog stands or imitation something else, which can only mean complete disregard for station design.

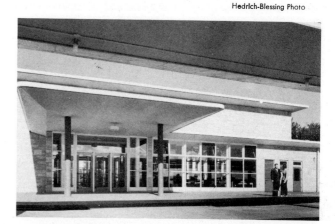

Merge Studios

thought to their stations. It would appear that railroad stations are still, as ARCHITECTURAL RECORD pointed out five years ago, a neglected architectural opportunity

Holabird and Root's station for Burlington, Iowa, upper photograph (AR, Oct., 1944), gives a hint of what might happen if the railroads gave the same attention to stations that they do to trains. The Santa Fe ticket office in Los Angeles (AR, June, 1947), by Maynard Lyndon, architect, typifies recent attention by railroads to the places where they sell tickets

CANADA MAKES A START

The Canadian National Railways is building a number of fine little stations, such as this one at Midland, Ontario, designed by John Schofield, chief architect. Designs are direct and unpretentious, and show evidence of consideration for economical maintenance, as in England

This Canadian Pacific Railway station at Leaside, Toronto, Ont., also shows evidence of the direct approach to station design

One suspects, incidentally, a desire by the railroads to keep the really good stations out of the public press. The very enthusiasm with which good stations are received frightens railroad executives; they are already over sensitive to public demand; they shudder to think of petitions for new stations from every whistle stop in the land.

Railroad executives have already amply demonstrated that they are no strangers in the field of design. They have paid out important commissions to industrial designers like Henry Dreyfuss and Raymond Loewy for locomotive and car design, for streamlined trains and modern coaches and handsome ticket offices. One cannot quarrel with the judgment that spends its money first for the trains in which the public rides, or perhaps for the places in which railroads do their actual selling. And there is a certain promise that when, as and if they turn their attention to stations, the railroads will demand the best design talent, will be willing to let stations look like stations, not Spanish missions, and will again make America proud of its railroad plant.

Another station for Canadian National Railways, this one at Ahuntsic, P. Q. The same design will also be used for Pointe aux Trembles, P. Q., and other locations

Gottscho-Schleisner Photos

STATION ON AN EASTERN
MAIN LINE

Lester Tichy, Architect

BUILT early during the war, this small station has two principal elements: a north-bound platform, which carries a completely new building; and a south-bound side, whose existing station building was radically rebuilt. The two sides of the station are linked by an underpass, whose butterfly-type entrance canopies contrast pleasantly with the straightforward and clean brick structures of the station buildings proper.

The north-bound platform building illustrated on this page stresses such details as efficient maintenance, economical operation and excellent visibility for passengers and personnel alike. The ticket office (right) is a fine example of neat and carefully considered design planned to facilitate its business

Gottscho-Schleisner Photos

The sequence of photographs on these two pages shows, first, the wide and well-protected north-bound platform; then the amusing underpass design with its corrugated transite surfaces; and, finally, the redesigned south-bound platform building with its former pitched roof, which was extended to afford greater protection to the platform itself

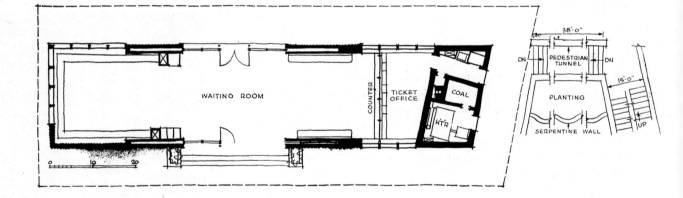

The plans are simple, and set a new standard for clean station design. An ample use of glass, which affords an almost uninterrupted vision of the platforms and train approaches from all parts of the buildings, has replaced the former unsightly bay windows common to older stations. All planning is very open, so that great crowds can pass through the station buildings rapidly without obstacles

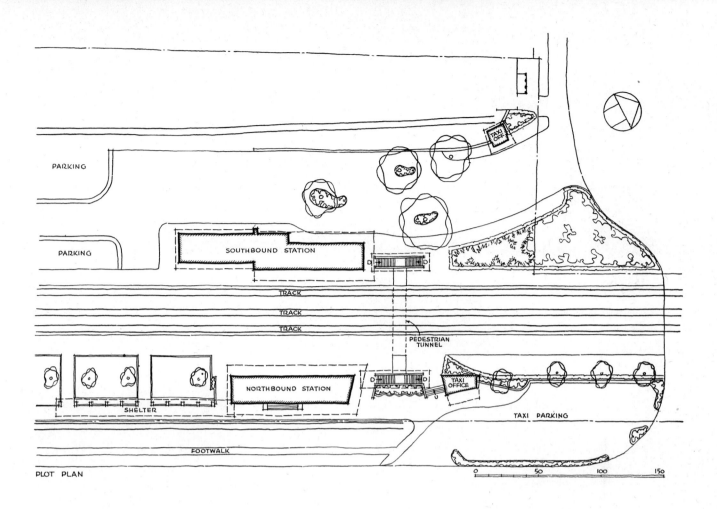

PARKING

PARKING

SOUTHBOUND STATION

TAXI
OFF.

TRACK

TRACK

TRACK

PEDESTRIAN
TUNNEL

NORTHBOUND STATION

TAXI
OFFICE

SHELTER

TAXI PARKING

FOOTWALK

PLOT PLAN

0   50   100   150

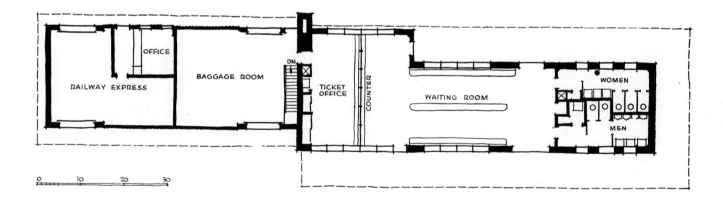

OFFICE

RAILWAY EXPRESS

BAGGAGE ROOM

DN.

TICKET
OFFICE

COUNTER

WAITING ROOM

WOMEN

MEN

0   10   20   30

Gottscho-Schleisner Photos

Although the south-bound platform building represents an alteration rather than a new design, its entire character has been completely ''revamped.'' All interior details, such as wall-paneling, cantilevered seats, terrazzo floors, and wide glass areas are impressive for their simplicity and ease of maintenance. The lettering within the station—an important point in railroad design—is distinguished for its clarity

The view of the remodeled building from the road approach shows how pleasantly the old structure was integrated with the new, modern design. It also indicates a possible manner of modernizing existing, antiquated railroad buildings where there are not funds for a more radical revision

DESIGNED TO ATTRACT ATTENTION

Wayne's Associated Service
Aiea, Oahu, T. H.

Wimberly and Cook, Architects
J. Grant Morgan, Structural Engineer

OWNER AND ARCHITECTS agreed at the outset that this service station must be of "eye-arresting design." Located on a main highway near Pearl Harbor, it had to attract attention to compete with several other service stations in the vicinity. Yet economy of construction was a main requirement.

Three major devices were used as attention-getters: a flaring pump canopy, wide open shop and sales areas, and highly unusual show windows (page 321). The canopy is supported by steel pipe frames; construction is of steel wide-flange roof beams with a 3 by 6 T & G roof deck and a suspended lath and plaster ceiling. On top of it is a specially designed sign panel intended to eliminate the possibility of the unattractive signs so frequently used by service stations. Wash rack and lubrication hoist are housed together in a high-ceilinged unit with adjacent storage and toilet facilities. A small office and parts sales room occupy a connecting low wing.

Main structure is of locally made buff-colored concrete block walls with wood roof framing, using steel members for beams in long span. Mild Hawaiian climate eliminated need for doors and heating facilities

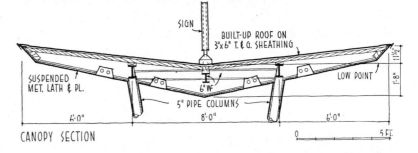

CANOPY SECTION

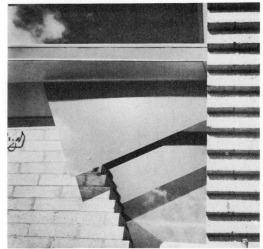

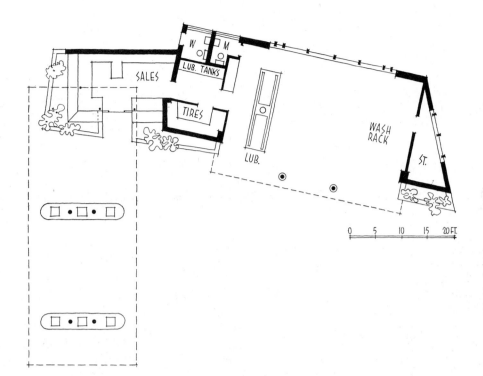

R. Wenkam

Show windows in office wing (right) were constructed of an inexpensive line of store front moldings and heat absorbing glass. Design was deliberately unusual, partly for effect and partly as an experiment in solving problem of show window reflections. Louvers (below) screen storage room windows

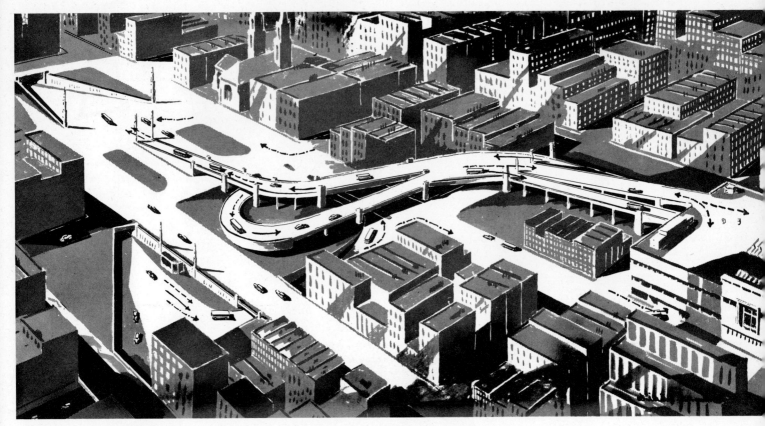

William Brower

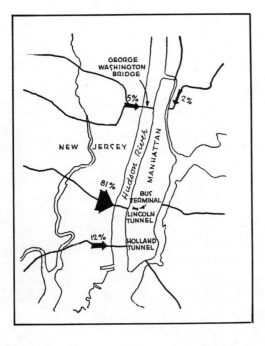

NEW YORK'S

Every five seconds a huge inter-city bus will arrive at the new Union Bus Terminal planned by the Port of New York Authority for New York City. At peak capacity it is anticipated that there will be 750 bus arrivals and an equal number of departures per hour.

This mighty terminal under construction around the corner from Times Square will provide 60,000 daily travelers with direct access to the city's vast underground communication system and to surface transportation. It will be also within walking distance of the majority of New York City's largest department stores and theaters and many of its principal office buildings.

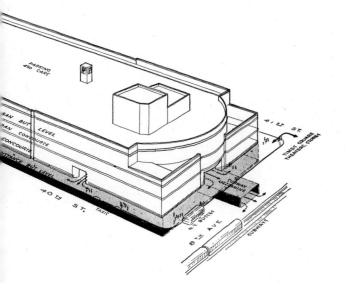

The Port of New York Authority

NEW UNION BUS TERMINAL

Connected by direct elevated ramp approaches to the Lincoln Tunnel, through which 81 per cent of bus traffic to midtown Manhattan passes, the new terminal will consolidate the movement of some 2100 whopping suburban and long-distance buses which daily manipulate and congest New York City's crowded streets to reach individual terminals scattered throughout the Times Square district. As a further measure of traffic relief the terminal will have a roof parking area for 450 privately owned automobiles. It is estimated that the elimination of traffic tie-ups will save commuters and shoppers from five to 20 minutes per trip.

The block long steel and brick structure will have four different floors with interior bus roadways and loading and unloading platforms on two levels. Long-distance buses, 15 per cent of the terminal load, will enter and leave the building at the Ninth Avenue street level. Suburban buses, 85 per cent of the load, will shuttle back and forth between the tunnel portals and the third floor level of the terminal by means of ramps.

Centralized around the concourses of the building will be all modern comfort conveniences for local and long-distance passengers including recreation facilities and an extensive shopping center.

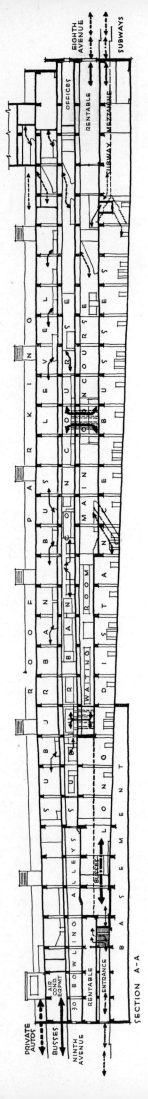

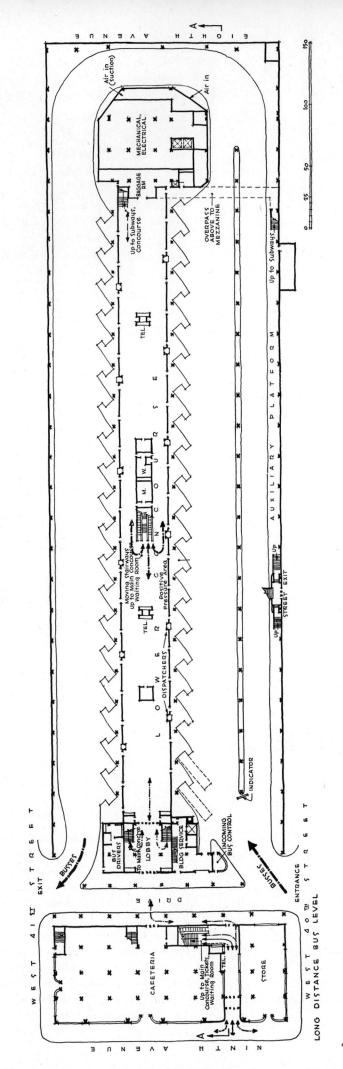

Section shows vertical relationship of main elements of the terminal. Employees' facilities and mechanical control are in the basement.

Incoming bus control flashes on the indicator at the entrance of terminal the number of dock that each incoming bus is to occupy. Electronic signal system keeps bus control constantly informed of docks in use. Buses will normally both discharge and load passengers at docks which open off the lower concourse. Company bus dispatchers are located in booths off the docks. Convenient moving stair access is provided between lower concourse and main concourse level. There is also a convenient entrance for long-distance travelers from Ninth Avenue and stairway access from the subway mezzanine level. Baggage is lifted from lower concourse to the main concourse.

The auxiliary platform along the outside wall will take care of special excursions, conventions, etc. Stairs from this platform lead directly to 40th Street, or waiting room, or subway mezzanine.

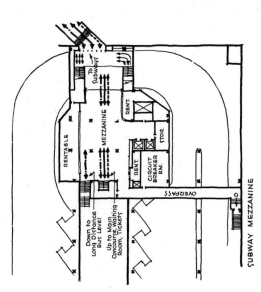

SUBWAY MEZZANINE

The maximum practical upward incline of the bus ramp from the mouth of the Lincoln Tunnel to the terminal established the floor elevation of the suburban bus level at the Ninth Avenue end of the building. As this elevation was insufficient to provide proper ceiling height for the concourses underneath, the suburban bus level continues on an upward incline for some distance into the terminal.

The existing elevation of Ninth Avenue, from which long-distance buses enter the terminal, fixed the elevation of the long-distance bus level at the Ninth Avenue end. Sections of the overhead main concourse level were cut away to provide head room for buses at entrance and exit points. As illustrated in section, the long-distance bus level slopes downward to provide bus headroom under the main waiting room, and continuing the downward incline, allows buses to swing under subway mezzanine to reach docks on the exit side of the level.

The steel structure of the terminal is of straightforward column, girder, and beam type with allowances for sloping levels and some eccentric column spacing due principally to bus circulation lanes. In the 800 ft. length of the building there are three expansion joints.

Road surfaces of the elevated ramps connecting the terminal to the tunnel entrance and exit will be heated to prevent the formation of ice.

The subway mezzanine is an integral and important element of the terminal traffic system as it provides direct access from the building to all of Greater New York

Main concourse, at the level of Eighth Avenue, 40th, and 41st Streets entrances, distributes travelers, commuters, and shoppers up to the suburban bus level and parking lot, or down to the long-haul level by means of 13 moving stairways and numerous auxiliary stairways. This level includes a large waiting room, ticket booths, information office, restaurant, shops and other conveniences and services for local and long-distance passengers

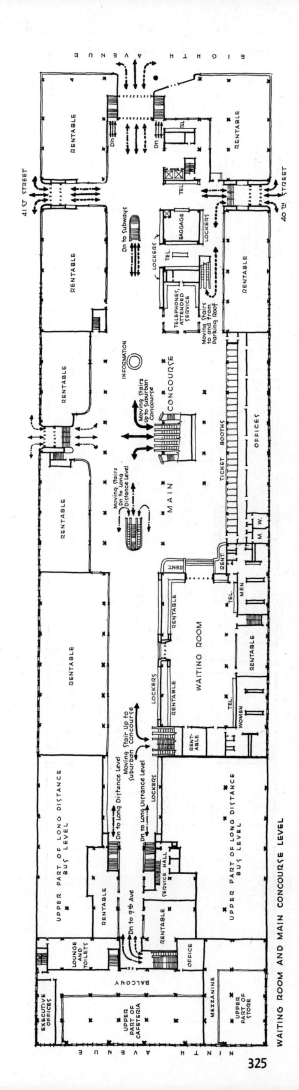

WAITING ROOM AND MAIN CONCOURSE LEVEL

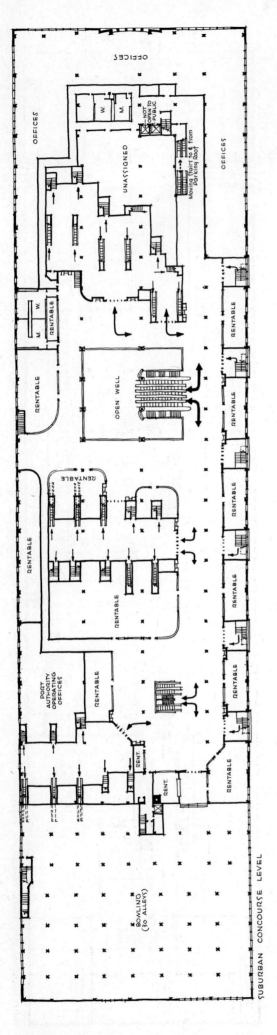

SUBURBAN CONCOURSE LEVEL

BOWLING
(30 ALLEYS)

OFFICES

OFFICES

OFFICES

UNASSIGNED

NOT OPEN TO PUBLIC

Moving Stairs to & from Parking Roof

RENTABLE

RENTABLE

RENTABLE

RENTABLE

RENTABLE

RENTABLE

RENTABLE

OPEN WELL

RENTABLE

RENTABLE

PORT AUTHORITY OPERATING OFFICES

RENT.

RENT.

W.

M.

W.

M.

Suburban commuters and shoppers are separated into three major sorting areas on the suburban concourse level. 14 moving stairways and 16 stairs provide access from these areas to the short-haul loading platforms. On this upper concourse as in the main concourse there are numerous shops, and recreation facilities including a 30 alley bowling center. Moving stairway traffic to and from roof parking area is isolated from bus passengers.

Suburban bus traffic which comprises 85 per cent of the load of the terminal will enter and depart from the suburban bus level by means of elevated concrete ramps which connect directly with the Lincoln tunnel portals. 84 bus loading and unloading spaces have been planned. Loading will be done from the island platforms which are connected by moving stairways and stairs to the suburban concourse below. One long platform, the length of the building, has been provided for unloading traffic. Stairs lead directly from this platform down to the suburban concourse level. During peak unloading periods, however, island platforms with reversible escalators will also be used.

Buses will not be serviced in the terminal building, but batteries, air and water will be available for use in the case of emergency.

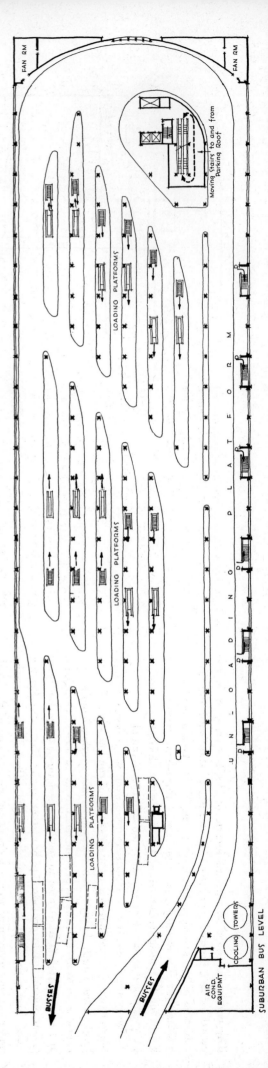

SUBURBAN BUS LEVEL

FAN RM

FAN RM

LOADING PLATFORMS

LOADING PLATFORMS

LOADING PLATFORMS

UNLOADING PLATFORM

Moving Stairs to and from Parking Roof

BUSSES

BUSSES

AIR COND. EQUIPMT

COOLING TOWERS

Times Square skyscrapers provide an impressive silhouette as excavation work for the terminal foundations proceeds. The Port Authority located and renovated apartments for dispossessed families

Sketch of main concourse shows escalators leading to suburban concourse level. Provision has been made for air conditioning waiting room and rentable areas. Individual vending machines will be recessed flush with walls and finished in special harmonizing colors

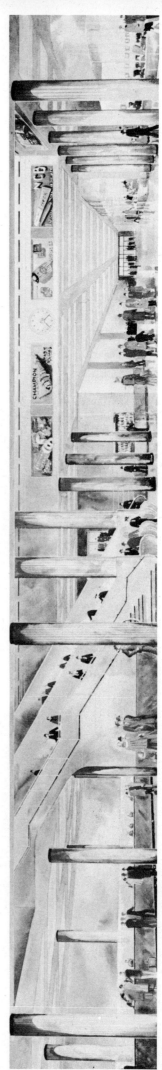

Particular attention has been given to the ventilation of bus loading levels. In the lower level, fresh air enters through bus entrance and exit openings off Ninth Avenue to be expelled from the roof through vents located under the subway mezzanine. In the upper level, continuous unglazed openings in both long sides of the building will afford the source of supply. Six huge exhaust units are located in the roof on the long axis of the building. Concourses opening to the loading areas will be "pressurized" with fresh air to prevent the entrance of exhaust fumes.

Electronic indicators will advise the incoming long-distance bus control which docks are in use. An announcing system for bus arrivals and departures will have outlets at strategic points.

Interior finishes reflect the careful consideration given to economical building maintenance. Waiting rooms, concours es, etc., will have marble wainscote 4 ft. 6 in. high with enamel steel panels above to ceiling. Wearing surfaces, hand rails, trim, and concourse column finish will be of aluminum. Terrazzo floors will be used with non-slip aggregate on sloping surfaces. Ceilings are of suspended acoustical metal pan units with lighting fixtures set flush. Stairs will have terrazzo treads with abrasive strips. The building exterior will be of brick with a 5 ft. granite wainscote and limestone trim.

The importance of rentable areas as a source of revenue has been carefully studied and emphasized in the working out of the plan. All available space has been developed for concession use. As in any good merchandising system, concessions have been played up — made more attractive and more easily accessible — where pedestrian traffic is heaviest. This has never been done, however, to the inconvenience of the traveler, but rather from the standpoint of providing him with extra service, and added time-saving facilities. Shop fronts, restaurants, magazine and shoe shine stands will all be designed and planned to harmonize with interior design and decoration.

Photographs on pages 328 and 329 did not appear in the August 1949 issue of the *Architectural Record*, since the Port Authority Bus Terminal was still under construction at that time. These photographs have been included for book publication in order to show the actual appearance of the completed building.

1. Ticket windows on main concourse.

2. Moving stairways leading to and from suburban concourse.

3. Passengers boarding buses from loading platforms on suburban bus level.

4. View of the completed Port Authority Bus Terminal from a nearby building shows the 8th Avenue facade and the roof parking area In the background are the entrance to the Lincoln Tunnel and the elevated ramps leading to and from the Terminal.

4

Right, transmitter tower, Station WBZ, Boston, Mass.; 649 ft. tall, it is surmounted by a three-section turnstile TV antenna which is supported by a two-section pylon FM antenna. Combined antennas are 76 ft. long, weigh 7442 lb., atop a heavy-duty steel tower which expands from a 29-in. square top to a 75-ft. square base carried on concrete foundations

RADIO AND TELEVISION BUILDINGS

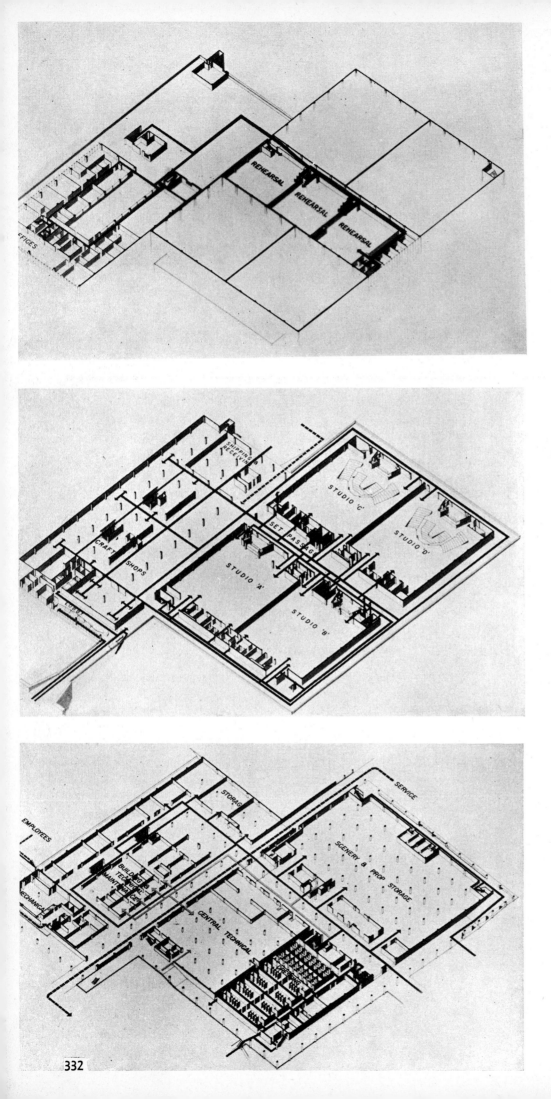

Plant is built around core of four studios on second floor, each containing 12,100 sq ft. Ramps and extra-size elevators facilitate flow of stage sets and materials from shops to studios and back to storage

PREVIEW OF C.B.S. TELEVISION CITY

Pereira and Luckman, Architects

A FLEXIBLE, EXPANDABLE PLANT for TV production on a gigantic scale is the objective of the new C.B.S. Television City now rising on Gilmore Island, Los Angeles. The first unit is scheduled for completion in October, will house four huge studios, three rehearsal halls, carpenter shops and facilities for writers, directors, producers. Additional units, including a 13-story administration building, are to be added as TV expands. Exterior walls of a number of the first structures are built with hinged iron connections at supporting points, so they may be moved later. Walls separating many of the interior areas are movable so room sizes may be changed. Basic concept of the plan is a free flow of bulky sets and materials on a production-line basis. A grouping of long, relatively narrow buildings approximately 150 ft wide was selected, with a wide traffic platform encircling the studio area at second floor level. The first unit in Television City is described by William Pereira as "an experimental workshop," since many facilities will be relocated, changed or expanded as experience in this growing field dictates.

Concrete platform extends around second floor, handles heavy traffic flow to and from studios. Initial plant covers 15 acres, will later be expanded to cover 25

Ezra Stoller

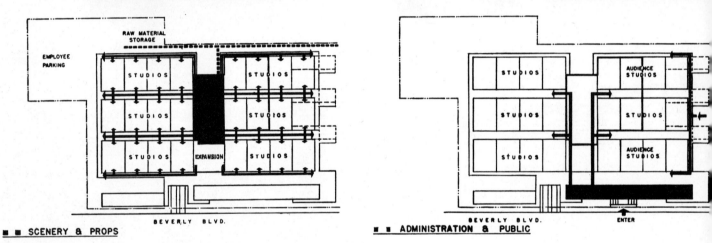

■ ■ SCENERY & PROPS

BEVERLY BLVD.

■ ■ ADMINISTRATION & PUBLIC

BEVERLY BLVD.

ENTER

Flow diagrams were prepared to aid in charting TV production activities. Rehearsal hall (below) contains 4550 sq ft, has movable walls

REHEARSAL HALL

DANCE REHEARSAL HALL

Size, shape and number of stages in TV studios can be altered to meet changing requirements and audience seating can be varied, or removed entirely. Electronic system controls complex stage lighting installation. Construction of the $35 million plant started in December 1950

Photo by Ezra Stoller

THERE are just enough similarities between radio and television broadcasting to confuse the building designer. However, radio is concerned with reproducing *sound*, while TV's greatest problem, not thoroughly licked though commercially quite feasible, is satisfactory *visual* reproduction. Visual broadcasting entails not only photogenic scenes and performers; to create its illusion TV has borrowed techniques and performers from the legitimate theater and the movies; in many studios properties are literally borrowed from the neighborhood retail store, after the fashion of an amateur dramatic club. Radio has borrowed performers from the theater and, often, the audience. Radio requires a studio sized and acoustically treated to suit the performance, containing a few props, sound effects, microphones, and enough light for reading scripts. In the 'live' studio TV requires a blaze of light, stage sets, many props, usually three cameras per show, all movable on dollies; mikes on booms, also mounted on dollies (these can't appear on the receiver screen); and a host of performers and production personnel: actors, camera and mike operators, dolly pullers, electricians, property men, stagehands, and assistant directors. Cameras, mikes, and lights demand complex wiring which usually covers the floor like a mass of snakes; no better system has been found; changing the camera cable's length causes serious technical difficulty.

Congestion of TV equipment, wiring, and personnel is so great that a studio audience is tolerated only when it is indispensable to a show. The program director in charge of a production works from the glass-walled control booth, supervising the performance and numerous control technicians simultaneously, and talking to the studio staff over an intercommunication system. The sponsor is usually in a separate booth to minimize interference with the broadcast.

Partly because technical changes are foreseen and partly due to complexity of broadcasting channel allocation, the Federal Communications Commission has granted no TV licenses in recent months. Impatient though broadcasters are with this 'freeze,' in the long run it should save both them and the public money and confusion. By early summer the Commission reportedly expects to decide on TV allocations in the VHF (very high frequency) channels; by late summer the freeze may be lifted. This would mean rapidly accelerated construction of TV facilities this fall. UHF (ultra-high frequency) broadcasting, a rumored possibility, depends upon development of suitable power. The following figures, obtained from FCC, tell the story as of March 31, 1949:

TELEVISION STATIONS IN THE U. S. A.		RADIO STATIONS, FM	
Now operating, fully licensed	7	Now on the air	724
Operating		Authorized but not yet op't'g	199
Special Temporary Authority	52	Total now authorized	923
Total now operating	59		
Authorized but not yet op't'g	62	**RADIO STATIONS, AM**	
Total now authorized	121	Now on the air	1974
License applications pending	323	Authorized but not yet op't'g	175
Total authorized & pending	444	Total now authorized	2149

Considering its relative youth, licensing difficulties, high building costs, fantastic equipment cost, and the frequent introduction of substantially improved equipment natural in so young an industry, the TV situation is phenomenal. Color television (for which two systems — one mechanical, one electronic — are understood to be now feasible) can further complicate matters.

Preoccupation with technicalities of visual broadcasting has been accompanied by a low level of intrinsic quality of TV programs. Coincidentally, the purely architectural worth of many TV buildings also parallels program quality; the same factors contribute to this condition and, if only for the promotion value of a good building, the same dependence upon public opinion may bring improvement.

Sky-high equipment cost, newness, and experimentation lead to much remodeling of buildings for TV, particularly for big-city studios where network programs originate and where land and building costs are highest. Architectural opportunities are somewhat limited in the case of these large studios, but medium-sized studios offer many. By far the greatest number of TV stations now contemplated is medium-sized, each containing a

George W. Warnecke & Co. ,courtesy Monitor Roofing Co

Contrast the elegance of the competently engineered transmitter tower on page 330 with this typical hodge-podge of receiving antennas on the roof of a New York apartment house (left)

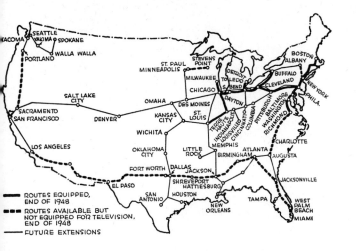

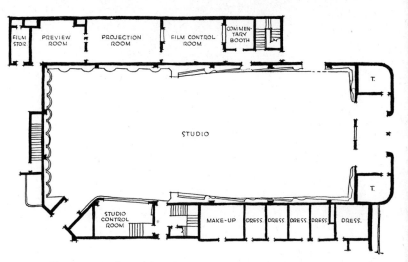

Above left, routes of coaxial cables and micro-wave relay facilities for television networks

Three ways of providing for television: above, NBC's Studio F, Hollywood, Calif., a converted radio studio; below, WFIL-TV, Philadelphia Inquirer station, built new, will also televise from the adjacent Philadelphia Arena and has remote transmitter in the Widener Building; bottom of page, part plan of WCBS-TV's New York studios in remodeled office space in the top of Grand Central Station

relatively small studio, mobile facilities, rebroadcasting facilities, control and transmission equipment, and offices. After these principal network links are established small studios will come along. Whether a small station can be designed to grow efficiently is an unresolved question.

For all the technicality of TV problems there is sound consulting advice available in the form of lighting, air conditioning, and sound control experts. Coordination of all types of equipment, and of spaces and techniques both borrowed and inherent in TV, is an architectural problem about which the TV station manager has much to say. He has opinions on the staggering circulation problem. He is an authority as well as a client; his decisions carry much weight, which may account for some makeshifts — even mistakes — which characterize many TV buildings. Certainly those stations in the design of which good architects have been employed demonstrate the value of competent architectural effort.

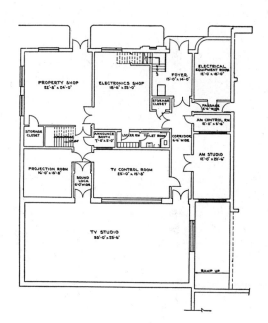

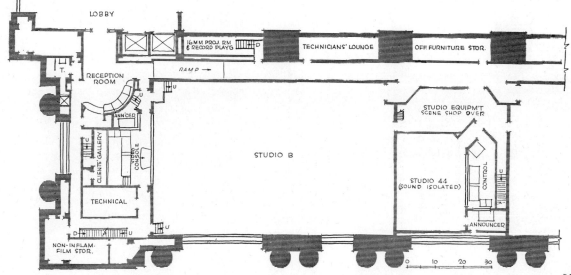

WHAM, THE RADIO CITY OF ROCHESTER, N. Y.

W. G. Kaelber & L. A. Waasdorp, Architects

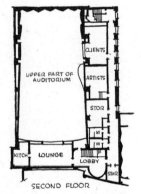

SECOND FLOOR

THE recently completed Stromberg-Carlson station, WHAM, provides for AM and FM radio and television. The five smaller radio studios and large auditorium studio are sound-isolated, with floating walls, floors and ceilings inside the reinforced concrete structure. TV studio, approximately 45 by 55 ft., was included in initial design but was completed after the remainder of the building, in time for telecasting to start in late spring, 1949. Access for bringing large props and scenery into the TV studio seems restricted, but some programs may be handled from Studio A. Note economical layout of TV equipment, film studio, vault, shop, transmitter.

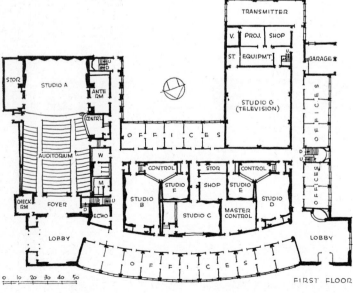

FIRST FLOOR

DESIGN OF TELEVISION STATIONS

By J. P. Allinson

THE financial importance of television buildings is indicated not only by their increasing number but also by the high cost of their equipment; telecasting equipment, air conditioning, lighting and sound control equipment for the 59 stations now licensed runs well up into the hundreds of thousands of dollars. Add the expense of actual construction and the dollar outlay becomes truly impressive. Whatever the opinion of TV as a cultural medium (and a few recent programs have had critical acclaim), the 2,000,000 estimated viewers of the last Presidential election constitute an audience which cannot be ignored. The industry generally is in a developmental stage — its youth, scarcity of suitable space, and astronomical costs not only complicate the design problem but also make it necessary to limit this article to a survey of ideas in the field at the moment.

TYPES OF STATIONS

Network Originating Studios Many of the networks (ABC, CBS, NBC, Mutual, Dumont, and Don Lee) have recently completed or are about to open new plants. Several have tremendous expansion plans; most consider their present facilities experimental. The large central station in which network programs originate is most complex, likely to be scattered among several floors or even several buildings in the downtown part of a large city. Often it is a remodeling job, designed by the network's architectural staff. The typical large station contains numerous studios, each with a control booth, central control facilities, and a full complement of technical, production, and administrative areas. Such close scheduling of TV broadcasts is necessary, in order to make maximum use of the costly space and equipment, that *circulation* assumes paramount importance, and

The author and the editors wish to thank the following individuals and organizations for their assistance in compiling the information contained in this Building Types Study, for permission to reproduce drawings and photographs, and for their help in checking preliminary copy.
Television Networks: ABC, CBS, Don Lee-Mutual, Dumont, NBC and their engineering and publicity departments; TV Stations KNBH, WABD, WPIX, WRGB; Paul Adanti, General Manager, WHEN; L. E. Littlejohn, Chief Engineer, WFIL-TV; Kliegl Bros. Lighting; Television Associates Inc.; Anemostat Corp. of America; the editors of "Communications", "Electronics", "Televiser Monthly", and of General Electric's "Television Show Business" and RCA's "Broadcast News" and "RCA Review;" and J. W. Eriksen, Engineer, The Austin Co. Organization chart, top right, appears courtesy NBC.

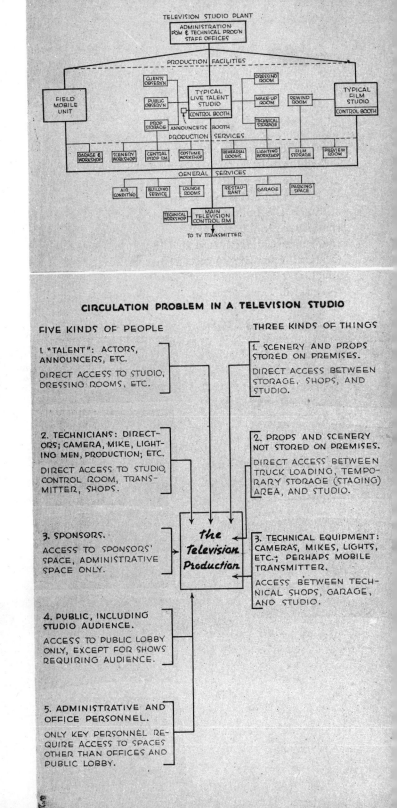

1.

Requirements for live-talent studio; sketch by Engineering Dept., NBC. A, scene being televised; B, cameras; C, microphone boom; D, camera picking up titles and video effects; E, lighting controls; F, lights (only a few shown) adjusted from E; G, slide projector for rear projection of scenery; H, audio and video control; I, program direction

the *traffic department* becomes the nerve center where schedules, distribution of programs through the network, etc., are handled.

People and things (see diagram) must flow easily through the building; control is essential. Executives and managerial personnel, sponsors, visitors, and studio audiences ordinarily use one set of entrances to the station; operating personnel — technicians and production staff — another; talent — actors, performers — a third. The diagram indicates the necessity for keeping the various kinds of traffic separate. In a one-story building, production shops and storage rooms might be on the opposite side from spaces reserved for talent, who should be able to enter directly from the street or parking space to their dressing rooms. Costume storage, make-up and artists' lounge rooms should be adjacent; if on another floor, a quick-change room should be pro-

vided near the studio. Ample rehearsal space is needed.

Production spaces are like those in the legitimate theater, but have to be larger and more accessible because the TV show is put on for one performance only. not for a long run, which means storage for many types of properties and scenery and delivery space for many more; carpentry and paint shops for the continuous making or revamping of scenery for new productions, and wide corridors, sound locks, doors, etc., for moving large units expeditiously from shop or shipping entrance to studio. Production personnel includes stagehands, prop men, etc., who have no occasion to enter talent's quarters but must have direct access to the studio. Technicians include those who work in the studio itself — camera and microphone operators and lighting men — and those who man the control rooms — video and audio operators, etc. — both of whom have contact

2. Live studio, KGO-TV (ABC) in San Francisco, view from control room showing sound-deadened walls, ceiling; portable and ceiling lights, air ducts, 3 cameras; at bottom, monitors as seen by video technicians. 3. Proposed alteration of Civic Theater, Chicago, for ABC telecasts. 4. Daytime studio from audience seating. WABD (Dumont), New York. 5. Making a telecast, KNBH (NBC), Hollywood

2   3

with the performers in the studio only. Technical spaces include not only the studio and master control rooms but also the transmitter room, equipment spaces and shops for working on equipment. It is convenient to have the garage for the mobile truck transmitter accessible to the technical shops. The entire production is supervised by a director (who works from the studio control room), one or more assistants (who work in the studio) and a script girl who is constantly at the director's elbow. The director talks to his assistants, lighting and production chiefs, and camera and microphone men over some type of intercom system: pocket radio, wired phone headsets, in some cases a low-volume loudspeaker.

In most studios audiences are not admitted, because they are the source of unwanted noise and because the congestion of equipment and personnel in the studio is so great that an audience cannot be allowed. Only in a few, and these mostly of the theater type for shows which demand audiences, is the public admitted. TV cameras require a great deal of space in which to maneuver — they are mounted on dollies which are pulled by men — and this also restricts the amount of space which can be given over to an audience. Audience circulation through the building must be very closely controlled. Many station operators would like to place similar limitations on sponsors as well, but this is rather difficult to achieve. Usually the sponsor has a booth completely separated from the studio and control room, with a glass wall into the studio for direct observation. CBS, in its new Grand Central studios in New York, places the sponsors in the control room itself, a practice which makes most program directors shudder. Regulations governing places of assembly must be respected.

Films, slides, commercials, etc., are dubbed into the TV program as it goes over the air from a telecine room, and announcers have a small studio; these are all grouped around the control room. In a large station, much dubbing in may be controlled from the master control room; it may also be done from the studio control. The transmitter and tower may be at the station or remote.

Very Small Stations At the opposite end of the TV building scale is the small local station for receiving network programs and making spot announcements, etc. This type is likely to be located at the ideal transmitter site, which may not be "downtown." Space requirements include a room for telecasting equipment and transmission, for network pick-up equipment, etc.; a small announce booth, telecine space and film storage. Personnel is usually limited; commercial and administrative offices are combined; minimum toilet facilities are provided. There may be a small room for costuming, make-up, etc., for the rare occasion when the local mayor will make a personal appearance on TV.

If there is any likelihood of televising local sports or other events, the station will have a mobile transmitter truck, which will require a garage. Often this space is so designed that the truck can drive virtually into the studio itself; on occasion the truck control equipment might be used instead of a studio control console (there is a difference of opinion on this practice). More common practice is to install, when the station is located at the transmitter site, a microwave receiver to pick up signals from the mobile transmitter. Switching between all the different types of programs is handled by the combination transmitter and master-control operator.

If the station transmitter has a downtown location, a small studio is probably essential because the possibility of telecasting simple studio shows is increased. Another variation, which interests a great many TV operators, has an out-of-town transmitter site and, downtown, a small plant containing film and slide projection facilities, small studio, announce booth, and control room which serves as master control, coordinating all program sources. The plant can be linked to the

5

4

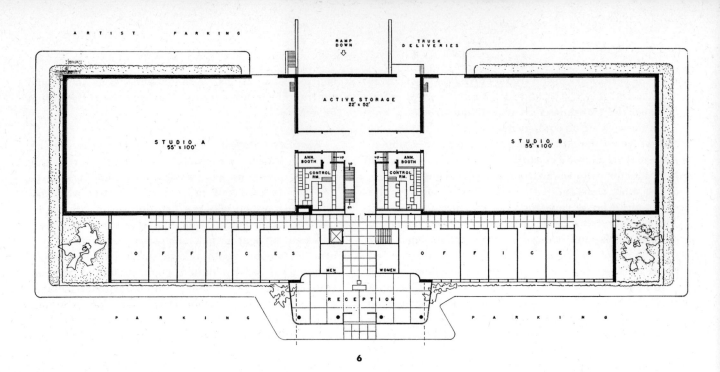

6

transmitter by microwave; mobile signals can be received and coordinated at the downtown plant or at the transmitter. All these variations on the small station assume a tie-in to one or more of the networks; cost of producing a "live talent" show is prohibitive for the small operator. As the accompanying map shows, coaxial cables and microwave relays essential for direct distribution of network programs are not likely to cover the entire country as rapidly as the demand for TV stations requires. The industry's answer to this dilemma is *kinescope recording,* or precision photography of actual TV programs. The technical difficulties are being solved, and kinescope promises to become a major source of network-quality programs.

Intermediate Stations Between the two types outlined — definitions here are arbitrary, assumed solely for convenience — lies a third principal type. It may be considered an expansion of the small station; it incorporates many features of the key network station, but is not considered adequate for full-scale network program origination. Although this type may contain more than one "live" studio, it can be planned quite successfully for a single, fairly large studio and control room around which are grouped announce booth, telecine room, network receiving equipment and transmitter room; from the one control room all master switching between studio, film, and remote programs can also be handled. The distinction between this and some variations on the small studio lies principally in technical facilities for programming. The studio itself is ordinarily larger to accommodate the desired 3 image orthicon TV cameras and mike on a telescoping boom, but otherwise total space requirements are little greater.

The telecine room here will probably contain two "multiplexers," or angular mirror setups for film and slide projectors which make possible the use of a single stationary TV camera (rather than a moving TV camera to be shuttled back and forth between movie projectors, which is common in smaller studios). Facilities for film processing, airing and editing should also be provided. It should be possible to add a second studio efficiently in the future; this may be a rehearsal room at the beginning. An eventual master control room and more office space should also be envisioned at the outset, and some provision must be made for the ultimate wiring system.

Even for the minimum, it is often advisable to plan for two studios, either both the same size or one fairly large — say 25 or 30 by 40 feet — and one small, for one-set performances. Adding the master control room eases coordination of technical facilities, permits operation by one man during long network periods, permits equipment repairs and maintenance without disturbing facilities; and one man can keep continuous watch over equipment performance. The projection room is best located next the master control room; when two studios are planned, a satisfactory working arrangement is to have this pair of spaces between the studios, with the studio control rooms above.

10. Studio suggested by William Foss, TV consultant, to use mobile unit controls at first, to which more equipment and another studio may be added efficiently

10

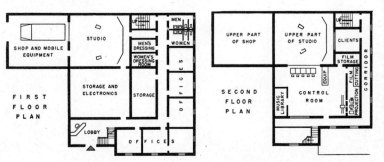

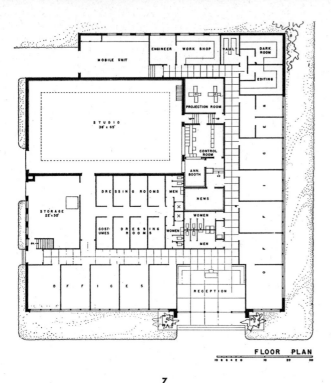

FLOOR PLAN

7

FLOOR PLAN

8

BUILDING DESIGN CONSIDERATIONS

Whatever the station size, rigid economy and compactness are essential. Equipment cannot be skimped, but little can be spent on impressive architecture and even such considerations as noise control and acoustics are handled inexpensively. Compactness also helps the plant to run smoothly, reducing operating costs. Many of the schemes illustrated are admittedly faulty because many existing studios are remodeling jobs or revamped radio studios, in which space and structure impose serious limitations.

The building designer will cooperate with the station manager or engineer, network advisors to affiliates, the video engineer, and probably a TV consultant. He will learn that a TV station requires three or four times as much space as a comparable radio station. Space estimates are difficult to make, but NBC engineers, for instance, suggest that a single live-talent studio entails five times the studio area for auxiliary spaces; that for a station containing three live studios the proportion is reduced to three times studio area. Production methods are almost certain to change, so flexibility of the original space and provision for expansion are important. TV plants have been developed both horizontally (all principal areas on one main floor) and vertically (multi-story). The horizontal plant offers production advantages, is easily expanded, but requires much land. Multi-story schemes may cost less initially but are difficult to expand; when enlarged, the plant's facilities may be scattered, leading to difficulty — and consequent high cost — of operation.

9

6, 7, 8. Floor plans of typical very large, intermediate, and small stations developed by Rene Brugnoni, Archt., and Ben Adler, TV Consultant. 6 has rehearsal rooms, building equipment, etc., in basement; master control, equipment, etc., on second floor. 7 has scene shops etc., under storage and dressing rooms, elevator to storage space. 8 envisages use of mobile equipment for control. 9. Plan, WXEL, station now under construction, Parma, Ohio; Rene Brugnoni, Archt. Note resemblance to typical schemes; also close relation between control and transmitter space. Studio wall opens up for supervision of telecasts from adjacent sports field

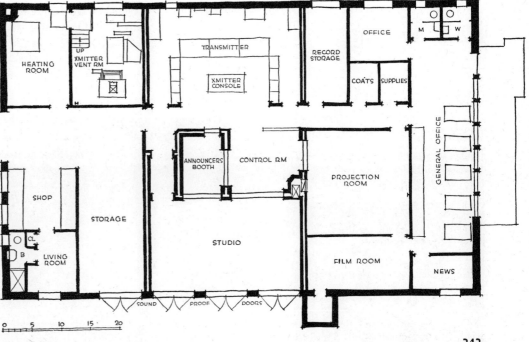

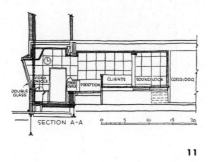

SECTION A-A

11

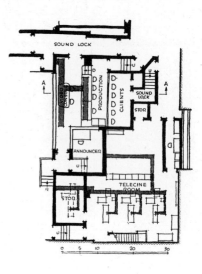

Below: 12. Control room equipment and sightlines suggested by General Electric engineers

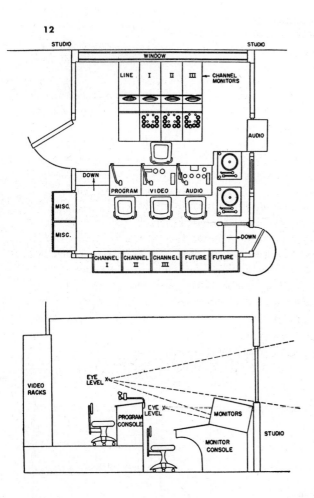

Above: 11. Section and plan through control room, new CBS studios in New York. Sponsors are separated from program director only by a rail, which is not common practice. Shaded areas show ducts for electronic connections in control room and telecine studio

Considerable parking area on the site is desirable. Convenient access for truck deliveries and garage space for the mobile TV unit are musts. Noise in the locality, airborne or carried into the studio by the soil or building structure, may cause trouble; occasionally this problem may render undesirable an otherwise satisfactory location. If the building has other tenants, their noise-producing activities must be considered; pumps, fans, printing presses and industrial machinery are offenders.

"Live" Studios Technically, video and audio equipment constitutes the heart of the TV plant, but building design usually centers around the studio for live talent. Here the practical requirements of TV — sometimes as many as eight sets ready at one time in one studio, room for the numerous operating, producing and acting personnel, equipment, and lighting evolved from stage and movie techniques — take precedence over such matters as acoustics. For a non-audience studio, NBC finds an 18-foot ceiling the absolute minimum, with some disadvantages; 22 feet is preferred, 25 desired, and for

14

Control Rooms. 13, 14, Studio 8G control, WNBT, New York, is on mezzanine. 15, WABD Studio A. 16, Master control, WFIL, Philadelphia

13

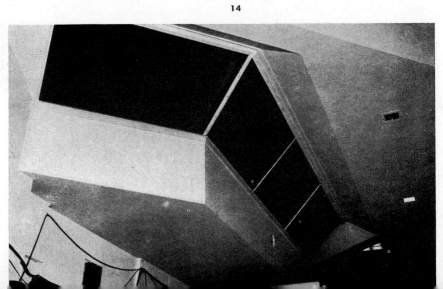

19

18

19. Installing equipment, telecine studio, KNBH; note floor chases for electronic wiring. 18, Telecine studio, WHEN, Syracuse, N.Y.; stairs lead to control room. 17. Transmitter building, Station KNBH, Hollywood, Calif. Note "turnstile" TV antenna

17

some studios designed to permit up-angle shots, 35 feet. Some telecasters believe there is no maximum, others that more than 25 feet is wasted; if sets are to be flied or if lights are to be manipulated from a suspended catwalk more height is needed; air conditioning such high rooms is costly. All these factors must be weighed. In area, 25 x 40 ft. is probably the smallest practicable, 30 x 50 is a desirable minimum, 40 x 60 or 40 x 80 is preferred; yet many stations have smaller studios. Entrances should be protected by sound locks and even if the studio is not sound-isolated, it is often surrounded by corridors, storage rooms or offices to reduce noise penetration. Building equipment, which is more fully discussed below, has some definite effects upon studio design.

Auditorium or Theater Studios Shows which demand audiences introduce the problem of providing for 300 to 500 people — seldom more — extraneous to the production, who cannot be admitted to the studio floor and whose convenience has less importance than that

15

16

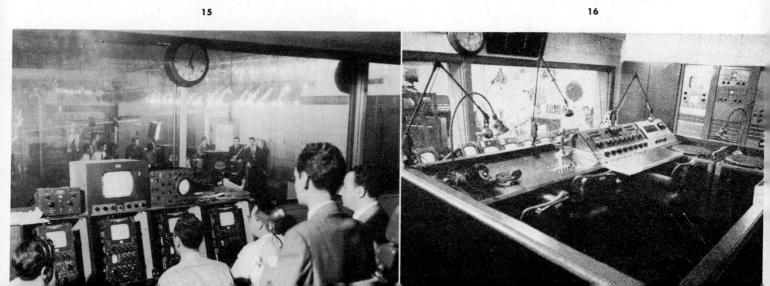

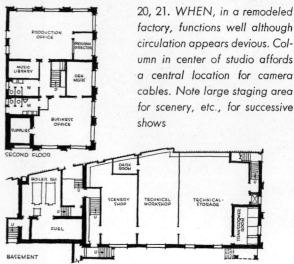

20, 21. WHEN, in a remodeled factory, functions well although circulation appears devious. Column in center of studio affords a central location for camera cables. Note large staging area for scenery, etc., for successive shows

20

of the audience which sees the telecast on a $199 receiver. The studio audience cannot be close to the performance because cameras and microphones must move about freely. It is often seated in a steep balcony (which may require a high ceiling), separated from the studio floor by a rail. Since many productions in this type of studio are musical, the acoustic properties may receive more attention. Several radio studios have been adapted for TV audience shows and function fairly well. Adaptation of legitimate theaters has both proponents and opponents; lighting and microphone installations are difficult enough, but providing for the desired three TV cameras becomes a real problem. There is usually one camera in the center; ideally this should be able to "dolly in" for close-ups, which may necessitate a runway similar to that in a burlesque theater. To give roundness to the televised actors and reality to the telecast performance, the other cameras may be at the sides of the auditorium, one perhaps lower than another. Only after experimenting with camera angles can camera platforms be built in with surety. The control room in a remodeled theater might be in a side box; in a new theater it might be under the raised audience space.

Film or Projection Studio These have in the past consisted of a room in which movie and slide projectors are positioned against glazed ports in one wall, on the other side of which a TV camera has been shuttled back and forth to pick up succeeding reels. Recently multiplexers (previously mentioned) have been developed; space requirements for these appear on accompanying plans. Much movie film is 35 mm. and inflammable; for this, fireproof storage vaults, vented to the outdoors, are needed. 16 mm. film, non-inflammable, is also used and requires cabinets only for storage. Both film projection and kinescope recording (which is to TV as transcription is to radio) necessitate processing, cutting and rewind space.

Announce Booth Usually placed so it has a view through double glazing into both studio and control room, the announce booth in some large stations is isolated from the studio. Occasionally it is supervised only from the master control room. Whatever its location, the booth is usually an interior room for a single person, who requires an audio and a video monitor like those in the control room.

Control Rooms The studio control room contains video consoles which house part of the electronic equipment and monitors which show the picture recorded by each TV camera; racks for more electronic equipment; more consoles for audio control; at least two "turntables" (record players); a monitor TV screen on which the actual telecast appears; and room for two or three video operators, an audio operator, the program direc-

25. Control room, WHEN, showing windows into film room and announce booth. Operating desk (another variation on program director's equipment) in foreground, video console just visible at lower right corner

25

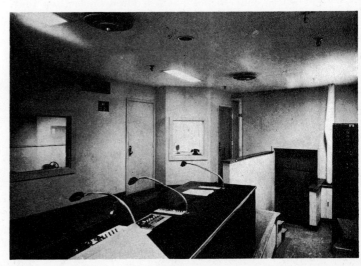

21

23

tor, and often a script girl. For a large studio the control room might be 16 x 24 ft.; for a medium-sized studio, 14 x 16 ft. Equipment is usually though not always set on two levels, with the director and audio operator 2 ft. above the other operators, so the director can see over the video technicians' heads. Ceiling height is 8 ft. above the higher level. In most cases the control room is centered on one long wall of the studio, with a double-glazed window set with its sill 3′ 10″ to 5 ft. above the studio floor, and with the lower control room floor 2 to 4 ft. above the studio floor. In other instances, the studio control room is a full story above the studio floor; sometimes the window is flush with the studio wall, sometimes it projects into the studio and is glazed on three sides; there are those who believe the director should work entirely from the monitors, in a control room which has no view at all of the studio.

The master control room, required where there are more than two studios, is similar in equipment to studio control, but need not have a direct view into studios. Here switching from one to another program and ultimate refining of the telecast are done. This may be a very large space; for a two-studio station, 15 x 25 ft. to 18 x 26 ft. should suffice. In a one-studio station master and studio control may be combined, or there may be one control room for the live studio and a combined master-and-film-studio control. The combination can be accommodated in a 16 x 17 ft. room with an additional equipment room about 9 x 17 ft. Master control consoles may be arranged in U shape for operating convenience. In WJZ-TV's new studios, the film studio has a separate control room from which film may be fed into any studio as well as telecast independently. In the very small station everything is controlled from one room, which may also contain part of the transmitter equipment.

Transmitter Rooms, Technical Shops and Offices Method of operation and size of the station govern transmitter room requirements; for a one-studio station, all transmitter equipment and personnel can be accommodated

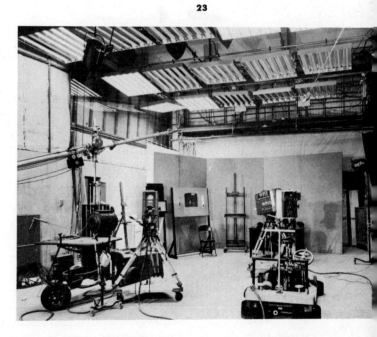

24. Lighting catwalk and fixtures suspended on rods, WCBS-TV, New York. Fixture positions are set from below with poles or from ladders

24

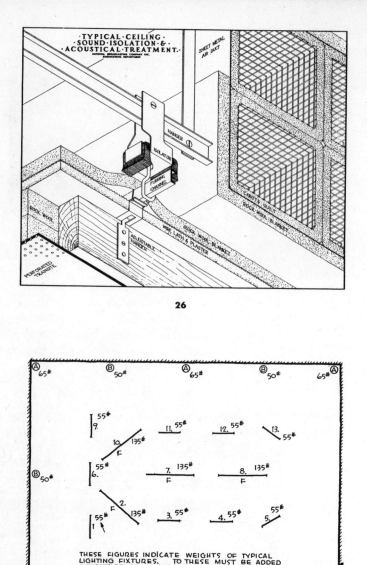

Figure showing TYPICAL·CEILING·SOUND·ISOLATION·& ·ACOUSTICAL·TREATMENT· with labels including SHEET METAL AIR DUCT, HANGER, ISOLATOR, FURRING CHANNEL, ROCK WOOL, ADJUSTABLE HANGER, WIRE LATH & PLASTER, ROCK WOOL BLANKET, CABOT'S QUILT, PERFORATED TRANSITE.

26

26. Standard sound-isolating construction, NBC; note method of subdividing air duct. 27. Typical lighting fixture layout for a small live studio; fixture weights are obtained from manufacturers. 28, 29. Air conditioning and lighting considerations; method shown in 29 is seldom practicable. 30. In Navy experimental studio for teaching by television, subjects televised are relatively fixed in position, hence lighting is nearly constant in direction and center-ceiling air outlets become possible

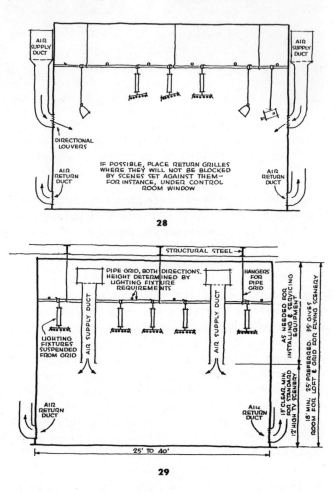

Figure 28: AIR SUPPLY DUCT, DIRECTIONAL LOUVERS, AIR RETURN DUCT. IF POSSIBLE, PLACE RETURN GRILLES WHERE THEY WILL NOT BE BLOCKED BY SCENES SET AGAINST THEM—FOR INSTANCE, UNDER CONTROL ROOM WINDOW

28

Figure 29: STRUCTURAL STEEL, PIPE GRID, BOTH DIRECTIONS. HEIGHT DETERMINED BY LIGHTING FIXTURE REQUIREMENTS, HANGERS FOR PIPE GRID, LIGHTING FIXTURES SUSPENDED FROM GRID, AIR SUPPLY DUCT, AIR RETURN DUCT, AS NEEDED FOR INSTALLING & SERVICING EQUIPMENT, 13' CLEAR, MIN. FOR STANDARD 12' HIGH TV SCENERY, 18' MIN. 25' PREFERRED, 35' GIVES ROOM FOR LOFT & GRID FOR FLYING SCENERY. 25' TO 40'

29

Figure 27: Lighting fixture layout. Weights marked 65#, 50#, 55#, 135# at various positions.

THESE FIGURES INDICATE WEIGHTS OF TYPICAL LIGHTING FIXTURES. TO THESE MUST BE ADDED WEIGHT OF GRID, SUPPORTS, CATWALK, ETC. TO DETERMINE LOAD SUSPENDED FROM STRUCTURE ABOVE

——— INCANDESCENT FLOOD REFLECTOR GRID
——— HIGH INTENSITY FLUORESCENT BANKS
Ⓐ 2 KW SPOTLIGHTS   Ⓑ 3/4 KW SPOTLIGHTS

27

in a room approximately 24 x 30 ft. In other cases the room must be appreciably larger. Occasionally station operation makes it advisable to include some transmitter equipment in the master control room, sometimes in a combined studio-master control. An engineering workshop is needed for equipment maintenance and storage, and the chief engineer usually needs a private office. When the transmitter tower is not at the studio loca-

30

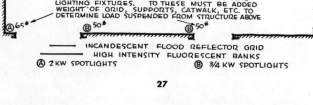

tion, part of the equipment may be at the studio and part at the transmitter building, or all at the transmitter, where an announce booth may also be included. A direct line of sight is required for relaying signals from studio to remote transmitter by microwave but not when signals travel by coaxial cable.

Production and Talent Areas For live talent (actors, lecturers, performers), provisions are much like those in the legitimate theater: direct access from building entrance, dressing and make-up rooms, toilets, a lounge, all dependent in size and number upon the extent to which live shows are contemplated. Production areas are also similar to those in the theater, with the added considerations that shows must change quickly (meaning immediate, easy access), that many articles are borrowed or rented for one performance only (necessitating truck deliveries convenient to the studio), and that many of these objects are large and weighty (requiring wide entrances, floors capable of bearing heavy loads and with durable surfacing in studio, shops and delivery areas). Spaces required include a scene dock for plywood flats 12 ft. high and up to 5′ 9″ wide; carpentry shop about 30 x 30 ft. for making stock sets; a large scene studio with paint frame, up to 40 x 80 ft., for setting up and painting sets; rooms for costume storage and possible dyeing and sewing. Sizes noted are for large stations; in smaller plants they might be reduced.

Cameras, Lighting, Electrical System

Introduction of the new image-orthicon TV camera recently has changed many studio requirements. The old iconoscope camera demanded much higher levels of studio illumination. At the same time, lighting units themselves have been undergoing change. Current good practice employs a mixture of fluorescent and incandescent lamps in fixtures suspended from a pipe grid which is hung from the studio ceiling; the proportion of each type is the subject of divergent opinions and must be determined for each job. In addition, some portable lamps on standards are used to give roundness to the televised subject. Fixtures are preferably adjustable in direction and height, and although dimmers have not been common, they are included in many recent installations. There is a growing practice of concentrating all responsibility for lighting in one individual, which means some method of remote control for the fixtures. This introduces complex lighting switching; and while some studios have installed catwalks at the level of the ceiling fixtures for manually adjusting lights, in others this is done from ladders. Some lights are adjusted by means of pulleys and cables; sometimes there is a wall-mounted pinrail to which the cables or ropes run. In a TV studio there is no chance to adjust lighting during the performance as there is on the movie stage; once set, the lighting stays. The lighting pipe grid is usually designed to carry 40 lbs. per square ft. of floor area; special tracks, monorails, etc., have also been used, although the need to cut costs may rule these out. Structurally, the ceiling must be capable of supporting the weight of the grid plus weight of fixtures.

To permit utmost flexibility of lighting, a great number of wall receptacles is essential. Three-outlet units ten ft. apart, entirely around the room, are recommended. One authority recommends two rows, one about 2 ft. above the floor, the other slightly below ceiling fixture level; another suggests a single row about 5 ft. above the floor. The studio power load is in the neighborhood of 15 to 25 watts per square ft. of staging area.

Camera cables have to maintain a constant length, so camera plug-ins are often concentrated in one spot, directly under the control room window where they cannot be blocked by scenery. In large studios several locations may be needed. In the control room, wiring may be carried in floor trenches; the same is true of movie-projector units in the film room. Future expansion must be considered when such permanent installations are made.

Air Conditioning and Sound Control

Air conditioning remains important to TV studios even with the reductions in light levels made possible by the new cameras. However, the only problems peculiar to TV are sound isolation and air distribution in studios. The air system creates noise or vibration in ducts, at supply and return grilles, and at pumps, compressors or fans. All reciprocating or rotating machinery should be sound-isolated; flexible connections are desirable between ducts and blowers; ducts are invariably lined with sound-absorbent material and often subdivided internally to reduce noise. Air is distributed at low velocity to eliminate hissing and ducts are oversized, careful attention being paid to design of turning vanes, corners, dampers, etc. Where ducts pass through the structure they are well isolated to prevent noise transmission. In the studio, the portion of the space above lighting fixture level is often not conditioned; directional supply outlets are located below the fixtures. If they did not interfere with mobility and direction of lights, it would be ideal to employ centrally located air supply grilles, but this is so difficult that high wall locations are more common. Return grilles near the floor may be blocked by scenery; nevertheless both floor-level and high-wall returns are used.

In discussing studio design some of the sound control problems have been covered: sound locks, sound-isolating corridors, etc. In the studio the ambient noise level is higher than a radio studio would tolerate, due to sounds from moving scenery, cameras, etc., and to movement and control of personnel. Directional microphones have been developed to cope with this, but it is also advisable to have the studio acoustically as dead as possible. Common practice is to line the entire walls with mineral wool blanket; sometimes alternating panels of live and dead materials are used, but sets, equipment, etc., negate such acoustic refinement. A sensible precaution is to protect the acoustic surfacing with a dado of perforated asbestos board, or at least a handrail. The floor is necessarily acoustically live. Control rooms are acoustically treated, usually to make them as completely dead as possible, sometimes to attempt reproduction of "living room" conditions — but not all TV receivers are in living rooms. Control room and sponsor's booth entrances should have sound locks.

Other equipment problems, such as placing the microphones so they will not cast shadows on the hero's face or the sponsor's product, are not strictly architectural. Nevertheless, the TV operator is so anxious to find solutions that the architect with an idea will find a ready audience.

WBZ RADIO AND TELEVISION CENTER

Architectural Dept., Westinghouse Electric Corp., Designers

Boston, Massachusetts

In 25 YEARS of broadcasting WBZ has grown from a simple monks-cloth-draped penthouse at Westinghouse's East Springfield works, first to quarters in a succession of hotels, now to this new plant on Boston's Charles River, housing WBZ-WBZA, WBZ-FM, WBZ-TV. Television studio (45 by 50 by 23 ft. high, sound-deadened with mineral wool on walls and ceiling) and control, projection and production spaces are grouped so facilities common to TV and radio can be used jointly. Circulation is particularly well handled. Auditorium-studio A, primarily radio, has TV camera and lighting outlets, seats 160, is 35 by 68 by 18 ft. high with stage 22 by 30 ft. TV film, network, studio and remote shows are controlled in TV equipment room. Studio flooring, left, is rubber tile to take heavy traffic.

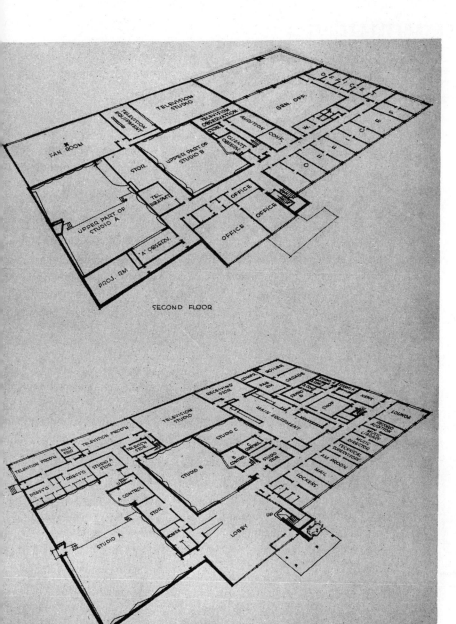

SECOND FLOOR

FIRST FLOOR

Above, WBZ-TV mobile truck. Below, film projection room: TV cameras, movie and slide projectors and multiplexers; film camera control consoles in foreground. In plan, note segregation of public, administrative, talent, technical and production traffic; also receiving space near equipment room and TV studio, actors' rooms serving TV and radio studios.

WICU   Erie, Pa.

DUMONT NETWORK AFFILIATE

Nelson and Goldberg,   *Engineer and Architect*

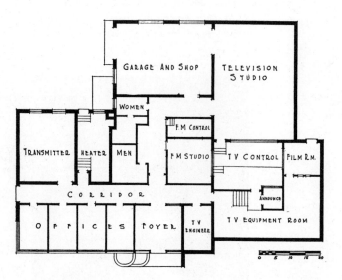

STATION WICU, completed late in April, 1949, is a small, limited-budget, one-studio television plant. Its plan is organized to permit operation with minimum personnel; special provisions for audiences are omitted because most live shows will come from networks. On occasion a few live shows may originate in WICU and others may be televised from local sources. When necessary, the studio can hold about 100 people. Limiting the local live program has made possible omission of some production and talent spaces and reduction of others. Grouping both studios (one for the FM component of the telecast), FM control, film room, announce booth and TV equipment about the TV control room helps reduce operating personnel. Equipment room is designed for double present requirements and transmitter room is located so it can be enlarged readily. Acoustic treatment is kept to a minimum in FM studio, eliminated in TV studio, where portable drapes and scenery are relied upon to deaden sound. Air conditioning has not been installed, though provision is made for future packaged air conditioners; at present recirculating air heating and individual ventilators change the air in non-fenestrated rooms; transmitter room has a power exhaust for heat generated by the equipment. Construction cost approximately $12 per square foot.

In contrast, the 3-million-dollar Mutual-Don Lee

KHJ *Hollywood, Calif.*

MUTUAL—DON LEE

PRODUCTION CENTER

Claude Beelman, Architect; **Herman Spackler, Associate**

building is a two-story, 14-studio radio and TV center where live shows originate. Covering a whole city block, it has ample parking space at the rear (not shown) and is noteworthy for its excellent circulation. Studio audiences may enter any of the theater-studios from the street; talent can proceed directly to dressing rooms and stages; administrative personnel is on second floor, which contains executive, business and sales offices, audition rooms, publicity department, and (on mezzanines) clients' booths and echo rooms for theaters. Each theater is 115 by 65 by 33 ft. high, has a 60 by 65 ft. stage for a 100-piece orchestra, and seats 350 people; all are permanently equipped for TV. There are four theaters, four non-audience studios, three commentator-and-disc-jockey studios, and three announce booths. Master control, set behind a sound-proof window into the main lobby, is 33 ft. long, 10 ft. high, weighs 8½ tons; through more than 800 switching positions a single engineer can handle as many as six programs running simultaneously through the board over 14 outgoing and incoming network lines, as well as circuits from studios, recording studios, cue circuits, video circuits, remote circuits, and house monitors. Basement houses sound-isolated air conditioning apparatus, storage space, employees' lounges, etc. Large studios are all "floated" construction for sound isolation.

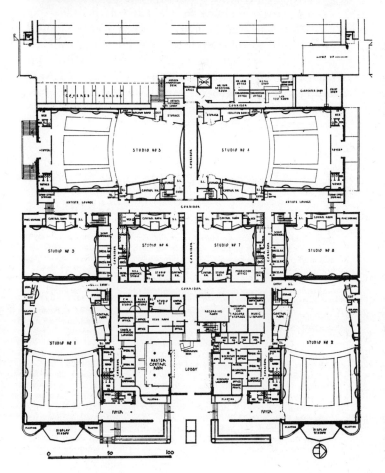

Tile and face-brick walls and concrete floor slab are carried by a peripheral grade beam, 12 by 24 in. in size, which rests on footing posts, all of concrete. Roof (built up, on gypsum decking) is framed with 24 in. open-web steel joists; top flanges are extended to carry overhangs; clear span is 45 ft.; interior partitions are non-load-bearing. Beneath floor are chases for radio wiring and air conditioning ducts

KWKC, SMALL FM RADIO STATION IN ABILENE, TEXAS

Hughes & Olds, Architects and Engineers

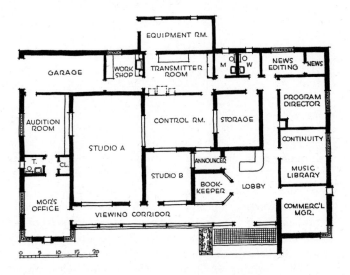

STATION KWKC, built in 1948, is a radio studio and transmitter building for the Citizens Broadcasting Co. The two studios and announce booth grouped around the control room can be augmented by converting adjacent storage space; like the other studios, this has been constructed with acoustically surfaced walls and ceiling, with mineral wool insulation in the studding. News ticker, though well isolated, is nevertheless convenient in a small station.

CONDENSED BIBLIOGRAPHY: BUILDING FOR TELEVISION

Note: Television has progressed so rapidly that few publications on its building requirements exist, and most of these are outdated. Much information is contained in periodicals; space permits listing only a few articles from such sources. Additional information can be obtained from the editors of the various magazines.

ARTICLES, BOOKS

American Television Directory, The, American Television Soc., 17 E. 45 St., New York, N. Y. 1946

Challenge of Television, The. John Flory. Educational Screen vol. 23, p284.

Facilities Housing for TV. Brugnoni and Adler. Broadcast News.

Forecasts in FM and TV. Columbia Broadcasting System, New York, N. Y. 1945

Official Yearbook of the Television Industry. Television Broadcasters Ass'n., 500 Fifth Ave., New York, N. Y.

Planning the Television Station. A. N. Goldsmith. Televiser, Nov–Dec 1945

Practical Equipment Layouts for TV Stations. Broadcast News.

Radio Broadcasting and Television annotated bibliography). Oscar Rose, ed. H. W. Wilson Co. N. Y. 1947

Story of a Penthouse Station. S. H. Cuff. Televiser, Jan–Feb 1946

Telecasting and Color. Kingdon S. Tyler. Harcourt-Brace. N. Y. 1946

Television Encyclopedia. Stanley Kempner, ed. Fairchild Pub. Co. N. Y. 1948

Television Show Business. Judy Dupuy. General Electric Co. Schenectady, N. Y. 1945

Television Station Costs. Wm. Foss. Electronics, Dec 1948

Television Studio (revolving stages). Arch. Forum. May 1944, p6.

Truth about Color Television, The. A. B. Dumont Laboratories. N. Y. 1946

WFIL's TV Studios. L. E. Littlejohn. Broadcast News, Sept 1947, Oct 1948

PERIODICALS

Broadcast News, Radio Corp. of Am., Engineering Products Dept., Camden, N. J.

Broadcasting, National Press Bldg., Washington 4, D. C.

Communications, 52 Vanderbilt Ave., New York 17, N. Y.

Educational Screen, 64 E. Lake St., Chicago, Ill.

Electronics, 330 W. 42 St., New York 18, N. Y.

FM-TV, Savings Bank Bldg., Great Barrington, Mass.

International Projectionist, 19 W. 44 St., New York, N. Y.

Radio Daily, 1501 Broadway, New York 18, N. Y.

RCA Review, Radio Corp. of Am., Laboratories Div., Princeton, N. J.

Tele-Tech, 480 Lexington Ave., New York 17, N. Y.

Televiser, 1780 Broadway, New York 19, N. Y.

Section V

THEATERS

"Island Theater," Hamilton, Bermuda

A BERMUDA THEATER WITH ``FLOATING SCREEN''

Schlanger & Hoffberg, Architects; Reisner & Urbahn, Architects

THE ISLAND demanded that the theater conform to its coral-rock and pink-stucco architectural mode; the cramped lot demanded exploitation of every angular inch (not one right angle in the entire plan); and luck smiled on the enterprise, to give it quiet charm.

Entering, through a neat clean range of plexiglass floors flanked by a marble wall and by reeded wooden screens, the patron finds himself in a cultivated place. An upper, mezzanine lounge gives an open view to the entrance for those awaiting friends; both this and the lower lounge are served by toilets carefully stacked to conserve piping and water, both being premium items.

In the auditorium the effect is perhaps best of all. The screen "floated" as seen in details on page 361, is unmasked; the patented arrangement of screen and surround gives synchronous lighting of the surround by light spilled from the picture, destroying sharp contrast, fading hard outline, varying with picture intensity. During short features, this surround is softly lighted up by bulbs from behind.

No irrelevant decoration is allowed to interfere with this pleasant dramatic effect.

Elliot Clarke Photos

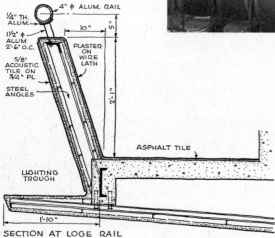

¼" TH. ALUM.

4" φ ALUM. RAIL

1½" φ ALUM 2'-6" O.C.

5/8" ACOUSTIC TILE ON ¾" PL.

STEEL ANGLES

PLASTER ON WIRE LATH

10"

5"

2'-1"

ASPHALT TILE

LIGHTING TROUGH

1'-10"

SECTION AT LOGE RAIL

The theater seats 650, including 200 in the radial mezzanine. Walls are gray in the corrugated plaster section near the screen, cream elsewhere; ceiling is sand-finished plaster painted gray-green; chairs are upholstered in blue-green, coated fabric on seats, mohair on backs. The mezzanine parapet fascia (detail at left) is hard plaster, painted gray, and angled to reflect sound downward. Downlights light house and aisles

The loge lounge, shown below, commands a good view of main entrance and lobby and forms a convenient meeting place. A second lounge, not shown, is located directly below (see plans and section, opposite page), with patrons' facilities stacked to conserve piping

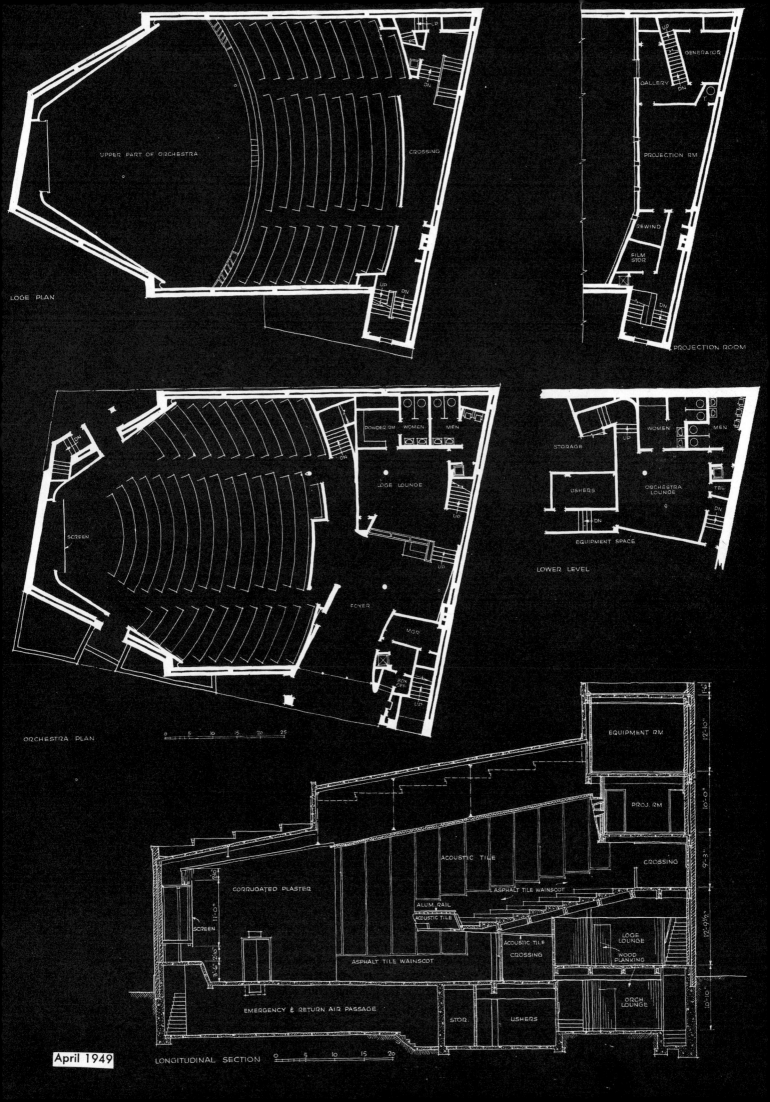

LOGE PLAN

UPPER PART OF ORCHESTRA

CROSSING

UP
DN

UP DN

PROJECTION RM

GENERATOR

GALLERY

UP
DN
T

REWIND

FILM STOR

DN

PROJECTION ROOM

SCREEN

DN

POWDER RM   WOMEN   MEN

LOGE LOUNGE

UP

UP

FOYER

MGR

UP

BOX OFF

UP

STORAGE

UP

WOMEN   MEN

USHERS

ORCHESTRA LOUNGE

TEL

DN

DN

EQUIPMENT SPACE

LOWER LEVEL

ORCHESTRA PLAN

0   5   10   15   20   25

EQUIPMENT RM

PROJ. RM

CROSSING

ACOUSTIC TILE

ASPHALT TILE WAINSCOT

ALUM. RAIL

CORRUGATED PLASTER

ACOUSTIC TILE

ACOUSTIC TILE

LOGE LOUNGE

CROSSING

WOOD PLANKING

SCREEN

ASPHALT TILE WAINSCOT

EMERGENCY & RETURN AIR PASSAGE

STOR.   USHERS

ORCH. LOUNGE

LONGITUDINAL SECTION

0   5   10   15   20

April 1949

Instead of a marquee, the theater has an open vestibule or portico, tied to the foyer by a flagstone floor which is continued as far as the auditorium doors. The plate glass entrance doors have bronze hand and kick plates, and the free-standing display case (seen at extreme left of bottom photo on this page) is also bronze. Foyer walls are green marble on the auditorium side, natural-finish oak boards opposite; vestibule walls are white marble. Across-page: plans and sections of the unique "floating screen," and a projection view showing the soft lighting of the surround used for short features

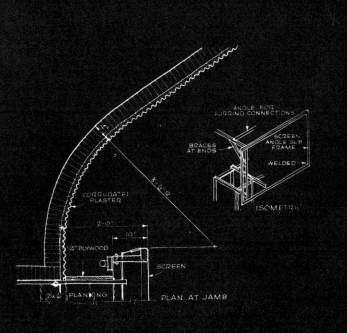

ANGLE FOR
FURRING CONNECTIONS

BRACES
AT ENDS

SCREEN
ANGLE SUB
FRAME

WELDED

ISOMETRIC

CORRUGATED
PLASTER

3'-0" R

2'-0"

10"

¼" PLYWOOD

SCREEN

2"x6" PLANKING

PLAN AT JAMB

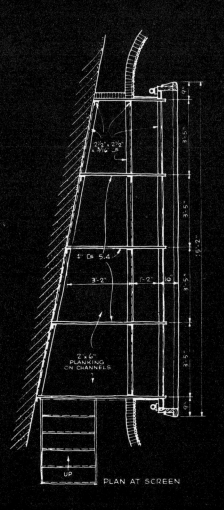

9"

3'-5"

2½" x 2½" x 3/16" Ls

3'-5"

15'-2"

1" Cs 5.4

3'-2"   1'-2"   6"   3'-5"

2"x6"
PLANKING
ON CHANNELS

9"

UP

PLAN AT SCREEN

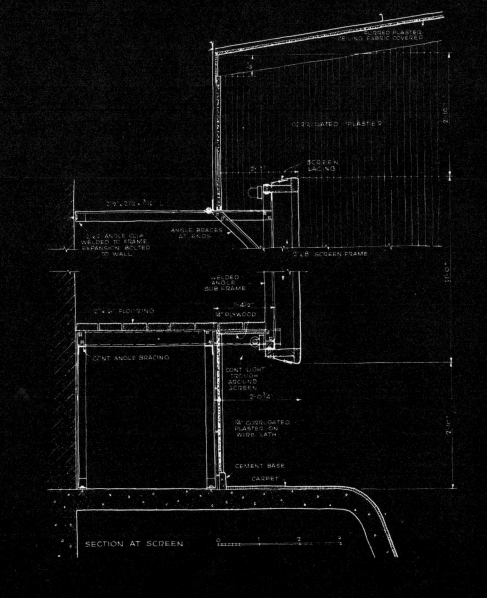

FURRED PLASTER
CEILING FABRIC COVERED

2'-10"

CORRUGATED PLASTER

SCREEN
LACING

2½"x2½"x3/16" L

2"x2" ANGLE CLIP
WELDED TO FRAME
EXPANSION BOLTED
TO WALL

ANGLE BRACES
AT ENDS

2"x8" SCREEN FRAME

WELDED
ANGLE
SUB FRAME

2"x6" FLOORING

1'-4½"
¼" PLYWOOD

11'-0"

CONT ANGLE BRACING

CONT LIGHT
TROUGH
AROUND
SCREEN

2'-0¾"

¼" CORRUGATED
PLASTER ON
WIRE LATH

2'-10"

CEMENT BASE

CARPET

SECTION AT SCREEN   0   1   2   3

Tacna Theater, Lima

PROJECTING PARAMOUNT PICTURES IN PERU

Schlanger & Hoffberg, Architects   *Reisner & Urbahn, Architects*

Not in New York and not in Hollywood but set against the Andes at Lima, Peru, is to be found the motion picture theater boasting the flattest balconies ever developed for designed seeing conditions in a theater, according to *Better Theaters*. Theater architect Schlanger (frequent RECORD contributor) achieved this by a combination of staggered seating and by the first use of a "reverse curve floor" in the *orchestra*, making the flat balconies possible. (See longitudinal section, page 365.) Meanwhile his associates, Reisner and Urbahn, helped contend with an export situation which meant that countless items had to be shipped pre-

assembled. This included glass, mirrors, neon tubes pre-bent, stainless steel work, even millwork such as candy counters. Glass mosaic, liberally used in lobbies, was pasted in 2-ft. squares, and skillfully assembled by native workmen who never had handled glass mosaic before. In concrete, however, they had previous training and skill, could have produced curved stairs without the supporting posts in the design.

Seating 2000, the theater lacks features such as Continental seating, because Paramount International, working with the Peru owners, asked conformity to the New York building code.

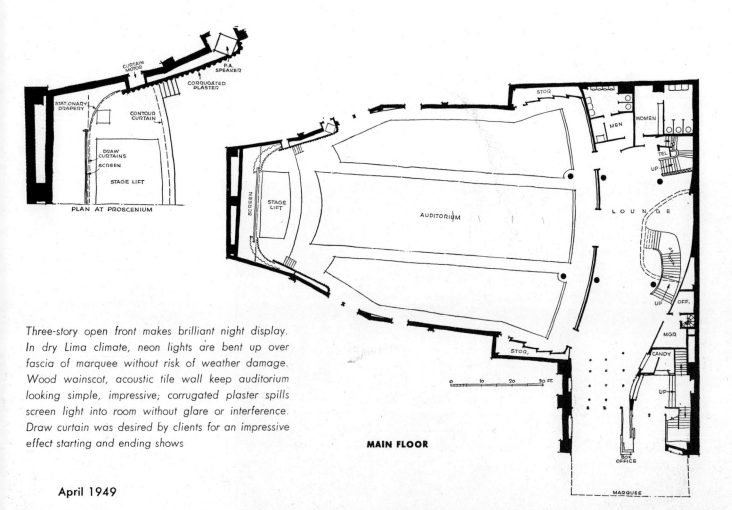

Three-story open front makes brilliant night display. In dry Lima climate, neon lights are bent up over fascia of marquee without risk of weather damage. Wood wainscot, acoustic tile wall keep auditorium looking simple, impressive; corrugated plaster spills screen light into room without glare or interference. Draw curtain was desired by clients for an impressive effect starting and ending shows

MAIN FLOOR

Lobbies and Lounges

Every one of the three levels has a complete lounge development of its own, and for all of them the architects designed all equipment, including chairs, which were manufactured in the U. S. but upholstered in Peru. As indicated in the sketch, the second-balcony lounge carries the spectacular hung lighting grid containing fluorescent lights, and has its own planting boxes as a "suspended" interior feature. (Another set of planting boxes, set on the marquee, is directly outside of the mezzanine lounge)

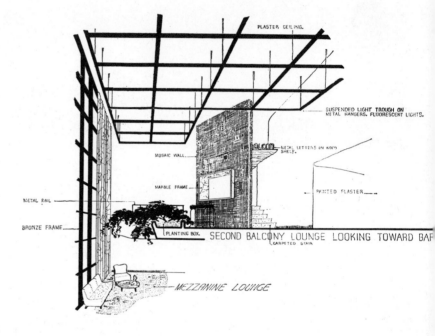

Main lounge (left) is set off by four great columns faced with glass mosaic (the first the local workmen had ever set, and set well). Stair at right is seen again overleaf on page 366

"Flattest balconies ever developed for designed seeing conditions in a theater" were made possible by staggered seating carefully calculated, and by reverse-curve flatness of orchestra floor in foreground. By lowering the ceiling such flat-balcony design diminishes cubage, reduces construction cost, improves acoustics, and helps the air conditioning, an important factor in a dry climate

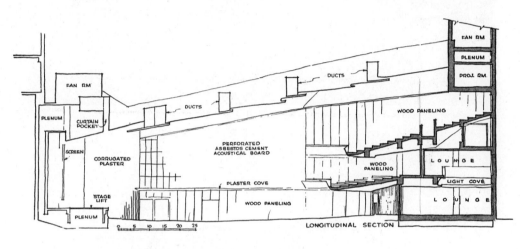

LONGITUDINAL SECTION

0 5 10 15 20 25

FIRST BALCONY PLAN

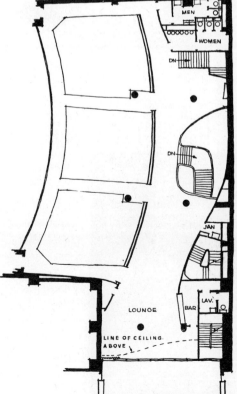

SECOND BALCONY PLAN

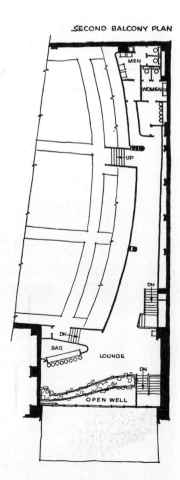

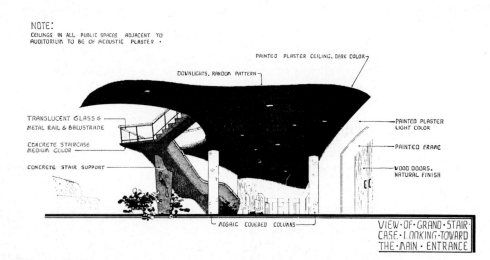

NOTE:
CEILINGS IN ALL PUBLIC SPACES ADJACENT TO
AUDITORIUM TO BE OF ACOUSTIC PLASTER •

PAINTED PLASTER CEILING. DARK COLOR

DOWNLIGHTS, RANDOM PATTERN

TRANSLUCENT GLASS &
METAL RAIL & BALUSTRADE

PAINTED PLASTER
LIGHT COLOR

CONCRETE STAIRCASE
MEDIUM COLOR

PAINTED FRAME

CONCRETE STAIR SUPPORT

WOOD DOORS.
NATURAL FINISH

MOSAIC COVERED COLUMNS

VIEW·OF·GRAND·STAIR·
CASE·LOOKING·TOWARD
THE·MAIN·ENTRANCE

Virtuosity with concrete of the Peruvian
workmen was found to be so high that
this curved stair to mezzanine could have
been built without the supporting column
designed by the architects. On the other
hand it was impossible to carry out the
original design, indicated in the sketch,
for a stair rail of tempered glass. There
was substituted the detail on next page

April 1949

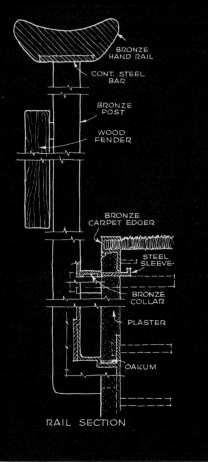

BRONZE
HAND RAIL

CONT. STEEL
BAR

BRONZE
POST

WOOD
FENDER

BRONZE
CARPET EDGER

STEEL
SLEEVE

BRONZE
COLLAR

PLASTER

OAKUM

RAIL SECTION

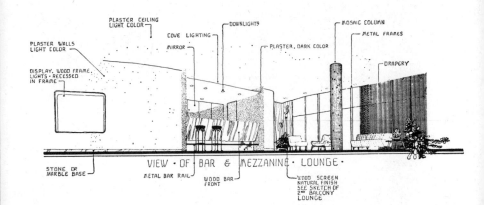

PLASTER CEILING
LIGHT COLOR

PLASTER WALLS
LIGHT COLOR

DISPLAY. WOOD FRAME.
LIGHTS - RECESSED
IN FRAME

COVE LIGHTING

MIRROR

DOWNLIGHTS

PLASTER. DARK COLOR

MOSAIC COLUMN

METAL FRAMES

DRAPERY

STONE OR
MARBLE BASE

METAL BAR RAIL

WOOD BAR
FRONT

WOOD SCREEN
NATURAL FINISH
SEE SKETCH OF
2ND BALCONY
LOUNGE

VIEW · OF · BAR & · MEZZANINE · LOUNGE ·

Features such as the bronze handrail seen in the stair detail were made in Peru, but were cast instead of tubular. Sections were faithful to the architects' drawings though there was some difficulty in obtaining perfectly smooth finish

In the case of furniture, display cases, attraction boxes, and other similar equipment seen in the sketch of the mezzanine lounge (above) and of the main exit (below) all was shipped prefabricated from the United States

Although the total effect is obviously suited to a palace of amusement, with due glitter and dramatization, there is a more consistent and knowing hand displayed than in most theaters in this country. A new slogan might be, ''go South!''

THEATERS

A NEW ARCHITECTURE FOR

THE MOVIE THEATER

Raymond Loewy Associates.

THE moving picture theater, now just about entering its second generation, looks to be due for some changes. The new generation will have to improve on the old, or the race may find itself dying out.

For science is right now giving the movie industry its worst scare since the movies began, with television making movie patrons "stay home in droves." The theater will have to, and should be able to, enlist science in its own behalf, and there are indications of important changes in the concept of a theater.

These changes should prove to be directly within the bailiwick of the theater architect. They certainly will not be mere dolling up of the theater; in fact they will probably be strictly in the functional order. And the progressive architect, with his eye on purpose and with science at his elbow, should be just the man for the job.

The basic weapon of the theater is "theater". The race with television will eventually settle down to a matter of real entertainment values, of dramatic impact of offerings, of intensity of illusion created.

Here the theater is still out in front of television. Its task is to remain ahead, to heighten its dramatic quality, to lure the television owner out of his home for better entertainment value.

So far the television set provides sight and sound, but not much "theater." It has caught on and is rapidly gaining new converts, but it is still an amazing new scientific toy. One still sits in a living room, amidst all the distractions of the home, and sees his show on a little screen. It is fine for sports and news events and perhaps style shows, but not for dramatic entertainment. As one man said recently, "I bought a television set almost a year ago, and hadn't been to a movie since, until last night. I guess I had forgotten how good the movies were."

Well, the movies are good, but they will have to be better. And while much of the improvement will have to come from Hollywood, the final battle will be in the local movie house, which must be redesigned for a better dramatic value.

To Free the Movie Art

Suppose, for example, that the movie industry were to accept a progressive suggestion that comes from the theater architect, Ben Schlanger. He points to the restrictive effect of a picture always of the same proportions, the same size, always seen in a dark frame. Why not, while reaching for dramatic impact, break completely away from this photo-album prison, and make the screen a fluid medium of art?

One step he suggests is to increase its size; it could easily be made 20 or 25 per cent larger. Already, it will be noted, there is a major change for the theater.

The larger screen would not mean simply a larger frame. The frame would be eliminated. In making the picture, the cinematographer would assume freedom within the larger area to use whatever picture size — or picture shape — best suited his subject matter. He might spread his picture to full width for a great mob scene, or for a chorus line. He might vignette a more intimate scene at relatively small size. The canvas broadens or closes in, brightens or darkens with its subject. Or the scene might move across the screen area to heighten the illusion of motion, which now is achieved only by having the background in motion.

To understand the effect on the theater itself, it is necessary to look into the vignetting idea. A year ago Ben Schlanger told the Society of Motion Picture Engineers:

"For the motion picture, where it may be better to present more realism, the vignette may well be a suitable representation of the peripheral portion of our field of vision. In real life there is no opaque masking frame in front of us all the time. The vignette is more like what one experiences visually.

"In still photography the vignette commonly fades to pure white at the extreme edges of the picture. This type of vignette would prove disturbing for the motion picture because of the competition created by stronger light at the edge. The vignette recommended here is one that diminishes the light value toward the edges of the picture. Light and color values seem to dim out in the visual peripheral. Colors do not change in hue, rather they seem to become grayer. The reduced light value proposed for the peripheral vignette is also the means of creating transitional light intensity between the bright picture and the picture environment. . . ."

Schlanger has even considered that the vignetted light might extend beyond the screen itself to the surrounding surfaces in the theater. Obviously, then, we should need something different from the gargoyled proscenium arch of the first-generation movie house.

The lighting of the screen surround is an immediate problem, not waiting for the adoption of Schlanger's idea of vignettes. And so is the architectural phase of the auditorium as a housing for dramatic entertainment.

A florid architectural style only competes with the illusion on the screen; here certainly is a place for modern functional design.

Its functionalism might begin with a better surround for the screen, one which would contribute toward the solution of a really pressing lighting problem. Experts have told the RECORD recently that no movie theater in the country is well lighted.

The science of seeing tells us how violent are lighting conditions in the typical theater. The eye dislikes the brightness contrast of the lighted screen in the darkened frame. Schlanger's vignette idea would soften the contrasts around the screen quite naturally. But that could, and should, be done right now, with present films. Schlanger has used textured ribbed surfaces near the screen to pick up light in an automatic relation to screen light values. Another possibility is a dimly lighted background behind the screen and extending beyond it. Still another, presented in this study (page 388), is keeping the auditorium better lighted while the film is running. The author makes what is really the first attempt to apply scientific lighting to the movie theater. Besides eye comfort, and therefore better illusion, better lighting would also improve convenience, simple safety, and perhaps propriety in the theater of today. Television

In the older theater the dramatic impact is diluted by florid auditorium decorations, by the fixed screen seen as a white spot in a dark frame. Ben Schlanger has suggested a vignetting idea in which the screen becomes fluid, the dark frame eliminated, the auditorium a neutral background. Picture size might be large or small, fixed or in motion, with lighted vignette edges adding dramatic impact

set owners quickly learn not to darken the room completely, for the same reasons. Now perhaps television is telling theater owners something they might well have known long ago.

Acoustics is another major area for theater improvement. And most theaters, while having an adequate level of projected sound, leave much to be desired as to quality, particularly as regards that "intimate" quality of sound which makes it seem to come from the screen. Here again the second generation movie theater, seeking to enhance its dramatic quality, might well profit from the science of auditorium acoustics, which has been developed largely since most movie houses were built. The article in this Study shows how much architectural design is involved in good acoustics, and how good acoustics are achieved.

Then, too, science has gone ahead in many other technical matters of design which can make their contribution to better theaters. Sight lines that permit the patron to see the action without being distracted by heads in front, air conditioning to make him unconscious of surrounding temperature conditions or even odors, seating to make him settle back comfortably to be entertained.

In considering the future of the movie theater, some have mentioned its community aspects, in the light of social appeal to lure the family out of the home. They are inclined to cite the social side of the old theaters of Europe, something that is still strong in the opera. Certainly the theater, even the movie theater of the modern age, is associated with "going out." And going out is not to be outmoded by the television set, even though the set in the home is highly regarded as a means of keeping the younger generation off the streets. Probably the younger generation, nevertheless, will be loath to desert the familiar movie entertainment, and perfectly willing to be lured out of the home.

How much of the social side of the theater can be translated into design is not readily discerned. Obviously, however, there are many matters that bear on the appeal to the patron. The cheerful, bright theater marquee has always been a tradition of the theater, is still highly regarded by theater people. It can be vastly improved in design certainly, perhaps also in advertising appeal. The lobby and waiting rooms and washrooms might all be subjected to some scrutiny, now that patrons need to be lured instead of herded into the theater. All of these are clearly related to social aspects of the theater as an institution.

Perhaps also the new science of community planning may offer something to the theater. The movie house is a logical nucleus for an entertainment center that might offer many other varieties of amusement and social activities.

At any rate it is very clear that the theater architect will be giving a newly serious attention to the true function of the theater, and that will lead him into a new consideration of all of the sciences and arts that will add something to the quality of entertainment. The theater owner will be thinking of these things, too; he certainly will get over any idea he may have had that the function of the architect is to design a shell to cover so many seats. He will need the architect as never before.

In general one effective answer of the movie industry to the competition of television is simply better. theaters, truly functional in design, using modern technology to heighten dramatic quality of entertainment. Theater in the Museum of Modern Art, New York City, Goodwin and Stone, architects

FACE AND FUNCTION LIFTED

Wareham Theater, Wareham, Mass.

William Riseman Associates, Designers

ONE immediate way for the movie industry to lift its face is shown in the three examples of remodeling on the following pages. The "Before and After" story of the Wareham, Strand and Astor Theaters, all redesigned by William Riseman Associates, is a fascinating example of what can be done with little money and much skill to entice the movie-goer when everything else fails.

By scrapping the dreary decorations of the original, superseding them with clean lines, pleasant materials, good lettering and attractive display areas, the designers succeeded in turning a drab local movie into a smart and inviting picture theater. Most successful is the change in the entrance and in the auditorium (see next page). The stairway and passage interior is not quite so interesting in design as the rest. However, the patterned carpet presents easier maintenance problems than a one-color flooring. The whole atmosphere of the theater has been vastly, and profitably, lifted from the banal.

The changes in the auditorium have been less radical than these pictures seem to indicate. The distracting wall decorations have been removed and plain wall surfaces now direct the eye toward the screen. In place of the old and inefficient central-aisle scheme, the designers have provided a two-aisle layout to provide a maximum number of desirable center seats, as well as for better circulation. The lighting appears to be somewhat low in intensity, and not sufficiently general — not a very serious fault in so small a theater

The old Warr Theater façade was removed in its entirety, replaced by the **strikingly** handsome stone, wood, glass and flagstone entrance at the left

George M. Cushing, Jr. Photos

Recessed ceiling spots turn the entrance lobby into a friendly island of light

MAINSTREET CLEAN-UP

The fascinatingly overdone auditorium (below) turned the stage into a minor side-show. Now the screen is the center of focus, as it obviously should be (above)

Strand Theater, Hartford, Conn.

William Riseman Associates, Designers

THE Strand Theater in Hartford represents a much more radical overhauling than the small Wareham Theater. While the entrance marquee remains flashy and not too legible, the interiors have been revamped drastically to produce a pleasant and restful atmosphere. Most interesting in this alteration is the change in the auditorium, where a gaudy Arabian-Nights palace was turned into an efficient and simple theater.

Despite the continued ''brilliant display'' of the entrance, the overall design has been toned down and made a little more legible. Note the improvement in display facilities

The mezzanine in the rear of the auditorium is now a most striking architectural success. Most successful in this redecoration has been the revamping of the auditorium itself. By cleverly exposing the structure of the building and filling in the mezzanine walls with glass, the architects have achieved a beautiful dramatic effect. But the new setting for the screen, and its subdued lighting, contrasts most strikingly with the former pretentiousness and false ''opulence'' of this theater. The old Strand Theater might have been almost anything, including a circus. The new Strand is unmistakably a movie theater, and a very good one at that

The candy counter (above) is typical of the cleaned-up design, attractive and productive

In place of the gloomy, badly-lit stairs, the designers have provided a handsome access to the mezzanine, inviting rather than repelling

George M. Cushing, Jr. Photos

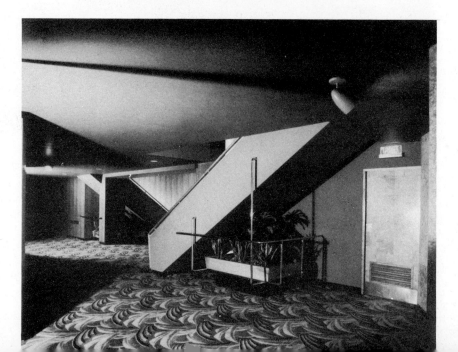

Although the lettering problem still remains to be solved, the new entrance is a striking advance over the old "design"

ORDER OUT OF CHAOS

Astor Theater, Boston, Mass.

William Riseman Associates, Designers

IF you had approached the old Tremont Theater in Boston, in a moment of recklessness, you would have had great difficulty (1) in finding it; (2) in locating its entrance; and (3) in discovering what picture was being shown. In the new Astor Theater such a chaotic condition has been substantially cleared up. The entrance is visible. Its lettering competes moderately well with that of adjoining restaurants, dancing schools and stores. And there is no way of mistaking what movie

is being exhibited or where to find the entrance.

How great the change-over has been is clear from the "Before and After" views of the lobby (over-page). It is hard to reconstruct the bleak institutional interior from the photographs of the comfortable new lobby. This remodeling job should be valuable to movie exhibitors in showing what can be done to give both the new look and a new life to even the most outdated and uninviting old picture-house.

The use of fine wood, corrugated transite, indoor planting and subtle lighting makes it almost unbelievable that these two areas are identical. Compare the former candy stand with the new counter

George M. Cushing, Jr. Photos

A THEATER DESIGNED WITH LIGHT METERS

Studio Theater, New York, N. Y.   **Ben Schlanger, Architect**

Gottscho-Schleissner Photos

MANHATTAN'S new Studio Theater is an experiment in reflected lighting. Its auditorium walls are left almost entirely undecorated, to avoid competition with the screen image. But though they are not decorated, the walls and ceiling surfaces around the screen are carefully slanted and textured to reflect the brightness of the screen image into the auditorium itself. Corrugations in the walls were designed at the exact angle that would reflect the light emanating from the screen to illuminate the seating area. Secondary lighting to maintain a low overall brightness throughout performances was cut down to a minimum.

One of the pleasing results of this scheme lies in the fact that the relationship between screen brightness and overall auditorium illumination remains constant, even if the scenes projected are of low light intensity. Tests are now being made to determine the success of this highly promising lighting design.

The seating arrangement is not very unusual, with a stadium-type layout in the rear. It is interesting to examine the slight irregularities in the seating pattern, caused by Architect Schlanger's analysis of sightlines from each individual seat. To adjust the seating pattern to the requirements of unobstructed vision, odd-sized seats have been used occasionally together with chairs of standard width

A LUXURY THEATER DESIGNED LIKE A CLUB

Park Avenue Theater, New York City

William I. Hohauser, Architect & Engineer

WHEN this luxury theater was first built, it was intended to have the character of a private club, with reserved tickets obtainable by subscription. For practical reasons, this policy of exclusiveness was abandoned early in the game, but the club atmosphere remained.

The entrance marquee is extremely simple, and lacks the vulgarity usually associated with movie houses. Since the Park Avenue Theater is a specialty job, with an exhibition policy that concentrates upon exceptional movies, it is not necessary to provide advertising signs that spell out the name of the current show. The customers know that the picture is likely to be good, and display cases at the entrance give additional details.

The entrance lobby itself is simple and spacious, and the inside lounges are more lavishly decorated. Nevertheless they are relaxing, quiet and pleasant.

In the basement there is a comfortable lounge where coffee is served and where customers can watch the latest television programs while waiting for the picture to start. Here again the club atmosphere has been successfully maintained.

The auditorium is remarkable in several respects. First, the seating is unusually comfortable, and the rows of seats are spaced far apart. In the mezzanine there are 125 love seats which, according to the architect, accommodate "two people in parlor comfort."

Gary Wagner

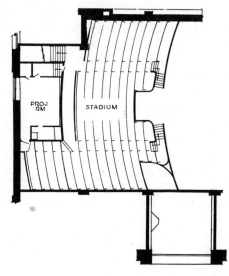

The seating plan is carefully worked out, and seats are staggered and placed at an angle to the screen. Hearing aids are provided for those who need them.

The theater is serviced by a 60-ton air conditioning system, supplemented with sterilamps. The lighting is well developed, and seats are easy to find even when the auditorium is darkened for the showing of the film. The shape of the auditorium was controlled by the existing structure and this accounts for the perhaps excessive width in relation to length, involving an excessive sight angle for some seats. The theater demonstrates that the feeling of luxury can be attained without resorting to exuberant ornamentation.

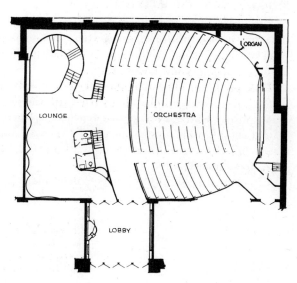

ACOUSTICAL DESIGN OF THE THEATER

By Vern O. Knudsen* and Cyril M. Harris †

IN planning for good acoustics the architect will avoid errors in design if he sets up a check list of the necessary and sufficient measures to be taken. These steps, approximately in chronological order, are as follows:

1. The selection of the site in the quietest surroundings consistent with other requirements.

2. A noise survey to determine how much sound-insulation must be incorporated.

3. The arrangement of the rooms within the building.

4. The selection of the proper sound-insulation constructions.

5. The control of the noise within the building, including solid-borne as well as air-borne noise.

6. The design of the shape and size of each room that will insure the most advantageous flow of properly diffused sound to all auditors, and that will enhance the esthetic qualities of speech and music.

7. The selection and distribution of the absorptive and reflective materials and constructions that will provide the optimum conditions for the growth, the decay, and the steady-state distribution of sound in each room.

8. The supervision of the installation of acoustical plaster, plastic absorbents, or other materials whose absorptivity is dependent on the manner of application.

9. The installation of sound-amplification equipment under the supervision of a competent engineer, wherever such equipment is necessary.

10. The inspection of the finished building, including tests to determine whether the required sound-insulation, sound-absorption, and the other acoustical properties have been satisfactorily attained.

11. Maintenance instructions, in writing, to be left with the building manager.

ROOM DESIGN AND ACOUSTICS

The shape of a room is one of the important factors affecting its acoustical properties. Hence the determination of the most desirable shape is a problem that the architect should know how to solve.

Floor plan. The optimum ratio of length to width for a room is not a fixed number, but varies with the size and shape of the seating area; it also depends on whether a sound-amplification system is used. For most rooms, ratios of length to width of between 2:1 and 1.2:1 have been found satisfactory.

Circular and elliptically shaped floor plans nearly always give rise to focusing effects, non-uniform distribution of sound, and echoes. The focusing defect is even more pronounced in elliptical plans. In both elliptical and circular plans, the acoustical conditions can be improved by addition of convex diffusing surfaces.

In order to bring a large audience as close as possible to the stage of an auditorium, it is advantageous to design a floor plan with diverging side walls. Reflections from these walls can aid in the establishment of a higher sound level at the rear of the auditorium, but these reflections must be carefully controlled. Path-length differences of 65 ft. or more between direct and reflected sound give rise to echoes. Path-length differences from about 50 to 65 ft. produce a blurring quality which may result in a lack of "intimacy," especially for auditors in the front seating area. Intimacy is a qualitative term used to describe the extent to which sound appears to come from the screen in a motion picture theater. If the included angle of the sound received by an auditor is small, then he will judge the auditorium to have intimacy. In this respect, reflections from the side walls are more significant than those from the ceiling, for one's ability to localize sounds in the horizontal direction is somewhat greater than it is in the vertical direction.

Elevation of Seats. Since an audience constitutes a highly absorptive surface, sound waves which graze it are greatly attenuated. Hence, it is good design in an auditorium, from a standpoint of hearing as well as seeing, to elevate the seats in order to provide a free flow of direct sound from the source to the listeners. A good line of sight will do this. It is advantageous to stagger the seats as well. The first few rows can be level since they will have a good line for both sight and sound. The higher the source is elevated, the farther back the level area can be extended.

Ceilings. The ceiling and walls should provide favorable reflections of sound, especially for the seats far removed from the stage. In some instances, the ceiling should also aid in the diffusion of sound. However, if adequate means of diffusion are furnished by the floor and wall surfaces, and no additional diffusion is needed by the ceiling, it may be utilized to the utmost for the advantageous reflection of sound. Lecture rooms and chamber music rooms are types of rooms in which a low, smooth, highly-reflective ceiling may be used to good advantage.

* Professor of Physics and Dean of the Graduate Division, University of California at Los Angeles. † Member of the Technical Staff, Bell Telephone Laboratories, Murray Hill, N. J. The text and figures are taken from a forthcoming book, "Acoustical Designing in Architecture," to be published next spring by John Wiley & Sons. NOTE: reproduction of text or illustrations is forbidden, except upon express permission by the publishers.

There is no simple (or even complicated) formula for calculating the optimum ceiling height of a room. Consideration must be given to the optimum volume. In general, the ceiling height of a room to be used for speech and music should be about one-third to two-thirds of the width of the room — the lower ratio for very large rooms, and the higher ratio for small rooms. If the ceiling of an auditorium is too high, not only will the volume-per-seat be excessive, but long-delayed reflections from this surface can be the source of echoes.

Ceiling splays in the front of a room, or appropriately tilted portions of the ceiling, can be devised so as to reinforce the sound reaching the rear parts of an auditorium. They serve the same purpose as do the front splays of the side walls. The law of reflection (angle of reflection equals angle of incidence) can be used to determine the most propitious angle of inclination. Similarly, a splay between the ceiling and the rear wall can be designed to reinforce the sound in the rear of the room, and at the same time to prevent echoes from the rear wall. This is illustrated in Fig. 1.

Concave surfaces such as domes, cylindrical arches, barreled ceilings, etc., should be avoided wherever possible, see Fig. 2. If they are required by the architectural style, as in a Jewish Synagogue, then the radius of curvature should be either at least two times the ceiling height, or less than one-half the ceiling height. If coves, bays, or other small concave surfaces are employed, their radii of curvature should be quite small compared to the ceiling height. The most serious defects (sound foci or echoes) occur when the radius of curvature of a ceiling surface is about equal to the ceiling height.

In order to avoid flutter echoes, a smooth ceiling should not be strictly parallel to the floor. If the floor and ceiling are both smooth, level and highly reflective, the flutter between the floor and ceiling will be very prominent.

Side Walls. The side walls should reinforce the sound that reaches the rear parts of a large room. While the location of the walls is determined largely by the general contour of the floor plans, the angle that any portion of the surface of these walls makes with the center-line need not be, if splays are employed. The law of reflection can be used to determine the proper angle for the wall surfaces so that they will guide sound to those seats where the sound level is not adequate. The side walls should be designed so that the sounds they reflect to the audience will not be too long delayed. Some parts of the side walls may be suspected of causing echoes or unduly delayed reflections; this may happen in very large auditoriums. In such instances the suspected surfaces should not be smooth and reflective. Instead they should either be made "acoustically rough" to diffuse the sound, or they should be covered with highly absorptive material.

Flutter echoes frequently occur between the side walls. They can be avoided by a number of means: by diverging, non-parallel, or tilted walls; by splayed, or V'd, walls. Splays not only serve to prevent flutter, but they can contribute both to desirably directed reflections and to the diffusion of sound within the room. As little as ⅝-in. splay to the running foot will prevent flutter.

Rear Wall. In the design of all rooms, large concave rear walls should be avoided. Unfortunately, they are of common occurence because it seems so simple and economical to most architects to have the rear wall following the curvature of the last row of seats. Walls having this shape are responsible for troublesome echoes and delayed reflections in many theaters and auditoriums. This is illustrated in the upper part of Fig. 1. Often these reflections from concave rear walls are concentrated in regions near the microphones of the sound-amplification system, causing feedback trouble and howling. These detrimental reflections can be converted into beneficial ones by introducing a ceiling splay between the ceiling and the rear wall, as shown in the lower sectional drawing of Fig. 1. Concave surfaces in certain situations can be made as effective as splays, and they are sometimes better adapted than splays to the general appearance of the room. However, unless properly designed, they can lead to focusing effects. In some designs, splays between the ceiling and side walls are useful in preventing long-delayed reflections and in directing advantageous reflections to the audiences.

If reflections from either a vertical or tilted wall are capable of producing echoes, the offending surface should be treated with absorptive material. There will still be some reflection from this surface but the sound

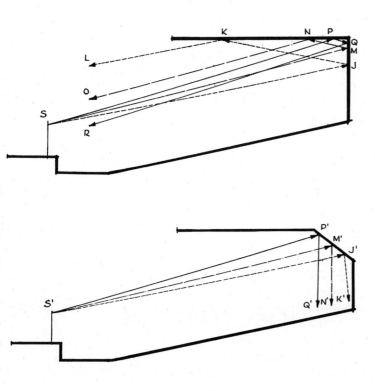

Fig. 1. Reflection of sound from rear surfaces of an auditorium, showing how a suitable ceiling splay can be used to prevent echoes from reaching the front seating area, and at the same time to reinforce sound for the last few rows of seats

level is thus reduced so greatly that its detrimental effects are negligible.

Balcony Recess. Good design of a balcony recess usually requires a shallow depth and a high opening. For an auditorium or legitimate theater, the depth should not exceed twice the height of the opening. This permits sound to flow readily into the space under the balcony. Good design also requires that the reverberation time in the balcony recess approximate that of the main part of the auditorium.

By applying the above rules, it is possible to design the recess so that the sound level in this space is about the same as it is in other equally distant parts of the auditorium. However, if the opening is low and the recess relatively deep, the sound level will be considerably lower in this area, especially at the rear of the recess. In large auditoriums and theaters it is advisable to "break up" the rear wall in order to provide proper diffusion of sound throughout the balcony recess. A large unbroken concave rear wall always should be avoided, since it invariably gives rise to a non-uniform distribution of sound. Trouble of this kind also may arise from large vertical surfaces of glass in front of the standee rail. If the chairs are highly absorptive, as they should be, it usually will not be necessary to add any absorptive material to the balcony recess other than the absorptive material on the rear wall. If the chairs are not absorptive, it may be necessary to add some absorptive material to the soffit or side walls of the recess in order to provide the optimum reverberation in this space. When this is done it is desirable to distribute this material in panels, strips, or patches.

The balcony rail (front) should not be overlooked in working out the acoustical design of an auditorium. Since it is frequently a large concave surface having a width that is large compared with the shorter wavelengths of speech and music, the balcony front can give rise to an echo or "slap-back." By tilting this surface downward and making it convex it is sometimes possible to utilize the resulting reflections to increase the sound level at the rear of the auditorium. Otherwise, the front should be highly absorptive or have a contour such that reflections from it will be diffused and not concentrated in small areas.

Control of Reverberation. Sound which originates in, or enters, an enclosed space is repeatedly reflected by its boundaries. At each reflection, a fraction of the acoustical energy is absorbed. Nevertheless, the sound may persist for many seconds before it dies away to inaudibility. The greater the volume of the room, and the less absorption it contains, the longer will be the reverberation.

A limited amount of reverberation is desirable in most rooms. However, excessive reverberation is one of the most damaging and annoying defects that can be inflicted upon a theater.

The reverberation characteristics of a room can be controlled by the amount and placement of absorptive material within it. The total amount of absorption in a properly designed room determines the rate at which sound will decay in it. Proper distribution of the absorption aids in controlling the diffusion of sound and also the nature of the time fluctuations of the sound during its decay.

The first step in planning the acoustical treatment of a room is to determine the optimum reverberation time (see page 157 of November 1948 issue) and to find the total number of square-foot-units (sabins) of absorption required to give this time. A large part of this absorption will be furnished by agents other than acoustical materials, for example, by the chairs, rugs, audience, walls, ceiling, etc. It is customary to assume that the size of the audience in an auditorium will be equal to two-thirds of the seating capacity. Then the amount of absorption that must be added is the difference between the total required units and the number of units furnished by the above-named agents.

The questions remain: Where should the material be placed, and what materials should be used?

As a general rule, the surfaces surrounding the stage should reinforce, by useful reflections, the "voices" of the performers, though on the other hand, the rear wall must be designed so that long-delayed reflections from it are prevented from reaching the audience. This requirement usually necessitates the use of a highly absorptive rear wall; the portion of the wall above the wainscot (the wainscot should extend not more than about one foot above the heads of the audience) should have an

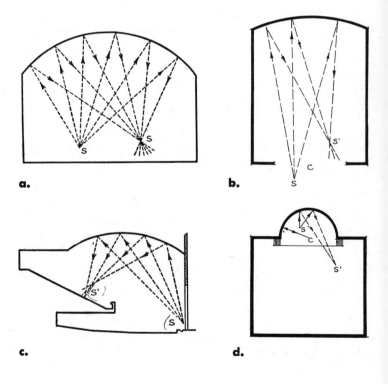

Fig. 2. (a) Reflection of sound from a barreled ceiling with a radius equal to the height of the room. (b) Reflection of sound from a concave rear wall. (c) Reflection of sound from a domed ceiling. (d) Reflection from a cylindrical wall behind speaker

average absorption coefficient in excess of 0.75. In auditoriums where the acoustical design indicates the desirability of tilting forward the rear wall so that reflections from this surface may be beneficially utilized, very much less absorptive material is needed and it should be applied in patches or panels. After allowances have been made for the rear wall treatment, the remainder of the required additional absorption should be distributed on the side wall — preferably in patches, strips, or panels having dimension of the order of 3 to 5 ft. The application of the absorptive material in the form of patches not only promotes diffusion but it helps to suppress flutter echoes.

It is important to choose materials that will provide the optimum reverberation time throughout the entire relevant range of frequencies, *not* at just one frequency.

THE LITTLE THEATER

In the little theater, the architect has an opportunity to design a structure that will embody the highest attainable standards of acoustics. If the seating capacity is limited to 300, the volume of the auditorium should not exceed 50,000 cu. ft. All seats are located on one floor, the rear portion of which should have a steep slope so that auditors will have good sight-lines and good sound-lines in all parts of the auditorium. The ceiling should not be more than 20 ft. high and should be left smooth. A highly reflective finish material will serve to direct the sound toward the rear seats. Diverging walls

Fig. 3. Plan and section of a little theater of good acoustics design. Auditorium is isolated from street noises by lobby and exit passage, both lined with absorptive treatment. Ceiling splays are angled to reinforce sound at the rear with reflected sound waves

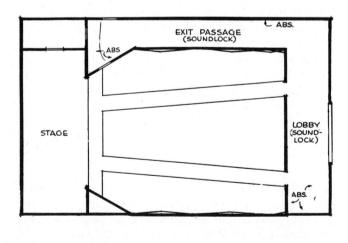

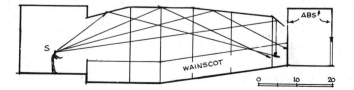

are desirable but not as necessary as in larger theaters. The lower 8 or 10 ft. of the side walls should be of reflective material. The front portions of these walls should not be pierced with boxes.

The chairs should be upholstered with absorptive cloth, such as mohair, over deep porous padding. The absorption of each chair should be three to four square-foot-units (sabins) at all frequencies about 512 cycles, and two to three sabins at frequencies of 128 and 256 cycles. The reverberation time of the theater will then be nearly independent of the size of the audience. Even during rehearsals the reverberation will be close to the optimum value.

The benefits associated with the small volume (less than 50,000 cubic ft. for the audience space) should not be nullified by making the stage recess so large that the sound is dissipated before it reaches the seating area. The volume of the stage should be reduced to a minimum consistent with other requirements. Stage settings with rear, side, and overhead reflective surfaces, should be designed so as to confine the sound to a small volume and reflect it to the audience. The use of plywood flats, or heavily-painted canvas flats is advantageous for the ceiling as well as the side and rear walls of the stage set. Designers of stage sets should be instructed not to ignore these pertinent requirements for good acoustics, which are especially necessary when the stage is large.

The stage floor should be elevated as high as possible, consistent with good sight-lines from all seats; this usually will allow an elevation of about 42 in. above the front level portion of the main floor. Orchestra pits should be avoided whenever possible; if indispensable, it is advisable that they be covered with a sound-reflective apron (plywood or heavily painted canvas) when not in use.

The optimum times of reverberation for the auditorium in a little theater having a volume of about 40,000 cu. ft. (the volume of stage is not included) are approximately 1.5 seconds at 128 cycles, and 1.0 second at 512 to 4096 cycles. These values are a compromise between those given by the curves for "speech" and "average music."

The exclusion of both outside and indoor noise should receive study whether the site is quiet or noisy. The average level of noise in the empty auditorium should not exceed 35 db, and if the highest standards of acoustics are required, this level should be reduced to 30 db.

A sketch of a plan and section for a little theater, based on a study of the requirements for ideal acoustics, is shown in Fig. 3. The auditorium is isolated by two walls on the sides that are adjacent to streets. These walls, in combination with the promenade and lobby which they enclose (and which, with heavily carpeted floors, act as sound locks), provide an average transmission-loss of at least 60 db.

The splayed walls and ceiling of the proscenium, the flat ceiling of the auditorium, and the lower portion of the side walls are designed to reflect useful sound upon the audience, and accordingly are finished with reflective materials (suspended plaster ceiling, furred-out plaster walls, and plywood waiscot applied to randomly spaced wood strips). The aisles are covered with cork carpet in order to reduce the noise of footfalls, and the floor under the seats is covered with linoleum to reduce the noise of scuffing feet. No special absorptive materials were needed in this theater to provide the optimum reverberation times — the total absorption furnished by the audience, chairs, and the materials for the walls, floors, and ceiling did not differ more than 5 per cent from total required absorption. The desirable outcome followed from the choice of a small volume per seat for the theater (148 cu. ft.) and the highly absorptive upholstered chairs.

THE LEGITIMATE THEATER

In this section, consideration will be given to legitimate theaters that are larger than the one described in the preceding section. Although the same general principles of design apply here with equal relevance, there is one important point of difference. In legitimate theaters, because of their larger size, speech is at a lower sound level than it is in little theaters. In fact, it frequently is not loud enough for good audition.

Therefore it is of the utmost importance to design the shape of the auditorium so that it will provide the audience with the greatest possible amount of direct and of beneficially-reflected sound. The divergence of the side walls, the slope of the overhead proscenium splay, and the slope of the main ceiling of the auditorium should be carefully designed to reinforce the sound propagated to the audience, giving some preferential reflection of sound for the rear seats under and in the balcony.

It is good acoustical design to keep the balcony overhang (depth) less than twice the height of the balcony opening, and to keep the balcony soffit reflective and inclined downward toward the rear wall. Heavily upholstered chairs, carpets on the aisles, and such absorptive treatment of the rear wall as is required to prevent objectionable reflections, ordinarily will provide satisfactory reverberation characteristics in the balcony recess. When the ratio of depth to opening-height does not exceed two, this space can be regarded as an integral part of the auditorium, and it then is not necessary to make separate calculations of reverberation in the two spaces — the main part of the auditorium and the balcony recess. In routine calculations of reverberation time, it is customary to regard these two spaces as one single volume and the stage recess as another. It is important that the stage have approximately the same reverberation characteristic as the auditorium. If a theater is to be used for musical as well as dramatic productions, the reverberation characteristic should be based upon the requirements for both speech and music, and the absorptive materials should be carefully located so as to favor a uniform average rate of decay in all parts of the theater.

Fig. 4 shows an acoustical study of a longitudinal section of a theater in which the ceiling surfaces have been designed to reinforce sound by reflection. The overhang of the balcony is short, and the opening under the balcony is high, so that adequate sound will reach the rear seats under the soffit. These seats, which are usually the poorest ones in most theaters, are further benefited in this design by the reflections of sound from both the splayed walls and ceiling of the proscenium. The main part of the ceiling has a gently rising slope in order to provide the most favorable reflection of sound. Heavily upholstered chairs are used throughout, and the aisles are carpeted over a ½ in. carpet pad. Most of the absorption required to provide the optimum reverberation is applied to the rear wall, under and above the balcony, to prevent echoes and interfering reflections from these surfaces. A 2-in. or 3-in. mineral wool blanket covered with perforated plywood, or similar facing, is suitable here. The highly absorptive material should not extend below the height of the heads of the audience. Below this level the rear wall is paneled wainscot, which together with the similar side-wall wainscot, provides much of the required low-frequency absorption. Calculations like those on p. 157 of Nov. '48 issue must be made in order to determine the kind and amount of additional absorptive material, if any, that is required to give the optimum reverberation characteristic. The directions and procedures outlined in the preceding section for sound insulation and for other acoustical aspects of the little theater also apply to the larger legitimate theaters.

The size of the auditorium should not exceed 100,000 cu. ft. without the use of a sound-amplification system. This recommended upper limit is not a critical value that must be precisely adhered to, but to exceed this volume without the assistance of sound amplification is a risky venture.

MOTION PICTURE THEATERS

Because sound is reproduced in motion picture theaters by means of electro-acoustical equipment that can furnish adequate sound levels in all parts of even very large theaters, the acoustical design of the cinema is not so dependent upon beneficial reflections from the walls, proscenium, splays, and ceiling as is the design of the legitimate theater. The average sound level of speech in the cinema is usually about 65 db for dialogue, which is 10 to 15 db higher than the average unamplified speech level in the legitimate theater. The acoustical power required to maintain this level depends on the size of the theater.

The general considerations of shape already mentioned apply to motion picture theaters. Furthermore, certain admonitions are especially pertinent here. For example, concave rear walls, parallel side walls, parallel ceiling and floor, and surfaces that give long-delayed reflections in the seating area should be avoided. Long, narrow theaters often have very poor acoustics: they are likely to require so much acoustical power from the sound system, in order to give adequate sound level in the rear seats, that the loudness will be excessive in the front and central seats.

Lengths greater than about 150 ft. should be avoided

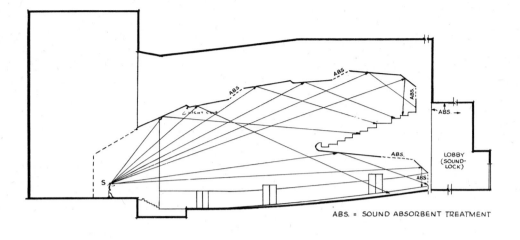

Fig. 4. Section of a legitimate theater; ceiling surfaces designed to reinforce sound by reflection. Balcony overhang is short, opening under it is high. Absorptive treatment at rear prevents echoes from reaching stage

ABS. = SOUND ABSORBENT TREATMENT

in order to avoid a noticeable delay in the arrival of the sound to persons in the rear of the theater. It requires about one-seventh second for sound to travel 150 ft. The lack of synchronism between sight and sound becomes quite annoying when the difference exceeds about one-seventh second. Since the length of the theater may be as great as double the width, it is necessary to design the side walls, floor and ceiling so as to minimize the attenuation of the sound that is transmitted toward the rear seats. Sound which is propagated over an absorptive surface, such as an audience or an acoustically treated ceiling, is greatly attenuated. Hence the floor should rise steeply toward the rear, the loudspeakers and screen should be well elevated, and the ceiling and side walls should neither be highly absorptive, nor obstruct unduly the flow of sound from front to rear. Splays, and other functional deviations in the wall and ceiling contours can be used to give the proper diffusion without hindering the efficient transmission of sound to the rear of the auditorium.

The Motion Picture Research Council recommends, for proper viewing and listening conditions, that the first row of seats be at least 20 ft. from the screen — for screen widths not greater than 16 ft. For wider screens, the first row of seats should be back an additional 15 in. for each foot of screen width over 16 ft.

If there is a balcony, its depth should not be more than three times the height of the balcony opening. A relatively deeper overhang can be tolerated here than it can for a legitimate theater since the average speech levels in a cinema are somewhat higher. The balcony soffit should slope downward toward the rear, and should not be absorptive. The optimum reverberation times for movie theaters are given on p. 159, Nov. '48.

Absorptive material should be applied to the rear wall to eliminate "slap back." Additional absorptive material may be applied to the side walls.

Treatment of the walls behind the screen with highly absorptive material prevents sound which is radiated from the back of the loudspeakers from being reflected to the audience. It also suppresses acoustical resonances that occur on some stages. Mineral-wool blankets have

been used in many theaters to treat this area. The absorption characteristics of an acoustical material can be enhanced, especially at low frequencies, by furring it out from the wall. If a blanket consisting of glass wool is used, it should be at least 2 or 3 in. thick and have a density of about 4 lb. per cu. ft. The floor between the screen and the first row of seats also should be highly absorptive, in order to prevent sound from reaching the audience in the front seats by reflection from this area. Such reflections contribute to the loss of "intimacy" — that is, the loss of feeling that the sound is actually coming from the screen. They may be suppressed by covering the stage floor with heavy carpets over 1 in. pads.

In many respects the acoustical problems of motion picture and legitimate theaters are similar. Both should be properly insulated against noise, but in general a slightly greater noise level can be tolerated in motion picture theaters than in legitimate theaters because of the higher speech level. The average "film (background) noise" level is about 35 db, while the average audience noise level in a cinema is about 40 to 45 db.

Since the projection booth is a potential source of noise, all available interior surfaces should be heavily treated with fireproof acoustical material, as a 2 to 3 in. mineral-wool blanket covered with perforated Transite. Double panels of glass of different thicknesses should be employed in the portholes. The windows should fit tightly in their frames so that there are no threshold cracks. It also is helpful to cover with absorptive material the peripheral surfaces separating the double windows. The wall between the projection room and the auditorium should have a transmission loss of not less than 35 db at 128 cycles, and not less than 45 db at 512 to 2048 cycles.

The acoustical designing of theaters can and should be based on the well established science of architectural acoustics. The principles and procedures outlined in this article are derived from that science. If they are carefully followed in the designing and constructing of a theater, there need be no anxiety about the acoustical outcome of that theater — the acoustics will be good.

LIGHTING MOVIE THEATER INTERIORS

H. L. Logan

Manager, Dept. of Applied Research,
Holophane Co., Inc., New York City

Lighting designs for motion picture theaters apparently fail to furnish an optimum visual environment simply because the science of seeing has not been applied. The brightness of theater interiors needs to be related to that of the screen; so the author establishes a theoretical basis for what brightness values should be and then proposes a practical arrangement for attaining them. As yet, the author's suggestions have not been applied as a whole to a specific theater. The recent organization of an Illuminating Engineering Society committee to study motion picture theater lighting adds emphasis to the importance of the problem outlined in the following article, which is based on a paper presented by the author at a recent meeting of the Society of Motion Picture Engineers.

ARCHITECTS and engineers concerned with the design of motion picture theaters generally agree that the continuous lighting of the present-day theater is inadequate — in fact, they go so far as to say that the properly lighted movie theater doesn't exist.

The trend of thought is, first of all, that there isn't sufficient, properly controlled light from the surround to permit best reception of screen images (ability of the eye to resolve detail and to distinguish contrasts increases as the brightness of the surround approaches that of the object viewed); and also that lighting of the interior is insufficient for safe and convenient movement of patrons in and out of seats. It is also believed that more light is needed to provide a comfortable atmosphere and to create a life-like illusion within the theater.

Criterion for Lighting

Conventional brightness rules do not seem to apply to the lighting of motion picture theaters, since the rules are either for critical seeing tasks, or are otherwise irrelevant; so an altogether different approach is necessary. The rational lighting analysis that follows is based on the premise that the eye adapts itself to the average screen brightness with film running. Thus if the average screen brightness is known, the illumination needed for the interior can be related to that value. To obtain average screen brightness values, typical films were run and the brightnesses were measured with a specially developed instrument.

If the lowest mean brightness that is to be met, namely that of black-and-white newsreels, is used as the reference value, the brightness of the screen with film running can be taken as 1 foot-lambert. One-tenth of that value can be allowed, according to available research data,* for brightness of the walls, ceiling and floor of the theater, as long as the

*The Scientific Basis of Illuminating Engineering, Parry Moon McGraw-Hill Book Co., Inc., New York, 1936, p. 441.

Fig. 1. Perspective of a hypothetically average motion picture theater illustrating the field of view of a patron sitting in the position indicated in the section and plan of Fig. 3 (on page 390) by a cross. The maximum brightness at any point within 30° of the line of sight of an observer should not exceed 0.1 foot-lambert so as to give adequate viewing

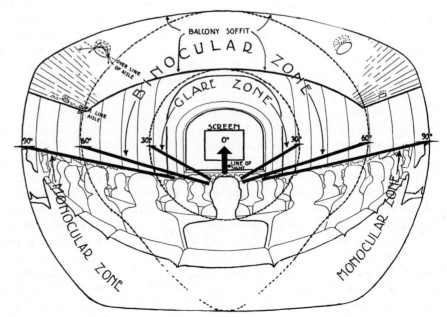

light is very uniformly distributed. This recommended value falls within the permissible range for optimum resolution of detail, but at the same time the amount of diffused light afforded does not tend to "wash out" screen images. The brightness of 0.1 foot-lambert should be continued right up to the edge of the screen.

Experiments in the Walt Disney studios were said to have shown that lighting between the screen and proscenium creates the illusion of great depth in pictures. This area should be lighted so as to appear as a pale gray mist. The lighting preferably should be uniform, but if that cannot be accomplished because of job conditions, then the brightness should be least near the screen and rise to 0.1 foot-lambert for theater walls.

Light Distribution

In order to attain satisfactory house lighting while the film is running, the distribution of light must be carefully controlled because the brightness level of 0.1 foot-lambert must be the actual maximum brightness at any point within 30° of the line of sight of a patron watching the screen (Fig. 1). This control not only will involve the careful selection of location for the light sources, but also the careful choice of materials for walls, ceiling and floor to reflect the proper quantity of light efficiently and thus permit the use of small lamps having very low brightness.

The lighting problem eases somewhat as screen brightnesses become higher. If, for example, colored films replace black-and-white entirely, house lighting can be about double the 0.1 foot-lambert value.

A brightness of 0.1 foot-lambert is too low for patrons' eyes to adapt to quickly when they come from outdoors, unless there is a long foyer in which the lighting intensity decreases steadily as the people move along.

Some improvement in the situation can be obtained in any case if the brightness of foyer surfaces at the end of the theater is set at 2 foot-lamberts. This should be succeeded by a brightness of 1 foot-lambert for the surfaces of the extreme rear of the auditorium behind the last row of seats (the crossover). This 1 foot-lambert brightness should decrease to 0.5 foot-lambert on the aisle floors within 10 ft. of the rear end of the aisle, and to the prevailing 0.1 foot-lambert within 20 ft. From then on, up to the front of the auditorium, the floor brightness of the aisles should remain at 0.1 foot-lambert. This arrangement of brightnesses is illustrated in Fig. 3 with a suggested system of lighting outlets to accomplish it.

Control of Lighting

Higher house brightnesses would be possible if motion picture theaters were designed to permit them. This might sometimes require the screen to be

louvered or hooded (after the fashion of traffic lights, or the miniature screens used for sales promotion in camera stores). At first thought, louvering would appear to reduce the number of seats by narrowing the angle of view, but this would not be necessary because the principal louvering would be against the ceiling to prevent the direct illumination of the ceiling lights from striking the screen. The actual amount of hooding required could also be reduced by sinking the lights into the ceiling, so that the depth of the coffer acts as a louver against the screen (see Figs. 1 and 3). The coffering would have the advantage of hiding the main ceiling lights from the balcony patrons.

An examination of Figs. 1 and 3 will show that such ceiling lights in the main ceiling cannot come into the field of view of any patron on the main floor as long as none is placed in the forward 30 per cent of the ceiling. This prohibition also prevents stray light of the ceiling sources from reaching the screen.

Figs. 1 and 3 also show that the lights in the main ceiling and those in the balcony soffit, when recessed in properly designed coffers, are hidden from most patrons. In the few cases where the lens can become visible, it is at the upper edge of a patron's field of view where it is farthest from the line of sight, and the least effective in reducing visual efficiency and comfort. The sides of the light coffers should be painted dark gray to prevent them from being bright enough to disturb patrons. Concealed downlights also could be used. In many theaters the use of lens units in coffers or downlights would be sufficient, in combination with the fact that screens are usually placed 6 to 10 ft. behind the proscenium arch, to make special louvering of the screen unnecessary.

In addition, it would be desirable to give all surfaces that are parallel to and face the screen, such as the balcony face and rear wall of the theater, a low reflecting finish (about 20 per cent) to make their contribution to screen brightness negligible. Surfaces parallel to, but facing away from the screen, such as the backs of the seats, should be given a reflection factor about equal to the floor, or 30 per cent.

Finally, the walls and ceiling should be sloped away from the screen as far as possible and given a ribbed surface. One side of each rib should face away from the screen and be given a reflection factor of 50 per cent. The other side of the rib that would face in the general direction of the screen could be dark gray

Fig. 2. Graph shows sequence of brightness changes for type of film used to relate theater interior brightness to that of the screen. Since one-tenth of average screen brightness can be the value allowed for the interior surfaces, the standard level recommended for theaters is 0.1 foot-lambert

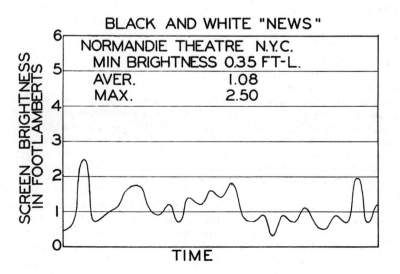

BLACK AND WHITE "NEWS"

NORMANDIE THEATRE N.Y.C.
MIN BRIGHTNESS 0.35 FT-L.
AVER.   1.08
MAX.   2.50

SCREEN BRIGHTNESS IN FOOTLAMBERTS

TIME

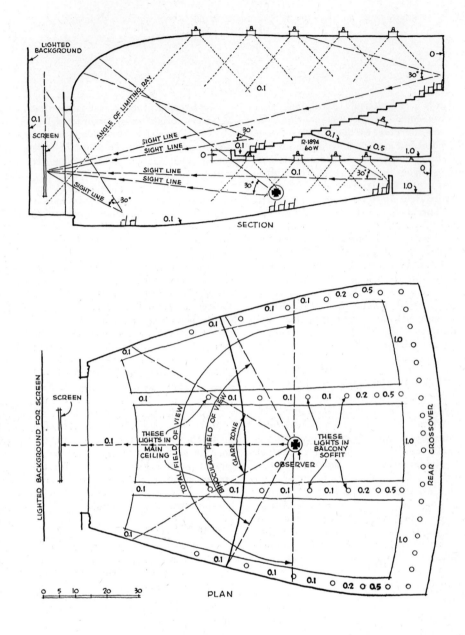

Fig. 3. *Section, plan of theater showing recommended brightness values and suggested lighting arrangement to attain them. Section gives sight lines of closest and farthest observers and of an observer (indicated by the circled cross) in what is termed a "standard" position. Indicated on the section are the 30 degree angles made with the sight lines, showing that no luminous part of any lighting unit comes within this angle. Finally it shows that no direct light from a lighting unit can reach the screen. Figures 0.1, etc., are the brightness levels in foot-lamberts*

with a 10 per cent reflection factor. This permits light to be accepted by these surfaces without its getting back to the screen. Floor coverings should have a reflection factor of 30 per cent.

Ceiling lights should begin no closer to the screen than about one third the depth of the house. They should be arranged throughout the remaining two thirds of the ceiling over the aisles so that the aisles would get the benefit of the principal illumination and no patron could be directly under a light to receive a high light on back of head and shoulders that might be disturbing to others. This also would light up the walls when the side aisles run along the walls. Where there are no side aisles, the lights should also run in such relation to the walls as to light them uniformly. Similar lights should be installed under the balcony (over the aisles), and along the back crossover.

Illumination on the ceiling would be diffused light coming from the walls and floor. If the ceiling were finished white it would acquire a brightness about equal to moonlight.

It would be desirable to raise the ceiling brightness to 0.1 foot-lambert, but most attempts to do this raise more problems than they solve. Where the scale of the interior permits lighting the ceiling, it can be done by a series of similar, well-designed, stepped coves. This is impractical in the average motion picture auditorium, and it is better to let the ceiling remain dark than to run into the great brightness variations that accompany most attempts at ceiling illumination.

It is easier to meet the visual requirements of continuous motion picture theater lighting with incandescent lamps than with fluorescent, as the extraordinary degree of control required is diffi-

cult with fluorescent. Fluorescent lighting can be used for the decorative and intermission lighting. Furthermore, the incandescent equipment can be dimmed easily so that after the computed installation is made, the exact point at which the house lighting no longer handicaps the screen can be determined by experiment.

In conclusion, the brightness level of 0.1 foot-lambert suggested for house lighting (about three times full moonlight) would call for an illumination level of from 0.3 to 0.4 foot-candles, on the basis of the reflection factors recommended. This can be secured, from 60-watt, incandescent lamps on about 15-ft. centers average, in controlled, coffered, direct-lighting equipment. Where the brightness level is to rise, as at the rear stretch of the aisles and the rear crossover, the lights should be spaced proportionately closer.

SUBURBAN MOVIE HOUSE

Carmel Hill Theater

Monte Vista Village, Monterey, California

Thomas S. Elston, Jr.,
Architect

Morley Baer Photos

THIS simple, straightforward movie theater is the pleasant result of a project for a workable, comfortable theater at minimum cost. The owner desired that it be informal, for about 300 people, and have facilities for serving coffee. It was to be planned for single showings of selected, adult type films.

In the search for an inexpensive structural system for the basic plan, glued laminated wood arches were finally selected as the type most attractive if exposed on the interior. The arch form lends itself well to the scheme, with center height for the screen and low side heights. For the interior finish, wood sheathing was left exposed and stained. The exterior was surfaced with oiled redwood siding, composition shingle roofing. Use of fire separation walls, usually required by code, was avoided by setbacks from property line and limitation of seats to 299.

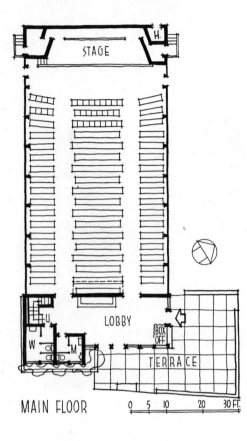

MAIN FLOOR

0 5 10   20   30 FT.

Morley Baer Photos

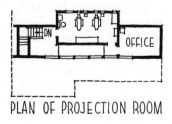

PLAN OF PROJECTION ROOM

Several dual-purpose and space-saving elements helped to reduce costs of the theater. Lobby (above) has bar for serving coffee, terrace to extend its area. Box office fits in corner, faces parking lot. Plastered walls are integral-color lightweight aggregate, left unfinished to double as acoustic treatment. Floor is single-pour concrete slab with embedded radiant heating. Lighting troughs in auditorium (right) serve also as raceway for electrical conduit

Western Photo

IT was once thought that only cities with more than 50,000 people could support a drive-in theater. To-day many towns of less than 2000 draw sufficient patronage from outlying rural areas to make them profitable. Costs for drive-in theaters range from about 25,000 to half a million dollars. With success, owners often get their entire investment back in three years or so. Some financing institutions are now said to loan money on the theater's own value, without collateral.

Vic Stein Photos

Baseline Theater, San Bernardino, Calif., William Glenn Balch, archt., Louis L. Bryan, assoc. General layout of ramps and speakers is shown in photo above and plan, right. Waiting area at entry keeps cars off highway; several exits ease after-show traffic congestion. Aluminum fencing surrounds the site. Photos at left (top to bottom) show principle elements of theater: entry with attraction sign and screen structure; seating area for walk-in patrons — entrance is below screen; ticket booth serves two lanes of cars simultaneously; and bottom, interior of snack bar. Photo second from bottom shows cars parked, ready for show, at Gilmore Theater, Los Angeles, Calif., also by Balch and Bryan

LOCATION OF SITE

A sufficient area of inexpensive land is the prime consideration in selecting a site. Location is generally better close to town, but theaters have been successful several miles from city limits. Many states and communities are developing codes regulating location and design of drive-ins; these should be carefully investigated. Other factors to check include: proximity to other drive-ins; nature of soil; natural drainage; simple, cheap excavation and grading; nearness to railroads or

Capacity and size: Maximum capacity is limited by number of ramps possible with clear view of screen. Picture size is limited to lenses and projection equipment available. Until larger and brighter pictures are possible, about 1000 to 1300 cars is maximum. Smaller theaters generally average about 450 cars, larger ones near cities, 650 to 1000 cars. *Motion Picture Herald* (Feb. 14, 1948) recommends roughly 100 ft of width for each 100 cars, and the following depths (based on full radii ramps, 38 ft o.c., and speaker posts 17 ft o.c.):

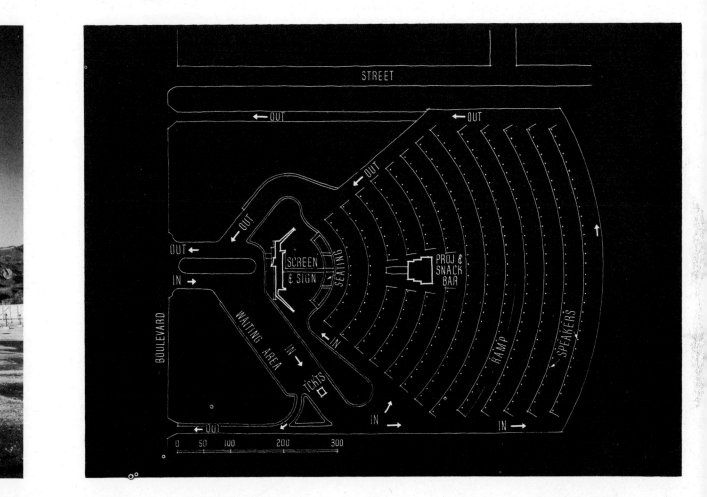

other distracting noises or odors; electricity — 220 volt, 3-phase service is needed. Drive-ins are usually best located on secondary roads connecting with major highways to prevent traffic congestion. Outside city limits, septic tanks must often be used for waste disposal, wells for water supply. Theater size should be derived from potential patronage; an average of 3.28 patrons per car was reported by *Theater Catalog, 1949–50 Edition*, from a survey conducted in the Minneapolis area.

PLOT LAYOUT

Ramps: The theater area is a series of ramps, laid out one behind the other in arcs. They are graded to elevate the front of each row of cars, permitting vision of screen above cars ahead. Sight lines and road grades must be established by size and terrain.

Capacity	No. of Ramps	Screen to rear of ramps
500 cars	10	510 ft
586	11	548
670	12	586
778	13	624
886	14	662
1000	15	700

Entrances and exits: Provide waiting space or extra wide entrance drives to get cars off highways; say for around 30 to 40 per cent of capacity. An escape exit drive by ticket office gives patron a means of getting out when cars are stacked behind him. On leaving ramps, it is best to have cars drive forward for exit. Several well lighted exits will ease traffic congestion. Often front-footage is retained for commercial use.

Surfacing: Drives should minimize dust and not be

Photos courtesy of H. H. Robertson Co.

slippery when wet. Crushed stone topped with gravel, oil treated or black topped, is often used.

Ticket booths: Ticket selling must get patrons in quickly to start show on time. One ticket booth can usually serve up to 300 car capacity, two up to 600, three up to 800, and four up to 1000 cars.

Screens: Screen towers should be placed so pictures cannot be seen from highway. Screen widths vary from 40 to 60 ft, depending on number of ramps and topography. Sizes often used are: 48 by 37 ft for 650 cars, 56 by 42 ft for 950 cars. It is desirable to face screen east or north; this blocks evening sun, permits earlier show. Height above ground is determined by ramp and sight angles. Tilting screen at top minimizes distortion. Manager's office and caretaker's apartment are often located in screen tower.

The screen may be of almost any material which will take a good covering of white paint; provisions should be made for frequent and rapid repainting. Asbestos sheets, aluminum and steel decking have been used. Minimize joints to prevent distortion and streaking. The structure should withstand at least 25 lb per sq ft wind pressure and be fire-resistant. Wood frames, structural steel, reinforced concrete, even telephone poles are used. Prefabricated units are available.

Seating area: If near residential areas, provide seating for walk-in patrons, in front of screen or by concession. A children's playground is desirable.

Courtesy Timber Engineering Co.   Courtesy Macomber, Inc.

Screen towers may be fabricated of any one of a variety of materials; typical construction is shown above in wood (left) and steel (right). Structures must be wind and fire resistant for safety

Cactus Drive-in Theater, Albuquerque, N. M., Jack Corgan, archt. Fluted surfaces and relief forms ·are used to give play of shadow in the desert terrain. The screen tower (above left) is finished with cellular steel panels. Flat steel plates with welded joints are used for the white-painted screen surface (below left). Auxiliary buildings are also constructed of cellular steel panels. Fences enclosing the area are of brick

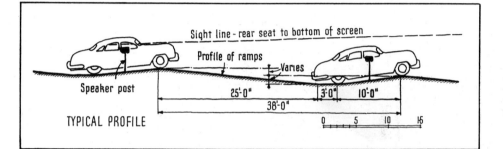

TYPICAL PROFILE

Sight line - rear seat to bottom of screen

Profile of ramps

Varies

Speaker post

25'-0"   3'-0" 10'-0"

38'-0"

0   5   10   15

Jimmie Willis Photo

Simplest ramp layout shown in diagram and photo above; Circle Drive-in Theater, Waco, Texas, Jack Corgan, archt. Radiating fanwise from screen, ramps elevate car front for clear view over other rows. Low projection booth clears sight-lines

Projection booth: Picture size and focal length of lens control placement and design of projection booth. It is often placed about 280 ft from screen, centered in lot. Special lenses can project greater distances. Projection angle depends on ramp layout. The booth must house two operators, two projectors, a large generator, and an amplification system for speakers. Heat becomes a problem in throwing pictures such distances; water cooled equipment is often needed.

Speaker units: Sound is best served by "in-car" speakers on posts about 16 to 18 ft o.c. Each serves two cars. Speakers may be removed from posts and hooked inside cars. Underground cables supply power. Aisle and signal lights are built into many commercial models. Electric car-heaters may be used for cool weather.

Concessions: Attractive, clean and roomy snack bars can

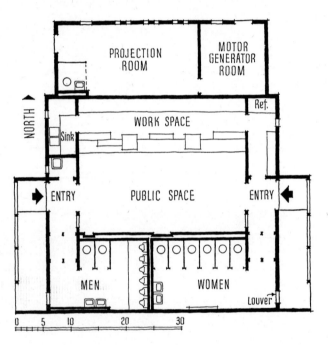

be an important source of income. Large numbers must be served quickly during intermissions and before showings. A terrace in front of concession allows continued viewing. Illumination must not detract from screen during showing. Service carts are used for ramp service; signal lights or an intercommunication system may be used for calling car-hops.

Storage: Space is needed for clean-up and repair equipment, and for supplies. If speakers, junction boxes and projection equipment are removed for winter, safe, dry storage is needed on site or in a warehouse. If left in place, waterproof covers should be used. Sprays for insect control, and fire extinguishers should be on hand.

Design notes: Illuminated signs should be placed near highway, but so as not to form a traffic hazard. The back of the screen is often used for advertising. Fencing should be high enough to cut off headlights of cars on highways. Simple, neat landscaping can help maintain desirability in the community, and attract customers.

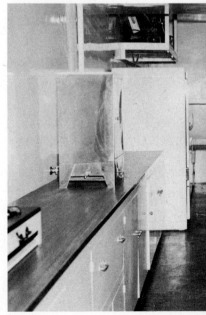

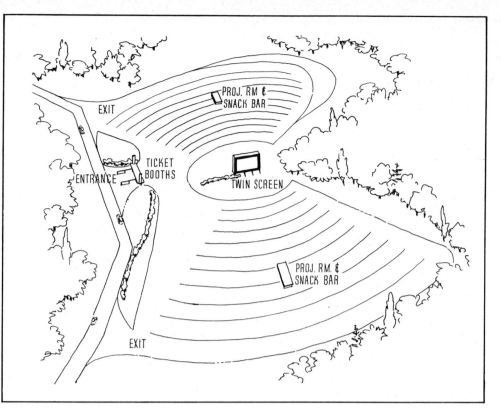

Courtesy R. C. Mahon Co.

Far left: plan of concession building, Baseline Theater. Projection booth, snack bar and toilet facilities are housed in single structure. Left: playground for children and picnic tables (top), Compton Theater, Los Angeles, Calif. Interior of snack bar (center), San Pedro Theater, Los Angeles, Calif., is closed in to prevent distraction from movie. Dispensing machines are used for quick service. Typical kitchen shown at bottom, Gage Theater, Los Angeles, Calif. All are the work of William Glenn Balch, archt., Louis L. Bryan, assoc. Sketches at right show schemes for expanding drive-in theaters by R. J. Haberstroh, engr. (above) and William Glenn Balch (below)

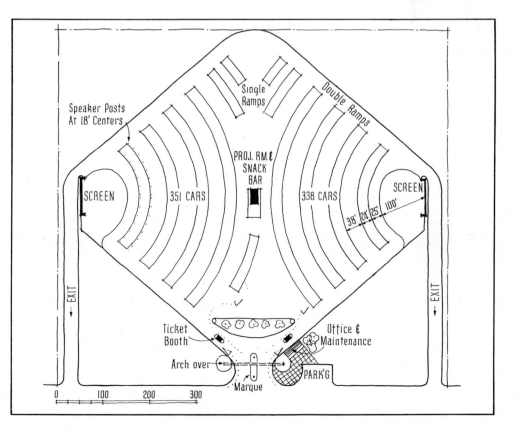

INDEX

INDEX